Proceedings of the 8th International Congress on Mathematical Education

Actas del 8º Congreso Internacional de Educación Matemática

Sevilla
14-21
July / *julio*
1996

Edited by / *Editado por:*

Claudi Alsina
José Mª Alvarez
Mogens Niss
Antonio Pérez
Luis Rico
Anna Sfard

In memoriam / *a la memoria del*
Prof. Gonzalo Sánchez Vázquez

Cover Design / Diseño de la Portada:
José Ignacio García Severón

Cover Picture / Fotografía de la Portada:
Ismael Roldán Castro

Published by / Publicado por:
S.A.E.M. 'THALES'

Printed by / Imprime:
Doble Cero Sevilla, S.L.

ISBN:
84-923760-2-3

Depósito Legal: SE-1686-98

CONTENTS

ÍNDICE

PREFACE / *PREFACIO*

This book constitutes the Proceedings of the 8th International Congress on Mathematical Education (ICME-8) which was held at Seville, Spain, from July 14 to 21, 1996.

The sequence of quadrennial ICMEs had previously taken place in Lyon (France), Exeter (United Kingdom), Karlsruhe (Germany), Berkeley (United States of America), Adelaide (Australia), Budapest (Hungary) and Québec (Canada) so it was the first occasion for the iberoamerican community to host such exceptional event of mathematics education.

Following the usual procedures, the Executive Committee of the International Commission on Mathematical Instruction (ICMI) accepted the candidature of Seville for hosting ICME-8 under the auspices of the Federación Española de Sociedades de Profesores de Matemáticas (FESPM) and the actual organization of the Sociedad Andaluza de Educación Matemática "Thales" (SAEM-Thales). All aspects of the Congress organization were delegated to the Thales Society that united incredible efforts and energies in the big job of hosting an ICME. A National Spanish Committee for ICME-8, a Local Organizing Committee and a considerable number of specific Committees and subcommittees were working for four years in the preparation of the congress.

It is necessary to say that behind the ICME-8 as a project there was always the enthusiasm, the work and the leadership of Professor Gonzalo Sánchez Vázquez who as President of FESMP and SAEM-Thales devoted his last years of life to this event. Unfortunately Prof. Sánchez was very ill during ICME-8 and died few months later. His presence was really missed during the congress but memories of what he did for ICME-8 and for the iberoamerican mathematics education will remind for ever.

As on previous congresses, the Executive Committee of ICMI set up in International Program Committee (IPC-ICME8) who was responsible for making the major scientific planning of the program. Taking into account the main trends and achievements of previous ICMEs, the IPC structured a rich scientific program keeping in mind traditional perspectives like the value of meeting in face-to-face groups allowing to discussions or the idea of presenting a big picture of mathematics education by including all kind of researches, experiences, materials, informations, etc., facing different levels, subjects and issues. Innovative aspects were introduced in the program after a critical review of previous congresses and a very large and wide scientific schedule was settled, giving special emphasis on achievements and trends that arose in Mathematics Education during the years 1992-1996.

The IPC invited four distinguished plenary speakers, a group of participants for an International Round Table, sixty speakers to present regular lectures of 45-minutes on a large range of matters, 26 working groups, 26 topic groups, 3 national presentations and a large number of reports from ICMI studies, ICMI Study Groups, special meetings, etc.

Working and topic groups covered a broad range of practical or theoretical key issues with an up-to-date perspective and ensuring an international coverage. All groups were planned by a team of people comprising a chief organizer, a local spanish organizer and an advisory team. While working groups had four 90-minute sessions to discuss some relevant problems in mathematics education, topic groups had two sessions to report on latest results and tendencies on various concrete topics.

Reports of ICMI studies celebrated before ICME-8 were presented and the official ICMI Study Groups (PME, HPM, IOWME, WFMC) organized special sessions to report on their on-going activities. Three national presentations of Australia, Hungary and Spain were made.

A general invitation was extended in the announcements of ICME-8 to all participants to submit proposals for projects or short presentations in the form of a poster, or a videotape or a piece of computer software. A large number was accepted and displayed. A book of abstracts was printed and distributed to all participants and visits to poster's displays were scheduled and attended by many people.

The main venue for ICME-8 was the campus of Reina Mercedes of the University of Seville where participants had the opportunity to attend regular lectures, working and topic groups, national presentations, ICMI sessions, projects, workshops, exhibitions, poster sessions, meetings... and the daily happy hours. Plenary sessions, the International Round Table, the opening and closing ceremonies, a reception and a great flamenco perfomance took place at the Congress Palace of Seville. Most students residences of the University and many hotels in Seville were used to host participants and accompaning persons who had also the opportunity in the excursion day to tour some exceptional cultural settings in Andalucia.

This book of Proceedings of the 8th International Congress on Mathematical Education includes the texts of the four plenary lectures, reports of the various groups presentations and debates, abstracts of regular lectures and tries to report on almost all activities on the program. Like most proceedings this volume intends to give an overview of the full congress and to facilitate, even to those who participated actively in some sections of the program, useful informations and conclusions that arose during the congress in all parallel activities taking place. Full text of a large number of regular lectures will appear in the companion volume on Selected Lectures from the 8th International Congress on Mathematical Education.

The editors want to thank all the people who provided reports for these Proceedings and would like to thank once more to all participants of ICME-8 who contributed to the success of the congress and with this to the improvement of mathematics education.

The editors
May 1998

CODES OF COUNTRIES

CÓDIGOS DE PAÍSES

[ANG]	ANGOLA
[ARG]	ARGENTINA
[AUS]	AUSTRALIA
[AUT]	AUSTRIA
[BAR]	BARBADOS
[BEL]	BELGIUM / BELGICA
[BGR]	BULGARY / BULGARIA
[BOL]	BOLIVIA
[BRA]	BRAZIL / BRASIL
[BRN]	BRUNEI DARUSSALAM
[CAN]	CANADA
[CAY]	CAYMAN ISLANDS / ISLAS CAIMAN
[CIV]	IVORY COAST / COSTA DE MARFIL
[COL]	COLOMBIA
[CRI]	COSTA RICA
[CRO]	CROACIA
[CUB]	CUBA
[CYP]	CYPRUS / CHIPRE
[CZR]	CZECH REPUBLIC / REPUBLICA CHECA
[CHE]	SWITZERLAND / SUIZA
[CHL]	CHILE
[CHN]	CHINA
[DEU]	GERMANY / ALEMANIA
[DNK]	DENMARK / DINAMARCA
[DOM]	DOMINICAN REPUBLIC / REPUBLICA DOMINICANA
[EGY]	EGYPT / EGIPTO
[ESP]	SPAIN / ESPAÑA
[EST]	ESTONIA
[FIN]	FINLAND / FINLANDIA
[FRA]	FRANCE / FRANCIA
[GBR]	UNITED KINGDOM / REINO UNIDO
[GRC]	GREECE / GRECIA
[GTM]	GUATEMALA
[GYN]	GUAYANA
[HKG]	HONG KONG
[HON]	HONDURAS

[HUN]	Hungary / Hungria
[IND]	India
[INS]	Indonesia
[IRL]	Ireland / Irlanda
[IRN]	Iran
[ISL]	Iceland / Islandia
[ISR]	Israel
[ITA]	Italy / Italia
[JAM]	Jamaica
[JPN]	Japan / Japon
[KEN]	Kenya / Kenia
[KOR]	Korea / Corea
[KWT]	Kuwait
[LBN]	Lebanon / Libano
[LIT]	Lituania
[LUX]	Luxenbourg / Luxemburgo
[MAC]	Macau
[MAR]	Morocco / Marruecos
[MAU]	Mauritania
[MEX]	Mexico
[MOL]	Moldavia
[MOZ]	Mozambique
[MWI]	Malawi
[MYS]	Malaysia / Malasia
[NLD]	Netherlands / Holanda
[NOR]	Norway / Noruega
[NZL]	New Zealand / Nueva Zelanda
[PAK]	Pakistan
[PAL]	Palestinian Authority / Autoridad Palestina
[PAN]	Panama
[PAR]	Paraguay
[PER]	Peru
[PHI]	Phillipines / Filipinas
[PNG]	Papua New Guinea / Papua Nueva Guinea
[POL]	Poland / Polonia
[PRI]	Puerto Rico
[PRT]	Portugal
[QAT]	Qatar
[ROM]	Romania / Rumania
[RUS]	Russia / Rusia
[SAL]	El Salvador
[SAU]	Saudi Arabia / Arabia Saudi
[SGP]	Singapore / Singapur

[SLN]	SLOVENIA / ESLOVENIA
[SVK]	SLOVAKIA / ESLOVAQUIA
[SWE]	SWEDEN / SUECIA
[SWZ]	SWAZILAND / SUAZILANDIA
[THA]	THAILAND / TAILANDIA
[TPI]	TAIPEI - CHINA
[TRI]	TRINIDAD & TOBAGO
[TUN]	TUNISIA / TUNEZ
[TUR]	TURKEY / TURQUIA
[UAE]	UNITED ARABIAN EMIRATES / EMIRATOS ARABES UNIDOS
[UGA]	UGANDA
[UKR]	UKRAINIA / UCRANIA
[URY]	URUGUAY
[USA]	U.S.A. / ESTADOS UNIDOS
[VEN]	VENEZUELA
[VNM]	VIETNAM
[YEM]	YEMEN
[ZAF]	SOUTH AFRICA / SUDAFRICA
[ZWE]	ZIMBABWE

Timetable

Timetable 8:30-10:00	Monday	Tuesday WG	Wednesday WG	Thursday	Friday WG	Saturday WG	Sunday
	Opening Ceremony (10:00)	BREAK			BREAK		Plenary 3 (10:00)
10:30-11:30	Plenary 1	Reg. Lect.	Reg. Lect.		Reg. Lect.	Reg. Lect.	Plenary 4
	Plenary 2	BREAK			BREAK		Closing Ceremony (ending: -14:00)
12:00-13:30		Reg.Lect.	Reg. Lect.		TG	TG	
	International Round Table (16:00)	BREAK		Official Congress Tour	BREAK		
17:00-18:30		Meetings ICMI Studies	Meetings ICMI Assembly		Meetings Projects	Meetings Projects	
	Welcome Cocktail (18:00)	BREAK			BREAK		
19:00-21:00	Cultural Performance (19:30)	Working Groups ICMI — Special Sessions	Working Groups ICMI — ICMI Studies — Workshops — Special Sessions		Posters Presentations	Working Groups ICMI — ICMI Studies — Workshops — Special Sessions	
21:00		Happy Hour	Happy Hour		Happy Hour	Happy Hour	

EXHIBITS

Exhibits: 10:00-20:00

HORARIO

Hora	Lunes	Martes	Miercoles	Jueves	Viernes	Sabado	Domingo
8:30-10:00		WG	WG		WG	WG	
	Sesión Inaug. (10:00)	DESCANSO			DESCANSO		Plenaria 3 (10:00)
10:30-11:30		Conf.Ord.	Conf.Ord.		Conf.Ord.	Conf.Ord.	Plenaria 4
	Plenaria 1						
	Plenaria 2	DESCANSO			DESCANSO		Sesión de Clausura (fin: -14:00)
12:00-13:30		Conf.Ord.	Conf.Ord.	Excursión Oficial del Congreso	TG	TG	
	Mesa Redonda Internacional (16:00)	DESCANSO			DESCANSO		
17:00-18:30		Encuentros	Encuentros		Encuentros	Encuentros	
		Seminario ICMI	Asamblea ICMI		Proyectos	Proyectos	
	Cocktail (18:00)	DESCANSO			DESCANSO		
19:00-21:00	ACTO INAUGU-RAL (19:30)	Grupos de Trabajo ICMI	Grupos de Trabajo ICMI		Presentación de Posters	Grupos de Trabajo ICMI	
			Seminario ICMI			Seminario ICMI	
		Sesiones Especiales	Talleres			Talleres	
			Sesiones Especiales			Sesiones Especiales	
21:00		Happy Hour	Happy Hour		Happy Hour	Happy Hour	

EXPOSICIONES

Exposiciones: 10:00-20:00

PRESIDENTIAL ADDRESS BY MIGUEL DE GUZMÁN
ICME EXECUTIVE COMMITTEE

Excmo. Sr. Presidente de la Junta de Andalucía, D. Manuel Chaves González,

Excma. Sra. Alcaldesa de la Ciudad de Sevilla, Dña. Soledad Becerril Bustamante,

Excmo. Sr. Consejero de Educación y Ciencia de la Junta de Andalucía, D. Manuel Pezzi Ceretto,

Excmo. y Mgfco. Sr. Rector de la Universidad de Sevilla, D. Miguel Florencio Lara,

Excmo. Sr. Secretario General de la Organización de Estados Iberoamericanos para la Educación, la Ciencia y la Cultura, D. José Torreblanca Prieto,

Ms. Anna Sierpinska, miembro del Comité Ejecutivo del ICMI,

Ilmo. Sr. Presidente del Comité Internacional de Programa del ICME-8, D. Claudi Alsina Catalá

Sr. Presidente del Comité de Organización del ICME-8, D. Antonio Pérez Jiménez,

Sras., Sres.,

Es para mí un honor y un gran placer, en nombre del Comité Ejecutivo de la Comisión Internacional de Educación Matemática, ofrecer mi más cordial bienvenida a todos los participantes de este Congreso. En su organización han tomado parte muy activa muchas personas y muchas instituciones, tanto locales como nacionales e internacionales. Quiero expresar también nuestra más profunda gratitud a todas las personas y organizaciones de Sevilla, de Andalucía, de España, que nos han ofrecido su proverbial hospitalidad para celebrar nuestra reunión en esta magnífica ciudad.

I have said and written already several times that I would like to call the meeting we are opening right now a Great Solidarity Congress in Mathematics Education.

The idea started at the Executive Committee Meeting of the ICMI held in Québec. It was the purpose of the Executive Committee to launch a campaign to stimulate the whole community of people working on Mathematics Education toward a spirit of solidarity.

This solidarity should make itself effective in many different ways, perhaps the main one in helping to establish programs on mathematics and mathematics education where this help was most needed, as the Solidarity Fund is doing in several countries.

But another very important way could be to help those people who usually cannot attend meetings and congresses like this one to come to the next one.

My words in Québec were rather utopic: take one, pay two, that is when you register to attend, please help another person who cannot afford in any way to come here.

But utopy means having a direction along which we can proceed with hope.

When I finished my words in Quebec, a person approached me with these words:

"Miguel, te prometo que en Sevilla haremos todo lo posible porque este proyecto de solidaridad comience a hacerse real".

"Miguel, I promise you that in Seville we shall make every possible effort to start making real your proposal of solidarity".

That person was Gonzalo Sánchez Vázquez, the same one who, through his constant and contagious enthusiasm, has been most effective to make possible this congress in Seville.

And now here we are at the beginning of the Congress. And although Gonzalo cannot be with us right now, we know that it is thanks to Gonzalo and to the spirit he has been able to instill into a great segment of the professors and teachers of mathematics in Spain through the creation, mainly due also to him, of the Federación Española de Sociedades de Profesores de Matemáticas, we all know, I say, that it is thanks to Gonzalo and to the solidarity spirit of Gonzalo and of many others like him that we are now here.

For this and for many other reasons I want to express in the name of ICMI our warmest thanks.

Being solidary is being together, especially in order to share with others that can be helped with what we are, with what we have. We are together in a Congress which deals with teaching and learning. Teaching is in a very real way being solidary, since teaching is sharing our knowledge, our perceptions, our feelings.

An also for sharing are we here. During these days we shall have very many opportunities for doing it.

We shall share the heat and the sweat, but also the joy and the wonder to be in Seville, where people are open and prepared to do almost everything for us.
But please do not ask them for winter temperatures.

And when the Congress shall be over and the heat already forgotten, we shall keep forever the wonderful memories of having been together for these days in Seville, having shared many experiences, having learned very much from each other, having established many links which will be very useful for our future work.

I wish all of you a very pleasant and fruitful work at this Congress.

WELCOME ADDRESS BY CLAUDI ALSINA
INTERNATIONAL PROGRAM COMMITTEE

Dear authorities, dear colleagues:

As chair of the International Program Committee I would like to welcome all of you to ICME-8 and to take the opportunity to thank some people for their work in the preparation of the scientific program.

I want to thank first of all Gonzalo Sánchez Vázquez, the Sociedad Thales, the Federación Española de Sociedades de Profesores de Matemáticas, ICMI and all the institutions which made all this possible. I thank you Seville for this ICME-8 which represents the reality of a dream.

The IPC has benefited from the contributions of Luis Balbuena, Lida Barrett, Werner Blum, Zhang Dianzhou, Miguel de Guzmán, Milan Hejny, Bernard Hodgson, Jeremy Kilpatrick, Colette Laborde, Mogens Niss, Antonio Pérez, Luis Rico, Toshio Sawada, Anna Sfard and Carlos Vasco. Luis Rico, Ricardo Luengo and their committees oversaw the selection process of Projects and Short Communications and Antonio Aranda and his group created the real local organization of the scientific program in Seville.

Our scientific program involves, in statistical terms, 30 people working in committees, 4 plenary speakers, 60 regular lecturers, 52 chief organizers and 52 local organizers of working and topic groups, 250 advisers for the groups, more than 1000 people making presentations or short communications, plus ICMI groups, ICMI studies, National presentations, Projects, Exhibits, Special Meetings, etc. This is counting... but a simple arithmetic shows that, indeed all of you are involved in ICME8. We have been working 4 years but now... you are the program! And you are the reason for organizing ICME's.

All of us come to ICME's every four years because we love Mathematics Education and we strongly believe in the future of our field. We are not coming here to show final results or closed theorems... but ways of progressing.

But, in some sense, our main job comes after each ICME. When we go back to our students and to our institutions and we have the responsibility of showing, everyday, the joy of learning and teaching mathematics.

On behalf of the International Program Committee and, perhaps, on behalf of the mathematics students of all levels and in countries throughout the world, thank you for making ICME8 possible and for sharing, daily, your enthusiasm for Mathematics Education with all of us... and with all of them.

WHITHER MATHEMATICS EDUCATION?

Anna Sierpinska

Montréal

In my schooldays, when I had lost one sheft
I shot his fellow of the self-same flight
The self-same way, with more advised watch,
To find the other forth; and by adventuring both
I oft found both.
W. Shakespeare, *The Merchant of Venise*, Act 1, Sc. 1.

As a motto for this talk I chose a Shakespearean verse from The Merchant of Venise. I chose it because it mentions the advantages that can sometimes be gained from re-doing the same thing 'with a more advised watch'.

Foreword

When preparing for this talk I decided to have a look at some older writings in mathematics education, like the first volume of Educational Studies in Mathematics or the UNESCO publications. This is how I came accross the 1971 Unesco Source book edited by Willy Servais and Tamas Varga. This book contains a full exposition of the New Math reform. The book left me wondering. We have the feeling that a lot of progress has been done in mathematics education in the last 25 years or so. Sometimes it is even said that the development of mathematics education as a domain of research started about 25 years ago. But as I looked at Servais and Varga's book I started wondering if there is indeed such a big difference in kind between what we are doing today and what these people were doing. Just as we do it today, these people were questioning their predecessors, justifying their ideologies with theories and experimental research, referring themselves to Piaget, Vygotsky and Bruner, designing teaching projects and trying them out. We may not like the New Math reformers' ideology, their views on curriculum, their epistemology of mathematics, but we still maintain ideologies. My questions were: Where are we different, can one speak of progress?

In this talk I shall start with the notion that developments in mathematics education can be seen as evolution of what I shall call 'programs'. What is referred to as 'Constructivism' can be seen as a program; 'Problem Solving' could be seen as a program. Servais and Varga's exposition of the New Math reform looked very much like a presentation of a program in exactly the same sense as these other two. It was a program of research and action, not just another curricular reform, and here is the probable source of my questions above.

A program will be seen as evolving on three planes: the plane of ideology, the plane of theory and the plane of didactic action.

I shall then look at a few of the directions in which mathematics education has evolved in the wake of the criticism of the New Math program.

The most striking feature of the New Math program was its idealism. Its failure has made mathematics educators look at reality with more respect. A program which has taken reality perhaps the most seriously into account is Interactionism. We shall have a look at this program and we shall see an example of a research within this program. We shall end with a conclusion that trying to bend reality to an ideology goes counter the aim of establishing mathematics education as a domain of research producing scientific knowledge.

We shall then proceed with an overview of a few revisions that have been made in mathematics education with respect to the New Math program:
- a revision of the ideology: a new view of the unity of mathematics
- revision of theories

We shall end with the issue of language and communication in the mathematics classroom, which seems to be all the rage in mathematics education lately, but which, in fact, has been around for a very long time already.

Introduction: *Programs and Slogans*

The striking thing as we look back at the history of mathematics education is that it could be seen as a history of popular movements, characterized by ideas presented in the lapidary form of slogans or buzzwords: Practice makes Perfect, Forward to Basics!, Mathematical Power, Teaching Mathematics in Real Life Contexts, Knowing Mathematics is Doing Mathematics, Problem Solving must be the Focus of School Mathematics!, Metacognition, Epistemological Obstacle, Culture,

Ethnomathematics, Situated Cognition, Cooperative Learning, Mathematical Discourse, Mathematical Discussion, Communication in the Mathematics Classroom, Writing in the Mathematics Classroom, etc. In a recent publication these movements were called 'monomaniacal enthusiasms' marked by a belief that a single idea can solve all mathematics education problems at once (Pimm 1996). This would not be, of course, a very flattering picture of mathematics education. But there must be some reason for this phenomenon. It occurred to me, when I was going through some old and some new literature in preparation for this talk, that these slogans and buzzwords can result from a popularization, and thereby an unavoidable trivialization, of *developing research programs* that need not be so trivial. Trivialization could be avoided only if research remained behind the closed doors of laboratories and experimental schools, in the sphere of pure theory and controlled action without targeting some impact on the level of ordinary teaching practices. But action geared towards the change of practices is normally built on ideologies and creates ideologies, because 'change' means improvement and improvement is understood within a system of values which constitutes an ideology. Ideologies, on their turn, express themselves, in the popular culture, by slogans and buzzwords.

Unlike a research program, say in the sense of Lakatos, a program in mathematics education is strongly linked to some project of action, meant to bring about some improvement. These two concepts: action and improvement, I think, distinguish mathematics education as a domain of research from academic disciplines.

A program in mathematics education characterizes itself by a certain ideology, a certain activity of theory building and theory verification, and an activity that could be called 'didactic'.

Three planes of a program in mathematics education: *Ideology, Theory, Action*

On the plane of *ideology*, a program in mathematics education either explicitly puts forward or implicitly assumes certain ideals or standards. It has a vision of
- a Model Learner of mathematics; for example, the learner as an autonomous thinker or an explorer of mathematics;
- a Model Teacher; e.g. a guide, a model intellectual, a mentor, a coach or 'a moderator and observer of children's thinking' rather than a 'conveyer of information', a participant in the research;
- a Model Classroom, e.g. a team working on shared problems, communicating and discussing them;

- a Model Curriculum, e.g. school mathematics as a horizontally and vertically integrated domain rather than a piecemeal collection of topics, teaching mathematics in contexts, teaching applied mathematics, teaching mathematics with applications, or teaching focused on problem solving, etc.

Programs use different *theoretical systems of reference* to support their ideologies and create theories for didactic action. These theoretical systems of reference include theories of all human activities and institutions that are at play in mathematics education. Thus we find here theories of cognitive development, theories of learning, theories of understanding, epistemologies of mathematics in general and of particular mathematical ideas, theories of meaning, theories of teaching, theories of symbolically mediated human interaction or communication, theories of the functioning of knowledge in systems and institutions of education, psychology, social psychology, anthropology, theories of culture. In interaction with knowledge drawn from these theories, mathematics education programs create 'theories for action', or certain systems of guidelines for the design of didactic action.

The *didactic action* is meant to bring the reality closer to the ideals. The term 'didactic' here is meant to be used in its very traditional sense: An act is didactic if it is meant to teach somebody something, especially a moral lesson. We may extend the notion of moral lesson to encompass such things as: 'If I touch the stove, I may get burned', or 'Telling lies doesn't pay' as well as such things as: 'If a function is differentiable in a point, then it must be continuous in this point'. A specific didactic action can be *direct*, when the moral lesson is verbalized by the person who undertook this action, or it can be *indirect*, when the person to whom the action was addressed has drawn (and verbalized) the moral by him or herself. Examples of direct didactic action can be: admonition (do this, don't do that...), warning about the unpleasant consequences of a behavior, lecturing, organizing the material for the student, pointing to what is important in it and what is not, highlighting the connections between different parts of the material. Examples of indirect didactic action include telling the child a story in which the behavior we want to promote is rewarded, and the behavior that we want the child to abandon is punished; exploiting naturally arising situations to teach the child or student something (e.g. turning the child's or student's questions into exploratory tasks for him or herself); artificially creating situations in which the child or the student will experience the need to learn something; e.g. by confronting him or her with a paradox, or generally, by putting the child or student in 'trouble', i.e. in problem situations where his or her old knowledge will not work anymore.

Design and justification of an indirect didactic action as a 'result' in mathematics education

It is much more difficult to devise an indirect didactic action than a direct one. In fact, it is quite an art. I would even say that, if anything in mathematics education corresponds to the invention and proof of a new theorem in mathematics, it is the design and justification of an indirect didactic action. Of course, just as there are important and less important results in mathematics, there are important and less important such inventions in mathematics education.

Here are a couple of examples of indirect didactic actions, one being a result of a design; the other exploiting a situation that naturally arose in the classroom.

Example 1: Mechanical and Organic problem solvers

In a research on problem solving published in 1945 (Duncker, cited in Peel 1971, p. 164) a distinction was made between two types of problem solvers: those who use methods that were called 'mechanical' and those who use methods that were called 'organic'. 'In an organic solution the thinker begins from the original problem and successively restates it by asking what it means and what is necessary. Each successive restatement is more precise in terms of the data available and takes the thinker to a final solution. Mechanical solutions, on the other hand, begin by asking what is given and then by casting about for theorems that might apply' (Peel, ibid.). Problems can be devised which lead the mechanical solver to an error thus giving him or her an opportunity to revise his or her method. If one takes a problem like the following:

> I go for a car ride travelling one hour at 40 m.p.h. and for the next hour at 30 m.p.h. What is my average speed over the journey?

It will not be possible to discriminate between mechanical and organic problem solvers. However, with a slight modification we already get this possibility.

> I go for a car ride travelling a distance of 120 miles at 40 m.p.h. and then back by the same route at 30 m.p.h. What is my average speed over the journey?

[The proof of this statement is straightforward and I leave it to the listeners].

Example 2. Vectors in affine spaces and vectors in vector spaces

(Exploitation of a student's question to discuss a subtle conceptual distinction in linear algebra)

The class was working on vectorial interpretations of linear equations in a linear algebra course. The question was:

Suppose x, y and z represent coordinates of a vector in the 3-dimensional vector space $\mathbf{R}^3$. What does an equation like 2x-3y+z=2 represent?

The equation was rewritten as

$$\begin{bmatrix} x \\ y \\ z-2 \end{bmatrix} \cdot \begin{bmatrix} 2 \\ -3 \\ 1 \end{bmatrix} = 0$$

The teacher said that, therefore, the equation can be seen as representing the set of all vectors [x,y,z] such that the vector [x,y,z-2] is perpendicular to the fixed vector [2,-3,1]. These vectors form a plane. A student then reacted: 'Rather an infinity of planes! Because there are infinitely many planes perpendicular to any given vector!', making gestures with his hands:

The teacher then proposed to do a similar exercise in two dimensions: Could you draw some vectors that satisfy the equation 2x-3y=2? Students drew the line 2x-3y=2 by finding two points satisfying the equation just as they usually did it in high school, and then drew some arrows on it, like this:

Now, it was clear that the teacher and the students had different spaces in mind, and therefore, different conceptions of vector. The distinction between the two had then to be discussed and clarified.

The difficult tensions between ideals, reality and theory

One of the functions of the theoretical activity in a program is verification of how realistic its ideology is. If a certain ideal is difficult to reach in reality, the program would ask itself the question: what is the obstacle? Is there a discrepancy between the ideal promoted by the program and the prevailing culture of the classrooms? For example, the Model Learner is an autonomous thinker and explorer, whereas the dominant routine of classroom interaction is some kind of Socratic dialogue or the funneling pattern of questioning. How much change would be needed to remove a given obstacle? How deeply is the obstacle rooted in the given culture, the customs and beliefs, and in the institutional establishment of the educational system? Is it in the power of local didactic actions on the level of the classroom to make the necessary changes? The conclusion of this reflection could be that a given ideal is impossible to attain.

The ideal of the learner as researcher in mathematics and the whole class as a research team was very much promoted by the New Math program in the 60s (Brailly 1968-9). But a closer look at the actual practices aspiring to this ideal revealed that very often the student is not so much discovering mathematics for him or herself as guessing the answer that the teacher is hinting at through a funnel-like series of questions (cf. Ausubel 1964). The apparent progress in the child's learning can be nothing more than a repetition of the answer given in actual fact by the teacher ('effet Topaze', Brousseau, 1986, p. 288) or a result of the observer's modeling in scientific terms of the child's behavior which was, in itself, motivated by banal meanings ('effet Jourdain', ibid, p. 289).

Ideologies are, however, very hard to overthrow, and programs sometimes rather change their theoretical explanations than the ideology. Alternative explanations of the failure of the system to attain an ideal are found and appropriate didactic actions are undertaken. For example, it may be argued that the behavior of the learners and teachers depend to a large extent on assessment. Assessment determines what and how the learner learns. If what is assessed are computational and technical algebraic skills, the learning will be based on drill and the fundamental principle of teaching will be the behaviorist 'practice makes perfect'. The idea is then: 'Let us change the forms of assessment', and didactic action is funneled in this direction (National Council of Teachers of Mathematics 1995; Kulm 1991).

The idea is not left without verification, however, by today's skeptical researchers, and at least in one case that I know research has shown that even a radical change of the tasks given to children (investigative projects, open problems rather than closed exercises) does not necessarily change the forms of assessment in the long run: Teachers may tend to continue to check certain easily identifiable features of students' work, not all of which are relevant to the judgment of students' thinking (Morgan 1992).

The Interactionist program: a radical approach to the reality of mathematics classes

Instead of blaming teachers for their incorrigible laziness or their incomprehensible reluctance to turn into researchers in the psychology of mathematics education some programs propose to study the deep reasons for their behavior, and, in particular, to understand and describe the reality in which they live. The reality of the classroom may be different for the teacher from what it is for the researcher. The two realities may be composed of different objects. A cognitively oriented researcher will see the classroom as a collection of individual minds. For the teacher, 'students' or 'class', collectively, constitute a unit, an identifiable object (Bromme 1994). When the teacher says: 'The class did well today', it does not mean that every single student in the class displayed signs of understanding. It may mean that at least one student responded in an expected way and the teacher was able to put this response in front of the class as a new standard, or *format of classroom interaction*, that the class will live up to until further notice (Bruner 1985; Krummheuer 1995; Sierpinska 1997).

This view of the classroom as a microculture in which meanings emerge in shared activities the interpretation of which is negotiated, formatted and eventually conventionalized in interactions between the teacher and the students, is characteristic of a program that has received the label of 'interactionism'. The main theoretical systems of reference of this program are inspired by symbolic interactionism of H. Blumer and G.H. Mead, J.S. Bruner's theory of interaction formats in language acquisition, and Goffman's frame analysis among others. Its research methodology draws upon the qualitative, naturalistic approaches based on exploration and inspection of phenomena, where a theoretical model is constructed and continually reconstructed during the study (Hammersley 1989, p. 155; see also Cobb & Whitenack 1996).

The aim of much of the research in the interactionist program is to achieve a better understanding of the phenomena of teaching and learning mathematics as it occurs in ordinary school setting. There is less focus on the building of theories for action and design of didactic action itself. Related to this is the program's reluctance to propose some explicit ideology. One could say that interactionism is programmatically 'a-ideological'. It has an in-built 'distaste for solving educational problems by organizing teachers' and students' and schools' lives for them, especially if it is done without first finding out how teaching at schools functions and why it functions as it does' (a paraphrase of a sentence in Hammersley 1989, p. 79). The outcomes of the research in the interactionist program lead not to recommendations for action but to description and discussion of different possibilities.

The microsociological, interactionist approach had an influence in France, on the development, by G. Brousseau, of the concept of 'contrat didactique', explanatory of the elective failure (*échec électif)* in mathematics (Sarrazy 1995). In Germany its impact led to the research program started by H. Bauersfeld focusing on microethnographical studies of teacher-student interactions (see Cobb & Bauersfeld 1995). Studies of classroom interaction seem to have been popular in the UK and the US in the 60's and 70's and this interest continues to this day but the research was not always specific to mathematics classes (e.g. Fey 1969; Coulthard & Sinclair 1975; Edwards & Mercer 1987). This trend was, for some time, overshadowed by the constructivist program, but it is resurfacing now with the collaboration between several German and American researchers (Cobb & Bauersfeld, ibid.). Its scope had broadened to encompass the study of classroom cultures and the mechanisms of their emergence and stability, in particular, the emergence and stability of the mathematical meanings in these cultures. A phenomenon that is presently receiving much attention is that of the establishment of socio-mathematical norms in the classroom interactions (Voigt 1995; Yackel & Cobb 1996).

Interactionist ideas, and especially the works of Goffman (1974) lead to a much more down-to-earth view of the teaching-learning process and the mathematics classroom in particular. Goffman's notion of 'frame' comes in handy in explaining how people interpret situations, and their roles, rights and obligations in them.

From the first days in school the child starts constructing the frame of the classroom: 'This is the teacher, I am a student; the teacher will be asking me questions; of course, it's silly, because she knows all the answers, so these are not real questions, they are classroom questions, and my job as a student is to give those answers that the teacher is expecting of me. I have to keep a straight face, I have to participate in this game. If, suddenly, the teacher sat back, and started to think out loud, reflecting on a problem, and asked the students questions without knowing the answers, I would be very surprised, and maybe I would even feel very uncomfortable'. This frame organizes the meaning, for the child, of what is going on. It also organizes his or her involvement in the given situation (Goffman 1974, p. 345).

How much should one get involved in the activity proposed by the teacher? How much involvement should one show? There must be a certain level of involvement that is appropriate. Is it appropriate to be totally carried away by this activity?

Answers to these questions may be different in different cultures. Very often the teacher is expected to portray a greater involvement than the students. So the teacher talks all the time; the pauses are short for fear of 'disengaging herself from the frame' (ibid., p. 350). It may be considered improper for students to get engrossed in the activities that the teacher is proposing; they risk the label of 'teacher's pets' if they do. Teachers know that. This is why so many activities proposed for the classroom start with a game of some sort, thus 'upkeying' the investigation to playing a game (see example in Brousseau 1986, p. 449). It may not appear 'cool' to get seriously involved in a mathematical research. But it's okay to get carried away by a game; it's 'cool' to play and to win.

Also the New Math reformers were stressing very much the playful aspects of doing mathematics:

> Essential to this approach is freedom of expression, arising from playful activity. To realize and enjoy the beauty of mathematics, pupils must be given sufficient opportunity for free, playful, creative activity, where each can bring out his own measure of wit, taste, fantasy, and display thereby his personality (Varga, 1971, p. 16).

Playing and games were important in Diénès's theory of the psychodynamic process of artificial genesis of mathematical concepts in six stages: the stage of structured play or game; the stage of isomorphic games; the stage of abstraction; the stage of schematisation, formulation and symbolisation; the stage of axiomatisation; the stage of generalisation (Brousseau, 1980, p. 41-2).

Example of a research within the interactionist program: DATSIT! And ARUSURE? formattings

In our research at Concordia University in Montreal on one-on-one tutoring in elementary linear algebra with the help of a textbook we observed two kinds of formatting of interaction between the student-as-learner-from-a-text and the tutor (these were not the only two kinds of formatting, of course) (see Sierpinska 1997). We called them DATSIT!-formatting and ARUSURE?-formatting. The following transcripts are intended to illustrate these formattings. In both cases the student is reading an introductory section on linear independence of vectors in R^n.

DATSIT!-formatting

The section on linear independence/dependence in the book read by tutor P I and student Endy1 was preceded by a section on homogeneous systems of equations and introduced by an explanation conveying the idea that the new notion is nothing really new, because it reduces to a certain type of question about the solutions of homogeneous systems of equations. The Student Endy1 has finished reading the definitions and a solved example, where the question: 'Is the following set of three 3-dimensional vectors linearly dependent or dependent?' was answered by solving and analyzing the solution of a homogeneous system of equations. The tutor then proceeded, as was his habit, to a small revision or repetition of what had been read.

Tutor P I : *So, a set of vectors is said to be linearly independent when...* (voice rising)?
Endy 1: (shyly) *When there is only a trivial solution.*
P I: *That's it!*
Endy 1: (amazed) *Oh, that's it?*

ARUSURE?-formatting

After having finished reading the definitions of dependent and independent sets of vectors, the student Sandy 3 exclaims:

Sandy 3: *It seems to me that it can happen only in very special cases!*
Tutor P III: *What can happen only in special cases?*
Sandy 3: *That the sum of some vectors multiplied by some numbers can give zero* (points to $a_1v_1+...+ a_nv_n=0$). *It can happen only very exceptionally.*
P III: *Are you sure? Could we try some examples?*

The next hour was occupied by taking vectors, trying to see if it is possible to obtain a zero by multiplying them by some numbers, getting convinced that it is rare but not impossible, concluding that for two vectors to be dependent it is enough that one of them is a multiple of the other, and that in the plane three vectors are always dependent, etc. The book was put aside.

The tutor could have responded: 'Oh come on! Just read on, you'll soon find out you're not completely right'. But the tutor is not doing that, he is taking the student's doubts seriously. By taking them seriously he conveys to him the message that his questioning behavior is all right, that it is welcome. As this kind of interaction is repeated, it becomes a standard or an accepted format of interaction.

These are real life examples of DATSIT! and ARUSURE? formattings. Maybe we could imagine some others, to explain the idea a little better. Suppose a child is reading a text on the division of a natural number by a fraction of the form 1/n. There is a lot of pictures, diagrams in the book, problems of the type: Johnny has 4 pizzas. How many friends can he invite to come over for a snack if each is to be given one third of the pizza. After all this, a framed formula appears: $a:1/n = a*n$. The teacher verifies if the child has learned the lesson: 'So, to divide a number by a fraction... what do you do?'. The student replies, shyly: 'I multiply the number by the denominator?'. The teacher replies: 'That's it!'. The student is a bit astonished but from now on, he multiplies by the denominator, even though the reason why the operation is still called 'division' eludes him. This would be an example of DATSIT!-formatting. Suppose now that, after having gone through the same text and seen the formula, another student says: 'No, that's impossible. Division is supposed to make smaller, not bigger. You divide a piece of cake to share with some friends, you get a smaller piece of cake. Here, they divided 4 by one third and they got 12! That's bigger. There must be some mistake in the book. This must be multiplication, not division'. The teacher says: 'Are you sure that division makes smaller? What does division mean, anyway? Can we try some examples?'. That would be the ARUSURE?-formatting between the teacher and a student-as-learner-from-a-text.

Formatting is a mechanism of stabilization of meaning in interaction that depends on both parties involved in the interaction. In our case, ARUSURE?-formatting worked for the pair P III and Sandy 3; it may not have worked for other combinations. The teacher can establish as a standard or format of interaction only what is already there in some form in the behavior of the students.

In the opinion of most mathematics educators, the ARUSURE?-formatting is the one to be encouraged and the DATSIT!-formatting should be decried as leading to superficial, instrumental understanding. However, the tutor P I, who systematically uses the DATSIT! formatting in teaching undergraduate classes in large sections, has a very high level of success: his students do well on the final exams and very few fail (one or two). It is very difficult to convince P I that there is something wrong with his way of interacting with students. On the other hand, the ARUSURE?-formatting of the interactions with the whole class at the undergraduate level is most of the time impossible. If one student in P III's class reacts like Sandy 3 with questions related to the sense of some statement, and then they embark on the usual ARUSURE?-interaction, the large majority of the class is not seeing it as a standard of behavior to be followed. Other students tend to consider the Sandy 3-like student as a nuisance, who is delaying everybody else in getting on with the course. In this case, unlike in the cheerful 'DATSIT!' -formatting, it is much less obvious that the teacher sets Sandy 3's behavior as a standard. The ARUSURE? formatting with more than one student works only in very special situations, for example, in small graduate classes where students are studying mathematics for its own sake, and where all students normally have the ambition to understand and are not taking the course just as an annoying prerequisite.

Conclusion: Trying to bend reality to an ideology and the question of scientificity of research in mathematics education

The awareness of all the subtle rules and patterns that govern the life of a classroom is indispensable in planning and designing teaching-learning activities, if one does not want to live another disillusionment with ideals such as the one of the classroom as a research team with the teacher as a guide.

The New Math program was perhaps the last desperate effort of mathematics education to bend reality to an idealistic vision. Its failure has brought about the realization that the educational system cannot be manipulated at will according to our whims and dreams. The educational systems of our societies exist and function under constraints that have to be studied and understood and taken into account when taking any action on them. And, in fact, as Chevallard (1985, p. 10) said, this 'determinism' of the educational system must be assumed in order to be able to claim that research in mathematics education produces a scientific knowledge. Every science has an object of study, which must be provided with a certain existential independence from the scientist. For mathematics education this object is the part of the educational system which is related to the teaching of *mathematics.* If the fate of a reform depended on just the good will of teachers and students and having a wise minister of education, research in mathematics education wouldn't even be necessary. All one would need is a police to enforce the law.

But, whatever we say about the New Math phenomenon we have to admit that many developments in mathematics education in the last two or three decades appear to have their roots in it. Some programs started as reactions against its ideology. Others - as theoretical explanations of its failure. Many were made possible thanks to the infrastructure of experienced people and institutions established during the New Math reforms period (Moon 1986; Artigue 1994).

A new view of unity in mathematics

The crucial point of the ideology of the New Math program was to unify the school mathematics, whose main disadvantage, reformers said, is its piecemeal character. The action undertaken to meet this idea was, as is well known, to organise the curriculum on several unifying, fundamental concepts such as set, relation, function, group, vector. The basis of unity was thus the structure of the existing and codified mathematical knowledge. The model mathematics of the New Math program was the academic discipline of mathematics in its most orthodox form.

This view of unified mathematics was perhaps the most criticized element of the New Math reform. In the aftermath of its failure, programs were started that committed themselves to the study of mathematical practices outside of universities and outside of schools and to the demonstration that these practices have an undeniable cultural value. This research has uncovered the existence of spheres of mental activity that, for not satisfying the canons of Greek, or Cartesian, or Boolean rationality, have nonetheless a definite rationality of their own. Programs linked to 'ethnomathematics', 'teaching mathematics in contexts', 'realistic mathematics', capitalize on this rehabilitation of everyday mathematical practices in different cultures in promoting their models of curricula, organization of classroom work, assessment through projects, taking into account the knowledge and mathematical skills that children bring to school from their out-of-school experiences.

Of course, these programs have their opponents, whose ideal of mathematics does not correspond to such pan-mathematical views (mathematics everywhere). For these opponents, when somebody is using numbers in calculating or measuring or even planning a calculation or a measurement, or playing with numbers and creating geometrical patterns, he or she is not yet doing mathematics. They say that mathematics starts with reflection on these practices, generalization and proof.

Moreover, the criticism of the piecemeal character of traditional school mathematics has never been given up, and the ideal of unity remained in force albeit with a changed notion of what actually constitutes this unity. In fact, there could be several views on what constitutes the unity of mathematics. Roughly two have been identified above. One goes in the direction of universalism: the pan-mathematics or 'mathematics everywhere' perspective. The other sees unity in the mathematical ways of thinking that can manifest themselves in any domain of human activity. In particular, it sees integration among mathematical domains, like geometry, algebra, analysis, not in that their concepts can all be expressed on the basis of the language of sets, relations and functions, but because the geometric, algebraic and analytic modes of thinking are in constant interaction, and one cannot, and, in fact, never could be a specialist in one without knowing anything about and using the other. Both movements have turned away from a synchronic and static view of the finished and written down mathematical knowledge towards a diachronic and dynamic view of mathematics as a specific activity and a specific process of theory building, theory verification, and theory application.

Revision of theories leading to new theories

The failure of the New Math program was a rude awakening to a reality that turned out to be a complete unknown. But the program was justifying its ideologies and didactic actions by theories and experimental research. One way to understand the failure was to have a second look at these theories. Another was to study the reality of mathematics classes, and the actual processes of 'discovery' or 'construction' of mathematical concepts without the student being discretely guided by some inspired teacher (Diénès or Polyá). Another reaction to the failure was to produce some home grown 'theories for didactic action', that would be specific for mathematics and for education and not just compilations of theories borrowed from psychology, sociology or general education.

From Diénès' 'six stages' to Brousseau's theory of didactic situations: an example of a theoretical refutation of a theory for action in mathematics education.

The verification of theories was not always oriented towards checking their fitness with reality. Criticism and refutation were sometimes done on the theoretical level, for example, by demonstrating an internal logical flaw. This was the fate of the well known theory of psychodynamic process of concept formation in six stages of Diénès, or rather of its interpretations by the mathematics educators who were trying to apply it in practice in France. The refutation, by Brousseau (1980, p. 40), of Diénès' theory was accompanied by the proposal of an alternative theory, also aimed at the creation of the conditions for an artificial genesis of mathematical concepts in the mathematics classroom, the *theory of didactic situations.*

Brousseau's argument is theoretical; it does not refer to some observable facts that would contradict the statements of the theory. But the heuristic genesis of this argument is empirical, according to the author's account: The very fact that he arrived at the idea that there must be something wrong with Diénès' theory, has its roots in observation of classes, and in his understanding of those subtle workings of the actual teaching and learning processes, their contractual character, that make the classroom interactions proceed smoothly while at the same time students do not learn at all or learn something totally different from what is aimed at.

These facts in the development of mathematics education programs could well be but instances of two more general regularities or phenomena. One is that a theory is never refuted if an alternative theory is not already there, waiting to replace it. The second has to do with the role of experience, whether the everyday teacher's experience or the more systematic and planned observation and experiment. Sometimes, on the basis of a theoretical analysis alone, it could be seen that some didactic actions are bound for failure. However, very often, these theoretical arguments only leap to our eyes after the action was undertaken and failed. Of course, sometimes this happens because we did not reflect on the planned action well enough prior to the experience. More often than not, however, the experience suggests and inspires the creation of a theory or of new elements of an existing theory which only allow to construct the refuting argument.

Revision of theories leading to shift in focus: Constructivism, Problem Solving, Theory of Situations

By studying children's *actual* conceptualizations of quantitative relations (as opposed to those fancied by the school-readiness tests of the psychologists) researchers have come to realize that in the New Math program perhaps the most important consequence of Piaget's epistemological constructivism was forgotten, namely, that knowledge is always an answer to *one's own* problem.

Children and students at school have problems that are not purely mathematical but more often than not social: They are the problems of survival and success in the school institution and not the problems of researchers who want to establish or find the truth. As children and students interpret their school tasks, they stumble upon things that are problems for them, and it is these problems that they solve. For example, when a child is given the task to solve an arithmetical story problem, his or her problem can be: 'What am I supposed to do here? Add? No, we were doing subtractions all day yesterday, so I better subtract. Now, this number is smaller than this other one, so I better subtract this one'. The teacher may have expected the students to read and carefully analyze the story and match the operation with the context, i.e. she would have expected that the students' problem will be mathematical modelisation of the situation from the story, but this student's problem was to correctly guess what operation is being practiced today in class. More generally, in many cases, the student's problem is, to a large extent, to find the hidden rules of the game that is taking place in the classroom, to unravel the expectations of the teacher, the constraints in which the teacher acts, and to adapt oneself to these rules, expectations and constraints.

What the students learn is the result of solving their own problems. They learn mathematical knowledge if the problems they have are mathematical.

How do we, as teachers, make the students have mathematical problems?

The question of how do we make students have mathematical problems has occupied mathematics educators in all their programs of research. But certainly the programs related to the problem solving approach, constructivism and the theory of didactic situations have been especially preoccupied with it on their 'theory-for-action' level.

While the focus of constructivism is on the developing child, the problem solving program and theory of situations are looking at the acquisition, by students, of a certain culturally shared or taken-as-shared knowledge. They both focus very much on didactic action and on the design and verification of classroom activities, but they have different views on the goals of these activities.

Most importantly, the problem solving approach gives a different role to tasks and problems than the theory of situations does. In fact, the theory of situations speaks of 'situations' of which problems constitute only a part, but even then they may not be problems in the classical sense of mathematics problems like

'For what values of a does the pair of equations
$$x^2-y^2=0$$
$$(x-a)^2+y^2=1$$
have 0,1,2,3,4, or 5 solutions?'.

(Schoenfeld 1990)

To give an example of a didactic 'situation' in the sense of the theory of situations, let us take one proposed by Brousseau himself (Brousseau 1986, p. 449).

Example

The objective of the proposed situation is to have students engage in producing a mathematical argument in geometry as opposed to an empirical argument of the type: it's clear from the drawing or from the construction. The idea of the project is to put students in a situation where the observation of drawings alone leads to a false statement, and this falsity can only be proved by remaining on the level of discursive knowledge. The situation is the following. Students are asked to draw a rather large triangle ABC in which one of the angles is obtuse and greater than 150°. In this triangle the students are then asked to draw the perpendicular bisectors of the sides. It is difficult to make very precise drawings and the three bisectors form another triangle, a very small one, A'B'C'. Now the teacher gives the students another problem, in form of a competition: Who can find a triangle ABC for which the triangle A'B'C' is substantially bigger? After a number of unsuccessful trials, some students put up a conjecture that there must be some reason for not being able to make this triangle any bigger. A debate may start where the proponents of the conjecture are trying to find this reason, and the arguments of the debate don't refer to the drawing anymore, since it is misleading, but to the properties of perpendicular bisectors as loci of points equidistant from two fixed points. In this situation, the usual contract between the students and the teacher, where the teacher is proposing only problems that have solutions, is broken. The teacher is now in the role of an older (or smarter) friend who has taken the students for a ride. The only way the students can save their faces is to beat the smart guy with his own weapon, and find the mathematical reason for which the proposed task is impossible.

What the student is supposed to learn in the problem solving approach is skills of problem solving in general and he or she is expected to experience mathematics the way mathematicians do. A problem is not chosen specifically to overcome a certain obstacle or to have the students use as a tool some concept that will later on become thematized as subject matter. These problems are just considered as 'challenging' - they are non-routine, and they are demanding intellectually, they force the student to use the knowledge introduced in the course in a way that is not just repeating a routine technique or a method. The problem of the two equations with a parameter above is not even a non-standard problem, yet it could be used in a problem solving course. The purpose of offering it to the students is to convince them maybe about the advantages of a heuristic strategy called 'draw a diagram whenever possible', suggested by Polyá. One kind of problems in the problem-solving approach that is closer to those intended in the theory of situations, are problems of the type 'discover a flaw, find the error'. These problems normally do address a certain definite misconception, and solving the problem helps to overcome this misconception, by bringing it to the level of awareness.

Theory of situations forces the educator and the designer of didactic action to think about the essence of mathematical concepts: what kinds of problems are they meant to solve, in what contexts are they applicable, what was their historical genesis? This kind of epistemological analysis is necessary in devising the so-called artificial genesis of a mathematical concept in students.

Example

Suppose that in a linear algebra course, you have to teach the notion of kernel of a linear transformation. You can start by giving the students the definition and then some exercises to calculate the kernels of some simple linear mappings. But will the students see what is the point of having this new notion at all? So you start thinking about the essence of this notion, and, for example, you come to the conclusion that the kernel measures the aspects of the vector that are ignored by the transformation, or how far is the transformation from being a one-to-one transformation. So, rather than starting by giving the formal definition, you start by posing a problem, for example: How much does the given transformation deform the space? How would you characterize the difference between vectors which, after the transformation, become indistinguishable?

But, in fact, thinking about the essence of mathematical concepts has occupied mathematics educators in all programs, whether it was done from a synchronic or a diachronic point of view. Of course, views change, and, for example, the essence of the notion of function had been seen, in turn, in its unifying character for all of mathematics (recall the famous slogan of *funktionales Denken)*, or it was seen as a model for relationships between variable magnitudes, a special kind of relation, a triple (domain, co-domain, rule), a machine turning inputs into outputs, a process, etc.

Of course, the outcomes of this work of thinking about the essence of a mathematical concept can be different depending on the epistemology of mathematics adopted by the program. In the constructivist approach, for example, the notion of number has sometimes been replaced by the notion of 'number sense'. In the Vygotskian tradition as maintained by, for example, Davydov, 'the basic concept underlying the domain of real numbers studied in middle school is quantity...'. This idea is supported by the view that historically and culturally, 'the concept of number arises within the context of measurement of a continuous quantity so that a multiple relationship is established between that quantity and a part of it that is used as a unit of measure'. Of course, seeing the essence of number in the notion of quantity (for the purposes of teaching at the elementary level) had been in the tradition of teaching mathematics for a very long time, it is not an invention of Davydov. One can find it in many older texts on the teaching of arithmetic to school children. One example is Warren Colburn's book *First Lessons in Arithmetic on the Plan of Pestalozzi, with some Improvements,* first published in USA in 1821, and still selling in thousands of copies a hundred years later (cf. Bidwell & Clason 1970, p. 13).

Let us, however, come back to reality. Even with the best of designs of didactic action, some of our students will look at mathematical problems as someone else's problems, not their own. I am not even talking about students whose personal and family problems overwhelm anything they could be doing at school. I am talking about those students who never miss a class, conscienciously take notes and do their assignments yet never invest much of their heart and intellect in what they are doing. When we observe gifted or motivated students doing mathematics, we see that they don't wait for the teacher to provide them with an interesting question, problem or situation. Of course, they grab any such opportunity and enjoy it, but most of the time they turn ordinary problems into their own problems by transforming them, extending them, linking them to other problems, etc.

They, in a sense, 'open up' these ordinary, seemingly closed problems, and by opening them up, these problems become their own. They talk to problems, they ask them questions, and, in return, they gain knowledge by solving them. In fact, 'openness' is not a property of a problem. Openness is a property of the relation between the solver and the problem. I am not sure I should be saying this, but it could well be that our efforts to make our students have mathematical problems are lost on students who are not motivated and superfluous in case of those who are.

The problematization of language and communication in the mathematics classroom

There is a lot of talk about 'communication' in mathematics education nowadays. Communication is seen as the most important aspect of learning, education, assessment. Education is defined as a communicative process. So is assessment.

> Assessment is a communication process in which assessors - whether students themselves, techers, or others - learn something about what students know and can do and in which students learn something about what assessors value (NCTM 1995, p. 13).
> [E]ducation is best understood as a communicative process that consists largely in the growth of shared mental contexts and terms of reference through which the various discourses of education (the various 'subjects' and their associated academic abilities) come to be intelligible to those who use them (Edwards & Mercer 1987, p. 63).

The discursive aspects of knowledge are stressed or knowledge is equated with discourse. What children have to learn at school is the 'mathematical discourse'. It is considered sometimes that 'mathematics is a language and... [since] language is best learned in a community of other learners' it is clear why having the students talk mathematically in the classroom is seen as so important. The ideal of a classroom is 'a discourse community'. What should control the flow of ideas in the classroom are 'student-defended conjectures and experience-gathered evidence' not textbooks (Elliot & Kenney 1996, p. ix).

From the interactionist point of view, communication is important because of the assumption that how we communicate partly determines what we communicate. Depending on the format of interaction between the teacher and the students in a primary classroom in the context of, say, addition, the students will be learning 'number facts' or 'mathematical argumentation'.

We have the feeling that the problematization of language and communication in the mathematics classroom is a recent invention. But if we look at the 1979 survey paper by Austin and Howson then we see how long-standing and well researched is this issue. It is important to note that the range of methodologies developed and used for research into classroom interaction was quite large. Methods of observing and recording verbal classroom interaction were devised. Not only statistical but also qualitative methods were used, concentrating on language behavior during teacher-student interaction.

But certainly there is a lot more stress on (a) the linguistic character of knowledge, and (b) students' talk in the classroom, learning through talking or writing, etc. However, this focus may bring about some risks.

One is the neglect of the non-linguistic aspects of mathematical notions. In fact, a good part of mathematical thinking requires not so much linguistic skills as a lot of imagination. Take, for example, the notion of variable and all the notions that follow: dependence, relationship, change, rate of change, etc. Of course, one could say that there is nothing more linguistic than a variable: it is a letter. But is it really? Okay, it is a letter denoting an arbitrary element of a set. Or something whose values can change. Does all this help to understand that the equation $2x+3y=1$ represents a straight line? Or that $x=r \cos(t)$, $y=r \sin(t)$ represents a circle? We all know how difficult it is to 'explain' the notion of variable to a student who has problems with it. We use all sorts of means, metaphors, pictures, or even dynamic computer representations. Very often we fail and maybe we are bound to fail because words or pictures are like snapshots of a flying arrow: They are pictures of the arrow, not of the movement. They are pictures of a concrete object, not of an arbitrary object. Arbitrariness and movement cannot be conveyed with linguistic means; Zeno's paradox of the arrow can be seen as pointing to exactly this impossibility.

Another thing that may escape our attention in our preoccupation with communication is silence: silent speech and thinking to oneself, not out loud; listening to others; reading mathematical texts, yes, also reading textbooks. The stress put on active participation of students in the building of the mathematical cultures of the classrooms through speaking, discussing and writing in the recent programs in mathematics education has left the passive learning, through reading and listening to others, a little bit in the shadow. Teachers who are making their students work with textbooks are even frowned upon, as if 'textbook classes' necessarily promoted rote learning.

Already the New Math reformers were expressing fears that the stress on 'active learning' may lead to neglecting the culture of reading mathematical texts and listening to oral presentations of mathematics.

In learning mathematics, as in learning languages, the active aspects - expressing our own ideas, using mathematics and language as a tool - are of paramount importance, but they have to be supplemented by passive aspects - understanding the ideas of others, assimilating them, allowing them to bear fruit. Developing in students the habit of learning from books or from oral exposition is an important component of mathematical education. Those who have sufficient experience in the active aspects are more likely to behave actively during these passive periods. For example, they put the book aside before a proof starts and try to construct the proof themselves; or try to find examples from general statements, or to generalize from examples. On the other hand, they who have acquired competence in the technique of reading (or listening to) mathematics, gain a powerful means therein for widening the scope of their mathematical understanding; this widening is likely to help in their more active work, their rediscovering mathematics or discovering it anew (Varga, 1971, p. 28).

Moreover, they were realizing, and Krygowska was voicing this realization at the ICME congress in Nice in 1968 that reading mathematical texts is a specific skill that needs to be allotted special time and attention in the teaching of mathematics; most children and students cannot be left alone to figure it out for themselves (Krygowaska 1969).

Conclusion

Mathematics education as a whole is a web of many programs, some collaborating, some competing. These programs focus on different things. Some - on the cognitive aspects of learning mathematics, the conceptions and understandings that students built of mathematical notions. Others - on the growth of knowledge through the use of material and cultural tools, like measurement devices or language or computers. Others still - on mathematical interactions between people and culture. Yet others focus on design and experimentation of didactic action, and building theories for this action. Programs have distinct ideologies, epistemologies of mathematics, theories for and of action, methodologies, and different standards of validation of their results. A piece of research may not be understandable for an outsider if he or she is not able to place it in some program he or she knows about, or if he or she is not informed about the basic assumptions and underlying frameworks of the research. This is why research reports in mathematics education often start with expositions of the programs to which they belong.

Very many articles in mathematics education journals as well as books are devoted to the presentation and discussion of a particular program or comparing it with other programs. Research descriptions are used only as documents supporting this or that claim, or illustrations stressing this or that point. This is because programs in mathematics education do not belong to established paradigms; they are all in the state of development. The work of presentation and discussion is not done merely in the aim of popularizing a program; it is substantially contributing to the development of the program through a clearer articulation of its stance, through becoming aware of the hidden assumptions, through a sharper statement of the goals and methods of didactic action, etc.

All this is an important work to be done in a domain of scientific research in statu nascendi. However, this work is not producing results in the form of design and justification of didactic action. It is producing improvements of theories to back up the design and the justification, or it is producing academic debates about theories, methodologies and programs in general, i.e. it is producing 'meta-results' rather than results proper.

This 'foundationalism' of mathematics education, or the concern of mathematics education with its theoretical foundations is a symptom of its uncertainty about its scientific character. In spite of the achievements and developments that date not from 25 or 30 years ago but from much earlier, mathematics education still does not feel as an established academic discipline. Could it be, however, that things are the other way round? Could it be that mathematics education has trouble becoming an established and recognized academic discipline because it is overly concerned with its foundations? Wouldn't it help if mathematics education produced more results than meta-results and also valued its results at least equally as its meta-results?

References

Artigue, M.: 1998, Research in Mathematics Education through the Eyes of Mathematicians, in A. Sierpinska & J. Kilpatrick (eds.), *Mathematics Education as a Research Domain: A Search for Identity* (pp. 477-489), Kluwer Academic Publishers, Dortrecht.

Austin, J.L. & Howson, A.G.: 1979, 'Language and Mathematical Education', *Educational Studies in Mathematics 10,* 161-197.

Ausubel, D.P.: 1964, 'Some Psychological and Educational Limitations of Learning by Discovery', *The Arithmetics Teacher 11,* 290-302.

Bidwell, J.K. & Clason, R.G. (eds.): 1970. *Readings in the History of Mathematics Education,* National Council of Teachers of Mathematics, Washington, D.C.

Braillly, A.: 1968-9, 'Un Exemple d'Exploitation d'une Situation', *Educational Studies in Mathematics 1,* 237-243.

Bromme, R.: 1994, 'Beyond Subject Matter: A Psychological Topology of Teachers' Professional Knowledge', in R. Biehler, R.W. Scholz, R. Sträßer & B. Winkelmann (eds.), *Didactics of Mathematics as a Scientific Discipline* (pp. 73-88), Kluwer Academic Publishers, Dortrecht.

Brousseau, G.: 1980, 'Problèmes de l'Enseignement des Décimaux', *Recherches en Didactique des Mathématiques 1.1*, 11-60.

Brousseau, G.: 1986, *Théorisation des Phénomènes d'Enseignement des Mathématiques.* Thèse pour Obtenir le Grade de Docteur d'Etat ès Sciences.

Bruner, J.S.: 1985, 'The Role of Interaction Formats in Language Acquisition', in J.P. Forgas (ed.), *Language and Social Situations,* Springer-Verlag, New York.

Chevallard, Y.: 1985, *La Transposition Didactique du Savoir Savant au Savoir Enseigné*, La Pensée Sauvage éditions, Grenoble.

Cobb, P. & Bauersfeld, H. (eds.): 1995, *The Emergence of Mathematical Meaning: Interaction in Classroom Cultures,* Lawrence Erlbaum Associates, Publishers, Hillsdale, New Jersey.

Cobb, P. & Whitenack, J.W.: 1996, 'A Method for Conducting Longitudinal Analyses of Classroom Videorecordings and Transcripts', *Educational Studies in Mathematics 30.3*, 213-228.

Coulthard, R.M. & Sinclair, J.: 1975, *Towards an Analysis of Discourse,* Oxford University Press, London.

Davydov, V.V.: 1982, 'The Psychological Characteristics of the Formation of Elementary Mathematical Operations in Children', in T.P. Carpenter, J.M. Moser, T.A. Romberg (Eds.), *Addition and Subtraction: A Cognitive Perspective* (pp. 224-238), Lawrence Erlbaum Associates, Publishers, Hillsdale, New Jersey.

Duncker, K.: 1945, *On Problem Solving,* Psychological Monograph, vol. 58, no. 15, American Psychological Association.

Edwards, D. & Mercer, N.: 1987, *Common Knowledge. The Development of Understanding in the Classroom,* Routledge, London and New York.

Elliot, P.C. & Kenney, M.J. (eds.): 1996, Communication in Mathematics, *K-12 and Beyond. The 1996 NCTM Yearbook,* National Council of Teachers of Mathematics, Reston, Virginia.

Fey, J.T.: 1969, *Patterns of Verbal Communication in Mathematics Classes,* PhD thesis, Columbia University.

Goffman, E.: 1974, *Frame Analysis: An Essay on the Organisation of Experience,* Harvard University Press, Cambridge, Massachussetts.

Hammersley, M.: 1989, *The Dilemma of Qualitative Method, Herbert Blumer and the Chicago Tradition*, Routledge, London and New York.

Krummheuer, G.: 1995, 'The Ethnography of Argumentation', in P. Cobb & H. Bauersfeld (eds.), *The Emergence of Mathematical Meaning: Interaction in Classroom Cultures* (pp. 229-270), Lawrence Erlbaum Associates, Publishers, Hillsdale, New Jersey.

Krygowska, Z.: 1969, 'Le Texte Mathématique dans l'Enseignement', *Educational Studies in Mathematics 2*, 360-370.

Kulm, G. (Ed.): 1991, *Assessing Higher Order Thinking in Mathematics*, American Association for the Advancement of Science, Washington, D.C.

Moon, B.: 1986, *The 'New Maths' Curriculum Controversy, An International Story*, The Falmer Press, London.

Morgan, C.: 1992, 'Written Reports of Mathematical Problem Solving', A contribution to ICME 7, Working group 7: *Language and Communication in the Mathematics Classroom*, Québec, Canada.

National Council of Teachers of Mathematics: 1995, *Assessment Standards for School Mathematics*. National Council of Teachers of Mathematics, Reston, Virginia.

Peel, E.A.: 1971, 'Psychological and Educational Research Bearing on Mathematics Teaching, in W. Servais & T. Varga (Eds.), *Teaching School Mathematics* (pp. 151-177), A UNESCO Source Book, Penguin Books Inc., Middlesex, England.

Pimm, D.: 1996, 'Diverse Communications', in P.C. Elliot & M.J. Kenney (Eds.), *Communication in Mathematics, K-12 and Beyond* (pp. 11-19), NCTM, Reston, Virginia.

Sarrazy, B.: 1995, 'Le Contrat Didactique', *Revue Française de Pédagogie* 112, 85-118.

Schoenfeld, A.H. 1985, *Mathematical Problem Solving*, Academic Press, New York.

Servais, W. & Varga, T.: 1971, *Teaching School Mathematics, A UNESCO Source Book*, Penguin Books Inc., Middlesex, England.

Sierpinska, A.: 1997, Formats of Interaction and Model Readers, *For the Learning of Mathematics 17.2*, 3-12.

Varga, T.: 1971, 'General Introduction', in W. Servais & T. Varga (eds.), *Teaching School Mathematics* (pp. 11-33), A UNESCO Source Book, Penguin Books Inc., Middlesex, England.

Voigt, J.: 1995, 'Thematic Patterns of Interaction and Sociomathematical Norms', in P. Cobb & H. Bauersfeld (eds.), *The Emergence of Mathematical Meaning: Interaction in Classroom Cultures* (pp. 163-202), Lawrence Erlbaum Associates, Publishers, Hillsdale, New Jersey.

Yackel, E. & Cobb, P.: 1996, 'Socio-mathematical Norms, Argumentation and Autonomy in Mathematics',
Journal for Research in Mathematics Education 27.4, 458-477.

EL PAPEL DEL MATEMÁTICO EN LA EDUCACIÓN MATEMÁTICA

Miguel de Guzmán

LA TAREA DE LA COMUNIDAD MATEMÁTICA

La tarea fundamental y general de la comunidad matemática consiste en contribuir de modo efectivo al **desarrollo integral de la cultura humana.**

Esto es precisamente lo que ha hecho desde el principio de su existencia. La matemática es, en el fondo, una exploración de las diversas estructuras complejas del universo. Analizar estas estructuras no ha sido en general un mero ejercicio especulativo o académico, sino un ejercicio práctico en el que se ha buscado muy pretendidamente la utilidad y el progreso de la cultura humana.

La matemática exploró inicialmente **la multiplicidad** presente en las cosas a su alrededor y para dominarla creó el número y la aritmética. El examen de las estructuras **del espacio y de la forma** condujeron al matemático hacia la geometría. El **estudio de las transformaciones y cambios en el tiempo** del mundo a su alrededor le condujeron al análisis matemático. El intento de enfrentarse y dominar hasta cierto punto **la incertidumbre** le condujo a la creación de la probabilidad y la estadística como herramientas para hacerlo eficazmente. El examen de las propias **estructuras mentales del pensamiento,** matemático o no, le llevaron hacia la construcción de la lógica, ...

Pero hay algo aún más profundo en el desarrollo de la matemática. La búsqueda de la **belleza intelectual,** esa belleza, como diría Platón "únicamente asequible por los ojos del alma", ha sido y siempre será uno de los estímulos más importantes en el quehacer incansable de la comunidad matemática. En la comunidad pitagórica este aspecto profundo de nuestra ciencia encaminó al matemático hacia los aspectos más hondos del ser y hacia la contemplación reverencial de la divinidad, que se presiente más o menos veladamente a través de la **armonía intelectual del universo.**

Pero la matemática se ha ejercitado también por razón de sus **aspectos lúdicos,** por sus **conexiones con el arte.** Se ha examinado **como modelo y como campo de trabajo por filósofos y por psicólogos,** etc. etc.

En resumen, las contribuciones de la matemática a la cultura humana han sido extraordinarias y extraordinariamente variadas y lo seguirán siendo aún más en el futuro. Como decía en 1923 Alfred N. Whitehead, uno de los grandes matemáticos y filósofos de nuestro siglo, con una visión certera y profética:

Si la civilización continúa avanzando, en los próximos 2000 años la novedad predominante en el pensamiento humano será el señorío de la intelección matemática.

La gran tarea de la matemática es, sin duda, seguir contribuyendo de múltiples formas, tan enriquecedoras como las que he mencionado, al progreso de la cultura humana.

LAS SUBTAREAS CONCRETAS

Entre las formas específicas de llevar adelante este objetivo global yo destacaría, para lo que aquí nos va a interesar, tres:

-resolver los problemas del campo y los que el desarrollo de la sociedad propone
-conservar y transmitir el legado matemático
-transferir a la sociedad los resultados de sus éxitos

Es claro que uno de los cometidos más importantes consiste en tratar de ir resolviendo aquellos problemas que de forma natural surgen en los diferentes campos de la matemática. Unos brotan de las preguntas propias del desarrollo interno de las matemáticas, otros aparecen propuestos por el progreso de otras ciencias que buscan constantemente su apoyo en la matemática. Otros surgen de la necesidad del desarrollo de nuevos instrumentos, de nuevas técnicas para diversos propósitos.

Junto a esta importante misión se presenta también la de ir estructurando los resultados y las teorías que van surgiendo, a fin de entenderlas mejor, de hacerlas más sencillas para poder profundizar más en ellas y para hacerlas así más asequibles a las generaciones posteriores.

La segunda subtarea importante consiste en conservar y transmitir el legado matemático acumulado durante los muchos siglos de crecimiento. La riqueza cultural que para la humanidad representa el acerbo de conocimientos y experiencias matemáticas a lo largo de varios milenios constituye un bien extraordinario para el hombre. Transmitirla de la mejor manera posible a las generaciones posteriores para hacerlas capaces de utilizarla y de ampliarla es un trabajo extraordinariamente complejo por razones diversas y fáciles de entender. He aquí algunas:

los **contenidos matemáticos** son estructuras elaboradas a través de un amplio esfuerzo colectivo que, en muchos casos, ha tenido lugar durante muchos siglos de esfuerzos de mentes muy privilegiadas. Es natural que la labor de transmisión presente problemas bien complicados

la transmisión de tales contenidos ha de hacerse poniendo la atención en las **personas concretas** a quienes van dirigidos, con características afectivas, cognitivas, ambientales, etc. muy diferentes que es necesario tener en cuenta

tales personas están inmersas **en una cultura y en una sociedad** bien específicas, con sus formas de existencia y de comunicación propias y marcadamente diferentes unas de otras.

La tercera subtarea mencionada consiste en **transmitir a la sociedad, de forma adecuada, los logros que la comunidad matemática obtiene.** Esto constituye también una seria obligación de la comunidad matemática en su conjunto. Se trata de ser útil a la sociedad, pero también es necesario ayudar a la sociedad a percibir el papel real que la matemática ha ejercido y sigue ejerciendo en el desarrollo general de la cultura humana a fin de que la sociedad, con esta persuasión, siga apoyando de modo efectivo la labor que la matemática realiza.

Es ésta una tarea extraordinariamente importante y delicada para la que no se puede delegar en personas ajenas a la comunidad matemática. Si la comunidad matemática, en su conjunto, descuida su presencia en la sociedad, ésta también acabará por considerar sin importancia el quehacer de los matemáticos y actuará de acuerdo con esta percepción. Es necesario que nos esforcemos por hacer bien conocida la presencia de la matemática en nuestra cultura, entre otras razones porque se trata de una realidad que para nosotros es patente.

LAS SUBCOMUNIDADES

Y correspondiendo a las diferentes tareas señaladas que la comunidad matemática en su conjunto ha de realizar, se pueden observar en ella varias subcomunidades suficientemente diferenciadas:

-personas dedicadas a la investigación de los problemas internos de la matemática o de los problemas provenientes de las aplicaciones

Este es el grupo que, un tanto impropiamente, se suele llamar de "matemáticos". Su interés principal consiste en resolver los problemas que van surgiendo en su campo y en estar atento, en comunicación con otros profesionales y científicos, a las posibles implicaciones y aplicaciones que su trabajo pueda tener

-personas dedicadas a la transmisión del saber y del quehacer matemático a las generaciones posteriores

El grupo de los maestros y profesores, cuya labor de introducción adecuada de los más jóvenes en el quehacer matemático y en el placer y utilidad que éste quehacer puede proporcionar es absolutamente esencial para el desarrollo y bienestar de la comunidad matemática

-personas dedicadas a la investigación en los problemas propios de tal transmisión

La existencia de un grupo que estudie intensamente los problemas de la transmisión del saber hacer matemático a otras generaciones, es decir el grupo de los investigadores en educación matemática, es un fenómeno reciente que está sólidamente motivado, a mi parecer, por las fuertes dificultades que esta transmisión ofrece, como antes he mencionado, por la necesidad creciente de una formación matemática más extensa y profunda para un segmento cada vez más amplio de personas y por las penosas experiencias que recientemente han experimentado generaciones de jóvenes con ocasión de la puesta en práctica masiva de procesos de aprendizaje que han demostrado al poco tiempo resultar ineficaces, cuando no seriamente perjudiciales

-usuarios de la matemática

Las personas que tratan de sacar el mejor partido posible de los resultados y las teorías de la matemática en su trabajo técnico, profesional, científico, que proponen cuestiones y problemas a la consideración de los investigadores matemáticos y que apoya de muchos modos la vida de la comunidad matemática

-educadores matemáticos de la sociedad (divulgadores)

Aquellas personas dentro de la comunidad matemática que, con especial sensibilidad, tratan de realizar la importante tarea de acercar a la sociedad los resultados de todo el esfuerzo de la comunidad matemática, a fin de hacer claro el papel de la matemática en la cultura humana en general y en la sociedad en la que vive.

La lista no es exhaustiva ni tampoco hay que pensar en que estos sean grupos disjuntos. Al contrario, lo deseable sería que las intersecciones de tales grupos fueran bien nutridas y que la comunicación y el posible paso por un grupo u otro de una persona en concreto fuera un hecho fácil y ordinario.

Lo ideal sería que cada uno de los miembros de la comunidad matemática tuviera la magnífica experiencia de formar parte simultáneamente o por algún período, de varias de estas subcomunidades. Y de hecho, como veremos más adelante, a lo largo de los siglos ha habido personas que han realizado con éxito esto que a algunos les puede parecer una utopía.

ALGUNAS PREGUNTAS EN RELACIÓN CON EL TEMA CENTRAL

El tema de mi intervención aquí es el papel del matemático en la educación matemática. Con relación a él se pueden indicar varias preguntas interesantes que trataré de responder:

-¿hay razones para que el matemático se preocupe por la educación?
Es decir, ¿puede el matemático encontrar motivaciones específicas que tengan que ver con su propia tarea para preocuparse y dedicarse él mismo a examinar a fondo la situación actual de la educación matemática en su entorno más próximo, en su país, en el mundo en general?

-¿puede aportar el matemático algo específico en los problemas alrededor de la educación matemática?
Es decir, ¿echaremos de menos algo verdaderamente importante si el matemático no nos dice su palabra en torno a los problemas en educación matemática, algo que otros no pueden aportar?

-¿en qué tareas podría participar más activamente?
Por su propia forma de ver, estar y hacer en la comunidad matemática, ¿tiene el matemático algún lugar relevante y especial a la hora de contribuir a aclarar los problemas y las tomas de decisión en torno a la educación matemática?

-¿por qué hay tan pocos que participen?
¿Qué circunstancias se dan en la actual estructura de la comunidad matemática para que sean relativamente escasos los matemáticos que colaboran activamente en el examen a fondo y en la solución de los problemas relacionados con la educación matemática?

-¿dónde están los buenos ejemplos?
¿Se pueden señalar matemáticos influyentes y reconocidos que se hayan ocupado activamente de los problemas relacionados con la educación matemática?

-¿existen problemas en las relaciones matemático-educador-investigador en educación matemática?
Es decir ¿se dan entre las diferentes subcomunidades matemáticas el grado de aceptación y respeto mutuo y el grado de colaboración que serían deseables?

-¿se pueden señalar algunas tareas que en la actualidad se estimen como más urgentes e importantes?
Posiblemente en prácticamente todos los campos de la educación matemática sería muy bueno escuchar con atención en todo momento lo que los matemáticos tengan que decir, pero en cada situación concreta habrá probablemente temas de urgencia en los que su intervención sea particularmente necesitada y bienvenida, ¿se pueden señalar algunos hoy día?

Trataré a continuación de decir esbozar tentativamente algunas respuestas en torno a estas preguntas.

UNA RAZÓN PODEROSA PARA LA IMPLICACIÓN DEL MATEMÁTICO: LA PROPIA ENSEÑANZA, LA PROPIA COMUNICACIÓN

La creación matemática tiene muchos puntos en común con la creación artística. La satisfacción del artista no puede reducirse a crear belleza y a contentarse con percibir la belleza que él ha creado. Necesita compartir su creación de la forma más perfecta posible.

Enseñar matemáticas tiene también este aspecto de comunicación y difusión de las creaciones matemáticas, ya procedan de uno mismo ya sean obra de otros. Parece natural que, en principio, el matemático creativo debería ser la persona mejor capacitada para percibir y transmitir la belleza de las creaciones matemáticas. Tratar de hacerse capaz de comunicar de manera adecuada la forma matemática que uno ha percibido implica interesarse a fondo por los modos más efectivos de educación matemática.

Enseñar matemáticas es también compartir esa visión personal a la que uno ha llegado tal vez tras muchos años de dedicación entusiasmada a un campo particular, hacer partícipes a otros de esos momentos de contemplación profunda, seguramente de algún modo única, con los que cada uno de los matemáticos se encuentra en su propio trabajo. Quien se hace capaz de realizar esta comunicación con éxito experimenta sin duda una enorme satisfacción. Y esto implica también interesarse por los modos más efectivos de transmisión de los conocimientos matemáticos, es decir por la educación matemática.

Posiblemente estas fuerzas han sido las que han impulsado en el fondo a los grandes comunicadores de la matemática, como Euler, por ejemplo, "el maestro de todos nosotros". Leer sus obras es como hacer una excursión por parajes admirables acompañados por un experto guía que nos conduce por senderos fáciles y nos hace descubrir al tiempo bellezas insospechadas a nuestro alrededor.

Pero, por otra parte, enseñar es realizar una labor de inculturación, de inmersión en la comunidad matemática de los más jóvenes de cada generación, a fin de que puedan aprender, en el taller mismo del matemático, el oficio propio del quehacer matemático. Al fin y al cabo, la matemática es mucho más un saber hacer que un mero saber. Y esto no se aprende con recetas escritas sino con el contacto con el maestro. Para ello el matemático que se ocupa de resolver los problemas propios de un campo matemático es sin duda la persona más adecuada.

También hay otro punto de vista, el del propio provecho personal, por el que el matemático podría tratar de interesarse por los problemas de la educación matemática. Todos solemos salir enriquecidos de nuestro propio ejercicio de enseñar. ¿Quién de nosotros no ha tenido ocasión de ser profundamente estimulado hacia una visión nueva, distinta, más honda, por las preguntas y observaciones de las propias personas a las que pensábamos estar enseñando? Ellas tienen muchas veces una mirada nueva sobre el mismo panorama que para nosotros ya parecía haber perdido los colores y el brillo inicial.

Littlewood, uno de los grandes analistas de nuestro siglo, cuenta cómo Marcel Riesz descubrió uno de sus famosos resultados en análisis armónico. Estaba Riesz simplemente jugando con la integral de una función analítica a fin de proponer un examen a sus alumnos cuando de ella saltó ante su asombrada mirada algo que le llamó poderosamente la atención. Este algo se llama ahora el teorema de Riesz y es una herramienta básica en análisis armónico.

De Polya es la observación de que el cálculo infinitesimal es tan profundo que nunca lo aprendemos verdaderamente, todo lo más, dice, sucede que llegamos a acostumbrarnos a él. Y Paul Halmos cuenta cómo por su mala memoria se ve obligado a aprender de nuevo cada año el curso que le toca explicar. Y con ello descubre cada vez que lo hace profundidades que antes se le habían pasado por alto.

Hay por lo tanto también razones puramente egoístas para que el matemático valore y se interese profundamente por los procesos de su propia enseñanza.

LAS APORTACIONES ESPECIFICAS DEL MATEMÁTICO A LA EDUCACIÓN MATEMÁTICA

Entremos ahora a examinar algunas de las posibles aportaciones específicas del matemático en torno a los problemas del aprendizaje.

-el ejemplo personal de inmersión en el quehacer propio de la matemática

El matemático debería tener razones para ser la persona más entusiasmada por su ciencia. A través de su propio trabajo creativo en el campo de su elección parece que debería estar en contacto más cercano con las raíz de esas satisfacciones que todos experimentamos en la mera contemplación de nuestra ciencia. La dedicación a la matemática no suele producir millonarios, pero sí personas intensamente enamoradas con aquello que por profesión hacen de tal modo que lo seguirían haciendo nadie les pagara por ello. La sociedad parece saberlo y aprovecharse de ello. Mi viejo profesor Ricardo Rodríguez San Juan al comentar la penuria de su sueldo en nuestra universidad me decía: "Guzmán, se están aprovechando de nuestra afición". Esta dedicación sin fisuras al quehacer de la ciencia y a su belleza es algo que nuestros estudiantes aprenden y estiman como por ósmosis. No hacen falta largos y convincentes discursos. Es el contacto con una de estas personas lo que transmite el contagio suficiente para que llegue el momento en que nuestros jóvenes digan: "Yo también iré por ahí. Esta es mi vocación."

La presencia visible de tales personas en el entorno educativo de la comunidad matemática representa una de nuestras riquezas más extraordinarias. Esta presencia constituye la más segura garantía de pervivencia y permanencia sana de nuestra ciencia en la cultura humana. Como cualquier otro arte, la matemática no puede morir. Dondequiera que haya hombres habrá también personas dedicadas a la matemática.

Afortunadamente nunca, en la larga historia de la matemática, nos han faltado los ejemplos de dedicación a la matemática, ya sean personas jóvenes y maltratadas por las circunstancias, como Abel o como Galois, ya sean personas que han tenido una vida larga y llena de éxitos matemáticos, como Euler o como Gauss.

-una guía sobre los contenidos y los procesos matemáticos más adecuados en la educación matemática

Cuando llega la hora de pensar en cambios de rumbo, de métodos, de contenidos en la educación matemática, sería muy irresponsable acudir tan sólo al especialista en métodos didácticos, al experto en la psicología de los procesos de aprendizaje matemático. Nos es absolutamente necesaria la ayuda de aquellas personas de nuestra comunidad matemática que tienen verdaderos motivos para percibir con mayor claridad cuáles puedan ser los elementos realmente obsoletos de nuestra enseñanza, por más tradición que los avale, cuáles son las ideas inertes que están lastrando nuestro trabajo y causando probablemente el tedio, la sensación de inutilidad, la frustración de muchos de nuestros alumnos y profesores. Es posible que haya equivocaciones individuales, opiniones sesgadas por visiones unilaterales, pero las opiniones elaboradas por los matemáticos deben constituir una guía imprescindible en las decisiones que se hayan de tomar.

-una visión global de la matemática integrada en la cultura humana

La matemática no es un meramente un conjunto de técnicas o de herramientas, por muy útiles que puedan resultar en nuestra civilización para alcanzar diversos fines. La matemática, antes lo he dicho, es una parte muy importante de la cultura humana. El matemático no debería ser el fontanero que arregla algunas porciones de un edificio que no entiende globalmente. El matemático debería ser el arquitecto que es capaz de contemplar y entender globalmente el edificio, su finalidad, su utilidad, su belleza, su sentido, su función, la expresión adecuada con aquello a lo que sirve, sus relaciones con el entorno, con la cultura de quien lo va a usar, con lo más íntimo de su personalidad ... Y para esta tarea necesitamos del matemático de visión amplia y profunda.

El matemático, hablo del matemático colectivo, debería tratar de percibir claramente, no sólo las relaciones de la matemática y de su campo con la mecánica, la biología, la economía, la ecología, etc., sino también con otros aspectos mucho más profundos de la persona humana como la filosofía, la ética.

También aquí ha habido guías matemáticos muy ilustres, comenzando con Pitágoras, a quien, como dice Whitehead, debemos probablemente lo que constituye la visión más certera que ha dado origen a la ciencia en el mundo occidental, la convicción de la inteligibilidad del universo y precisamente a través de la racionabilidad matemática.

LA NECESIDAD DE COLABORACIÓN CON LOS OTROS MIEMBROS DE LA COMUNIDAD MATEMÁTICA

Parece claro, por lo que hasta aquí he dicho, que la presencia del matemático en la exploración de los problemas es imprescindible. Pero no es menos claro que tal presencia ha de darse con un espíritu de colaboración, sin tratar de imponer, consciente de que su opinión ha de ser valorada conjuntamente con otras personas que también tienen luces muy valiosas que aportar. He aquí algunos aspectos que tratan de hacer patente la necesidad de ese **espíritu de colaboración**

-para orientar conjuntamente el proceso educativo hacia la persona concreta

En el matemático técnico se puede presentar una tendencia que, de no ser suficientemente equilibrada, resultará francamente perjudicial. Se trata de la inclinación a hacer girar toda la educación matemática exclusivamente en torno al contenido matemático, sin consideración de otros aspectos más personales y circunstanciales. El contenido es, ciertamente, un ingrediente fundamental que hay que considerar, pero claramente no el único.

En cualquier tipo de educación **el centro es la persona, con su idiosincrasia y sus circunstancias propias.** Es cierto que, en cualquier época y circunstancia habrá contenidos más adecuados que otros para el aprendizaje matemático de tal o cual nivel, y esto constituye un problema extraordinariamente importante que hay que resolver para obtener una educación matemática adecuada. Pero es necesario no perder de vista que la visión adecuada para resolverlo no es exclusivamente la del que está inmerso en los problemas de los diferentes campos de la matemática del momento. También tiene mucho que decir quien conoce más de cerca al estudiante, que debe ser el centro del proceso de aprendizaje.

Puede haber contenidos y formas de proceder en el pensamiento matemático que parecen adecuarse más al desarrollo de la matemática del momento, pero junto a ello hay que considerar otros muchos aspectos que desaconsejen la inmediata introducción de las formas de proceder que al matemático del momento le parecen insoslayables y las únicas aceptables.

-para ser capaz de percibir los efectos de las innovaciones propuestas

Lo que fue bueno ayer, tal vez no lo sea ya hoy. Lo que le parece adecuado que se introduzca y cambie rápidamente en la enseñanza, tal vez sea una buena utopía hacia la que hay que dirigir nuestros esfuerzos, pero con cierta parsimonia y con el convencimiento de que son las personas las que deben cambiar su visión primero. La educación matemática es, por la propia naturaleza tan compleja de su estructura, un proceso dotado de una fuerte dosis de sana inercia. Esa inercia nos puede parecer, y es que a veces así es, una verdadera rémora que impide la transformación y el crecimiento adecuados. Pero la educación no puede tener la misma flexibilidad que es propia, o debería ser propia de las tareas de la investigación científica. La educación, por su propia naturaleza, involucra a la vez a varias generaciones distintas de personas, y por ello es natural que los cambios globales se realicen muy paulatinamente. No valen las sugerencias escritas, los cambios legales, los planes de estudio más o menos inteligentes. Lo que vale fundamentalmente es la disposición de las personas, profesores, que han de estar en contacto con los estudiantes que son los que han de aprender y aceptar a su modo lo que del profesor puedan aprovechar. Y tal proceso evolutivo es necesariamente lento.

-para tratar de evitar los peligros de las visiones unilaterales

No fue hace mucho tiempo cuando un fuerte grupo de profesores de gran prestigio, en una buena parte pertenecientes al ámbito de la universidad, abogaron por cambios bastante drásticos sobre todo en lo que se refiere a los contenidos de la enseñanza primaria y secundaria. Hoy día , a distancia, nos parece como si una fuerza mágica hubiera arrastrado tras ellos a todo un ejército de maestros y profesores de diferentes niveles. En nuestro país, como en otros muchos, tales fuerzas lograron el apoyo de las autoridades educativas. Como por ensalmo surgieron fuerzas transformadoras que dinamizaron a cientos de miles de profesores en todo el mundo. Se llamó "matemática moderna". Muchos profesores, incluso muchísimos padres y madres de familia hicieron esfuerzos ingentes hacia la adaptación de lo que para ellos era tan arcano como para sus estudiantes y sus hijos... Y el paso del tiempo puso de manifiesto que una gran parte de todo el movimiento habría de conducir a resultados más bien indeseables.

Tal vez fueron muchas las circunstancias que hicieron posible en aquel tiempo no tan lejano que tuviera éxito un movimiento con tan graves consecuencias para la educación matemática de muchas personas, pero se puede pensar que no hubo un contraste previo, experimental, de los resultados a los que se encaminaba y que la atención al peso y al brillo de algunos de los matemáticos que abogaban por estos cambios fue capaz de deslumbrar a muchos.

La consecuencia de observaciones y experiencias como ésta no debe de ser el desaliento para los matemáticos que quieren intervenir en los problemas que la educación matemática tiene entre manos, que son muchos y bien serios, sino la conciencia de que es muy necesario para el matemático escuchar con sumo respeto las observaciones de quienes tienen que poner en práctica los programas y las ideas que a él se le puedan ocurrir como extraordinariamente convenientes.

ALGUNOS BUENOS EJEMPLOS DIVERSIDAD DE FORMAS DE ACTUACIÓN

Por fortuna ha habido en la larga historia de nuestra ciencia muchas personas, matemáticos y matemáticas eminentes cuya actividad puede iluminar poderosamente nuestra forma de proceder. Y al observar sus modos de actuar podemos constatar la gran diversidad de maneras que puede darse, de acuerdo con las posibilidades del tiempo y según los gustos y la idiosincrasia de cada persona. Mencionaré, en una visión probablemente muy sesgada, tan sólo unas pocas de estas personas.

No sabemos casi nada que se pueda considerar cierto acerca de **Pitágoras** como persona, pero, a juzgar por la estela que dejó, es absolutamente patente que Pitágoras tuvo que tener una capacidad de entusiasmo, de persuasión y de comunicación de su visión acerca de la matemática como no se ha dado probablemente en toda la historia de la ciencia.

De **Hypathia** también conocemos poco. Vivió en Alejandría a principios del siglo V. Fue una de las primeras mujeres matemáticas famosas y, por lo que sabemos, debió de ser extraordinariamente buena comunicadora y de una gran influencia entre sus alumnos. Tal como pensaron los oponentes de sus concepciones filosóficas, ejercía un enorme influjo sobre muchas personas. Esto les impulsó nada menos que a acabar con su vida violentamente.

Descartes escribió una obra de juventud, las llamadas *Reglas para la dirección del ingenio,* unas notas fundamentalmente para su propio uso, que quedaron inacabadas, ni siquiera tituladas y no publicadas en vida de su autor. Las *Reglas* son como un preludio, un torso de *El discurso del método.* En el *Discurso del Método* se entreveran diversos hilos de interés. En las *Reglas* se manifiesta un interés más puro por el gran problema de cómo pensar mejor y en ellas Descartes se manifiesta como un excelente precursor de George Polya al escudriñar a fondo las cuestiones relativas al pensamiento eficaz, sobre todo en las indagaciones matemáticas. Descartes, como el mismo Polya, se asoma también a la posibilidad de transferir tales formas de pensamiento a otros muchos aspectos de la investigación de la mente humana, tanto en el terreno científico como en el filosófico. Las visiones de Descartes enriquecieron sin duda la matemática, pero no menos la filosofía y otros aspectos de la ciencia. Sin duda Descartes puede proponerse como un gran ejemplo por imitar para nosotros en su enorme apertura y en la visión global de la matemática como un elemento muy fundamental de la cultura humana y en su preocupación por guiar el talento del modo más correcto hacia la solución de los problemas, matemáticos o no. **Leed a Euler. El es el maestro de todos nosotros.**

Euler es el gran maestro de todos los matemáticos posteriores a través de su obra. Y no solamente por el contenido, sino también por razón de la forma y modos de transmitir. La obra de Euler es en general, una muestra en ejemplos de lo que un buen enseñante de matemáticas debe hacer, tratando de colocarse inicialmente en la ignorancia del tema y de los métodos que va a emplear para comenzar en condiciones de igualdad con aquél a quien trata de conducir por el camino, haciéndole ver las dificultades con las que también él mismo se ha encontrado, llevándole a veces por senderos equivocados que él mismo ha recorrido antes, a fin de que aprenda también de las equivocaciones, extrayendo de las conclusiones a las que llega visiones muy generales que han de resultar válidas en otros muchos casos, etc.

Weierstrass es un gran ejemplo para los profesores de enseñanza secundaria. Por mucho tiempo fue Weierstrass profesor de Gymnasium y muy probablemente fue en él donde aprendió a transmitir eficazmente hasta el punto de crear una potentísima escuela matemática.

Felix Klein, uno de los gigantes matemáticos a caballo entre el siglo 19 y el 20, se interesó especialmente por la formación de profesores de enseñanza secundaria en su país y por la reforma de los estudios de matemática. Pero su influencia a través de la obra *Matemática elemental desde un punto de vista superior* se extendió rápidamente a muchos otros países. En España fue rápidamente traducida y publicada en la colección Biblioteca Matemática que promovió Julio Rey Pastor, uno de los matemáticos españoles que se han interesado por la educación matemática elemental. Yo mismo tuve la fortuna de estudiar los textos que él, en colaboración con Pedro Puig Adam, escribió para la enseñanza secundaria.

Henri Lebesgue es fundamentalmente conocido por su teoría de la medida, pero también se ocupó activamente de los problemas de la educación matemática, siendo él mismo un extraordinario didacta.

Hilbert, otra de las figuras más importantes entre los siglos 19 y 20, puso gran interés en escribir un libro muy interesante, donde expone una forma de hacer y contemplar la matemática que, desafortunadamente, fue hasta cierto punto barrida por el formalismo que sobrevino a los pocos años. En el prólogo de su *Geometría intuitiva*, obra que fue publicada en 1932, defiende a ultranza los orígenes intuitivos de la matemática, en particular de la geometría y la utilidad, no sólo para el investigador, sino también para quien desea percibir los resultados de la investigación en geometría. Y afirma explícitamente: *Este libro ha sido escrito para proporcionar un mayor goce de las matemáticas haciendo más fácil al lector penetrar hasta la esencia misma de las matemáticas sin tener que soportar una carga excesiva de laboriosos estudios.*

Poincaré es el gran ejemplo de matemático convencido de que las formas propias del pensamiento matemático presentan influencias profundas para el conjunto de la cultura humana. Poincaré no sólo enriqueció muchas ramas de la ciencia matemática, la mecánica, la astronomía, la física, ... sino que los mismos psicólogos en uno de los Congresos más importantes de principios de siglo, le pidieron que les iluminara sobre la naturaleza de la invención matemática.

El estudio de Poincaré fue la fuente de donde brotó toda una corriente de investigaciones sobre la forma de trabajo en matemáticas, sobre la naturaleza de la creatividad matemática, etc. **Hadamard,** otro gran matemático de la primera mitad de nuestro siglo, se ocupó de continuar y profundizar la labor de Poincaré con su magnífico trabajo *Psicología de la invención en el campo matemático*, que apareció en castellano apenas dos años después traducido por Luis Santaló. Hadamard, por otra parte, es autor de un magnífico texto de introducción a la geometría elemental, que demuestra su gran interés por la enseñanza de la matemática.

Otro de los grandes ejemplos de nuestros días es **George Polya**, cuya obra matemática en análisis matemático y en otras ramas es de gran profundidad. Su influencia sobre las corrientes actuales en educación matemática ha sido fundamental. Su pequeño libro *How to solve it*, en la vena de Descartes, Leibniz, Euler, Poincaré, Hadamard y de los grandes matemáticos que se han preocupado por escudriñar las formas misteriosas en que la mente humana actúa en el acto creativo, dio lugar a un torrente de publicaciones posteriores, entre otras la obra admirable de Polya mismo *Descubrimiento matemático*.

Sería interminable la lista de los buenos ejemplos de interés activo e influyente por los problemas de la educación matemática entre los matemáticos más eminentes. Pero quisiera citar uno que para todo el mundo de habla hispana es excepcionalmente importante. **Luis Santaló** ha sido y sigue siendo para nosotros el personaje que ha sabido aunar de una forma más influyente su altura matemática con el interés efectivo por la educación matemática. Todos los matemáticos conocen sus obras en torno a la geometría integral. Pero todo el mundo matemático de habla hispana conoce además a fondo sus muchas obras dedicadas a la enseñanza matemática. Y no sólo para discutir e iluminar sus problemas, sino incluso para aportar de forma muy directa textos elementales de nivel primario, secundario y terciario, en colaboración directa, por sí mismo o en colaboración con otros colegas cuyo quehacer directo se ubica en tales niveles.

Si en nuestro mundo iberoamericano pudiéramos contar con media docena de Santalós es absolutamente cierto que el panorama de nuestra educación matemática cambiaría de forma inmediata. Que él sea para nosotros un guía de dedicación, de apertura, de accesibilidad, de capacidad de comunicación y de entendimiento con todos.

POSIBLES TAREAS CONCRETAS AHORA

En la actualidad, en algunos países al menos, parecen respirarse aires de cambio en lo que se refiere a la implicación de los matemáticos en los problemas de la educación matemática. En Estados Unidos, por ejemplo, parece que se van oyendo voces cada vez más intensas pidiendo cambios en la cultura de la comunidad matemática. Varios organismos como el *Conference Board of the Mathematical Sciences* y potentes organizaciones como la *American Mathematical Society* y la *Mathematical Association of America* están coordinando sus esfuerzos, y junto con el foro MER *(Mathematicians and Education Reform)* han publicado ya en los últimos 5 años media docena de volúmenes impulsando una reforma con esta orientación. El título del volumen 5 de la colección es bien significativo, *Changing the Culture: Mathematics Education in the Research Community.*

Es claro que se está originando una corriente que estimulará con el tiempo a matemáticos de todo el mundo para contribuir en la misma dirección. Y son muchos los temas de urgente consideración en los que los matemáticos podrían, ya lo van haciendo algunos, colaborar muy eficazmente. A mí se me ocurre enumerar algunos de ellos:

-participar en la elaboración de nuevos diseños de aprendizaje matemático a nivel primario, secundario y terciario
Teniendo en cuenta la necesidad cada vez mayor del ciudadano de nuestros días de una adecuada formación matemática y de la extensión de esta educación a niveles cada vez más amplios y más altos, es necesario tratar seriamente de explorar y poner en práctica modos de

aprendizaje más efectivos que aquellos con los que hasta ahora hemos contado, y esta labor no se refiere exclusivamente a los niveles primarios y secundarios, sino probablemente es tanto o más urgente que se realice a niveles universitarios, en los que la atención a los problemas educativos ha sido probablemente menos intensa.

-elaborar modelos efectivos de incorporación de las herramientas actualmente a nuestra disposición
El fenómeno es interesante y evidente en muchas regiones. La inercia mayor a la utilización de las nuevas herramientas, el ordenador y otros instrumentos, en el aprendizaje matemático se presenta, no a nivel secundario, sino a nivel universitario. Sería muy importante explorar muy a fondo los beneficios y los inconvenientes que se pueden ocasionar con tales herramientas, los cambios en los contenidos aconsejables, los cambios en los énfasis, en las formas de aprendizaje de nuestros estudiantes a todos los niveles. Es claro que es muy necesario que los matemáticos intervengan muy activamente a fin de encaminar correctamente un movimiento que, si bien parece beneficioso en muchos aspectos, no está exento de peligros y de posibles exageraciones y dañosas desviaciones.

-colaborar activamente en la necesaria tarea de hacer la matemática más claramente visible en la sociedad actual
Como antes he dicho, esta es una obligación acuciante de la comunidad matemática entera, pero es claro que de donde pueden salir las personas capaces de realizar la tarea de hacer visible la matemática en nuestra cultura es especialmente del grupo de personas que trabajan en investigación matemática y de entre aquellos que más en contacto están con ellos.

Por otra parte, sería excelente para la comunidad matemática entera y para la sociedad misma en la que está inmersa, que hubiera alguien hoy día, en cada campo de la matemática capaz de realizar una labor como la de Felix Klein, pero a la inversa, explicándonos a todos lo que es

LA MATEMÁTICA SUPERIOR DESDE UN PUNTO DE VISTA ELEMENTAL

Afortunadamente se van produciendo obras que viene a responder a esta idea que han llegado ha comvertise en grandes éxitos de ventas a nivel mundial. Gracias a unos cuantos matemáticos creativos, buenos comunicadores, con grandes dotes expositivas, algunos temas profundos, intrincados, centrales a la matemática de hoy, como por ejemplo los sitemas dinamicos, parencen estar muy presentes en nuestro mundo actual, a veces, y así debe ser, gracias al atractivo y la potencia expresiva, el gancho de nombres como el caos, que logran transmitir algo del misterio profundo que el pensamiento matemático implica.

Y para terminar, quisiera expresar el intenso deseo de todos los que nos ocupamos de los problemas de la educación matemática de que sean muchos más los matemáticos que se dedican a la investigación que quieran enriquecer con su experencia y sus ideas esta tarea tan esencial para la sana evolución de la comunidad matemática entera.

INFORMATION TECHNOLOGY AND MATHEMATICS EDUCATION: ENTHUSIASMS, POSSIBILITIES AND REALITIES

David Tall

Mathematics education Research Centre
University of Warwick
Coventry, CV4 7AL, UK

This presentation addresses critical issues in the use of information technology in Mathematics Education. By reflecting on human thinking processes, it will consider developments of enthusiastic researchers using technology to teach mathematics as new facilities develop, the possible gains shown by this research and the realities that may be achieved in the classroom.

1. A time of great change

We live in changing times. Noble species which have been on the earth for millions of years such as the whale and the elephant are threatened with possible extinction by mankind and now a human sub-species, the mathematician, may be under threat from the competition of information technology.

Will *Homo Mathematicus* become extinct?

As the president of the Royal Society, Sir Michael Atiyah, has said:

Whereas the eighteenth and nineteenth centuries witnessed the gradual replacement of manual labour by machines, the late twentieth-century is seeing the mechanisation of intellectual activities. It is the brain rather than the hand that is being made redundant. (Atiyah, 1986, p.43.)

The performance of routine tasks traditionally taught in mathematics education has been taken over by technology in a spectacular way. The supermarket checkout assistant no longer adds up the cost of the items and calculates the change. Software using a machine bar-code reader not only does the arithmetic, it also prints out an itemised bill for the customer and automates stock-control for the trader. Does this means that traditional mathematical skills are becoming less important?

Information technology highlights the difference between being able to perform standard skills and beingable to "think mathematically". Current technology is no match for a creative mathematical mind. As Edward de Bono observed on a recent BBC TV "Brains Trust", the "poor engineering" of the human brain gives it the ability to make associative links and leaps of insight. Because of its logical and orderly design, today's technology is incapable of musing, as Einstein could imagine, *"what would happen if I were sitting on a train travelling at nearly the speed of light?"*

But can a computer *think*?

This imaginative strength is the product of the complex way in which the brain works, and in turn is linked to the way in which human learning occurs. Whereas the computer can be reprogrammed by replacing its software, erasing all previous data from the memory, the human mind is built up through a life-time of experience and evolves by building the new upon the old, subtly retaining elements of the old alongside the new. The corporate beliefs of the mathematical community therefore serve as a stabilising factor, preserving the familiar and taking time to adjust to new possibilities.

Meanwhile, technology changes at an extremely fast pace that predicting the next stage is a hazardous business:

If you take the way the Internet is changing month by month – if somebody can predict what's going to happen three months from now, nine months from now, even today, my hat's off to them. I think we've got a phenomenon here that is moving so rapidly that nobody knows exactly where it will go.

(Bill Gates, 1996).

The result is that enthusiasts are forever chasing the cutting edge of technology, often moving on to the next innovation before the wider community has absorbed the last one, and operating at a speed which means that the long-term effects are often not known until long after the changes have already been made.

So how can we attempt to make sense of the impact of information technology? My own chosen route is to be aware of technological changes and possibilities, but to see how they interact with the nature of human learning. As mathematics *educators* we need to know the realities as well as the possibilities for human learning in an age of information technology

2 Different forms of mathematical knowledge

The first step is to consider the nature of mathematical knowledge, to see how different parts of this knowledge structure are effected by technology.

Human evolution passed through several million years before the development of speech. The first form of mathematics was therefore *enactive*, involving physical manipulation of objects. This remains the first form to be encountered by the developing child and forms the initial stages of mathematics education. *Pictorial* representations in the form of cave paintings are 40,000 or 50,000 years old and *written language* developed in Phoenicia some 5,300 years ago, by which time arithmetic notation was already being used in trade and exchange. *Arithmetic* symbolism of various forms, for counting and measuring, developed in ancient civilisations such as those of Mesopotamia and Egypt, then two and a half thousand years ago the Greeks developed the abstract theory of *geometry* expressed *verbally* through Euclidean proof.

Manipulable *algebraic* symbols were introduced comparatively recently in the sixteenth century and the flowering of calculus occurred in the seventeenth. It is the ability to *calculate* with symbols that has contributed to the vast accelerarion of human achievement in the last three hundred years and it is this which has become the focus of mathematics education in schools.

It is only in the last century that the attempt has been made to reorganise the whole of mathematical knowledge into a *formal* theory, founded on verbal definitions and logical deductions.

Before the development of the computer, we therefore had various forms of mathematics, including:

(1) *Enactive mathematics,* with physical actions on actual objects.

(2) *Visual mathematics described verbally,* with physical properties of objects verbalised and built into a systematic deductive theory as in Euclidean geometry.

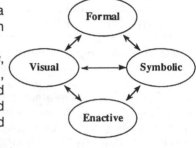

(3) *Symbolic mathematics,* (arithmetic, algebra, calculus etc.), arising from actions on real-world objects (such as counting) and developing through computation and symbol manipulation.

(4) A combination of (2) and (3) linking symbolism and graphical representation.

(5) *Formal mathematics,* with concepts *defined* by verbal-symbolic axioms and further properties *deduced* by formal proof.

These different forms of mathematics interrelate in a complex way, but they do have different characteristics which can give insight into the learning process.

3 New computer facilities

Computer technology developed in a sequence which contributed to different parts of this knowledge structure, setting successive agendas for mathematics education. The arrival of the computer first focused on the elementary *symbolism of numeric computation,* then had a *graphical* display added, followed quickly by an *enactive* interface allowing selection and manipulation of objects drawn onscreen. Software to enable *symbolic manipulation* required more sophisticated programming and has gone through several reincarnations to produce a more human user interface.

So far we have used the computer less in handling formal proof in mathematics education (with the honorable exception of the use of a language such as ISETL with the formal structure of set theory complete with quantifiers and logical implication.) "Theorem proving" and "theorem checking" software exist in certain contexts, and computers have been used to carry out lengthy checking procedures beyond the capacity of the individual, such as in the celebrated computer proof of the Four Colour Theorem (Appel and Haken, 1976). But standard computer technology still has the Achilles heel noted of the pioneering design of Charles Babbage in the nineteenth century:

The Analytical Engine has no pretensions whatever to originate anything. It can do whatever we know how to order it to perform. It can follow analysis; but it has no power of anticipating any analytical relations or truths. Its province is to assist us in making available what we are already acquainted with.   (Ada Lovelace, Observations on Mr Babbage's Analytical Engine, quoted in Evans, C, 1983, p. 31.)

Although modern computers provide an enactive human interface with manipulable visual display and symbolic facilities, it still needs the mind of a mathematician to perform thought experiments to decide what is important and what needs to be proved.

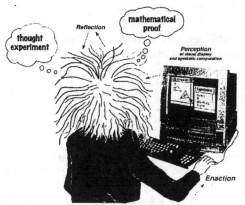

Creative human thought and algorithmic computer processing

4 Computers in mathematics education

Before computers became widely available, there was scepticism about their value in education:

It is unlikely that the majority of pupils in this age range will find [a computer] so efficient, useful and convenient a calculating aid as a slide rule or book of tables.   (Mathematical Association, *Mathematics 11 to 16,* 1974.)

Such illusions were soon shattered and slide rules and books of tables lingered for only a short time before they became obsolete.

4.1 *Numerical algorithms*

The first microcomputers (for instance, the Apple, in 1976) were sold with the BASIC language available for programming. So the first enthusiasms were for mathematicians and their students to program their own numerical methods. The enthusiasts believed that by *programming* the students could learn to understand the processes of mathematics. In reality there were too few computers for wide-spread student programming at the time and so the practice did not spread far. Research was produced to show that children programming in BASIC had a better insight into the use of letters as variables in algebra (eg Tall & Thomas, 1991). But BASIC has a bad press as a poorly structured language and by the time more computers became available the agenda changed and programming in BASIC was widely regarded as ancient history.

4.2 *Graphic visualisations*

In the early eighties high resolution graphics brought the next stage, including such things as graph plotters to represent functions and programming in Logo for children of all ages.

The visual possibilities also brought the experimental study of chaos and fractals by mathematicians and introduced new *graphical* approaches to the teaching of such things as geometry, statistics, calculus and differential equations. The student could now be helped by *visualising* mathematical ideas. This was a time of great creativity with mathematics educators writing little pieces of software to visualise mathematical concepts.

There was soon considerable evidence that a visual approach to graphs helped students to gain a wider conceptual understanding without necessarily affecting their ability to cope with the corresponding symbolisations. (e.g. Heid 1988, Palmiter 1991). But on the debt side there was also evidence that students who lacked the sophistication to interpret the meanings of the graphs could develop serious misconceptions.

A classic instance was the case of young children watching the cooling curve of a liquid on a display with fairly large pixels, seeing the move from one pixel to another as a sudden drop in temperature (Linn & Nachmias, 1987).

In the same way, when drawing graphs of functions, the choice of range to give a suitable picture becomes crucial and it is possible to misinterpret the meaning of the graph on the screen. (Goldenberg, 1988).

4.3 *Enactive control*

In 1984 the "mouse" was introduced to give the computer an enactive interface. Instead of having to type in a line of symbols, the user could now select, and control the display by intuitive hand-movements.

This allowed a completely different approach to learning which encouraged active exploration rather than first learning to do procedural computations.

For instance, statistics is often taught by procedural "cook-book" methods because few teachers, let alone students, have the experience to understand the underlying formalities. Yet software allowing an enactive exploratory environment can be used to give a "sense" of the nature of statistical data and to see how robust interpretations are when they are subject to variations. For example, in

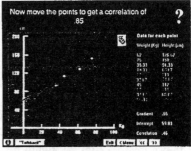

Visual statistics under enactive control

giving a line of "best fit" to data, and computing various rules such as "least squares fit" it is possible to use computer software to enactively move the line of fit until it looks good by eye, or to move data points around and to see how this causes variations in the various fitness measures.

In this way sophisticated mathematical concepts can be given an intuitive visuospatial meaning without (or before) the need to study the procedures that the computer was using for internal computation.

Interactive programs in geometry offer enactive exploratory environments giving new dynamic conceptualisations of geometric figures. For instance, a triangle ABC with the midpoints M , N of AB , AC joined could be pulled around by holding on, say, to the vertex A to see that the length of MN is always half that of BC. The figure takes on a new

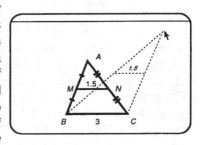

meaning which holds whatever position the triangle is moved to, subject to the given construction and provides a rich environment for exploration and hypothesising. However, note that the available actions involve selecting a point and pulling it round. There is no move that lifts up one triangle and, retaining its size and shape, allows it to be moved onto another (congruent) triangle. The environment does not contain the seeds of Euclidean transformations and leads to a different kind of mathematical knowledge from that required in the systematic building of theorems and Euclidean proofs.

4.4 Computer algebra systems

Computer algebra systems had been around in various guises before the *American Mathematical Monthly* carried a full page advertisement for the computer algebra system *MACSYMA,* in the fateful year 1984. It asserted that the software

> ... can simplify, factor or expand expressions, solve equations analytically or numerically, differentiate, compute definite and indefinite integrals, expand functions in Taylor or Laurent series.

In less than a decade, computers had successively developed *numerical, graphical and symbolic* facilities each offering new methods of conceptualising mathematical ideas and these came to be conceived as the three major representations in college calculus:

> One of the guiding principles is the 'Rule of Three,' which says that wherever possible topics should be taught graphically and numerically, as well as analytically. The aim is to produce a course where the three points of view are balanced, and where students see each major idea from several angles.　　　　　　　　　　　　　　　(Hughes Hallett 1991, p.121)

The American calculus reform is based on a wide range of software that uses various representations. There is no evidence that students learn to use the computer algebra systems to "think with", by formulating the solution of problems in a way that can be carried out by computer algorithms. (Davis et al, 1992). However, there is also evidence that many students using computer algebra systems do not understand what is going on internally and do not link the mathematical ideas in the same way as those with a more traditional experience. For instance, students may use graph-plotters to "see" solutions of equations, but not necessarily relate them to the symbolic meaning of the problem. Caldwell (1995) expected students to find the roots and asymptotes of the rational function

$$f(x) = \frac{x(x-4)}{(x+2)(x-2)}$$

by algebraic means, only to be given a substantial number of approximate solutions such as 0.01 and 3.98 read from the graph. Hunter et al. (1993) found that a third of the students using a computer algebra system could answer the following question before the course, but not after:

> 'What can you say about u if u=v+3, and v=1?'

As they had no practice in substituting values into expressions during the course, the skill seems to have atrophied.

The reality of the classroom can prove to be different from the possibilities envisioned by enthusiasts.

4.5 *Personal portable tools*

The technology migrated from desk-top machines to portable calculators and computers for personal use. Four function calculators progressed to include scientific functions, then programming facilities, then graphical representations.

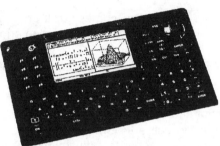

In 1996 we know hand-held computers which will do all the numeric and symbolic algorithms which were the staple diet of mathematics exams and includes an implementation of *Cabri Géometre* to explore geometric ideas. This offers most of the facilities discussed so far, with the added advantage that it can be used at will by the student at any time in any place, though it retains an input-line of commands and lacks the freedom of fully enactive computer environment.

4.6 *Multi-media*

The last two or three years have seen the development of multi-media interactive software to use for individual study. This, as yet only partially realised, facility promises to allow the learner to have a variety of materials giving explanations in text, words, video, within a software environment that offers interactive facilities to explore mathematical processes and concepts. It allows the possibilities of the return of smaller interactive units from the eighties to be embedded in a more coherent overall environment.

4.7 *The World Wide Web*

More recently the world-wide web has become a reality, allowing information and software to be passed from one individual to another round the globe. World-wide mathematical courses for multi-media interaction are becoming available. Students increasingly have freedom to access software at any time to suit their own timetable, offering yet new promises for the future. Currently the promise is often different from what happens in reality, as the internet gets clogged up with huge numbers of users and the bandwidth available is often too narrow to transfer large amounts of data for sound and pictures in real-time.

> People say the Internet is carrying multimedia today, but then dogs can walk on their hind legs.
>
> (Robert X. Cringely, Accidental Empires, 1996, p.344.)

Yet change comes quickly and greater capacity is around the corner so that the world-wide information superhighway seems to be inevitable.

5 Developing a theory to consider the evidence

So how do we make sense of this change? It is evident that information technology is here to stay and we as mathematics educators need to come to terms with its use. Many teachers at this moment are suspicious about technology which carries out processes that they have devoted a life-time to teach to their pupils. It is easy enough to express Luddite opinions and to fear the practicalities that will change our livelihood. At the same time we should attempt to develop some kind of understanding of the processes involved that enables us to make coherent judgements as to the best use of the new facilities.

In my own work I took a route dictated by the sequence of technological development. I had done some empirical work into students' understanding of limits and happened to enter the computer world as graphics arrives, and developed a graphical approach to the calculus. At the same time I was working on a Mathematical Association Committee with many colleagues who were devoted to programming numerical algorithms, and as time passed, we attempted to take in the new ideas of symbol manipulation. To put together the diverse threads of visualisation and symbolisation, I thought about how the human being operates, *perceiving* the real world, *acting* upon it for survival and *reflecting* on personal thoughts to maximise their effectiveness.

This combination of *perception*, action and *reflection* fitted together to help me formulate my own views on cognitive development. I saw the contrast between what I term "object-based mathematics" typified by geometry and "action-based mathematics" typified by the actions of counting and measuring in arithmetic. I also saw that reflecting on these experiences allow mature experts to develop a "property-based mathematics" with axioms and formal deductions. In the 1960s the "new math" tried to develop a "property-based" set-theoretic approach to the curriculum. It did not work. For learning at earlier stages a combination of enactive, visual and symbolic may offer a more practical solution. It happens that these may be well-served by a computer.

5.1 Enactive and visual mathematics

The computer can provide an enactive way to manipulate visual mathematical objects. This allows powerful "sense making" of subtle concepts at a primitive enactive level. It can provide what I have termed a "cognitive root" from which a progressively sophisticated theory can grow (Tall, 1989) This can happen not only in geometry, but in other areas of mathematics. For instance it can be illustrated by the notion of a solution of a first order differential equation, embedded in wider experiences of visualising and manipulating graphs.

At the root of this idea I see the formal notion of derivative in a primitive visual way as the gradient of the graph. I do not talk about tangents, or locally linear approximations, or any formal notions in the initial stages. Simply by magnifying graphs, on the computer screen, many can be seen to de "locally straight", that is, under high magnification, they are *perceived* as being straight. This can then be linked to numeric and symbolic approaches to give the notion of derivative a computable meaning. However, the root idea of local straightness can be used to visualise the solution of the reverse problem–to construct a graph given its gradient.

In this context, computer software can use the knowledge of the gradient to draw a small line segment of the gradient. If this is under the control of the user, say by moving around with the mouse or with the cursor keys, it becomes possible to stick together short lines end to end to build up a solution of the equation. The solution is "locally straight", in fact the picture is built up with approximate straight line segments, with its gradient given by the differential equation.

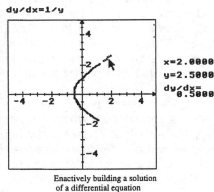

Enactively building a solution
of a differential equation

In this way the computer can provide an environment in which the learner can physically experience the ideas of the mathematics at a fundamental human level. This involves vision and bodily movement without the need at the time to concentrate on the symbolism and the computations required to produce a solution.

Having obtained such human insights, it is still necessary to be able to construct a solution in a more accurate quantitative manner. The symbolic solution of such a problem involves quite different mental activities.

5.2 Symbolic mathematics

Inspired by a succession of thinkers in the cognitive development of mathematical processes and concepts, including Dubinsky (1991) and Sfard (1991), I was fortunate to collaborate with Eddie Gray to develop a viewpoint that proved useful for analysing not only how individuals use symbolism, but also how we interact with the symbolism manipulated by a computer.

We noted, as had others before us, that symbols in arithmetic, algebra, calculus, and a wide range of other mathematical contexts had a certain characteristic. The following symbols illustrate this:

$5+4, \ 3 \times 4, \ 3a+2b,$

$$\lim_{x \to a} \frac{x^3 - a^3}{x - a}, \ \frac{d}{dx}\left(\frac{\sin x + \cos x}{x^2 + 3x + 1}\right), \ \int_0^{2\pi} e^{2x} \cos x \, dx, \ \sum_{n=1}^{\infty} \frac{1}{n^2},$$

These all play a dual role representing both a mathematical *process* to be carried out and the *result* of that *process*. For instance 5+4 evokes the *process* of addition to produce the *concept* of sum 5+4, which is 9, 3a+2b is both a process of evaluation and a concept of algebraic expression, and $\sum_{n=1}^{\infty} \frac{1}{n^2}$ is the process of evaluating an infinite sum to find the limit value (which happens to be $\frac{\Pi^2}{6}$).

The name *procept* was introduced for the combination of symbol, process and concept which occurs when a symbol evokes a process to give the resulting concept (Gray & Tall, 1994). We were interested in the way in which individuals interpret symbols in arithmetic, algebra and calculus, causing some students to find mathematics essentially easy yet others finding it increasingly difficult.

We emphasize that the cognitive notion of procept carries with it no implication as to how that cognitive structure is built. Indeed one of our purposes was to investigate the concept-building of such symbols. However, in pre-computer contexts, we often found that the meaning of symbols developed through a sequence of activities:

(a) *procedure*, where a finite succession of decisions and actions is built up into a coherent sequence,
(b) *process*, where increasingly efficient ways become available to achieve the same result, now seen as a whole,
(c) *procept*, where the symbols are conceived flexibly as processes to *do* and concepts to *think about.*

Initially the individual builds an "action schema" (in the sense of Piaget) as a coordinated sequence of actions. At the *procedural* level, the focus of attention concentrates on how to do each step and how this leads to the next. We use the term "procedure" for a specific finite sequence of decisions and actions. In contrast the term "process" is used in a more general sense, such as "the process of addition" or the "process of solving a linear equation". A process may have several different procedures which give the same result. For instance, the symbols $2(x+3)$ and $2x+6$ involve two different sequences of computation, but represent what we consider to be the same process. In this way the function $f(x)=2(x+3)$ is the same function as $g(x)=2x+6$ because they have identical input and output.

In the case of an addition such as 2+7, it might be performed in a variety of ways, say by counting two sets, then both together, or starting at 2 and counting on 7, or counting on 2 starting at 7, or simply knowing that 2+7makes 9. Now the symbol 2+7 may be seen not only as a *process* (of addition), but also as a *concept* (os sum), so that 2+7 not only *makes* 9, but 2+7 *is* 9. This can lead to a rich web of relationships, so that, if "2+something" is 9, then the "something" is 7, and on to other facts involving place value, such as 32+7=39 or 70+20=90. Meanwhile the child who sees addition only as a "counting-on" procedure is likely to see substraction as a "counting-back" procedure, counting back 9-2 in two steps as "8, 7", or 9-7 as count-back seven steps "8, 7, 6, 5, 4, 3, *2*" incorporating lengthy counting procedures that prove to be increasingly more difficult to carry out correctly.

Procedures allow individuals to *do* mathematics, but learning lots of separate procedures and selecting the appropriate one for a given purpose becomes increasingly burdensome. *Procepts* allow the individual not only to carry out procedures, but to regard symbols as mental objects, so they can not only *do* mathematics, they can also *think* about the concepts. For such a student with powerful mental connections, greater abstraction gives greater simplicity, whilst the less successful student is left with ever increasing complexity and the greater likelihood of failure.

A consequence of this is that those students who do *not* make enough appropriate mental connections have a far greater mental burden and fall back on the need to routinise mathematics to be able to "do" the procedure to get an answer. They can therefore "do" a problem in a limited context and see this as "success" but are not developing the long-term connections to be able to think about more sophisticated ideas.

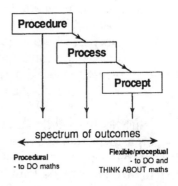

I conjecture that this is a major reason that many students are "damaged" by their experiences in school, apparently learning how to "do" mathematics but unable to ink together ideas which are, for them, either meaningless or too complex. Such students who require remedial help at college may benefit from a visual/graphical approach, which can increase their confidence as they are, at last, able to make sense of *something*. Yet such students may find it continuingly difficult to make sense of the symbolism and link it to the visual ideas. Meanwhile, more successful students who have some conceptions of the mathematical connections may benefit enormously by extending their powers, using computer software as a tool to think with.

Essentially I conjecture that our role as mathematics educators is not just to teach procedures (to "do" mathematics) but also flexible relationships between various ways of considering process and concept (to "think" mathematically").

5.3 Long-term difficulties with symbols

As the mathematical curriculum develops through arithmetic, algebra and calculus, the symbols operate in subtly different ways:
(i) *arithmetic procepts,* such as 5+4,3x4,$1/_2+2/_3$, or 1·54÷ 2·3, have explicit algorithms to obtain an answer, but become increasingly difficult for the procedural learner,
(ii) *algebraic procepts*, such as 2*a*+3*b*, do not have an "answer" (except by numerical substitution), but they can be manipulated using more general strategies, which again coerces the procedural learner into rote-learning of isolated techniques,
(iii) limit procepts, such as

$$\lim_{x \to a}\frac{x^3 - a^3}{x-a}, \; \frac{d}{dx}\left(\frac{\sin x + \cos x}{x^2 + 3x + 1}\right), \; \int_0^{2\pi} e^{2x}\cos x\, dx, \; \sum_{n=1}^{\infty}\frac{1}{n^2}$$

involve a potentially infinite process of "getting close" to a limit value, which may be computed by a numerical approximation and sometimes by a symbolic algorithm.

Each of these requires new ways of thinking about the symbolism, a change of conceptualisation that proves difficult for many. A child who thinks of a sum 4+3=7 as a counting procedure in which "4 plus 3 makes 7" may find it difficult to cope with a symbol such as $4+3x$ which does not "make" anything, except perhaps to "do the bit 4+3 that makes sense" and get $7x$. This leads to great confusions for many students starting algebra.

Likewise, a student who is used to "doing" mathematics in a finite number of steps may find it difficult to cope with the potential infinity of the limit process and seek the security of the symbolic algorithms in calculus, which at least operationally give an "answer".

Instead of being a comfortable sequence of successive logical steps, the mathematics curriculum is actually littered with subtle hurdles that are not always apparent to the expert.

Therefore there continues to be a role for the mathematics educator, to not only "teach" mathematics, but to be aware of the ways in which children *learn* mathematics and the pitfalls of the routine teaching of how to *do* procedures without also considering how to organise and *think* about the resultant concepts.

The Mutual Roles of the Visual and the Symbolic

The individual makes sense of the environment by perception to receive information, *reflection* to think about it, and *action* to manipulate it. When acting on objects, it is possible to focus either on the objects themselves and the results of the action, or on the actions. For instance, oneway to share three pizzas between four people is to cut two in half, give one half to each, then cut the remaining pizza into four, and give a quarter to each. Visually one can see each person having three quarters of a pizza. Alternatively, the action of dividing three by four can be expressed symbolically as a fraction.

Of the two, the visual conception gives an intuitive, yet primitive, idea of a fraction, whilst the symbolic conception is more subtle, but has long-term developmental possibilities leading to more sophisticated mathematical symbolism.

These two aspects of the same idea typify how the visual can provide a global, holistic idea in mathematics whilst the symbolic produces a sequential, operational method capable of great computational power. However, the two do not always fit together easily (think, for instance, of visual models appropriate for the sum or product of two fractions, or the extension of these ideas to negative

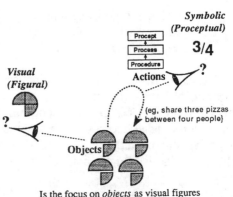

Is the focus on *objects* as visual figures or on the *actions* symbolised as procepts

rationals). A concentration mainly on symbols may lead to a rote procedural approach which grows in complexity as the number of unconnected rules increases. A concentration only on the visual may give an insight into what is going on in a restricted context perhaps with limited power to generalise.

The task of providing an appropriate blend of mathematical insight and computational power still remains elusive. In this task the computer can prove not only a mechanical tool to carry out complex algorithmic tasks, but also an environment to relate visual and symbolic ideas, to enable the growing individual to gain a new equilibrium with mathematical ideas in a new technological age. It is not a universal panacea, for different individuals have different ways of coping with the mathematical world, but it offers differing kinds of support which can be supportive to a wide spectrum of approaches.

6. The continued need for mathematics educators

The volatile nature of the development of information technology continues to defy prediction, both in general, and in mathematics:

> Anyone who presumes to describe the roles of technology in mathematics education faces challenges akin to describing a newly active volcano – the mathematical mountain is changing before our eyes...
>
> (Kaput, 1992, p.515.)

We may no longer need to prepare children to use regular mathematical routines as a central feature of their future employment, but they will need to grow in a way that enables them to survive in a new technological world. The evidence we have suggests that it is insufficient just to give individuals tools to carry out procedures if they are not properly integrated into a cognitive structure that can make sense of the relationship between the various processes, concepts and representations.

In this new world, the creative mathematician still has a full role to play with the cutting edge enthusiast pressing on with innovative possibilities. The reality of the learning process continues to require the reflective guidance of the good teacher.

The reflective guidance of a mathematics teacher

References

Appel, K. & Haken, W. (1976). 'The solution of the four colour map problem', *Scientific American* (October), 108-121.

Atiyah, M.F. (1986). 'Mathematics and the Computer Revolution'. In A.G. Howson & J.P. Kahane (Eds.), *The Influence of Computers and Informatics on Mathematics and its Teaching.* Cambridge: CUP.

Caldwell, J.H. (1995). 'Assessment and graphing calculators'. In L. Lum (ed.), *Proceedings of the Sixth Annual International Conference on Technology in Collegiate Mathematics,* (pp. 99-105). Reading MA: Addison-Wesley.

Cringely, R.X. (1996). *Accidental Empires, (How the boys of Silicon Valley make their millions, battle foreign competition, and still can't get a date),* New York: Penguin.

Davis, B., Porta, H. & Uhl, J. (1992). 'Calculus & Mathematics: addressing fundamental questions about technology', *Proceedings of the Fifth International Conference on Technology in Collegiate Mathematics,* (Addison-Wesley), 305-314.

Dubinsky, E. (1991). 'Reflective Abstraction in Advanced Mathematical Thinking'. In D.O. Tall (ed.) *Advanced Mathematical Thinking,* Kluwer: Dordrecht, 95-123.

Evans, C. (1983), *The Making of the Micro,* Oxford University Press.

Gates, W. (1996), quotation of a statement made in the TV programme, *Triumph of the Nerds,* broadcast internationally in Spring 1996.

Goldenberg, P. (1988). 'Mathematics, Metaphors and Human Factors: Mathematical, Technical and Pedagogical Challenges in the Educational Use of Graphical Representation of Functions', *Journal of Mathematical Behaviour,* **7** 2, 135.173.

Gray, E.M. & Tall, D.O. (1994). 'Duality, Ambiguity and Flexibility: A Proceptual View of Simple Arithmetic', *Journal for Research in Mathematics Education* 26, 115-141.

Heid, K. (1988). 'Resequencing skills and concepts in applied calculus using the computer as a tool', *Journal for Research in Mathematics Education* 19, 3-25.

Hughes Hallet, D. (1991). 'Visualization and Calculus Reform'. In W. Zimmermann & S. Cunningham (eds.), *Visualization in Teaching and Learning Mathematics,* MAA Notes No. 19, 121-126.

Hunter, M., Monaghan, J.D. & Roper, T. (1993). 'The effect of computer algebra use on students' algebraic thinking'. In R. Sutherland (ed.), *Working Papers for ESRC Algebra Seminar,* London: Institute of Education.

Kaput, J.J. (1992). 'Technology and Mathematics Education'. In D. Grouws (ed.) *Handbook on research in mathematics teaching and learning,* (pp. 515-556). New York: Macmillan.

Linn, M.C. & Nachmias, R. (1987). 'Evaluations of Science Laboratory Data: The Role of Computer-Presented Information', *Journal of Research in Science Teaching* 24 5, 491-506.

Mathematical Association, (1974). *Mathematics 11-16.*

Palmitter, J.R. (1991). 'Effects of Computer Algebra Systems on Concept and Skill Acquisition in Calculus', *Journal for Research in Mathematics Education* 22, 151-156.

Sfard, A. (1991). 'On the Dual Nature of Mathematical Conceptions: Reflections on processes and objects as different sides of the same coin', Educational Studies in Mathematics, 22 1, 1-36.

Tall, D.O. & Thomas, M.O.J. (1991). 'Encouraging versatile Thinking in Algebra using the Computer', *Educational Studies in Mathematics,* **22** 2, 125-147.

Tall, D.O. (1989). 'Concept Images, Generic Organizers, Computers & Curriculum Change', *For the Learning of Mathematics,* **9** 3, 37-42.

REAL PROBLEMS WITH REAL WORLD MATHEMATICS

Jan de Lange
Freudenthal Institute; Utrecht

1. Mathematics Education is changing.

Mathematics education is changing continuously (Romberg 1995, De Lange et al. 1993, Wirszup Streit 1992). That may come as no surprise. But it is worthwhile to reflect a bit on the changes of the recent past to learn for the immediate future. A Washington, USA, based quarterly, 21st Century Science and Technology, featured the following example of the evolution of (american) mathematics education in its 1993-1994 winter edition.

*in 1960: A logger sells a truckload of lumber for $100. His cost of production is four fifths of the price. What is his profit?

*in 1970 (traditional math): A logger sells a truckload of lumber for $100. His cost of production is four-fifths of this price; in other words, $80. What is his profit?

*in 1970 (new math): A logger exchanges a set L of lumber for a set M of money. The cardinality of set M is 100, and each element is worth $1. Make 100 dots representing the elements of set M. The set C of costs contains 20 fewer points than the set M. Represent the set C as a subset of M, and answer the following question: What is the cardinality of the set P of profits?

*in 1980: A logger sells a truckload of wood for $100. His cost of production is $20. Your assignment: Underline the number 20.

*in 1990 (outcome based education): By cutting down beautiful trees, a logger makes $20. What do you think of this way of making a living? (Topic for class participation: How did the forest birds and squirrels feel?)

The author of this list hopefully considered this as a tongue-in-cheek example of development of mathematics education in the US over the past decades. But it shows two serious issues that are at present in the focus of discussion:

–the role of the real world in mathematics education

–the problem of losing real mathematics when introducing the real world.

2. Real world problem is not a real problem.

Examples are abundant, in many curricula and in many countries, of the use of the real world, but quite often not in a 'real' way. By introducing the real world in a fake way we degradate the problem to an artificial non relevant problem. Let us look at two rather typical examples of this:

*One day a sales person drove 300 miles in $x^2 - 4$ hours. The following day, she drove 325 miles in $x + 2$ hours.

–Write and simplify a ratio comparing her average rate the first day with the average the second day.

In this case we are dealing with a very artificial problem that has no relevance to the students but also makes no sense. A mathematical problem has been 'dressed up' (Niss, 1993) as to resemble a real world problem. The mathematics may be real, but the problem is not.

Another example, taken from a standardized test for 16 year olds in the USA makes clear that the designers of the test do not seriously expect students to read and understand the text (Stanford Test 1994).

*It is 350 miles from Charlotville to New York City. Jim drove the distance in 7 hours. Which of the following represents the average number of miles per hour traveled?

a. $350 + 7$
b. $350 - 7$
c. 350×7
d. $350 \div 7$
e. none of the above

Everyone who takes the context into account, and certainly 16 year olds, will know that the average driving speed will be something around 50 miles per hour. And definitely not $350 + 7$ miles per hour, or $350 - 7$ miles per hour. The answer 350×7 makes clear how astray we can go if we do not take te process of integrating real mathematics into real world problems seriously. The students are treated as if they should not take the situation into account but disconnect the mathematics from the context.

3. The problem: creating suitable contexts.

The problem of how to find a good match between real world and real mathematics is not a new problem at all. Freudenthal's plenary address at the ICME 4 conference in Berkeley in 1980 was titled: Major problems of Mathematics Education (Freudenthal 1983a). In the vein of Hilbert, who in 1900 in Paris pronounced his celebrated 23 mathematical problems, Freudenthal addressed 13 main problems for the future. His 8th problem was stated as follows:

'How to create suitable contexts in order to teach mathematizing?' He recognized that this was not an easy question.

'The real world–what does it mean? Forgive me the careless expression. In teaching, mathematizing 'the real world' is represented by a meaningful (to the learners of course) context involving a mathematical problem.'

So one of the key issues in judging real world problems is if we have a mathematical problem in a meaningful context to the students. We will show some examples where a real world problem was judged by students as meaningful, and where real mathematics was involved.

4. Meaningful Contexts for Concept Development.

Consider a classroom with students of 8 to 9 years of age. The teacher introduces the problem to his students (see also Gravemeijer 1994):

*'Tonight your and other parents will visit the school–it's parents evening. Your parents will discuss all kind of things with the teachers. According to the forms that they have filled out we know that we can expect 81 parents. They will be received in the meeting room, and will be seated at tables. We still have to place the tables in the room. Every table can accomodate for 6 parents'. The teacher makes a small sketch on the blackboard:

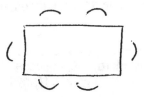

'The question is: How many tables do we need in the meeting room?'

The students start to work on the problem in groups of 3 and 4. The teacher walks around in the classroom, asking small questions about the process of solving the problem. The students were eager to engage in this process. After about ten minutes the teacher ends this part of the lesson. Students are asked to show and explain their solutions. They vary quite a bit. Badr just copied as many of the teacher's sketch on the blackboard as he needed to seat the parents:

Another student, Roy, started out the same way, but after drawing two tables he shifted to a more schematic representation: a rectangle with 6 inscribed. After drawing two of those 'tables' he realized that five tables would add up to 30, and considered this handy. So, via 30 to 60 and then on to 72 and 78. And finally he added the last three chairs.

A third student, Abdelaziz, went a step further in mathematizing the problem. Although he also started to draw the 'model table' from the blackboard he immediately schematized the problem and used his very recent knowledge of multiplication, by using multiples of 6. He wrote down: 6×6=36, then doubled the 36 to 72, and added another two tables to get a capacity of 84.

If we look from distance at these three 'different' solutions (and of course there were many more) we notice a different level using 'real' mathematics in this 'real world' problem. Many teachers would even argue that in the first solution no mathematics has been used at all. But visualizing and schematizing are also important mathematization tools that can be very powerful. The third solution makes the mathematics more visible and will be considered 'higher' level.

Solving this problem is not what this problem is all about. The problem was designed to prepare students for 'division' problems later on. It is part of the phenomenological exploration (Freudenthal 1983b) that will offer students the opportunity to re-construct or, better, re-invent mathematics.

After solving this first problem the teacher has the difficult and complex tasks to present a number of the different solutions. Without making too many explicit recommendations of which solution is the best. After this whole classroom discussion the next problem is presented.

*The 81 parents will be served coffee, of course. Each pot holds 7 cups of coffee. How many pots do we need?

From a mathematical point of view exactly the same problem. Instead of 81 ÷ 6 we now have to deal with 81 ÷ 7. Not so for the students. In the first place the context prohibits an easy pictorial solution: the students have a hard time drawing the coffee pots as Abdelaziz' solution shows:

Abdelaziz, who used the most formal solution in the table problem now goes completely to mental arithmetic with visual support. Badr, who had the most 'simple' solution with the tables, tries to use that schema again with the pots. He even represents them in the same way: a series of cups around the pot.

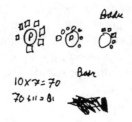

$10 \times 7 = 70$
$70 + 11 = 81$

But after two pots he seems to realice the discussion about multiplication as a means to speed things up and he jumps to:

$10 \times 7 = 70$

and adds: $70 + 11 = 81$, which gives him 12 pots.

The work of yet another student, Paul, shows a typical solution for this second round of the parents problem:

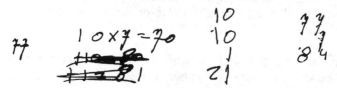

No visualization, but multiplication. Within one lesson one can easily see the progress that the students have made towards solving this class of real world problems and mathematizing in order to develop new mathematical concepts, in this case division.

An important aspect in judging these kind of examples is that they should be placed into context, which means that they are taken out of a series of problems (sometimes stretched out over years) to develop well defined mathematical concepts and activities. That holds also for our next example that was designed for students of age 12. The problem itself is neither very new, nor original (the Babylonians did these kind of problems already). But the place in the curriculum and the connections to earlier and later activities make this problem very powerful. The problem is presented in a visual way (see also Van Reeuwijk 1995):

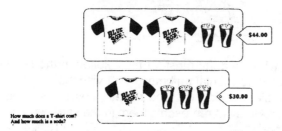

Students come with very ingenious and different solutions. They do not recognize the algebraic nature of the problem and are not hindered by this algebraic knowledge that makes the problem so difficult to teachers and mathematicians. Instead of using $2x + 2y = 44$ and $x + 3y = 30$, they are now supposed to solve the problem 'just' using common sense reasoning.

Observing many teachers solving this problem one notices that they have a mental picture of the system 2x + 2y = 44 and x + 3y = 30 and try to reason back from this solution. Students operate differently:

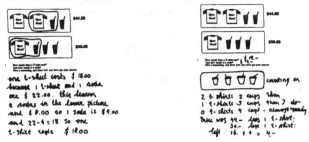

These two solutions are very different in nature: the first one notices that if two shirts and two cokes are 44, one plus one must equal 22. They take away one shirt and one coke from the second picture which leaves two cokes for 8 dollars. Done.

The second solution uses regularity as the starting point. The first picture shows 2 + 2, the second 1 + 3, so the 'third' picture must show 0 + 4. The price belonging with the third picture must be 16, fitting in the sequence: 44, 30, 16. The student shows good insight in where the essential part of the reasoning takes place: after noting that 2,2 followed by 1,3 leads to 0,4 he writes down: almost ready. Exactly.

One observation in a grade 6 (USA) classroom gave about five clearly different strategies, and a lot of representations including the standard algebra notation like: 2t + 2c = 44, etc. From a mathematical, formal point of view, one sometimes notices incorrect notations or language. But from an epistemological point of view these are only helpful. We sometimes have to make a choice between complete mathematical correctness (from a much higher standpoint) and epistemological correctness. In this case the choice is easy.

Much later students will handle in a formal way systems of equations. At that time they know how to reason algebraically, to understand equations, to use the proper mathematical notation, and even understand the concept of a variable. But in this case it will take about two years to reach that level of real mathematical understanding.

5. Realistic Mathematics Education.

The previous two examples may have given some impression about the philosophy we support to learn and teach mathematics, embedded in some 'real world' situation, and with the development of 'real mathematics' in mind, although as a long term product. So what are some tenets of this philosophy? In the first place a student should start with a real problem, real in the sense that the student is willing to engage and that the problem seems meaningful (Treffers 1987, Streefland 1990, Freudenthal 1993b, Gravemeijer 1994, Cobb 1994). It is very difficult to describe conditions for a suitable context. The context can be day to day life (every day life real world), cultural, scientific, artificial, mathematics and others. A possible role of the context can be to give the student support to define a model that he can use in his further mathematical development. Several of these models will be discussed lateron.

The real world problem will be used to develop mathematical concepts. This process can be called conceptual mathematization: the problem is not in the first meant to be solved for problem solving purposes, but the real meaning lies in the underlying exploration of new mathematical concepts (like in the previous examples) (De Lange 1987).

After the process of initial mathematization (to bring the problem from the real world to a more mathematical stated problem) the student will be put in the position and given the occasion for abstraction (in different levels of abstraction), formalization and generalization.

After some kind of abstraction and formalization of the concept the students will use the newly gained knowledge to be applied in new problems in different contexts. In this way, we serve some very important goals. First, the concepts are reinforced by applying them anew. Secondly, this process of applying in essential to achieve transfer skills with the students: only when they can apply certain concepts in different contexts they have mastered the concept.

Another key tenet of this philosophy is the fact that mathematics is seen as a unity. This means an integration of the different mathematical strands, and making the connections explicit.

And finally, there should be a balance between understanding concepts and processes, mathematical understanding, and mastering of basic facts and skill.

From the previous examples, it may come as no surprise that the teaching and learning process fitting with this philosophy is one of a high level of interaction on the classroom. Interaction between student and teacher, but also between teachers. This is no easy task, as there are other points that need special attention, and that were mentioned in my regular lecture at ICME 7 in Quebec in 1992 (De Lange 1993). We will focus on these problems next.

6. Some problems with Realistic Mathematics Education.

We borrow the following from the Proceedings of ICME 7 (De Lange 1993). Some of the problems encountered with the introduction and implementation of new curricula based on the 'realistic' philosophy are:

–the 'loss of teaching
–the 'loss' of basic skills and routines
–the 'loss' of (mathematical) structure
–the 'loss' of clarity of goals
–the complexity of 'authentic assessment'.

In the present article, we will focus on the first two points as they relate to the points of 'losing' real mathematics, and to what constitutes the 'real world'.

7. The problem of 'un'teaching.

Teaching is often interpreted as an activity mainly carried out by the teacher: he introduces the subject, gives one or two examples, may ask a question or two, and invites the students who have been passive listeners to become active by starting to complete exercise from the book. It is not unusual that most of the time this 'activity' is carried out in an individual way. The leson will be ended in a well-organized way, the 'closure', and the next lesson will be conducted in a similar scenario (De Lange 1992, USDE 1996).

Proper real world mathematics education makes teaching more complex. The teacher is not supposed to teach anymore. And learning the art of 'unteaching' has been proven to be very difficult and very personal.

Referring again to the above mentioned 'parents evening' and 'coke and t-shirt' problem, it will be clear that one cannot 'teach' the problems in a traditional way. This does not mean that we have a fixed scenario ready and available for the teacher who is eager to change and learn. The classroom in combination with the teacher will determine in which way an optimal result, consisting of interaction, individual work, group work, classroom discussion, student presentation, teacher presentation, and other activities, can be obtained.

The teacher's role is that of organization and facilitation– a process that cannot be described in detail for 'the' teacher. The teacher needs to make personal adaptation. To make things more difficult the teacher faces even more obstacles. Regularly teachers and students will be confronted with problems that have different 'correct' answers or one correct answer and different strategies.

To add to the complexity of classroom management the different strategies will include different levels of mathematical thinking. All these factors will lead to increased insecurity for the teacher. Add a feeling of loss of authority when a student presents an unexpected brilliant solution. To summarize: teaching mathematics in context in order to develop concepts is no easy task. The following example will make this even clearer.

8. Designing and teaching for re-inventing.

In Freudenthal's words we should start by offering the children an opportunity for a didactical phenomenological exploration. The students will explore, simplify, mathematize, and model the situation. Or even carry out a simulation in some way. All this in order to develop well-defined concepts. As soon as the goals and concepts have been identified, the problem of how to create suitable contexts in order to teach mathematizing is a real designer's problem.

How to put a simple concept like the vision line or line of sight in a suitable context in order to give the students an opportunity for a didactical phenomenological exploration was the problem for designers of an American-Dutch curriculum project (Romberg, De Lange et al 1997). The first idea was to present to the students the following photograph of a hiker sitting on the ledge of the Grand Canyon (Feijs, De Lange, Van Reeuwijk, Spence, Brendefur, 1994):

The Grand Canyon

The question asked to the students is: If the person looks straight down and ahead, he cannot see the river. Why?

An open question, not giving away the concept, but trying to 'seduce' students into a discussion why the person cannot see the river right ahead of him. Although many students engage in the discussion, and many answers make some sense ('because the rock is in the way', 'if he looks sideways he will see the river', 'he should walk closer to the edge') very few students re-invented the idea of vision line (Feijs, 1996). This did not come completely as a surprise. So one of the following problems made the vision lines very explicit by making them concrete. Again in the context of the canyon, and by actually modeling both the canyon and the vision lines. However, the whole process of re-invention was not considered to meet the minimum requirements: that at least some students in most classes will re-invent the vision line.

So the designers had to go back to the drawing board. This cyclic process is one of the characteristics of the methodology of developmental research, that is typical for the work of the Freudenthal Institute (Gravemeijer 1994). Classroom based observations leading to revisions, to theories about how children learn and teachers teach, to new designs based on a dynamic theory that is continuously changing, leading to new designs. After lengthy deliberations the designers decided to simulate the canyons, but not with a carton model but with tables representing the canyon:

Students are placed behind the tables and are asked to indicate with dots which part of the vertical wall is visible to them. So the dark student on the right indicated to the girl ('in the canyon') which part of the canyon wall he can see. And the same will take place with the student on the left for the opposing canyon wall. This activity (which is not easy to manage in a large classroom) turned out to be successful: several students indicated that they were arguing about and along lines. Some of them even used and/or invented names like visionline or line of sight.

So it seemed that the designers had solved the problem: how to create a suitable context. But the teacher has to be prepared for unexpected events at all times, which adds to the already existing problems. The picture tells the story:

Several points on the left canyon wall means that students start wondering about the relation (if any) between these points. The following hypotheses were formulated by the students in one classroom:

–the line is straight.
–the line is 'hollow'.
–the line reflects the top of a hill.

This discussion was not foreseen by the designers, as they were too obsessed by the re-invention of the vision line. So the teacher was on his own. As teachers frequently will be in problem oriented curricula. Without telling how the teacher 'solved' this problem it is no exaggeration to state that many very capable teachers will have a hard time solving it without some support from a teachers' guide or other additional support materials–and training.

But on the other side the rewards can be huge. The described exploration activities lead not only to conceptualization of visionlines and blind spot and blind area, but also to issues related to the steepness of the visionline in relation to the angle, and the ratios involved. Eventually, after three weeks the students will deal with the formal definition of a tangent. So again one should take into account the role and place (in time) of the real world problem in any curriculum before making any judgements.

9. The problem of basic skills.

Again looking back at the ICME 7, we noticed that the discussion about the role of basic skills is related to the implementation of realistic mathematics curricula, but it is ongoing in many countries in its own right. For many teachers this discussion has not been part of their daily practice. Basic skills are for them a matter of fact and form the kernel of math education.

The questions we need to address are: what are the basic skills for the 21st century? How do we develop and maintain basic skills? What is the role of the calculator? (De Lange 1993).

A report on mathematics at primary level in the Netherlands has clearly indicated that the new 'realistic' approach need not lead lower scores on basic skills tests. On the contrary, the research shows clearly that on most areas the students do better than before (Bokhove 1995). For secondary we can gain some insight on the scores of Dutch students on the primarily low level basic skills items of the Third International Mathematics and Science Study. Although the items do not fit with most of the curriculum, Dutch students performed well (Beaton et al. 1996).

How context can support the development of basic skills on a conceptual level will be shown next.

10. Problematizing for concept development.

As we noted in the beginning of this article not all uses of the real world make the problem a meaningful real world problem. As another example we can look at:

$$88 + 97 + 105 = 290\,(千克)$$

几个数连加，可以写成一个竖式。

The context, a couple of sacks of 88, 97 and 105 kg, has no functional relation with the addition problem. On the contrary. The formal addition procedure does not bear on the context at all. And no advantage is taken from the fact that the number make a mental, smart, addition much better suited for the purpose (90 + 100 + 100, and then –2, –3, +5).

A better example of problematizing we found in a recent article by an international group of renowned mathematics education researchers (Hiebert et al. 1996). The problem that the students have to solve is the following:

*Find the difference in the height of two children, Jorge and Paulo, who were 62 inches tall and 37 inches tall, respectively.

The context is the same, but the presentation different from the problem that was used in research in the Netherlands, some years earlier (Van den Heuvel–Panhuizen 1996).

FIGURE 1

One has to bear in mind that it is more than likely that students will react differently to the different representations of the same problem.

The first child to react to the question of the teacher, Gabriela, had solved the problem by counting up from 37 to 62. In the process, she counted by 1's and 10's, keeping track of her counts by drawing single dots to represent 1's and drawing sticks to represent 10's. She counted from 37 to 40, making three dots as she counted, then she counted from 40 to 60 by 10's, drawing 2 sticks to show the 2 10's. Finally she counted up to 62, making two more dots:

$$37 \cdots > 40$$
$$40 \; / \; / \; > 60$$
$$60 \cdots > 62$$

25

Another student, Roberto, had first drawn a picture of Jorge and Paulo and extended a horizontal line from the top of Paulo's head across to Jorge. His comments: 'I shrunk the big guy down by taking away the little guy from him. I took 3 10's from the 6 10's and 7 from this 10. That leaves 3 and these 2 are five and two 10's left is 25". Or, more visual:

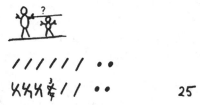

These students used sticks, but we need to stress the flexible use of different models. Another powerful model is the empty number line (Gravemeijer 1994). The same problem will be solved as follows:

First, add 20 to 37 to get 57. We need another jump of 5 to get to 62. The total is 20 + 5 = 25.

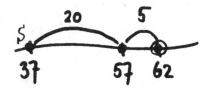

The second strategy:
Start at 62 and take away 30. This brings you at 32. Take away another 7 and you reach 25. The total difference in height is 25:

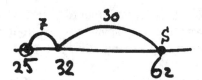

The third strategy:
Start at 62. Take away 2. Get 60. Take away 30. You are at 30. Take away 5. We are now at 25.

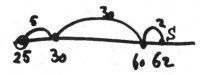

To show how this empty number line can work in classroom-reality we borrow student work from Germany (Selter 1996). The problem stated was the following:

*Cinema 8 has a total of 212 seats. 175 persons are already sitting there. How many empty seats are left?

The students show many different strategies, all involving the empty number line:

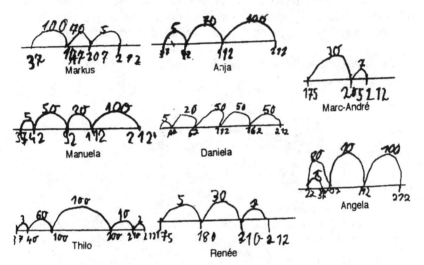

Anja and Markus take away hundreds, tens and ones separately, Danielle and Manuela use the splitting up strategy, Thilo also, but differently, while Marc-Andre uses the adding up strategy.

Another 'model' different from the sticks and empty number line is the money model. Let us go back to the two students from the American example, one student being 37 inches, the other 62 inches tall. The length of the taller student will be represented by bills and coins (6 bills of 10, 2 coins of 1) as follows:

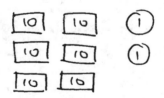

Now the student solves the problem by crossing out (subtracting) 3 bills of 10 which equals 30. Next he wants to cross out 7 but there are only 2 coins. So he crosses the two out and makes a firm note that he is still 5 short (notation: –5!). He writes down in the box:

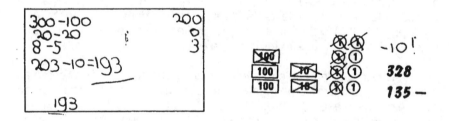

Again we would like to give a real classroom example representing this strategy, taken from a classroom in the Netherlands (Boswinkel 1996). The problem involved is the subtraction of 328 – 135.

We see that the student first takes away one of the 100 guilders and writes down: 300 – 100 = 200. Next he takes away 2 from the 10 stack: 20 – 20 = 0 and 5 from the guilders stack (8 – 5 = 3) while making a note (–10!) reminding him that he is 20 short. So the answer is 203 – 10 = 193.

Two issues need some further attention here. In the first place that we should offer the students a wide array of models to choose from, like the sticks, empty number line (a model resulting from the bead string) and the money model. And within these models they have freedom to use their own strategy. In this way students will be very flexible, and, as research seems to indicate, need less repetition and training in the traditional way, while their conceptual understanding is at a higher level.

The second point that needs careful attention is the place in the curriculum of context problems. As we indicated before there are two extremes: the first place is as the problem is used from the didactical phenomenological exploration. Than the problem is at the start of a (part of the) learning sequence. The problem of the lengths of the two students can only be used as a starting point in a relevant way to introduce subtraction if the students do know very little about subtraction. If the students are good in subtraction problems the same problem of the length of the two boys loses its meaning and relevance. The students will use mental arithmetic and make no connection to the context.

But the real world problem can also be placed at the end of a learning sequence. By 'end' we mean that the students know subtraction and need rich applications in order to reinforce the concept and to develop transfer skills. In order to be able to judge the relevance and meaningfulness of a problem we need to look at these issues in the first place.

11. Where is the real mathematics?

Recently another problem arose in the discussion about real world mathematics. Thomas (1996) indicated that mathematics in context is 'proto mathematics'. Sierpinska (1996) suggested that it could be that the restriction to 'real life contexts' hinders the attainment of the goals. And Verstappen (1996) claims that the use of higher mathematical tools and generalization is not an aim for the pure realist.

It is rather remarkable to see the coincidence in time. How come all of a sudden there is a surge in these and similar concerns? There may be more than one reason. Using and applying mathematics in a context has been 'trendy' for many years (Keitel 1993). With the result that many projects and ideas have emerged all proposing the ideas of mathematics in context. But among all the projects that have emerged only a limited number should be regarded as firm in philosophy, theory, practice and supporting research. We need to clarify more clearly under which conditions mathematics in context, or real world mathematics, will deliver real mathematics. And this has been our goal since the outset. As we wrote already a decade ago: '(in realistic mathematics education) the students are required to find some level of generalization' (De Lange 1987).

Realistic mathematics education should lead to excellent basic skills, as we have just discussed, but also to real mathematics. Our next example will show that we are dealing with real mathematics, in a meaningful context, at a somewhat higher level, students of 15/16 years of age.

12. Real problem with real mathematics

The problem we will discuss is taken from one of the many innovative curricula projects that have emerged in the USA in the last decade, in part because of funding of the National Science Foundation.

The project (ARISE) places applications in the heart of the curriculum and is meant for high school students.

*A new building has to be built on Main Street. A, B and C are buildings on side streets:

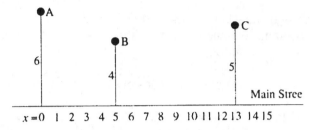

—Where on Main Street must the new building be located so that the average distance to A, B and C is as small as possible?

First we show the work of a student who solved the problem with a table:

Some teachers and others as well would argue that again no mathematics is used in this. This may be proto mathematics (Chevallard 1990) or common sense reasoning. This, of course, is true to a certain extent. Just like in the parents' evening problems, one has different levels of mathematical sophistication to solve the problem. But before making any definite judgements, let us look at the continuation of the problem, the next question asked:

*Use the table to find the minimax location.

The students answer makes perfectly clear that he understands the problem: –'The minimax location is at 6, that is where the furthest away point is closest'.

But let us now look at the next question:
*The same question: suppose the new building will be located at position ´ on Main Street.

–Give absolute value equations of the distance from ´ to A, B and C.

The students answer:

$$A: y = |x - 0| + 6 \Big/ y = |x| + 6$$
$$B: y = |x - 5| + 4$$
$$C: y = |x - 13| + 5$$

After having drawn the graphs, the students are asked to find the minimax location using the graphs. On the left we have the graphs, on the right the conclusion of the student:

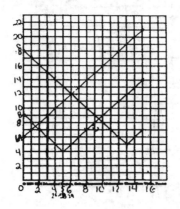

I can see at $x = 6$ that the two highest graphs are the lowest.

Real mathematics, a meaningful problem, and some good reasoning. Those are the characteristics we should be looking for. To design these problems, even at primary level (or maybe especially at primary level) is no easy task. The importance of the task in relation to the reflective inquiry and problematizing we are looking for, is the next point we would like to discuss.

13. The design and impact of a good problem.

The art of 'unteaching' is a real art and definitely one of the key issues to be addressed when implementing real world curricula (Simon 1995, Lampert 1989). It is imperative that the classroom atmosphere is one that stimulates reflective inquery, that the students are willing to engage in a classroom discussion, that they show a problem solving attitude. This means a complete culture change in most classrooms.

Hiebert et al. (1996) propose that the reflective inquiry and problematizing depends more on the students and the culture of the classroom than on the task. It may come as no surprise to the attentive reader that we tend to disagree with this statement. It is very difficult to change the classroom culture with tasks that are not in line with that culture. Proper tasks facilitate this process, sometimes to the extent that the classroom culture as far as the students are concerned changes faster than the teachers' culture. We are therefore tempted to conclude, after years of observing students in action with realistic mathematics education in different countries, that the reflective inquiry and problematizing depends on the task, and the place of the task in the curriculum, more than anything else.

This means that the 8th problem of Freudenthal, as stated in 1980, has only won in relevance for the present problems. And Sierspinska (1996), while questioning whether the restriction to real life context hinders the attainment of the goals, also supports Freudenthal when stating that we have to look for good questions and contexts in which these questions arise.

14. The Alhambra as a real life context with real mathematics.

Being so close to the Alhambra one cannot but look at the possibilities to see whether or not this magnificent building lends itself for relevant and meaningful mathematical activities. Having visited the Alhambra at an earlier occasion we struggled with this question. The following example was designed with 12 year olds (USA) in mind, but experiments with the materials were also carried out with graduate students at the University (Netherlands).

*The art of the Alhambra Palace in Spain is very mathematical. Or more precisely: geometrical. Beautiful starlike structures are connected to each other in a very ingenious way. Sometimes the stars have twelve points, sometimes eight or six.:

The students are given two transparencies with this shape, and they know the angles involved:

Then they are asked to construct this star shape, and how large all angles are in the starfigure. Just by reasoning.

Next they are asked whether or not they can form the 16 point star, with the same transparencies, and what they can tell about all the angles in this case:

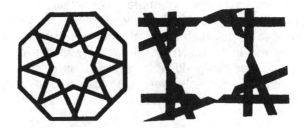

It is interesting to see how graduate students reacted to this problem. They were all math majors, and had a hard time working on this

problem. First they found it strange to work with transparencies (math is not a hands on science). Secondly they had no idea how this fitted with their existing knowledge. Thirdly they found reasoning in this case quite hard. And finally they did not know very well how to present the solution:

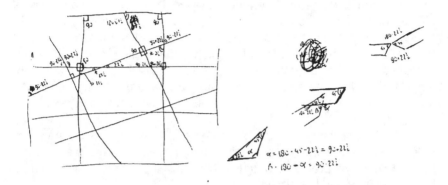

15. Reflecting on the context issues.

We would like to look at contexts as they appear in different places and roles. The place and role of the context in a curriculum, in a task or problem, at different grade levels, and in assessment.

For the context in the curriculum the time factor is essential. There is an essential difference between the role of the context when we are trying to develop new mathematical concepts, and when we are applying these new concepts in applications or otherwise. In that phase of exploration and problematizing the design of the proper context is very critical. Some contexts will work, others won't and we are still, and probably will be forever, finding out what works and what doesn't. And this will vary from culture to culture, to name a trivial point of attention.

Furthermore in this phase it would help if the context offers the student a model that can be used later as a model to solve other problems.

It may come as a surprise that in this phase the 'realness' of the context is not a very important issue. The context need not come from 'real life'. It may even be completely artificial. It just needs to be meaningful to the students.

When we are using mathematical concepts in applications the roles change. The context itself is not a critical issue so much, but the realness of the problem seems to have gained in this situation compared to the exploration phase. This does not implicate that designing suitable problems in context is easier in this situation.

If we zoom in and look at the role of the context within a specific problem or task we see different possibilities. There can be no context at all. But quite often in present day textbooks we see the problem of the 'dressed up' or 'camouflage' context. The context is just there to add some flavour to the problem. It makes it visually appealing by making a picture, or makes a situation around a simple problem. Even the problem about the lengths of the two students would fit under this category if it was offered to the students at a much later stage in their cognitive development.

The most intriguing use of contexts is when one really needs to reflext on the context in order to solve and truly understand the problem. In our opinion the problem about the three buildings in the main street fits in this category (De Lange 1995).

A point for future research seems to lie in the fact that one notices that different kinds of contexts seem to be used for different groups of students. For primary grades one tends to see more artificial, more 'very close' to the students contexts like shopping, school, music and sports. For older students (high school) the context s are becoming more real in the sense that they become scientific, and further away from the student. Not only do we notice this 'horizontal' separation, but one can also notice a vertical separation. By this we mean that the brighter the students are, the more real and scientific and farther away from the students the context can be. Although one can observe the effects in many schools, at least in the Netherlands it is not supported by any research. On the contrary, there is some (incidental) proof that young children can handle scientific contexts very well if the problem is challenging and meaningful.

In assessment the problems concerning context are easily underestimated. The rules in assessment are different from those in ordinary student materials. First the context in the problem will make it more difficult to identify what you actually are measuring. And of course this is the key issue in assessment. Furthermore the array of contexts you can choose from is considerably smaller than in ordinary lessons. Contexts should distract students, or harm them emotionally in any way. So one has to be careful when choosing AIDS, cancer, poorness, etc, as a context in assessment.

In short, the choice and role of context in assessment is very critical.

An example of a context that was appealing and meaningful to students, had good real mathematics, but draw criticism for choice of the context for political reasons.

16. A controversial context.

The example, meant for 16 year olds (De Lange 1987):

*In a certain country the defense budget is 30 million dollars for 1990. The total budget for that year is 500 million dollars. The following year the defense budget is 35 million, while the total is 605 million. Inflation during this period between the budgets was 10%.

–You are invited to lecture for a pacifist society. You want to explain that the defense budget has decreased last year.

This problem is quite complex: relative versus absolute, percentages, proportional reasoning. But the context derived its controversial character from the combination of this question with the following:

–You are invited to lecture to a military academy. Explain that the defense budget has increased during this year.

Reactions from teachers varied quite a bit. From: 'an excellent exercise, motivating, enlightening, showing the role of mathematics in politics', to: 'I refuse to teach my students how to manipulate'. And that this comment has some more support proves the adaptation of this problem when it appeared in the Mathematical Sciences Education Board (USA) publication: For Good Measure (1991). Mathematically the problem had remained te same, but the context was neutralized. In our opinion we should develop a critical attitude with our students and we need these kind of problems to develop that attitude.

17. The logger and his truckload revisited.

We started this article with a short historical lookback at the recent development of mathematics education by means of a real world problem, that lost its meaning over time, and its mathematics as well. How would that problem look at this moment, anno 1996? This would be my version:

*In an old math book (1960) we found a real world problem:

A logger sells a truckload of lumber for $100. His cost of production is four-fifths of the price. What is his profit?

We're now in 1996. Lumberprices have gone up. Profits are under pressure. Asked about his profit the same logger said: 'Yeah, prices of production have gone up dramatically. It takes me $750 to produce one truckload. And I still make the same profit.'

–Discuss different meanings of 'the same profit' and compute the(se) profit(s).

In this way we have a meaningful real world problem with real mathematics. And to achieve that is our goal for the years to come.

18. Summary

Our goal, wish, expectation for the next decade, reflecting on more than twenty years of experience, observations, research, and taking into account the present level of discussion, can be stated in very compact form:

We need the (not so) real worlds in order to develop real mathematics to be used in the real world.

References.

Beaton, A.E. and I. Mullis, M.O. Martin, E.J. Gonzales, D.N. Kelly, T.A. Smith (1996), *Mathematics Achievement in the Middle School Years*, Chestnut Hill, Boston College.

Bokhove, J. (1995), *Brief Sketch of Results Assessment Research Mathematics in Primary Education* (English translation by E. Feijs) in: Journal for Mathematics Education in the Netherlands, Nieuwe Wiskrant, 14-4, 4-9.

Boswinkel, N. (1996) Personal communication.

Chevallard, Y. (1990), *On Mathematics Education and Culture: Critical Afterthoughts*, Educational Studies in Mathematics, 21, 3-27.

Cobb, P. (1994), *Theories of Mathematical Learning and Constructivism: A Personal View.* Paper presented on Trends and Perspectives in Mathematics Education, Klagenfurt, Austria.

De Lange, J. (1987), *Mathematics, Insight and Meaning,* Utrecht, OW & OC.

De Lange, J. (1992), Higher Order (Un-)Teaching in: Wirszup, I. and R. Streit eds. (1992) *Developments in School Mathematics Education around the World,* Reston VA, NCTM.

De Lange, J. (1993), *Curriculum Change: An American Dutch Perspective,* in: Robitaille, D.F. and D.H. Wheeler and C. Kieran eds. Selected Lectures from the 7th International Congress on Mathematics Education, Quebec, Universite Laval.

De Lange, J. and C. Keitel, I. Huntley, M. Niss eds. (1993), *Innovation in Maths Education by Modelling and Applications,* Chichester, Ellis Horwood Limited.

De Lange, J. (1995), *Assessment: No Change Without Problems,* in: Romberg, T.A. ed. (1995), Reform in School Mathematics and Authentic Assessment, New York, SUNY Press, 87-172.

Feijs, E. and J. de Lange, M. van Reeuwijk, M. Spence, J. Brendefur (1993), *Shady Business (At a Different Angle),* Madison / Chicago / Utrecht, NCRMSE / EBEC / Freudenthal Institute.

Feijs, E. (1996), personal communication.

Freudenthal, H. (1983a), *major Problems in Mathematics Education,* in: Zweng, M. and T. Green, J. Kilpatrick, H. Pollak, M. Suydam eds. Proceedings of the Four International Congress on Mathematical Education, Boston, Birkhauser.

Freudenthal, H. (1983b), *Didactical Phenomenology of Mathematical Structures,* Dordrecht, Reidel.

Gravemeijer, K. (1994), *Developing Realistic Mathematics Education,* Utrecht, CD-b Press.

Hiebert, J. and T.P. Carpenter, E. Fennema, K. Fuson, P. Human, A. Olivier, D. Wearne (1996), *Problem Solving as a Basis for Reform in Curriculum and Instruction: the Case of Mathematics,* Educational Researcher, vol. 25 (4) 12-22.

Keitel, C. (1993), *Implicit Mathematical Models in Social Practice and Explicit mathematics Teaching by Applications,* in: De Lange, J. and C. Keitel, I. Huntley, M. Niss eds. (1993), Innovation in Maths Education by Modelling and Applications, Chichester, Ellis Horwood Limited.

Lampert, M. (1989), *Choosing and Using Mathematical Tools in Classroom Discourse,* in: J. Brophy, ed. Advances in Research on Teaching, vol. 1, Greenwich, JAI Press, 223-264.

Niss, M. (1993), *Assessment of Mathematical Applications and Modelling in Mathematics Teaching,* in: De Lange, J. and C. Keitel, I. Huntley, M. Niss eds. (1993), Innovation in Maths Education by Modelling and Applications, Chichester, Ellis Horwood Limited.

Romberg, T.A. ed. (1995), *Reform in School Mathematics and Authentic Assessment,* New York, SUNY Press.

Romberg, T.A. and J. de Lange eds. (1997), *Mathematics in Context,* Chicago, EBEC.

Selter, C. (in press), Taking Children's Thinking Seriously, *Educational Studies in Mathematics.*

Sierpinska, A. (1996), Mathematics: 'In Context', 'Pure' or 'With Applications'?, *For the Learning of Mathematics,* 15, 1 pp 2-15.

Simon, M.A. (1995), Reconstructing Mathematics Pedagogy from a Constructivist Perspective, *Journal for Research in Mathematics Education,* 26, 114-145.

Streefland, L. (1990), *Fractions for Realistic Mathematics Education,* Dordrecht, Kluwer Academic Publishers.

Thomas, R. (1996), Proto-Mathematics or/and Real Mathematics, *For the Learning of Mathematics,* 16, 2, pp 11-18.

Treffers, A. (1987), *Three Dimensions,* Dordrecht, Reidel.

USDE, National Center for Education (1996), *Pursuing Excellence,* Washington, USDE.

Van den Heuvel- Panhuizen (1996), *Assessment and Realistic Mathematics Education,* Utrecht, CD-b Press.

Van Reeuwijk, M. (1995), *Students' Knowledge of Algebra,* in: *Proceedings of PME 19,* vol. 1, Recife Brazil, July 1995, pp 135-150.

Verstappen, P. (1996), *Mathematics in Reality?,* in: ZDM 96, 2 pp 47-56

Wirszup, I. and R. Streit eds. (1992), *Developments in School Mathematics Education around the World,* Reston VA, NCTM.

COMMUNICATION IN THE CLASSROOM

COMUNICACIÓN EN CLASE

Chief Organizer / *Responsable:* Susan Pirie (CAN)
Advisory Panel / *Asesor:* Heinz Steinbring (DEU)
Local Organizer / *Coordinadora Local:* M. Victoria Sánchez (ESP)

The work group offers an opportunity of exchanging ideas and results, and discussing problems, in:

- empirical research into every day classroom communication by quantitative or qualitative methods, emphasizing a psychological, a sociological or a linguistic perspective;

- theoretical analysis into every day classroom communication, looking at it as a social event (a culture), as an environment for learning, as a language game, or with respect to distrubances or obstacles;

- interventions into classroom communication for reasons of research, investigation or improvement (change in teaching style, introduction of learning aids, different forms of social organization, etc.);

- empirical research into small group work or into individual work of pupils by means of overservation or (clinical) interview, with interest for, e.g., processes of problem solving, pupils cognitions or concepts.

FORMS OF MATHEMATICAL KNOWLEDGE

FORMAS DEL CONOCIMIENTO MATEMÁTICO

Chief Organizer / *Responsable*: Dina Tirosh (ISR)
Advisory Panel / *Asesores*: Tom Kieren (CAN), Lena Lindenskov (DNK)
Local Organizer / *Coordinador Local*: Javier Brihuega (ESP)

Introduction

This working group was mainly devoted to defining, discussing and contrasting psychological and philosophical issues related to various types of knowledge involved in mathematics learning and teaching (e.g., intuitive and formal; explicit and tacit; elementary and advanced; visual and analytical; knowing that; knowing how; knowing why and knowing to). Possible impacts of modern developments in epistemology and philosophy of mathematics on the learning and teaching of mathematics were discussed.

Structure

The first three sessions dealt with the following topics:
Session 1: Forms of mathematical knowledge: Theoretical and philosophical aspects.
Session 2: Forms of mathematical knowledge: Elementary vs. advanced.
Session 3: Forms of mathematical knowledge: The teachers' perspective.

Each of these sessions began with two keynote presentations that drew upon various aspects related to the theme of this session. The group then split up into two subgroups, each of which continued to discuss specific issues raised in the keynote presentations, and other related topics.

The last session (Session 4) was split into three parts. In the first part, five presentations were given in parallel, by Swapna Mukhopadhyay (USA), Greisy Winici and Rosa Leikin (Israel), Behiye Ubuz (UK), Pessia Tsamir (Israel) and Lyn English (Australia). In the second part two reactors, Michele Artigue (France) and Dina Tirosh (Israel), reflected on the keynote presentations and their ensuing discussions. The last part of this session was devoted to a general discussion.

Here, I shall briefly describe the keynote presentations and some of the issues discussed by one of the reactors (Michele Artigue).

Interactions between various forms of mathematical knowledge

The first two sessions related to various forms of knowledge, some of which are familiar from the mathematics education literature (e.g., instrumental, relational, conceptual, procedural, algorithmic, formal, intuitive, implicit, explicit, elementary, advanced, knowing that, knowing why and knowing how), while others were defined in the presentations. Implications of the differences between the various forms of mathematical knowledge for mathematics learning were a central issue in these two sessions.

Keynote presentation 1: *"Knowing that, knowing how, knowing why and knowing to"* by John Mason, The Open University (UK).

John Mason described three types of knowledge traditionally distinguished in philosophy: knowing that, knowing how and knowing why. He then argued that education driven by these three types of knowledge, sees knowledge as a static object, a collection of facts and approaches, which can be passed from generation to generation. He defined a fourth form of knowledge: knowing to act and identified various factors that enable us to know how to act in some way in certain situations or contexts. The main part of John Mason's presentation was devoted to an elaboration on the roles that habituation, enculturation, imagery, emotion, training and creative conjunction of present and past experience, play in this kind of practical knowledge.

Keynote presentation 2: *"Forms of knowledge in mathematics and mathematics education: A philosophical perspective"* by Paul Ernest, University of Exeter (UK).

Paul Ernest described and discussed the works of several distinguished philosophers of mathematics, psychologists and educators including Davis and Hersh, Lakatos, Tymoczko, and Kitcher for whom "knowing that" was concerned with explicit knowledge of propositions and "knowing how" referred to practical, tacit or personal knowledge. He suggested that most personal knowledge in mathematics is tacit, and discussed possible implications of this assertion to mathematics education (e.g., should the emphasis in mathematics education be on abstract and general knowledge or rather on concrete and content- specific knowledge?). A main part of Paul Ernest's presentation was devoted to issues related to ways of validating tacit knowledge and the roles that intrapersonal as well as interpersonal conversation and cultural conversation play in mathematics. Paul Ernest argued that mathematics educators should reconsider the rhetorical style of mathematics in the classroom in light of recent changes in mathematics itself.

Keynote presentation 3: *"What mathematical arguments are acceptable?* " by Tommy Dreyfus, Centre for Technological Education, and Sarah Kiro, Weizmann Institute of Science (Israel). This keynote presentation was a natural sequel to the previous one. Tommy Dreyfus and Sarah Kiro questioned the extent to which it is reasonable to demand (and to expect) formal proofs from students at the high school or college level. They demonstrated that studies on students' conceptions of proof and valid mathematical argumentations consistently show that very few students ever learn to appreciate the characteristics of formal proof and to construct such arguments themselves. The main part of their presentation was devoted to a description of various types of informal reasoning often used by students (e.g., intuitive, experimental, and visual) and to a discussion on possible criteria for evaluating such justifications, argumentations and explanations.

Keynote presentation 4: *"Elementary and advanced forms of mathematical knowledge"*, by Eddie Gray, Demetra Pitta and David Tall, University of Warwick, (UK).

This presentation described the development of mathematical knowledge from elementary arithmetic to higher mathematics. The authors first introduced a theory which is based on three essential components of cognition: object, action and property. They argued that the difference between those who succeed in both elementary and higher mathematics and those who fail is rooted in the ability to flexibly move between seeing symbols as a process and as a concept . In respect to elementary arithmetic, they presented evidence that children who succeed in elementary arithmetic could freely "move" between the objects counted, the process of counting, and the procept of numbers. Less successful children focused on the specific nature of the objects counted and associated them to real and imagined experiences. Gray, Pitta and Tall argued that at a more advanced level, a student should understand that in mathematics the existence of objects with certain properties can be assumed, and the mental objects are reconstructed through formal proof. At this level, less successful students are unable to focus on the generative power of definitions to construct the properties of the conceptual objects that are the essence of the formal theories. The concluding part of this presentation discussed the similarities and differences between the presenters' theory of forms of mathematical knowledge and other theories and approaches concerning this issue (e.g., Piaget's theory of different forms of abstraction and Fischbein's three dimensions of mathematical activity).

Teachers' forms of mathematical knowledge

Teaching is increasingly being recognized as a difficult profession that requires decision making and problem solving in a complex, dynamic and public environment for many hours every day. There is also growing recognition that mathematical knowledge alone does not guarantee better teaching and attempts are being made to define the various forms of knowledge needed for teaching. This session was devoted to differentiating and characterizing forms of knowledge needed for teaching, and ideas about forms of mathematical knowledge that are important for teachers to know.

Keynote presentation 5: *"Conceptualizing teachers' forms of knowledge"* by Thomas J. Cooney, University of Georgia, (USA).

In the introductory part of this presentation, Tom Cooney described and discussed attempts to characterize and differentiate various forms of teachers' knowledge (e.g., Shulman, Bromme). He described the structure of teachers' beliefs and argued that teachers need to become adaptive agents and that the structure in which knowledge is held (e.g., dualistically or relativistically) is critical to a teacher becoming a reflective practitioner. Then, Tom Cooney provided examples of several activities aimed at enabling teachers to develop types of knowledge that promote reflective thinking and offered a framework for conceptualizing teachers' professional knowledge. He argued that teachers' knowledge constitutes an often neglected but critical element in the process of teacher education, and that conceptualizing forms of teacher knowledge and how that knowledge is held will allow teacher education to move toward being an arena for disciplined inquiry.

Keynote presentation 6: *"Forms of mathematical knowledge : A teacher educator perspective"* by Anna O. Graeber, University of Maryland, (USA).

Anna Graeber's presentation focused on the question: What are the important ideas about forms of students' mathematical knowledge that teachers should acquire in their preservice education? She described several ideas about forms of students' mathematical knowledge that teacher educators should familiarize preservice teachers with, including different forms of mathematical knowledge that have been described in the mathematics education literature, the ideas that students' current knowledge is probably important if you want them to amend what they know, that different logical and experimental paths can lead to the same mathematical ideas and that knowledge is more enduring when it is learned in a meaningful context, through reasoning from primitive concepts, by explaining to others, and by reflecting on one's own knowledge growth. Anna Graeber suggested some implications of each of these ideas to teaching mathematics and listed experiences that might help preservice teachers appreciate students' typical ways of thinking in mathematics.

The necessity to go beyond hierarchical and dichotomous visions

Michele Artigue, from Universite Paris 7 and IUFM of Reims, France, integrated and compared the approaches and ideas concerning forms of mathematical knowledge that emerged during the earlier three sessions. She discussed the various shifts that have occurred over time in views of mathematical knowledge within the field of research in mathematics education, and related to two main shifts: the first was the transition from a structural and hierarchical conception towards a more dialectical vision focusing on the diversity of forms of knowledge, and the second was the transition between a global notion of knowledge towards a more local, situated one. Artigue discussed these approaches as they are reflected in the mathematics education literature in French.

Note: Papers and discussions of WG2 will appear in a special issue in Educational Studies in Mathematics on forms of mathematical knowledge: Learning for teaching with understanding.

STUDENTS' ATTITUDES AND MOTIVATION

ACTITUDES Y MOTIVACIÓN DEL ALUMNADO

Chief Organizer / *Responsable*: Fong Ho Kheong (SGP)
Advisory Panel / *Asesor:* Douglas McLeod (USA)
Local Organizer / *Coordinador Local:* Manuel Torralbo (ESP)

The working group will focus the discussions on the students' attitudes and motivation in front of the learning of mathematics and how to improve the situation in the future.

TEACHING MIXED-ABILITY CLASSES

ENSEÑAR EN CLASES CON HABILIDADES DIVERSAS

Chief Organizer / *Responsable*: Liora Linchevski (ISR)
Advisory Panel / *Asesores:* Margaret Cozzens (USA), Zmira Mevarech (ISR) Nada Stehlikova (CZR)
Local Organizer / *Coordinador Local*: Francisco Esteban (ESP)

Every session will be devoted to a different topic related to the Learning of Mathematics in Mixed-Ability classes as follows:

(a) ability grouping vs. mixed ability classrooms: a look from a theoretical and empirical perspectives;

(b) innovative methods designed for mixed ability classrooms;

(c) alternative assessments emerge from the mixed ability classes needs;

(d) teacher training for mixed ability classes.

GENDER AND MATHEMATICS

GÉNERO Y MATEMÁTICAS

Chief Organizer / *Responsable*: Barbro Grevholm (SWZ)
Advisory panel / *Asesores*: Jeff Evans (GBR) Roberta Mura (CAN)
Fidela Velázquez (ESP)
Local Organizer / *Coordinadora Local*: Eugenia Jiménez (ESP)

For the first time in the history of ICME conferences a working group had the title Gender and mathematics. It attracted 23 presenters and in total 75 participants, who all actively contributed to the collective knowledge. Since ICME 7 took place in 1992 there has been an ICMI Study conference on Gender and Mathematics Education and the working group was able to take advantage of the research presented in this conference (Grevholm & Hanna 1995; Hanna, 1996).

In the first session a panel of six speakers gave a background for the work and provided an up-to-date international context in order to inspire all participants to actively take part in the later sessions. Gila Hanna spoke about future research in gender and mathematics education and indicated that questions about enrolment and achievement at school and undergraduate levels in North America are no longer major concerns. She suggested that the research efforts should now be directed towards uncovering and understanding factors that seem to impede women's pursuit of doctoral degrees in mathematics. Elizabeth Quinlan presented data from women's participation in mathematics, science and technology education in Canada. A marked change has taken place towards a more equal distribution between men and women.

Tony Gardiner focussed on gender aspects of the Mathematics Olympiad in the UK. Jeff Evans reflected on the possibilities and opportunities offered by quantitative methods, including statistical modelling of medium and large scale surveys, secondary analysis of data, use of official statistics (e g on gender differences in maths performance), content analysis of semi-structured interview material, and textbooks or media output. He illustrated the use of the Worldwide Web as a source of official statistics that might facilitate international comparative studies.

Kari Hag presented the ideas from a Round table on Women and mathematics in the second European mathematics conference in 1996.

Jo Boaler reported upon two three-year case studies in the UK of schools that used radically different approaches to teaching mathematics. An open, project-based approach seemed to create a more rewarding context for girls in many respects.

In the second and third sessions the group divided into five subgroups each working on a specific theme headed by a chair and a secretary.

Subgroup 1 was organised by Fidela Velázquez and Jeff Evans and dealt with different research perspectives. Fidela Velázquez summarized and analysed different research perspectives while grouping them in five broad types. That is explanations based on genetic factors, psychological and social factors, and curricular and environmental factors, as well as factors which draw upon a feministic perspective and those which derive from meta-analysis.

Emanuila Gelfman's and Natalia Lobanenko's paper was presented by Raissa Lozinskaia. This concerned educational dialogue in relation to gender and mathematics and revealed teachers' opinions through interviews; fairytales were used to present mathematical ideas in textbooks.

Paul Ernest spoke about mathematics, philosophy, values and gender and argued that the values realised in the classroom are probably the dominant factor in determining the learner's image and appreciation of mathematics.

Subgroup 2 was organised by Sharlene Forbes and Elizabeth Quinlan and dealt with manifestations of gender inequities.

Lafina Cronje spoke about cognitive gender differences in Euclidean geometry. In her study there were no statistically significant gender differences in mean values, but analysis at item level produced gender differences in 20% of the items used. Sharlene Forbes spoke about gender and assessment and advocated that we need research to investigate the progression of students through various achievement levels. Her question was, is it time to develop a measure or index of lifetime mathematics achievement?

Miriam Seliktar considered the relationship between gender attitudes and achievements at college level and her study was focused on a large sample of students from one ethnic and sociocultural background. She questioned whether attitudes set early in the student's life can be changed later at high school or college level.

Subgroup 3 was organised by Lisbeth Lindberg, Gila Hanna and Marj Horne and dealt with ethnic, cultural and social conditions associated with equity issues.

Bharati Banerjee analysed the motivational aspects of mathematics teachers in relation to value profile and gender.

Lisbeth Lindberg spoke about the Swedish network Women and mathematics, started in 1990 and now with over 700 members from Scandianvia and the Baltic. She pointed out that this network could encourage others to build similar networks once they see outcomes such as those produced in the conference in Gothenburg this year.

Hanako Senuma spoke on her paper, written jointly with Eizo Nagasaki, using a longitudinal study on gender differences in changes in mathematics performance. Although no gender differences on average are found from 5th to 8th grades, there are four patterns of gender differences in grades 9 to 10.

Subgroup 4 was organised by Barbro Grevholm and Leigh Wood and dealt with international, regional and local cooperation in research.

Barbro Grevholm argued that research results that come from of many countries do not have to be replicated in every country. Perhaps progress could be made in the area of gender and mathematics if resources were used in regional and international cooperation. Have we come to the point where we are able to create this cooperation?

Neela Sukthankar presented a study of female students in Papua New Guinea concerning low female enrolment in tertiary institutions over the years.

Leigh Wood talked on a longitudinal study of sex differences at the Higher School Certificate in New South Wales, Australia. In mathematics females have outperformed males at all levels, except the highest. This is maybe due to government programs and to general changes in society, which carry over to schools.

Kyungmee Park talked about her study on gender differences in attitude and achievement scores among mathematically talented Korean students. Girls are outperforming boys in classroom tests, but in standardised tests there are no significant differences. The attitude surveys shows that boys have a more favorable disposition to technology use in mathematics learning and girls are more likely to believe that gender differences in mathematical abilities or achievement do not exist.

Subgroup 5 was organised by Gerd Brandell and Jo Boaler and focused on directions for change in educational contexts.

Gerd Brandell considered the development of gender inclusive teaching methods in engineering education, where the most far-reaching action is a new program in computer engineering admitting only women.

Maria Goulding discussed national gender differences in achievement at 16 in the UK with special reference to the inclusion of coursework in public examinations.

Marjatta Näätanen showed a video with the title "European Women of Mathematics (EWM) and why it is needed". Female mathematicians, who had worked in various countries gave their experiences and highlighted cultural differences.

Victor Parson discussed gender and mathematical problem-solving using a life history account. He found that gender variables are remarkably resilient in affecting members in a group problem-solving context.

In the final session chairs and secretaries from each of the five subgroups gave an overview of the discussions and pointed out the most vital issues covered and questions raised. As the groups had themes that could overlap some groups had touched on the same areas. Summarising these discussions, the following issues were covered:

Mathematics as a historical, social construction reflecting human interests, a subject that is not neutral and value-free. Mathematics as a school construction, where the hidden curriculum determines the masculine context and practise. Mathematics as a consumer product, where the technology used gives more and more consumers and the teachers are the best sellers. Mathematics in the context of cultural differences, where the Mediterranean world seems to be more open to women than the Anglo-Saxon world.

What do we measure in assessment and what does it mean? Focusing on mean scores can mask gender differences at item level in specific areas. Gender differences might appear when performance in the previous year is controlled for. There is an ongoing need to investigate gender differences and to develop more sophisticated techniques, both qualitative and quantitative in order to understand the overall picture and the longer-term outcomes for students.

Participation rates for women are higher than anticipated, at least at the undergraduate university level. There is a need to look closer at recruitment of women for graduate level in the light of current economic and social conditions in some countries. Gender differences may appear in spatial ability tests but are rectifiable with additional teaching as this a deficiency is caused by social and environmental factors.

We need to compare problems in different countries, what are the differences and what are the similarities? The gender balance must be looked at alongside social classes and cultural traditions. There is a need to look at the restricted curriculum, at textbooks, at costs for education, at the role of parents and of politicians and to realise the complexity of the issue.

How can we be sure that the information about what is known through research is available for teachers, parents and society? We need to make literature available and start courses, masters programmes and start really interesting research. Boys and girls are not homogeneous groups and we need to use a pluralistic approach. Differences in societies lead to differences in gender achievement. There is a need for an up-dated survey of good intervention programs and the dissemination of this knowledge.

Career information must be exchanged between countries. There are huge differences between countries in access and participation, in the degree of women in higher level mathematics, in either large scale or small scale differences.

What are the main changes that need to be done and what are the obstacles?

What are the ways forward? We have to use parents, the political situation, international experiences, and realise that we have to take small steps sometimes, and be prepared to handle the changing environment.

Gender and mathematics research has many important messages for all those involved in education and a good way to disseminate findings is to link this work to other concerns and initiatives.

In a final synthesis of what had been exposed from the groups Gilah Leder pointed at some challenges ahead:

1. We have identified and commented on interesting differences between countries, but our explanations are still very tentative. Are we ready for analysis and synthesis?

2. Breaking down the data we have suggests that we need quantitative as well as qualitative approaches. Yet for the last few days we have heard far more of the former than the latter.

3. We have focussed on what schools can do and what happens there and seem to have forgotten about the impact of society, parents, and politicians.

4. We have ignored the impact of technology. We must be vigilant that the technology increasingly introduced into the mathematics classroom does not lead to increased inequities.

5. We must go beyond the deficit model and conceive research studies within a pluralistic model and social justice model framework.

6. Looking back over the last few days, there is a feeling of us having achieved collectively, a coherent research program. How have we moved forward? As a group we have a unique opportunity to mold a focussed plan. The whole is greater than the sum of the parts. How do we achieve such cohesion and focus?

As chief organiser I would like to express my gratitude to chairs, secretaries and everyone among the participants for making the working group so rewarding. My message for everybody to take home with them is to try to keep alive the feeling of female solidarity that we experienced together also with the men among us. Find strength in this solidarity and support each other. Let the networks of researchers that vaguely showed here come to full bloom. Keep in touch with the groups. Concentrate more of your efforts on the task to find ways to change, when the question why is too complicated for us to fully answer. Publish as much as you can in your own language to reach all different groups and in English in the international journals and books. Plan national documents for teachers, parents and politicians with facts on gender and mathematics and ideas on how to work creatively. Let the ideas from those, who have already done this, inspire you. Together we are strong.

Note: This report was prepared by Barbro Grevholm and Jeff Evans. There will be a publication with contributions from the presenters in the working group.

References

Hanna, G. (1996). *Towards gender equity in mathematics education.* Dordrecht: Kluwer Academic Publishers.
Grevholm, B. & Hanna, G. (1995). *Gender and mathematics education.* An ICMI study in Stiftsgården Åkersberg, Höör, 1993. Lund: Lund University Press.

MATHEMATICS FOR GIFTED STUDENTS

MATEMÁTICAS PARA ALUMNOS CON TALENTO

Chief Organizer / *Responsable*: Vladimir Burjan (SVK) and Ivan Jezik (AUT)
Advesory Panel / *Asesores:* Fou Lai Lin (CHN-TWN), John Webb (ZAF)
Local Organizer / *Coordinador Local:* Diego Alonso Cánovas (ESP)

WG7 will focus on: the notion (phenomenon) of "giftedness" (who are mathematically gifted students? which are the characteristics? which types? how can we recognize?...); approaches to identification and fostering of mathematical giftedness within the educational systems; what mathematics should be the gifted taught and how?, which out-of-class and out-of-school activities must be organized for the mathematically gifted?

STUDENTS WITH SPECIAL NEEDS

MATEMÁTICAS PARA ALUMNOS CON NECESIDADES ESPECIALES

Chief Organizer / *Responsable*: Jens Holger Lorenz (DEU)
Advisory Panel / *Asesores*: Marie-Jeanne Perrin-Glorian (FRA), Nuria Rosich (ESP), Olof Magne (SWE).
Local Organizer / *Coordinador Local* : Luis Mª Casas García (ESP).

Because of the language favoured by the participants the working group split up after the first day into an English speaking subgroup and a Spanish speaking subgroup. This seemed necessary and appropriate as a large group of Spanish teachers attending the Working Group work in the field of special education andadded a great amount of experience to the discussion. The subgroups reassembled at the last day to share the ideas, plans and discussion of the others and to develop joint projects.

Naturally there is a wide variety of students needing special help and the approaches in different countries for dealing with this problem are multifacet as is shown by the papers presented (see list below). But to discuss the commonly shared ideas as well as the country specific methods was the main interest of the working group.

The topics which have been discussed intensively in the two subgroups were (not necessarily in this order):

1. Is there a common phenomenon, a unifying characteristic of students needing special education?

2. Is it possible to identify students with special needs?

3. What are the different approaches for the remediation of those students?

4. What is the mathematics to be taught to these students, i.e. is there a curriculum for subgroups of students (basic standards) in the different countries?

5. What are the pre- and inservice programs for teachers of special need students?

6. Are there any out of school programs for these students? ad 1) The experience of the participants showed the wide variety of student characteristics fitting the phenomenon of "special need students". The only common feature identifyable among these students was the need of additional help which can not be provided in regular classrooms. Students with special needs seem to lack the ability to make abstractions from concrete objects and from their experiences partly because of insufficient self-esteem. Participants reported of successful intervention based on self-directed, ego-fostering and success-oriented experiences which students with special needs made in their projects and schools.

Within this context a German study gave an overview of
– the main trends in mathematics education in the country's schools for learning disabled students, pariculary of
– the different subgroups of students in various types of schools
– the general teaching practice for these subgroups
– the tests used in a longitudinal experimental study including the tasks, the case studies and interviews (of which a video was shown), the consequences for teaching
– the realisation of the research study, in particular of the manipulatives, the individual strategies of the students and the productive exercises used in the project.

The dicussion centered around the different strategies used by students and their gain in solving arithmetic problems within the only three month teaching period. The group discusson focused on the problem of the children's ability to generalize afterwards and whether special need students are characterizable merely by a longer time need.

In contrast, a study from Sweden gave insight into the characteristics of cerebral palsied children in a rehabilitation centre and material used for arithmetic instruction. The teaching model consists of several "stones", i.e. training for the schemes for numbers, for memory, in particular the working memory, for reading and writing letters and numerals, for concentration, for the capability to keep attention, for the visual ability and spatial thinking, for automatization, for doing things quickly (very important for multiply handicapped students), for logical thinking and intuition and flexibility, and finally for motivation, each for the different types of dyscalculia (or dysmathematica, according to the famous Swedish researcher Olof Magne).

ad 2) The identification of students with special needs relies heavily on standardized tests but as these tests seem to be country (cultural context and language) specific, an exchange of identification procedures is not without problems. Apart from tests stating merely the (lack of) actual arithmetic ability of students there was no tests for the underlying or causal cognitive factors of dyscalculia.

ad 3) There was a report on a sophisticated method using the relationship between numerals and dot patterns which showed good results in the study. Several participants offered further dot-notations used in their countries. It was however argued that dot-notation could be crucial in the use of analogy problems and that most dot-notation does not use the power of five.

A four-year study was also reported on how children with arithmetic problems learn addition and several strategies have been identified which are also used by normal children as adding one, adding all, adding on, memorizing. Results of the four year study showed that

- the same strategies were used by children with learning problems
- these children went through the same stages within the four year period
- some children skipped some stages going from "counting all" to "memorizing".

A French study reported about ideas on symbolic character of mathematics, problem of going beyond the symbol, self-directed activities (or inactivities) of teachers of students with special needs and open situations.

ad 4) Because of the variety of students with special needs it was agreed that there is no fundamental mathematical content to be taught to all students. Mathematics should be adapted to the individual needs and capabilities of the single student. The experience of the participants showed that there could be even no main curricular approach to either the mildly vs. severely handicapped students and no prior distinction should be made.

ad 4 and 5) The teacher preservice and inservice training methods differed between the countries as did the out of school programs and facilities. Both problems in question have to take into account the idiosyncrasies of the social, historical and financial context of the country.

Additional interests raised and discussed by the subroups could be summarized als follows:

–visualization and lateralization and its impact on learning disabilities,

–abstract thinking and its lack caused by emotional/personality factors,

–the relation between mathematics and language.

–the historical context of the definition, identification and remediation of learning problems in general and dyscalculia in particular

.

Presentations of papers and short communications of participants at the WG 8

José E. Fernández del Campo (Spain): "Material for blind students"

José E. Fernández del Campo (Spain): "'Tinkunako': Un nuevo material para la iniciación al cálculo"

Pedro Soria Gamez (Spain): "Otra puerta hacia el álgebra. Material de números y de álgebra" (A door towards algebra)

Karin Guttman (Sweden): "Teaching mathematics to cerebral palsied children"

James Hanrahan (Canada): "A dot-notation method of teaching addition to children with moderate learning problems"

James Hanrahan (Canada): "Results of a four-year study on how children with learning problems learn addition"

Arturo Mandly Manso (Spain): "Remediation in the knowledge – motivation circle"

Kooe Nishimoto & Minoru Yoshida (Japan): "Concerning the characteristics of problem solving by students in school for the deaf"

Catherine A. Pearn & Marguerite Merrifield (Australia): "Mathematics intervention: The first three years"

Henri Planchon (France): "Qualitative aspects of mathematic activity" Andrés Sánchez Márquez (Spain): "The math in the blind child"

Petra Scherer (Germany): "Low attainers in mathematics – Diagnosing difficulties and using capabilities"

Helena Siwek (Polen): "The role of mathematical activities in development of lightly handicapped children"

Maria Sznajder & Lech Klosowski (Polen): "Difficulties for deaf children in forming mathematical notions: The computer as a means of communication between teacher and student"

María del Carmen Rodríguez Teijeiro (Spain): "Baccalaureate students with special needs"

María del Carmen Rodríguez Teijeiro (Spain): "Un ejemplo de actividades para alumnos con necesidades educativas especiales in matemáticas"

Alicia S. Villar (Argentina): "Mathematics for students with apprenticeship difficulties"

INNOVATION IN ASSESSMENT

INNOVACIÓN EN EVALUACIÓN

Chief Oraganizer / *Responsable:* Antoine Bodin (FRA)
Advesory Panel / *Asesores:* Kenneth Travers (USA), Bengt Johansson (SWE), Nitsa Movshovitz-Hadar (ISR), Vicente Riviere (ESP), Gill Close (UK)
Local Organizer / *Coordinadora Local:* Adela Jaime (ESP)

This working group concerns recent innovation in assessment of mathematics learning from the individual classroom up to national level. It will focus on assessment innovation which have improved assessment or learning for students, including why and how these happened. Small discussion groups will be based on specific assessment questions or methods actually used in school, which illustrate innovations in: written, oral and practical assessment; assessment of mental processes; self-assessment and peer assessment; adaptive / interactive testing; recording progress of large classes; methods for designing questions and tests; style of internal and external assessment; teachers' use of question data banks; use of learning theories to design assessments; scaling of tests results. Discussions will be summarised in plenary sessions.

Boundaries and aims of the group

The WG will be a forum for sharing an recording up-to-date information on innovations in assessment. It also aims to identify factors contributing to successful innovations and to disseminate these. It plans to build up a network of participants, indicating their interests, to facilitate sharing of information and collaboration. Our work will not overlap that of WG20 or TG26. It will not deal with international comparative studies or any administrative, social or political aspects of large scale assessment. It will not deal with any evaluation of systems, schools, curricula, etc. It will focus on assessment of students' learning from individual classroom level up to national level using both internal and external assessment. It will include only innovations in assessment which the contributors judge to have improved assessment or learning in their classrooms or countries. This subjective judgement will vary across countries as will the date when the innovation was introduced.

MATHEMATICS AND LANGUAGES

LENGUAJES Y MATEMÁTICAS

Chief Organizer / *Responsable*: José Francisco Quesada (ESP)
Advisory Panel / *Asesores:* Ferdinando Arzarello (ITA), Joop van Dormolen (ISR)
Local Organizer / *Coordinadora Local:*Alicia Bruno (ESP)

1.- Introduction: Why Mathematics and Languages?

This working group focused its attention on the role of languages in mathematics and mathematics education.

From a didactic point of view, teachers usually assume that knowledge is useful if it can be expressed in some ``conventional" language. In other words, teachers assume that someone knows something if he or she is able to explain what he or she knows. Also, every communication in the classroom is made by means of some language: teachers explain ideas, recommend strategies, ...; students read, calculate, write, ...; teachers hear what students say, read what students write, and so on.

In sum, language is the background that fixes the limits of our communication, and probably the limits of our knowledge.

Accordingly, one of the most important goals in this group was the discussion of the kinds of mathematics languages and their corresponding characteristics.

From another perspective, we can say that people have problems and, of course, they have to solve their problems. That is, people use mathematical knowledge, and most important for us, people express their mathematical knowledge using languages, basically verbal, graphic and/or numeric-algebraic ones. Therefore, another topic of interest in this group was the discussion of the relation between logic, mathematics and language. In other words, the position of mathematics within the philosophical triangle of World, Mind and Language.

Another line of discussion focused on the use of computational techniques in mathematics education. Computer languages are necessarily artificial languages (languages that try to be similar to mathematical languages). But, are these languages convenient for mathematics education? Even more, are professional mathematics software useful in the classroom (specially in non university classrooms)?

2.- Areas of interest

Accordingly, the working group was divided in two major areas, and each one concentrated in the following topics:

A) Mathematics Languages (the languages of mathematics):
(i) Typology of languages: main characteristics and their didactic potential.
(ii) Relations between psycholinguistic levels and cognitive strategies.
(iii) Relations between social, economic and linguistic factors in mathematics languages.
(iv) The role of metaphor in mathematical education.
(v) Syntax and semantics of mathematics languages.

B) Logic, Semiotics and Computers:
(i) World - Mind - Language: Where are mathematics?
(ii) Thinking /vs/ Speaking: What is first?
(iii) Formalization and representation of mathematics knowledge: natural languages and symbolism.
(iv) Artificial intelligence, and specifically, computational linguistics: lexical, syntactic, and semantic analysis of mathematics languages.
(v) Design of specific languages for educational mathematics software.

3.-Program, Structure and Contents

The first two sessions of the working group was dedicated to the the study of the state of the art in mathematics and languages.

Following the previous division, the first day concentrated on the analysis of The Languages of Mathematics.

Patricio Herbst spoke about Metaphor and mathematical discourse. In his talk, Herbs attempted to pose the question of the role of metaphor in mathematical discourse as a researchable problem. A discussion on mathematical discourse was sketched and illustrated with historical examples. According to Herbs, the problem of metaphor, posed with respect to the discourse in its form of archive and consequently as a discursive strategy, is: What does a particular metaphor do in a particular discourse? Max Black's interactive view of metaphor was sketched and used to address the question. Finally, the relevance of this problem to research in mathematics education was discussed by elaborating on the relation between mathematical discourses and mathematics as a web of social practices.

Joop van Dormolen, in his presentation Levels of Language, outlined a layered perspective in relation with the use of languages. Three main levels were distinguished: exemplary or demonstrative, relative and functional. This model has interesting consecuences for mathematical education, that can be summarized in the idea of adaptation to student's abilities.

In Mathematics and Language: A Study of Children Describing Geometric Patterns, Rosalyn M. Hyde discussed the difficulties children have with language in mathematics and listed a variety of ways of categorising the language used in the learning of mathematics. Also investigated was a number of related issues about pupils' development in talking about mathematics, variations by gender, age and ability, and, what it is that might be learnt by mathematics teachers from language teachers.

The second day concentrated on Logic, Semiotics and Computers, including the following three speakers:

Phyllis August-Rothman presented a full of suggestions paper titled A Definite Maybe, in which, she attempted to dispel the common misconception of the universality of mathematics and logic, as if they were language-free. According to August-Rothman, language can be either a conducive, enhancing molder or an inhibitor of clear, logical thought. The paucity of a language may result in ambiguities and confusion which must be identified and resolved if it is to serve in modeling, problem solving, and logic. The richness of a language, on the other hand, can encourage associative thinking in that language, as well as the ability to make distinctions.

Adam Vile was in charge of the second communication: Peirce, the interpretant (a tripartite division of experience) and mathematical meaning. According to Vile, in considering mathematics as a language one is accepting mathematics as a quasi-social phenomenon. Debates between social constructivists and followers of a Vygotskian position centre on the question of the primacy of social or individual and on whether mathematics is intrasubjective or intersubjective. Charles Sanders Peirce pre-empted this debate and modeled the division of experience in a way that transcends the question of whether knowledge is objective or subjective through the consideration of a third entity - the interpretant. Peirce saw logic and semiotics as equivalent and developed a theory of semiotics that took account of the dynamic and relative nature of meaning. In his presentation, Vile outlined the Peircian position and discussed briefly some recent developments of a semiotic picture of mathematics.

Finally, Jose F. Quesada spoke about Artificial Intelligence between Languages and Mathematics: the computational side of mathematics languages. The talk concentrated on the study of the relations between languages and mathematics from th Program, Structure and Contents

The perspective of Artificial Intelligence in general, and specifically, from the point of view of Natural Language Processing or Computational Linguistics. Natural Language Processing (NLP) is a very well founded field in Artificial Intelligence with more than 40 years of history. Its tecniques, models and results can be used in the design of computational environments aimed at the teaching of mathematics. The core idea is that natural language is the perfect interface between people and their computers; and the languages used in mathematics are very similar to natural languages, because they are in fact ambiguous, and they need a semantic interpretation. The communication presented the basic notions of NLP, including the state of the art of some projects that include research in AI, NLP and MPP (Massively Parallel Processing), the relations between Knowledge Engineering and their applications in the area of computer-based learning systems, and some guidelines for the application of these kinds of techniques to the field of mathematical education, including an architecture for the desing of mathematical educational software based on NLP models.

In the third session, the working group was divided in two parallel subgroups with more specific communications, including: Bill Atweh, Robert Bleicher and Tom Cooper: Sociolinguistics and mathematics interactions: A study of gender and socioeconomic factors; Dhamma (Susan) Colwell: Learning and using maths in second language; Candelaria Espinel and Alicia Bruno: Regla de Tres y Redes: Dos Mundos; Pablo Guerrero, Francisco Gutierrez and Blas Ruiz: El solitario de Abreu desde la teoria elemental de Grupos; Patricio Herbst: The Number-Line Metaphor in the Discourse of a Textbook Series; and Adam Vile: A semiotic perspective on the development of fluency.

Finally, the fourth session was an open and in some moments warm discussion chaired by Joop van Dormolen.

4.- Conclusions

It is very complex to obtain commonly accepted conclusions in a working group with such a heterogeneity. Nevertheless, there was a general agreement about the interest of this topic in mathematics education, that can be sketched with the following idea: mathematical teaching, learning, reasoning and thinking use languages. Also, the study of language and communication was proposed as one of the most important research trends in mathematical education by Anna Sierpinska in her plenary lecture at ICME8.

In a brief talk at the beginning of the last session, Jose F. Quesada proposed a schema (see Fig. 1) for the study of the relations between languages and mathematics. We can begin considering that mathematics is a language: we can think of things like symbols, meanings, discourses, social and cultural interactions, etc. Also, mathematics is knowledge: we have conceptual structures, theories, laws of thought, and so on. And mathematics is

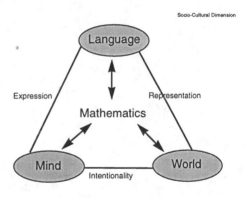

something real and useful: in his plenary lecture, Miguel de Guzman spoke about the origin of mathematical theories from concrete and everyday problems, and Anna Sierpinska concentrated on the notion of didactical actions.

From an eclectic perspective, we can (probably, we must) mix the three points of view: mathematics as a representation, a model and an activity. This may be used as a departing point toWhere a approach the classical question about Where are Mathematics?

The open discussion during this last session can be structured en three lines. The main ideas proposed in each one were: First, from a semiotic point of view, social aspects play a crucial role in mathematics languages. Second, from an epistemic perspective, it is worth to study the relations between knowledge, language and mathematics; and, in this goal the layered model proposed by Joop van Dormolen would be useful. Third, from a didactic point of view, language is a crucial component in the teaching--learning process: the problem of communication is partly discovering the register the other person is speaking.

CURRICULUM FROM SCRATCH (ZERO-BASED)

REVISIÓN DEL CURRICULUM PARTIENDO DE CERO

Chief Organizer / *Responsable:* Anthony Ralston (USA)
Advisory Panel / *Asesores:* Hugh Burkhardt (GBR), Nerida Ellerton (AUS),
Susan Groves (AUS), Rolf Hedren (SWZ)
Local Organizer / *Coordinador Local:* Salvador Guerrero (ESP)

The task of this Working Group was to explore the notion of developing a primary and secondary school mathematics curriculum from scratch, that is, without being inhibited in any way by the curriculum (subject matter or pedagogy) that exists anywhere. The long-term purpose of this essentially intellectual exercise is to provide a model curriculum not for implementation by anyone but as a goal toward which curriculum developers would strive as they struggle with making changes in curricula which, it is generally agreed by mathematics educators, are not satisfactory for the last decade of the twentieth century. The underlying force which motivates this exercise is the impact of technology on mathematics education, an impact which has, as yet, barely been felt but which is an important source of the general unease with current curricula.

During the first three sessions of the Working Group, there were nine presentations followed by a discussion of each. The titles and abstracts of these presentations follow:

1. A Zero-based Curriculum - What It is and How It Might Be Used
Anthony Ralston
State University of New York at Buffalo (USA) and Imperial College, London (UK)

Technology should have a more profound effect on the primary and secondary school mathematics curriculum than on any other subject studied prior to university. This has not happened, however, mainly due to the immense inertia in the educational systems of all countries. It is, therefore, worth considering what the school mathematics curriculum would look like if it were not constrained by current practice. A zero-based curriculum does this by requiring that all subject matter and pedagogical practice be justified on grounds other than that the topic is currently in the curriculum or that the methodology is that used presently.

The purpose of developing a zero-based curriculum is not to implement it anywhere immediately because that would be unrealistic. However, if, as expected, a zero-based curriculum looks very different from the current curriculum anywhere, then it provides a goal at which mathematics educators can aim. It could then inform a debate on how to change the mathematics curriculum from where it is to where we would like it to be and it might even suggest ways to get from here to there.

2. Implementing a Zero-based Curriculum: How Might It Be Effected? Hugh Burkhardt

University of Nottingham (UK) and University of California, Berkeley (USA)

In planning curriculum change, the process of implementation is often treated as straightforward. It is discussed, if at all, as a second stage -- or even an afterthought. There is much agreement on the goals of mathematics education, for example on the importance of problem solving and realistic applications of mathematics. Yet, in the great majority of classrooms, the curriculum still has very little of such elements. The implemented curriculum is far from the target curriculum. The Zero-based Curriculum will face this challenge acutely, because it represents a big change in well-grooved habits. It will require profound changes in the knowledge, beliefs and teaching skills of very large numbers of teachers of mathematics -- often 1 in 200 of the total population. Many other groups, from principals to parents and politicians must make changes, too. How might all this be tackled? What professional development can in-service training of various kinds achieve? What roles can materials play? What other 'tools' could help the change process? What are the implications for school and district organization? How can a proper rate of change be found, and implemented? How do we decide on the order -- what should go in and what should come out of the curriculum? What development and research is needed to find answers to these questions? How might it be done? This paper examines these issues from both theoretical and empirical points of view.

A case study considers the need for the integral use of computers and calculators in much of the curriculum - both as a challenge to change and a catalyst for it.

3. Are There Other Ways to Do Pencil-and-Paper Computation than with Column Arithmetic? Rolf Hedren
Dalarna University College (Sweden)
The following issues are discussed in this paper:

* The fact that most computations nowadays are carried out with the help of calculators and computers, and that many pupils use calculators and computers in their spare time.

* Constructivism tells us that our pupils do not passively receive knowledge but actively construct their own knowledge. They come to mathematics instruction with a lot of former experiences, and these experiences influence the new knowledge they are building.

* My research, like that of other researchers, shows that our pupils are able to find their own methods for calculation with paper and pencil. These methods are closer to those used in mental calculation and estimation. They also seem to give pupils an enhanced number sense.

* If we were in a position today to write a curriculum from scratch, this would in my opinion stress mental calculation, estimation, and the use of calculators from the first school year. The traditional algorithms for the four arithmetic operations would not be mentioned, but the teachers would be told to help their pupils to invent their own methods for calculation with paper and pencil.

4. Rethinking the Primary Mathematics Curriculum
Alistair McIntosh and Len Sparrow
Edith Cowan University (Australia)

We make three assumptions, all of which could be challenged : first, that we are considering an education suitable for all children in traditional Western culture, second, that schools will still exist, and third, that the current range of subjects will remain more or less as it is.

We envisage four aims for mathematics in the primary school: that students should experience it as living, useful, interesting and mainly involving the development of number sense.

For mathematics to be living students must become aware of it as evolving over time and differing according to the demands of different cultures: usefulness implies that students find it relevant and empowering in exploring and responding to their environment; interest will spring from students finding it accessible and yet having moments of wonder and beauty; and finally number sense involves acquiring confidence and competence in handling and processing numbers and calculations appropriately, with emphasis on estimation, mental computation and calculator use.

This paper explores the relevance and the practical implications of these assumptions for young children.

5. New Mathematics in a Zero-based Secondary Curriculum
Albert Goetz
Ramaz School, New York (USA)

The development of a zero-based secondary school mathematics curriculum requires the answer to the following question: As mathematics educators at the turn of the century, what is the mathematics that we want our students to know upon their completion of secondary school? Only when that question is answered satisfactorily can a curriculum be organized.

In this paper I first attempt to answer the question posed above. After a brief review of curriculum reform projects extant in the United States, including their strengths an weaknesses as seen from a zero-based perspective, I conclude with an outline designed to include, in a coherent and complete manner, the response to the initial question.

6. A Zero-Based Technology Enhanced Mathematics Curriculum for Secondary Mathematics
Franklin Demana and Bert K. Waits
Ohio State University (USA)

Technology will have a profound influence on our mathematics curriculum. Every secondary mathematics student will have a personal hand-held computer with an electronic writing pad (e.g.. Apple Newton) and built-in software for computer symbolic algebra (CAS) and computer interactive geometry as well as other mathematics software (spreadsheets, statistics, etc.). Without the past constraints of "paper and pencil" tradition driving the mathematics curriculum, our new, integrated curriculum can focus on mathematics as reasoning and problem solving. Reasoning would include a study of the structure and major theorems of mathematics. For example, the topic of "factoring" will still be studied (after all it is part of the fundamental theorem of algebra) but the tools used "to factor" will be either mental or CAS (much less time will spent on the process of factoring). Problem solving would include mathematical applications. In this respect, "algebra" will become viewed as a "language of representation" rather than paper and pencil symbolic manipulation. Technology tools will provide access to a great deal of modern mathematics in both the discrete and continuous worlds. For example matrix algebra and differential equation problem solving methods are now practical and part of our "elementary" secondary mathematics content. Other issues such as distance learning and the changing role of the traditional mathematics classroom are also discussed.

7. Developing Number Sense in a Calculator Rich Environment - Implications for Classroom Practice
Susie Groves
Deakin University (Australia)

For the past 20 years calculators have been recognised as having the potential to change profoundly both the nature of mathematics teaching and the curriculum. However, despite official endorsement, calculators have not been widely used in primary school mathematics, especially in the lower grades. It is no trivial matter to use technology effectively in classrooms - teachers need to rethink mathematics and children's learning of mathematics, as well as develop new (and substantially different) skills for teaching and assessment.

In Britain, the Calculator Aware Number Project (CAN) which commenced in 1986 under the direction of the late Hilary Shuard, began to explore what a curriculum might look like if it takes seriously the implications of the availability of calculators. While children were reported to have developed a wide range of strategies for carrying out calculations and to have reached a high level of numeracy for their age, the project found that the calculator's full potential could only be realised with a change in teachers' classroom practice.

In Australia, the Calculators in Primary Mathematics project was a long term project investigating the effects of the introduction of calculators on the learning and teaching of primary mathematics. The project involved a total of 79 kindergarten to grade 4 teachers and approximately 1000 children in six Melbourne schools during the period 1990-93. It was hypothesised that the presence of calculators would lead to children dealing at a much earlier age with large numbers, negatives and decimals and that, in order to accommodate this changing curriculum, teachers would need to alter radically the way in which they teach mathematics. This paper reports on the findings of the project - which confirm these hypotheses - and their implications for classroom practice in a zero-based context.

8. Pedagogy in a Calculator-Computer Environment
Pearla Nesher
University of Haifa and Ministry of Education (Israel)

It is obvious that the future mathematics curriculum will not regard the child as a calculating machine and will leave everything regarding algorithmic performance to the machine, either in the form of a hand calculator or a more advanced computer. It seems, therefore, that understanding mathematical concepts will form the core of future mathematics learning and will also be the major challenge to mathematics pedagogy.

Still, there remains a dilemma: Can one teach just for understanding without being occupied to some extent with calculations? At present, children at the primary level get their intuition about numbers and operations with numbers from being engaged with these operations. What will replace this if we still wish to establish their number sense and their intuition about mathematics (e.g. which arithmetic operation to perform)? In my paper I try to shed light on the relationship between understanding and performing algorithms in mathematical pedagogy. I also elaborate on the distinction between mathematical operations and standard algorithms in early arithmetic as the point of departure for discussing future pedagogy in primary school.

9. Redefining Teacher Education for the Zero-based Mathematics Curriculum
Alan Bloomfield
Cheltenham & Gloucester College of Higher Education (UK)
Susan E Sanders
Prifysgol Cymru Abertawe (UK)

This paper has as its premise that *the* teaching of mathematics will be influenced by views of what mathematics is, but should not be dependent on the age of the students. The paper is informed by theories of learning but not limited by current practice.

The paper begins by outlining position statements concerning the teaching of mathematics which include:

- Teachers of mathematics must feel confident about their own ability and knowledge of mathematics.

- Teachers of mathematics should enjoy both doing and teaching mathematics.

- Teachers of mathematics should use the potential of resources (e.g. information technology) to optimise learning.

- Teachers should have theoretical underpinnings for their pedagogical decisions.

In the next section a model of teacher education is developed which allows these goals to be achieved. This model has at its centre the concept of the 'learned teacher', expert in teaching mathematics, making decisions on what mathematics is taught and training future teachers of mathematics. These considerations have implications for the zero-based concepts of earlier papers.

The paper concludes with a discussion of the cultural contexts in which such a model could be situated.

In the final session of the Working Group, in addition to a general discussion of the previous three sessions, Karen Usiskin of Scott Foresman/Addison Wesley, a large US publisher of K-12 mathematics textbooks, gave a brief presentation, full of information, on how a commercial publisher might view a proposal some time in the future to publish a textbook series whose basis is a Zero-based Curriculum.

The Working Group will publish its Proceedings, including the full text of the nine papers whose abstracts are above and the main points of the discussion of each paper, some time early in 1997 through the auspices of the Shell Centre for Mathematics Education at the University of Nottingham, UK.

CURRICULUM CHANGES IN PRIMARY SCHOOL

CAMBIOS CURRICULARES EN LA ENSEÑANZA PRIMARIA

Chief Organizer / *Responsable:* Mary Lindquist (USA)
Advisory Panel / *Asesores:* Maria Canals (ESP), Michala Kaslova (CZR), Hans Nygaard Jensen (DNK)
Local Organizer / *Coordinadora Local:* Carmen Burgués (ESP)

The purpose of this working group was to consider the implications of the changing primary school curricula in terms of implications for content, pedagogy and the process of change. Approximately 150 participated in the Working Group.

SESSION 1

Thomas Carpenter (Planning Primary Curricula to Build on Children's Informal Mathematical Thinking) based the plenary talk on his research experience in working with children across his professional career, but most centrally on his experiences with the Cognitively Guided Instruction Project (CGI) at the University of Wisconsin. He noted that there exists a substantial body of evidence about the mathematical knowledge that children bring with them to school and set the scene for the Working Group by challenging us to consider how skilled teachers should work to develop curricular materials appropriate for children in these grades; how to formalize children's knowledge into a workable curriculum; and how to adjust reflection and discussion to be child centered in such settings. His talk focused on the role of notation in affording or constraining children's solutions of problems, how notation could help show children's thinking and how notation could be object of reflection.

Carpenter then illustrated these points with a variety of examples of children's work from the CGI project classrooms. These illustrations identified different student problem-solving strategies and showed a variety of levels of depth in students' understanding of concepts central to anyone's definition of the primary grades' curriculum in mathematics. He noted that these original notations provide a basis for building on a student's constructions and discussion of alternative strategies by students. This was contrasted with the more conventional approach of notation just being a way of "doing the problem." Considerable discussion was given to the allowance of students to utilize extended strings of "equality" like relationships, such as

$$50 + 40 \rightarrow 90 + 4 \rightarrow 94 + 8 \rightarrow 100 + 2 \rightarrow 102$$

in adding the numbers 54 + 48. Several felt that such notational conventions would allow students to adopt the incorrect notations associated with running equalities often seen in algebraic settings, strings that are not, in reality, real equality relationships.

Carpenter then discussed the findings of the CGI group in other curriculum areas, noting the work of Richard Lehrer in geometry, with the problem of finding all nets for a cube and for a tetrahedron. Again he noted the role that notation plays in providing an object for reflection and a point for discussion. He noted that we need to consider:

* How curriculum can be designed to provide children with an opportunity to build on their informal thinking?
* How can/should notation be introduced to support children's inventions?
* What role should student invention of notation play in the school curriculum in primary mathematics?

Members of the Working Group then posed a number of questions of Carpenter. There was considerable interest in the ways in which CGI teachers have worked to bridge children from their invented notations to the more formal notations found in standard curricula. He noted that the CGI has no specific recommendations. He indicated that some teachers are more flexible in letting the invented notations run for longer periods of time than others. The central question was, he felt, not one of a specific time, but rather one of children having control over their own learning and confidence in their strategies to shift from their notation to that developed by others.

SESSIONS 2 and 3

The next two days of the Working Group sessions were devoted to the presentation and discussion of papers contributed by group participants. In addition to the three questions proposed by Carpenter in his plenary talk, Working Group Leader Mary Lindquist asked that participants also consider the following questions raised by the participants in a general discussion the previous day:

* How do we approach administrators/politicians about research results concerning children's thinking and the role it should play in the primary grades?
* How can administrators better support teachers in their work to engender mathematical ways of thinking in primary aged children?
* How do we assist students who are slow in inventing their own notation and slow in joining into the investigation of mathematical situations?
* What should be the role of children's thinking in the formal development of the school mathematics curriculum? How do we help teachers teach in this way?

Subgroup 1. Douglas Grouws chaired the subgroup working with pedagogical issues associated with changing the curriculum. Papers were presented by Alison Millett, Graham Jones, Tom Cooper and Mary Briggs.

Millett (Using and Applying Mathematics) reported on a case study set in the context of the National Curriculum in England and Wales. She noted that the topic, Using and Applying Mathematics (UAM), in each of the three versions of the National Curriculum, had been problematic for teachers. Her study focused on a primary school, working on its own, in implementing this part of the curriculum recommendations. Questions of the research were: How do teachers interpret and implement instruction for UAM? What are the tensions between the intentions of UAM and the beliefs of teachers? What organizational features promoted or inhibited the implementation of UAM? Millett's study found that most teachers adopted an idiosyncratic approach to teaching for UAM, changes in teaching style were required if learning in UAM was to be encouraged, and schools needed to provide a stronger and more focused nurturing role in relation to curriculum development, giving teachers a variety of stimuli for reflection and opportunities to reflect on their practice with colleagues.

Jones (Using Children's Probabilistic Thinking in Instruction) reported on probability curriculum research, responding to the increase emphasis on this topic by Australia, UK and USA curriculum efforts. The grades 3- 5 project was informed by a research-based framework describing elementary- and middle-school students' thinking in probability. Underlying principles included the position that learning is optimized when students are encouraged to reorganize their thinking in situations that are problematic for them, and that mathematics learning is interactive as well as constructive. Jones and his colleagues (Jones, Johnson, Langrall, and Thornton) found that, following instruction, students showed significant growth in probabilistic thinking; however, there was considerable variation in the quality and degree of such growth.

Research by Heirdsfield and Cooper (Mental Computation and Curriculum Change) examined mental computation strategies in addition and subtraction used by students in grades 2-6 prior to and after instruction on algorithms. Clinical interviews revealed four strategies: counting, separation, aggregation and holistic. Although counting was dominant in grade 2, separation (left to right) in grade 3 and paper and pencil strategies in later grades were dominant. The results suggest that students can develop their own strategies, but these tend to be subsumed once formal algorithms are introduced.

Briggs (Raising the Roof) examined the learning of number concepts prior to (under age 5) and during Key Stage 1 (ages 5-7) of the National Curriculum in England and Wales. The aim of her research was to characterize the differences between teachers who do and do not incorporate large numbers when working with young children. She noted that some teachers of Key Stage 1 tended to be locked to National Curriculum statements even though many opportunities arose to introduce large numbers. Nursery teachers and other pre-school teachers were not as prone to this practice, but she speculated that may happen since expectations for children prior to Key Stage 1 have been set by the National Curriculum. In essence, NC statements could be a vehicle for constraining and even lowering teachers' expectations of students' mathematical thinking.

Subgroup 2. John Dossey chaired the subgroup working with content issues for the primary grade curriculum. Papers were presented in the content subgroup on the topics of by Joanne Mulligan, Kees Buys, and Jane Swafford.

Mulligan (Changes in the Number and Operations Curriculum in Australia) reported on the changes in bringing their primary curriculum to a more relation focused subject in number,space, measurement, chance, and data. The role of links and reflection has come more to the front and focus on procedural work with algorithms more to the back. Instructional sequences have tended to move from prescriptive to reflectional form with increased emphasis on building sophisticated strategies based on children's intuitions.

Buys (Considerations for an Alternative Program for Introducing Rational Numbers in Holland) reported on the work to reshape the teaching of fractions in grades 4 to 6 of their primary program. In particular, they are rethinking the sequence to allow for the teaching of applications first, multiplication/division second, and addition/subtraction third. This sequence allows for a greater emphasis on student intuition and construction of meaning and strategies for dealing with rational number situations. He illustrated his work with student solutions to a problem involving the partitioning of 1 1/2 liters of lemonade among 4 glasses each with a capacity of 1/3 liter. Students were supposed to tell how many glasses were filled and how much lemonade remained in the pitcher. Five different student solutions were presented and discussed relative to student understanding of the problem, student understanding of the underlying concepts, student understanding of notation and its use, and student ability to generalize and work with rational number concepts.

Swafford's talk (Algebra in the Primary Grades: Bridging Arithmetic to Algebra) dealt with a study carried out at the 6th grade level with a colleague Cindy Langrall. They focused on students' abilities to cognize three problem situations with algebraic overtones. They examined the students' abilities to recognize patterns, describe and explain the problem and its representation in tables and graphs. Finally, they examined students' abilities to generalize patterns, form equations, and solve the equations. Three problems were posed, one with refunds on soda cans, one that dealt with salary levels, and one that dealt with concert hall seating. The results showed that students at grade 6 level were able to create recognize and represent the problems, even in symbolic form; to explore them through tables and graphical methods; to find solutions through these forms of representation; and consider the use of variables as quantities that vary. However, they were unable to manipulate equations they had formed as a method of obtaining solutions.

Subgroup 3 Carmen Burgués chaired the third group that worked on issues germane to the Spanish primary curriculum. No papers were presented, but a rich discussion focused on the role of the teacher in curricular change and on the training necessary for educators in order to ensure changes are really made. The group organized their thoughts into aspects that should be taken into account in the change process. They consisted of the following:

* POSITIVE MOTIVATION OF TEACHERS
---they need to understand the needs of a change
---they need to know the process of change
---they must participate actively
---change must be well organized

* REAL CHANGE is SLOW
---it's a change of philosophy or conception of education
---it takes team work
---it changes the role of the teachers
---it can't provoke labor anxiety

* THE ADMINISTRATION NEEDS
---to control bureaucratization, which in general is large
---to provide adequate training, without declaring it compulsory
---to make possible the work of the groups by providing time tables
   and organization

* DESIRABLE CHARACTERISTICS to achieve REAL changes
---training model must facilitate a continuous change, avoiding
   "jumps"
---in addition to activities such as courses, we should consider
---with some priority, training of teachers by teachers
---groups integrated by teachers of the same educational level
---groups participate with expert teachers as well as building
   networks among many different groups of teachers in a variety of
   ways

SESSION 4

After reports from the subgroups, two plenary talks given by John
Dossey and Douglas Grouws helped us look ahead to implications of the
Third International Mathematics and Science Study (TIMSS) and to the
role of technology in planning for primary curriculum.

Dossey (Implications of the TIMSS Curriculum Study for the Primary
Curriculum) presented a preview of the data from the TIMSS curricular
study related to the curriculum contents of grade 4 mathematics at an
international level. He discussed how countries might make use of these
data in terms of comparing their curricula for the primary grades to that of
their international peers. He stressed that the past focus on achievement
results from international studies might be inappropriate in terms of the
wide variance in curricular contents, time of introduction, duration of focus,
and levels of expectation associated with the topics during their study.
Dossey noted the relationships were not tied directly to geographical,
economic, or political jurisdictions. The presentation provided an advance
organizer for the full study's release in the fall of 1996, a source not
previously available for those interested in primary mathematics curricula.

Grouws (Technology in the Primary Grades: A View to the Future) noted the roles that technology can play in assisting students to represent, select modes for viewing mathematical situations, to examine patterns, to analyze data and patterns, and to develop justification for various generalizations. He considered the role of textbooks and how they might change such as being used in combination with Web sites. Such use would have ramifications for teacher generation of activities, for greater roles for teachers in curricular decision making, and for funding patterns for classroom mathematics programs. Grouws then turned to the topic of wise technology use. He urged us to look for situations that cannot be presented or learned without the aid of technology, such as powerful videos and data sources and handlers. He questioned the use of technology, at the primary level, to manipulate models of concrete objects on a video screen. He concluded his presentation with a discussion of the implications of technology for situations involving equity and the opportunity to learn. Technology can either promote it or stifle it.

CURRICULUM CHANGES IN THE SECONDARY SCHOOL.

CAMBIOS CURRICULARES EN LA ENSEÑANZA SECUNDARIA

Chief Oragnizer / *Responsable:* Martin Kindt (NLD)
Advesory Panel / *Asesores:* Abraham Arcavi (ISR), Margaret Brown(UK),
Eizo Nagasaki (JPN), F. Villarroya (ESP).
Local Organizer / *Coordinador Local*: Francisco García (ESP)

In this group we will focus the discussions on the topics: algebra/calculus; Geometry; Discrete Mathematics (graph theory, combinatorics, probability, statistics, cryptography. There will be two simultaneous sessions in the first three meetings (12-16; 16-19) and the last session will be a plenary discussions on trends in currciulum changes all over the worl. In all sessions there will attention to what are the influences on new curricula of changing view on learning; changing societ, changing mathematics, changing technology.

LINKING MATHEMATICS WITH OTHER SCHOOL SUBJECTS

RELACIONES DE LAS MATEMÁTICAS CON OTRAS MATERIAS ESCOLARES

Chief Organizer / *Responsable:* Fred Goffree (NLD)
Advisory Panel / *Asesores:* Rolf Biehler (DEU), Mario Carretero(ESP),
Kurt Kreith (USA), Howard Tanner (GBR)
Local Organizer / *Coordinador Local:* Mariano Domínguez (ESP)

Introduction

The theme 'linking mathematics with other school subjects' is closely related to the themes of 'applications and modelling' and 'teaching statistics'. This point of view has been justified at previous ICME conferences, for instance in Theme Group 6 (Applications and modelling) in Adelaïde (ICME 5, 1984). In Theme Group 6 (Mathematics and other subjects (at school and university) in Budapest (ICME 6, 1988) the 'why' and 'how' of applications and modelling were elaborated by giving theoretical arguments and practical examples. Werner Blum presented his model to explain more clearly the concept of 'interrelations between mathematics and the real world'. Obstacles to the linking have been mentioned as well. In the organization of ICME 7 (Québec, 1992) the intention was to reduce the emphasis on the 'linking' or the 'interrelations'; instead, many working and topic groups were created which collectively covered the theme.

These groups included 'mathematical modelling in the classroom', 'improving students' attitudes and motivation', 'probability and statistics for the future citizen', 'ethno-mathematics and mathematics education', 'mathematics for work', 'teaching mathematics through project work', 'mathematics in the context of the total curriculum', 'art and mathematics'.

In Sevilla , however, it was planned that many of these lines would come together again, emphasizing the linking more. This led to the organising of sub-fields of 'real world and other school subjects', 'using contexts and (visual and mental) models', 'mathematizing', 'experiencing the power of mathematical knowledge and considering the ethics of using it'.

Preparation

In a prelimenary statement the possibilities and intentions of WG 14 were put forward. Different points of view could be taken, such as 'arguments and philosophies behind the linking', 'designing integrated maths teaching', 'the linking media like statistics', 'information technology and simulations', 'development and research', 'paradigms of integrated math lessons', 'the problems of low and high achievers', 'related theories of learning and teaching', 'the meaning of the didactical phenomenology according to H. Freudenthal', 'practising how to present mathematics in the context of another subject', 'investigating other school subjects in search of starting-points for mathematics education' and 'the problems of culture, language and media'. Each of these points of view could be considered from different school levels.

Following invitations on e-mail and the WG14 -page of the ICME-8 Internet website eighteen colleagues from Australia, Austria, Denmark , Germany, New Zealand, The Netherlands, U.K., Uruguay and USA offered to present a paper.

Using these papers as a basis together with the prelimenary statement and taking into account the available time in Sevilla, four sub-streams were created, each forming the focus for the work of a sub-group during the conference:

1. Secondary education;
2. Statistics;
3. Society and environment;
4. Modelling

Several key questions were also formulated: Why do we link Mathematics to other subjects? Is it - because we consider mathematics to be a tool rather than a discipline?

· to enable students to apply what they know?
· to make mathematics seem useful and therefore motivate students to learn?
· because we think that by learning mathematics in a variety of situations they will learn mathematics in a qualitatively different way which will facilitate transfer?
· to relate mathematics to students' interests and previous experiences thus building on real world knowledge rather than creating a separate mathematical domain?

that the learning skills involved in applying mathematics across the curriculum are the same skills which are involved in the creating of new mathematics? (See also Tanner's and Jones' paper: Can knowledge, skills and understanding developed in one world be applied in another?).

Procedure, sub-groups and papers

In the (plenary) first session Fred Goffree introduced the theme, the key questions and the programme for the following three sessions. Interested people in the audience were invited to prepare a five minute talk about their own work which they could present during the fourth session. Next each of the sub-organizers presented their own brief interpretations of the selected papers in their streams. Then the subgroups were constituted in different rooms. The presenters of papers introduced themselves and initial discussions were started.

For the second and third sessions, group members worked within their subgroups. The work of these subgroups was as follows.

The substream on secondary education was organized by John Gillespie (U.K.).

Both subgroup sessions were very well attended, with over 50 people at each session. In each session, three papers were presented, followed by vigorous discussion. In the first session, papers were presented by Ronald Keijzer (NL)- focusing on the development of number sense through everyday examples, Alicia Villar (Uruguay) - giving examples of links between mathematics and geography, and Pieter van der Zwaart (NL) on different way problems with maths content were tackled in the classroom and on the shopfloor. In the second session, Anna Chronaki (Greece) and John Gillespie (UK) gave two perspectives on links between mathematics and art, from research into artists' approaches, and from work in vocational classes.

Sonja Jones (UK) analysed three different styles of teaaching observed in thea application of maths in modelling fitness.

Contributions to the discussions included those from Margarita Oria de Chouhy Aguirre, who also provided English-Spanish translations throught the sessions which greatly aided theri accessibility for all, Julian Williams, Brian Hodgson, M.Victoria Ponza, Mirta Toruella, Rita Bastos, Dorit Patkin, Liliane E. Urschel de Prieto, Suzana Martins Paiva, Tracey Cooke, Susan Lamon, Drora Booth, Luis Carlos Cachafeiro Chamosa, Luisa Garcia de Andoin, Maxine Bridger, Sadie Bragg and those who presented the papers.

The substream on statistics was organized by Rolf Biehler (Germany). The session focussed on links with other subjects where statistics was interpreted in a broad sense including data analysis and use of data graphs in various subjects and mass media. Four papers were presented: Frances R. Curcio (USA): Building a theory of graphicacy: where are we now?, Sue Gordon(Australia): Teaching statistics to reluctant learners; Sharleen Forbes (New Zealand) Bringing real world into statistics assessment ; Jane M. Watson(Australia): Student analysis of variables in a media context.

Some of the more general question that were discussed include: What are new challenges for mathematics education as a servant to other school subjects such as to provide knowledge in methods of data analysis and competency in using graphs? How can data analysis create new opportunities of co-operation between various subjects? Which kind of internet resources for this purpose are available? How can we integrate real world examples into assessment? What are preferences of boys and girls with regard to real world content? How can links to other subjects overcome the problems of reluctant mathematics and statistics learners?

The substream on society and environment was organized by Howard Tanner (U.K.).

The stream was divided between those who used the environment as a context for learning mathematics and those who wished to model the environment mathematically. Alicia Villar and Jose Muniz described a mathematical walk through Montevideo city during which students met problems set in their environment. John Truran discussed the links between mathematics and science and the skills necessary to interpret the environment mathematically. Work done on field trips in alpine Australia was used to illustrate how children could make "thinking mathematically" one of their working cultures.

Howard Tanner and Sonia Jones considered situated cognition and described a project on mathematical modelling in which students explored the impact of farming, mining and industry on the ecology of their local river system.

Their paper explored the extent to which mathematics which had been learned in one environment could be used in another.

Eva Jablonka showed how values must enter into criteria for solution evaluation and that the use of a mathematical approach may in itself carry values. She questioned whether it was always appropriate to use mathematics to examine environmental problems which mathematics was partly responsible for causing.

Iben Christiansen's paper on ozone depletion referred to "the technocratic transformation" through which fundamental ethical/political questions concerning the formulation of goals are transformed into technical questions. The use of models might indicate the graveness of the problem but direct attention away from fundamental ideological issues.

The substream on modelling was organized by Steve Kennewell (U.K.). This stream was introduced by posing a number of questions which might frame the work. These included issues specific to the use of computer modelling tools such as:

How does computer modelling differ from mathematical modelling?

Is the computer modelling system just a tool for mathematical modelling, or does it change the way that we know the modelling process? Can powerful features of computer modelling tools aid the teaching of mathematics?

An important theme emerged from the papers presented, concerning the identification of dependent and independent variables in situations drawn from different subjects. Students commonly had difficulties with this part of the modelling process, but computer environments in which students could explore and create models provide cognitive scaffolding and support the making of valuable mistakes'. Programs such as spreadsheets make changes visible, allow testing of hypotheses and enable relationships to be refined easily. Students could be seen progressing through different levels of mathematical formalisation of variables, and cultural variations had been found in their use of graphical and algebraic approaches to studying relationships.

In the last session short, four short 5 - 10 minute sub-group reports were presented and most of the remaining time was taken up with five minutes presentations from the following: Christine Laurie (AUS), Geoff Vake (UK), Jun-ichiro Kawamaru (JAP), Estella Sonio Aliendro (ARG), Mirta Torruella (ARG), Drora Booth (AUS), Nema Victorie Ponza (ARG), Maxime Bridger (USA), Takayoki Kodero (JAP) and Hironori Ohsawa (JAP). Throughout the four sessions the working group was indebted to : Margarita O. de Chouly Aquirre (ARG), who acted as a most effective interpreter.

Reflection

Prior to the last session the papers and discusions in the sub-groups were discussed and analyzed in order to find the core of our theme. The outcome, in short statements, now follows:

I. About the nature of mathematical knowledge.

Applying mathematics in the real world and other school subjects, using skills of mathematizing and modelling, and using information technology and new media requires essentially new thinking about mathematical knowledge.

Possible starting points are: using mathematics and common sense to develop in connection, contextualized knowledge, the narrative way of knowing, mathematical enculturation, the ethical component and the dimension of personal responsibility.

II. About learning

Applying mathematics is not the same as learning mathematics. Being successful in applying as well as learning mathematics, requires the features of 'situated learning' to be taken into account. Reflection is a fundamental necessity the whilst the whole problem of transfer is central.

Moreover, during the learning process, time must be allowed for exploring the non-mathematical contexts and for taking into account students' personal beliefs and needs. Special attention has to be paid to the development and use of meta-cognitive skills.

III. About teaching

Teaching mathematics through its applications differs dramatically from teaching pure mathematics. Interactive exploration of new fields, situations and problems requires the teacher to be a guide, the students to be researchers, all being cooperative, communicative and reflective.

Through being active like this in the mathematics lessons, intercultural possibilities can be exploited or at least be taken into account. The use of the linking tools in relation to mathematical knowledge and its different levels, needs special consideration by the teacher as well.

Mathematics education has to be seen as 'development' as well as acquiring subject matter knowledge.

IV. About the curriculum

A lot of developing work has to be done in order to obtain access to a wide variety of non-mathematical contexts. Charting the 'other' domains for didactical elaboration (as Jablonka did in her paper: 'Mathematics and conflicts between economy and ecology') is necessary. This seems to be a good approach if experts are able to demonstrate the natural behaviour as that of reflective practitioners in these domains . They can show the use of the linking (mathematical) tools on the shop floor. Ethno-mathematics, cultural sources and the 'grand problems' of society, and of the environment, for example, provide many reasons for doing mathematics.

Subsequently didactical elaboration of the linking modes (application, exploration, historic (genetic) approach, technologic versus reflective approach, phenomenologic analysis etc.), need to be undertaken.

V. About the impact in/of society

If the problems to be solved are part of the world the problem solvers live in themselves, and their commitment and constraints will play a role during the learning process. What is learned in that case, is not only the mathematics. Politics, ethics, handling cultural differences, and other aspects of life will all colour the mathematical experiences. What will be remembered are, among other things, the narratives of the teaching-learning process.

Perspective

Considering the outcomes, the working group organizers want to propose a research and development agenda for future years, to include the following:

1. The continued mapping of the 'other' domains, finding reasons for mathematics education and providing didactical elaborations.
2. Asking and answering epistemological questions (e.g. concerning contextualized knowledge, (de)contextualized knowledge, common sense & mathematics).
3. Transfer questions (e.g. about situated learning and learning in contexts).
4. Case studies in classrooms (using narrative research methods and aiming for practical teacher knowledge).
5. Curriculum development (e.g. horizontal and related vertical mathematizing, creating learning strands).

6.Teacher training (in relation with 4).

7.Sharing experiences and meanings with other ICME subgroups (e.g. those concerning history of mathematics, modelling and applications, realistic mathematics education, information technology and computers.).

IMPACT OF TECHNOLOGY ON THE CURRICULUM

EL IMPACTO DE LA TECNOLOGÍA EN EL CURRICULUM DE MATEMÁTICAS

Chief Organizer/ *Responsable:*Michal Yerushalmy, Haifa University, (ISR)
Subgroup1: Modeling and Real-Life Applications - Koeno Gravemeijer Freudenthal Institute The Netherlands
Subgroup 2: Organizing Curriculum Around Big Ideas: Daniel Chazan, Michigan State University, (USA)
Subgroup 3: Novel Content With Technology: Paul Goldenberg, Education Development Center, MA. (USA)
Local Organizer / *Coordinador Local:* Jacinto Quevedo (ESP)

"Societies maintain educational systems for a variety of reasons.

These include aiding the personal growth and development of its citizens, preparing people for the world of work and transmitting the culture and values of the society. Given the reasons that societies maintain educational systems, and the ways in which mathematics curricula could be changed in light of changing technologies, what changes might, in fact, be desirable and for whom?" (Judah L. Schwartz) The aspects of desirable changes of curricular standards and the reform of school mathematics in different societies around the world lead the discussion of the technology workgroup. A common thread to many presentations was the analysis of **Curriculum organized around big mathematical ideas:**

Developments that re-think the organization and the emphasize of the current traditional content of the curriculum. We discussed a range of mathematical topics (arithmetic, geometry, algebra, statistics) which involve learners of different ages (middle school, secondary school, and practicing teachers). Common to all is a desire to teach conceptually, to organize instruction around a set of "big ideas" and to use technology as a tool towards this goal. Presenters shared the tensions and the dilemmas arise while developing and studying these reformed curricula: Patrick

Thompson provided examples to demonstrate why the introduction of technology to support curricular reform is not a neutral act in the same way as is, for example, introducing a new text. Thompson suggested that the curricular changes need not be for the better if reforms merely lay a new technology on top of old objectives. Examples from arithmetic and from the use of graphing technology demonstrated the tension between where the technology and where materials and instruction push the children. A tension between the ideas about mathematical relations as presented with various graphing tools and mathematical relations as traditionally appear in the curriculum was detailed by Biehler, who offered a new conceptual map to the learning of school algebra and statistics. The presentation outlined how does a big idea "Relation between variables" opposes the current curricular beliefs which lead to a complete separation of functional and statistical relations. This offered conceptual change is only available with the use of new tools. More presentations examined the nature of the mathematical ideas chosen for instruction, the design of technological environments to support student activity, and the design of the instruction of students to prepare them for the use of the technology. A special attention was given to the role of the function as a major big idea in a few reformed curricula. Major research findings regarding the function's approach algebra (reported by Heid) offered some comparative views and a discussion of the tension between what assumed to be basic skills of algebra and the capability of the technology in learners' hands.

When compared with their peers in traditional courses, students can achieve the goals of the new curricula, developing better conceptual understanding as well as more refined abilities in problem solving and mathematical modeling. Moreover, students can learn about mathematical concepts without prior mastery of related by-hand skills. In fact, the learning of related skills after technology-intensive exposure to the concepts may even occur more quickly than it would in a skills-only or in a simultaneous skills-and-concepts curriculum. Technology makes it possible to change radically the content of the school mathematics curriculum from one of skill acquisition to one that bases itself in families of functions and mathematical modeling. Having a conceptual organization of curriculum with technology, rather than skill oriented organization was reported to support teachers' professional growth. As described by Daniel Chazan regarding his own teaching of algebra (and similar findings by Pat Tinto regarding her work with geometry teachers) "This (the function) approach helped me express the problems I posed to students in a way that allowed them to understand the desired goals and at the same time it gave them resources which they could use to solve the problems even before being taught standard methods."

Within the general them of "big ideas" (mainly discussed in subgroup 2), two specific trends were the focus of the other two subgroups. In subgroup 1 presentations focused on Modeling and Real-life applications and illustrated the potential of an integration of technology in the mathematics curriculum that is based on "reality". The discussion focused on choices that can be made on the dimension "mathematics" - "reality", and on the dimension "invention" - "discovery". The first dimension, as defined by Gravenmejer, can be thought of as a continuum with attenuated reality dominated by the beamed mathematics at one end, and mathematics dominated by the "authenticity" of real-life situations at the other end. With the latter dimension the label "invention" is used to refer to situations where the students invent tools, models, or concepts to help them solve problems presented to them, and the label "discovery" is used to refer to a situation where the students discover something that is embodied in the courseware. The approaches to the use of software varied from open environments that represent real-life situations, via software that supports the modeling of real-life situations, to more focused programs where the reification of the actions with a certain model are to support the development of well defined mathematical concepts. The educational possibilities afforded by new connections between physical and simulation-based data to build intimacy with function representations were part of a few presented environments. Jim Kaput reviewed common technology which facilitated actions within notations and even bi-directionally linked them. Yet, Kaput argued, recent data indicate that students' difficulties with interpreting and productively using mathematical notations continue. Technology to link phenomena to notations, and the option that students themselves be immersed in generating such phenomena were demonstrated as part of learning by modelin reality.

Subgroup 3 focus grew out of the idea of several new developments that the ways of thinking that mathematicians use in finding mathematical facts should figure as prominently in students' learning as the facts themselves. The group discussed how can computational technology help students gain access to mathematical ideas and ways of thinking that were previously unmanageable. Colette Laborde offered a view on an expected new learning cycle: new tools generate new phenomena to be observed, new phenomena generate new questions which may be solved by means of the new tools which generate new phenomena. However, it was acknowledged that unfortunately this cycle does not work so nicely for learners as it does for mathematicians. Our challenge is to set the appropriate conditions to support making mathematics with technology be part of the learning of mathematics. The discussion of conditions include the consideration of such elements as students' previous knowledge, interface of the computer environments, the new type of objects and operations made available by technology, the kind of problems which can be given to students integrating technology and the meaning of the problems for the students. Interface plays a crucial role in the potential for mathematical learning and a prior analysis of the possible difficulties and understandings of learners must be carried out. Such analysis is productive if the software interface can be understood as an outcome of conceptual decisions rather than a collection of sophisticated facilities. Conceptual transparency of software design: visibility and invisibility of ideas, processes and concepts, as principle of design was offered by Yerushalmy to be a central factor in the ways mathematics is studied with technology. It seems to be an urgent task for software designers, curriculum developers and mathematics educators to interact and discuss the choice of appropriate software, analyzing the interface, and research the power of various software design principles to be a major component on a wide range curriculum reform. A few presentations (Sharon Dugdale overview of her long experience with teachers is quoted below) offered research finding about "..the rich opportunities for new and exciting mathematical inquiry made possible by computer technology, and effectiveness of the ability of teachers to select among a variety of software those tools applicable to a given problem situation, and to combine a variety of appropriate technological and non-technological tools to investigate different aspects of a problem."

The tensions among mathematics educators regarding the relations between the innovation and the traditional content and standards, and the type of research that may inform us about the standards of tomorrow in the current classroom, dominated the closing discussion of the technology group.

THE ROLE OF TECHNOLOGY IN THE MATHEMATICS CLASSROOM

EL PAPEL DE LA TECNOLOGÍA EN LA CLASE DE MATEMÁTICAS

Chief Organizer / *Responsable:* Marcello Borba (BRA)
Advesory Panel / *Asesores*: Manuel Armas (ESP), Jim Fey (USA), Maria Mascharello (ITA)
Local Organizer / *Coordinador Local:* Miguel de la Fuente (ESP)

The aim of this working group is to discuss both from a theoretical and practical point of view the changes in the mathematics classroom as computers and graphing calculators are introduced in the classroom.

MATHEMATICS AS A SERVICE SUBJECT AT THE TERTIARY LEVEL

MATEMÁTICAS INSTRUMENTALES EN EL NIVEL UNIVERSITARIO

Chief Organizer / *Responsable:* Eric Muller (CAN)
Advisory Panel / *Asesor:* J. Alvarez (COL), Fred Simons (NLD)
Local Organizer / *Coordinador Local:* Ceferino Ruíz (ESP)

Introduction

Eighty six individuals from eighteen countries actively participated in this Working Group. On the first day presentations were made in English by Lynn Steen [USA], Fred Simons [NDL], John Searl [GBR], and in Spanish by Jairo Alvarez [COL]. All speakers had transparencies in both official languages ably translated by the local organizer Ceferino Ruiz [ESP]. For the second and third days participants joined one of four subgroups in which each organizer paid special attention to getting everyone in the subgroup involved in the discussions

Subgroup and Subject	Led by
Mathematics in the formation of non-mathematics majors	Jairo Alvarez (in Spanish)
Technology (Computer Algebra Systems)	Fred Simons (in English)
Transition from school to university mathematics	John Searl (in English)
Teaching, accountability and attitudes	Eric Muller (in English)

On the fourth day the subgroups met for half an hour before reporting in both official languages in a plenary session.

Previous ICME and ICMI activities

In the last ten years, ICMI has shown substantial interest in the area of "Mathematics as a Service Subject at the Tertiary Level". In 1987 an ICMI Study was held in Udine, Italy with the title "Mathematics as a Service Subject". This Study produced two volumes [1] and [2]. The following year, in 1988, at ICME 6, in Budapest, Hungary, the Action Group 5 on "Tertiary (post-secondary) Academic Institutions" (see [3] pp. 159-176) had a subgroup on "mathematics for non-specialists". Four years later, in

1992, the Working Group 15 at ICME 7, in Quebec City, Canada, dealing with "Undergraduate Mathematics for Different Groups of Students", (see [4] pp. 186-190) ran two subgroups one in the area of "mathematics for non-specialists in the science field", and one in the area of "service courses for non-scientists".

In some parts of the world the enrollments in Mathematics Departments have grown at a very fast rate through the late sixties, seventies and early eighties. Much of this increase was due to a greater demand for Service Courses. This growth in enrollments produced a parallel increase in mathematics faculty positions. In many of these same countries, resources allocated to post secondary education have either diminished or the priorities within the institutions have changed. In response administrators are questioning the role, necessity and effectiveness of Service Courses offered by mathematics departments. For many of these departments the Service Courses have become increasingly a political issue, possibly impacting seriously on their faculty components. If this is the start of a new reality then a review of the roles and responsibilities of mathematics departments and their faculty in Service Courses is urgent and this Working Group timely.

Highlights of WG 17 discussions

a. Transition from school to university mathematics

There is a general concern by those who attended the Working Group that the gap between the expectations (often students' achievement in mathematics) between school and university staff has widened over the last few years. No data was presented to support this widely held view and it was not clear whether this perception is due to the increase in the percentage of populations going to university, more disciplines requiring university mathematics, a shift by the more mathematically able students away from areas requiring mathematics, changes in social norms influencing dedication to studies, or other factors. A number of institutions, in various parts of the world, have responded by providing additional resources to assist students to make the transition from school to university mathematics. Examples of such support include, the use of diagnostic tests followed by additional tutoring of weaker students, allowing students with difficulties to take more time over their program, formation of peer groups, and other types of intervention. In the Service Courses the situation is aggravated by the negative attitude towards mathematics that many students bring to its study, where they see mathematics as a difficult hurdle erected in the way to meeting their aspirations. This is especially true in disciplines which are oversubscribed and where mathematics is used as a means for student selection. The

Group identified a need for more school-university mathematics initiatives to generate increased cooperation and understanding between staffs of the various institutions.

b. Responsibilities of mathematics departments

Individuals in the group showed concern that, although the student enrollment increases in mathematics courses over the last two decades were generally due to increases in the number students in Service Courses, Mathematics Departments have made very little effort to hire individuals who are interested in developing appropriate courses and teaching these students. To many mathematics faculty the content of these courses is classified as "second hand mathematics". Mathematics departments should be encouraged to develop an explicit philosophy which values their Service Courses to the same extent as those for their mathematics majors. Hiring should reflect this philosophy and value the experience of mathematicians in other fields. A suggestion is that all candidates for new positions could be asked to give two lectures, one in their area of research and another, to a wider audience, exploring the interaction of mathematics with other disciplines. Mathematics departments should actively promote dialogues between their faculty and those of other departments. Additional support should be considered for those individuals who are in the early stages of developing these dialogues, for example, a lighter teaching load could be given to someone who is auditing courses in another discipline. Most university structures do not foster or facilitate cooperation between departments, especially between departments in different Faculties. The Group believes that this segregation is particularly damaging to mathematics as a discipline but also has important repercussions to mathematics departments when scarce resources are to be allocated between competing academic sectors of the university.

There was a consensus that the academic formation of mathematicians emphasizes a broad background of mathematics but lacks sadly in educating individuals to have a vision of the role of mathematics in the construction of scientific and technical knowledge. The Group recommends that all undergraduate mathematics majors be required to take mathematics courses aimed at developing this vision both from an epistemological perspective and from the study of concrete applications.

c. Responsibilities of individual mathematics faculty

It was the experience of those in the Group that many Service Courses tend to emphasize content at the expense of both basic processes of mathematical thinking and experience in the role of mathematics in the construction of scientific-technical knowledge. An example was provided in a presentation by Maria Ines Cavallero [ARG] based on work with Marta Anaya [ARG] which explores alternative didactic methods in traditional topics of mathematics for students in engineering. Mathematics departments should review their Service Courses to determine whether they develop individuals who will be able to use mathematics in a creative and independent way within their own disciplines. This suggests that mathematics faculty also need to take into consideration the aspiration of the students in these courses and respond by finding an appropriate level somewhere between a purely "formula based course" and a "mathematically coherent course". The Group recommends that faculty experiment with mathematics courses which are structured in a coherent way from the point of view of the discipline served and that their experiences be communicated to the mathematics community. Proposals for this kind of course are often set aside by mathematics faculty because they are seen to violate the traditional mathematics prerequisite structure. However it is possible that coherence from the point of view of the discipline served, may be more stimulating, meaningful, and accessible to the student than a mathematical coherence as seen by the faculty teaching the course.

Research results on the importance to the student of the mathematical coherence of a course would be helpful. Could it be that mathematical coherence is only a positive experience for a student who has mastered a broader area of mathematics than that required for the student's programme? Is it possible that softwares now provide opportunities for non standard approaches to mathematics, and allow student access to mathematical concepts in a non traditional sequence?

d. Technology - Symbolic Mathematical Systems

Recent developments in software such as Symbolic Mathematical Systems (SMS), more commonly known as Computer Algebra Systems, have substantially increased the types of well structured mathematical problems which can be solved routinely with little understanding. One finds that exercises in traditional Service Courses can be solved by just entering the correct expressions into a SMS. Such procedures have not much to do with mathematics. Furthermore the contents of these courses have seen little evolution in the past two decades and they reflect the needs of scientists and engineers as they existed prior to the advent of the computer. Because more recent developments in software make it easier to fully integrate numerical and analytic procedures, one should consider, when appropriate, starting with numerical aspects and then proceeding to show that in some, mostly rare, circumstances analytical solutions can be obtained. This balance between numerical and analytical approaches is particularly important in Service Courses as applications in other disciplines tend not to have exact solutions. The Group concluded that the use of SMS in undergraduate mathematics require new approaches, techniques and knowledge. Mathematicians, scientists, and engineers should come together to restructure the content of Service Courses for the Twenty First Century.

Symbolic and Mathematical Systems also provide a rich environment in which to explore and develop mathematical concepts. This suggests a different approach to the delivery of Service Courses. In the last ten years, the body of literature addressing the "how to" use SMS in undergraduate mathematics has increased substantially and faculty can now start to draw on the experiences of others, and adapt the situation to their own circumstance.

Conclusions

The Working Group succeeded at providing its participants with real opportunities to discuss and share experiences relating to their teaching of mathematics courses, by minimizing the number of presentations and maximizing the time in subgroups. Important issues dealing with the transition from high school to university mathematics, the responsibilities of mathematics departments and their teaching faculty towards these courses, and the impact of technology such as Computer Algebra Systems were explored.

References

"Mathematics as a Service Subject", Howson, A.G., et al., Cambridge University Press,(1988)
"Selected Papers on the Teaching of Mathematics as a Service Subject", Clements R.R., et al. (eds.), Springer-Verlag, (1988)

ADULTS RETURNING TO MATHEMATICAL EDUCATION

FORMACIÓN MATEMÁTICA PARA ADULTOS

Chief Organizer / *Responsable:* Gail Fitzsimons (AUS)
Advisory Panel / *Asesores*: Diana Coben (GBR), John O'Donoghue (IRL)
Local Organizer / *Coordinador Local:* Antonio Renguiano (ESP)

The Seville congress saw the inaugural meeting of this working group: Some 50 people participated during four sessions. The stated goal of this group was to propose a set of recommendations related to mathematics education for the different populations of adults returning to the educational system. This goal, and the title of the working group, implicitly included those entering formal education for the first time. Ideas were shared about the mathematics education needs of adults, acknowledging the appropriateness of judging adults' needs in differing ways for differing purposes and in different contexts. The inclusion of this working group on th ICME programme was seen as a recognition of the growing importance of a complex field which spans all educational levels, and which is likely to be linked with issues such as class, gender and race.

Work is being undertaken in many countries to develop systematic and critical foundation for research into adult learners specifically in relation to mathematics education. This research needs to be grounded in the work of those practising in the field, and the group welcomed the contributions of educators with experience of teaching mathematics to adults in any sector of the education, whether on a formal or an informal basis.

As the programme evolved it became apparent that there were two major subgroups with distinctive orientations: adults returning to, or embarking on, studies of basic mathematics; and those returning to study at the tertiary level. The programme was structured to accomodate plenary sessions on the first and final days, with parallel sessions running on the second and third days.

Day 1: An Overview of the Field

The first plenary session was intended to set the scene for the work of the group, illustrating aspects of research which may have implications for different levels of practice, and to allow participants to meet one another.

Roseanne Benn (GBR) presented a paper, Silent Murmurings, which used a framework of discourse theory to explore the issues surrounding adults' learning in a culturally diverse society. Diana Coben (GBR) reflected on research into adults' mathematics life histories, exploring the concept of common sense as developed by Geertz (1993) and Gramsci (1971), in a paper, Mathematics or Common Sense? Some Reflections on our Research into Adults' Mathematics Life Histories. Gelsa Knijnik (BRA) described and analysed her work with young and adult rural workers who are members of the Landless Peoples Movement in a paper entitled Mathematics Education and the Struggle for Land in Brazil. Katherine Safford (USA) presented a paper National Standards for K-12 Mathematics Education: What are the Implications for Adult Mathematics Education?. She raised the point that many adult mathematics instructors are unaware of the suggested reforms for school mathematics and the rationale behind them, and even if they are familiar with the concepts, may be reluctant about incorporating them into their own practice.

SUBGROUP 1

Adults in Basic Education

Adults beginning their formal studies or returning to study at the basic level have particular needs in mathematics, not the least being the development of confidence in their own abilities. Other facets of adults' life histories may also be addressed by practitioners. As Iddo Gal (ISR/USA) pointed out, one of the goals of adult education is to empower students and enable them to become more informed citizens. His paper, Statistical Literacy: The Promise and the Challenge, exemplified the means of pursuing such a goal. Along the same line, another paper by Ginsberg and Gal, presented by Linda Ginsberg (USA), Uncovering the Knowledge Adult Learners Bring to Class, focussed on the relationships among adults' pre-instructional knowledge about percent and associated mental mathematics and computational skills. Hans ter Heege (NDL) illustrated examples from classroom experiences based on research in his paper The Development of Activities for Adults Using a Second Language. Patricia Ward (IRL) presented a paper The Provision of Mathematical Education for People with Special Needs in the National Training & Development Institute in which she described compensatory support given to bridge the gaps between students' entry-level skills and the vocational programs offered. Tine Wedege (DNK) addressed the problem of developing relevant materials based on the everyday and work experience of adults who were early school leavers, in a paper entitled Professional Profile in Mathematics of Adults Returning to Education. A poster session was given by Pedro Plaza (ESP), illustrating the development work of the Adult School in Madrid. From a different perspective, Dave Tout and Beth Marr (AUS) addressed the issues associated with professional development for teachers of adult numeracy in their paper Changing Practice: Adult Numeracy Staff Development. One emerging issue here is the trend in some countries towards linking literacy and numeracy, resulting in the employment of teachers who do not necessarirly have strong backgrounds in mathematics.

SUBGROUP 2

Adults Returning to University

There are growing numbers of students enrolled in university courses who require additional assistance in mathematics. Among these are students referred to as "mature age" who are likely to have special needs arising from the discontinuity of their education. A paper on The Mature-Age Mathematically Underprepared Student: Profile, and the need for Mathematical Awareness in Advance was presented by Gail Godden and John Pegg (AUS). This paper considered the needs of mature age students in comparison with younger students, and also reviewed attempts made by institutions to meet the challenges presented. Gail Godden and Carmel Coady (AUS) discussed issues associated with Mature-Age Students in Service Statistics, with special reference to Health Science students who generally have poor mathematical backgrounds. An innovative practical solution to such problem was developed by Martin, Roberts and Pierce (Australia). Peter Martin presented the paper entitled Adult Students Involved in Activity Based Learning. Barbara Miller-Reilly (NZL), in her paper Reactions of Adults to Investigative Mathematics Courses, described a research project exploring reactions of students enrolled in a special course designed to meet the needs of adults returning to study. John O'Donoghue (IRL) presented a paper entitled An Assessment-Driven Open Learning System for Adult Learning Mathematics, with special reference to the education/employment interface in Ireland. This system seeks to integrate facets considered imporatnt to adult learners. Tony Watkins (GBR) outlined his university's successful program in a paper entitled Adult Students Returning to Study Mathematics for an Engineering Degree.

RECOMMENDATIONS

The final session allowed for participants to make recommendations about different populations of adults learning mathematics, as well as about the organisation of ICME and this working group in particular. The following is a synthesis of recommendations taken from the session.

It was recognised that this working group represents an emerging field concerned with extremely diverse populations of learners in terms of variables such as educational, social, cultural, and political backgrounds.

The following recommendations were made about the processes of teaching and learning.

1. Individuals should be empowered through learning mathematics.
2. The diverse needs of adults learning mathematics need to be taken into account.
3. Individual priorities of adults should be taken into account.
4. The curricuculum should be built on the experiences of individuals in their social and working lives.
5. A critical mathematics agenda should be developed, in order to enable learners to participate in critical citizenship.
6. Mathematics curricula should enable reflective and reflexive thinking through mathematics.
7. Learning and doing mathematics should be developed through a co-operative approach.
8. Mathematics curricula should reflect the way mathematics is actually performed by people in everyday life.

Mathematics educators in the field of adult numeracy and adults returning to study have much to contribute as a result of their experiences of working with students who have apparently been failed by their experiences of school mathematics and who have the maturity to reflect on these experiences.

It was recommended that the advice of adult educators be sought on a range of issues, in order to improve current and future practice in the area of compulsory education:
· effective teaching practices
· working with diverse groups
· curriculum development
· assessment tools
· teacher training
· instructional resources

Indeed, future ICME organisers might address this issue through scheduling formal study meetings for the various networks involved with adult learners on the official programme.

General recommendations were made concerning the recognition of adults learning mathematics and their teachers:

1. We commend the introduction of this working group, and encourage its continued support. We recommend that the name of the group be changed to "Adults in Mathematics Education."

2. We recommend that future organisers of ICME give greater recognition to the importance of the field, and its differentiation from school mathematics, by scheduling and least one regular lecture based on a theoretical frame work for teaching adult learners. Further, speakers in other sessions such as plenary addresses, panels, topic groups and other regular lectures, should be encouraged to incorporate issues of relevance to adult learners in recognition of the fact that not all learners are children.

3. We commend the congress organisers for the provision of opportunities for networking and sharing of ideas. Interested practitioners and researchers who wish to learn of other networks concerning adult learners may contact the chief organiser, Gail Fitzsimons.

4. We recommend the support of ongoing research in the field, which would ideally take the form of collaboration between current practitioners and university-based researchers, at the local, national, and international levels.

5. We recommend that individual governments recognise the importance of educating adults in mathematics, and provide adequate funding, including provision for the professional development of teachers.

ICME should be more clearly advertised to allow wider participation. Also, in order to overcome the problem that significant development may go unreported because of the language barrier, we recommend greater attention to the provision of translations through ICME. The working group organisers have taken note of the comments / recommendations specifically relating to the operation of this group.

References

Geertz, C. (1993). *Common sense as a Cultural System*. In C. Geertz, Local Knowledge: Further Essays in Interpretative Anthropology. London: Fontana.

Gramsci, A. (1971). *Selections from the Prison Notebooks of Antonio Gramsci*, Quintin Hoare and Geoffrey Nowell Smith (Eds. & Trans.). London: Lawrence and Wishart.

PREPARATION AND ENHANCEMENT OF TEACHERS

FORMACIÓN INICIAL Y PERMANENTE DEL PROFESORADO

Chief Organizer / *Responsable:* Marjorie Carss (AUS)
Advisory Panel / *Asesores:* Barbara Jaworski (GBR), Milan Koman(CZR)
Local Organizer / *Coordinador Local:* José Ramón Pascual (ESP)

The participants in Working Group 19 initially divided into three groups reflecting the focus of the papers prepared for the Congress. The groups working on Mathematics Teacher Knowledge and Beliefs and Mathematics Teacher Education Programs broke up into several subgroups whose discussions ranged across both areas. The third group discussed issues related to Mathematics Teacher Education and Information Technologies. The groups met separately for the four working days of the Congress, coming together for the initial meeting and to report in the second hour of the last session.

Mathematics Teacher Knowledge and Beliefs and Teacher Education Programs.

Discussions of the groups within these areas focussed mainly on the issues of teacher preparation. The two major groups divided further into several subgroups with specific interests in a level of education or issues of shared concern. The diversity of interests was reflected in the reports for the final session. This report is an attempt to reflect the wide range of issues addressed, problems identified and suggestions for future research and development.

1.   General concern was expressed with the low level of mathematics entry requirements for primary teacher education in all countries represented. While it was agreed that students should have more content knowledge on entry, this is not sufficient. Students also need to be competent mathematics thinkers, a quality that is not usually assessed by entry tests. It is important that all students understand the need to be both confident and competent in mathematics. The lack of basic understanding of mathematical concepts is as much a cause for concern as the lack of ability to "do" the mathematics they are to teach.

2. It was suggested that support groups (with negotiated roles) be established

. to assist students to bring their beliefs and feelings into the open (and to provide opportunities for teacher educators to share their experiences too);

. to engage in constant reflection and discussion about the mathematics they are learning;

. to realise that negative reactions are natural, and making mistakes can lead to a positive experience.

A major task for mathematics educators is to identify tasks which constantly challenge students to think mathematically.

3. Strategies suggested included the use of diagnostic software (such as "Diagnosis") to target students at risk; developing the expectation in students that they be able to explain their procedures to their peers; making use of computer assisted tutorials as one strategy for those who need to upgrade their basic learning and understanding; establishing the idea of having students take responsibility for identifying their own weaknesses and for setting their own learning goals.

4. There is a need for the teacher to be willing to develop in him/herself a more positive attitude to mathematics, a growing self confidence in problem solving and problem posing, and an ability to create situations suitable for problem solving.

5. Teachers need to be familiar with relevant psychological theories to aid them in understanding students' learning, both through self reflection and through understanding how children learn. (The group was adamant that this communication should be by mathematics educators, not educational psychologists.) Concern for the development of the whole child must be a priority.

6. Concern was expressed that current models of initial teacher education, with an increased school based element have led to the generation of an artisan model of teacher education as opposed to a professional model. This was considered to be a regressive and negative move.

7. The importance of attitudes and beliefs of student teachers was a major focus for the groups concerned with secondary teacher preparation.

8. A critical concern was how to help teacher education students understand the effects of attitudes and beliefs - both their own and their students, on learning. One group identified the need for much more research on the origins of attitudes to and beliefs about mathematics.

9. The problems of the diversity of school placements for practice teaching is a matter of concern, especially for secondary teachers where the models of teaching are sometimes in conflict with current research and policies.

10. In an information age a major problem for both teacher preparation and enhancement is how to change teacher perceptions of their role from transmitter of knowledge to facilitator of learning.

11. There was considerable discussion as to how much mathematics beginning teachers ought to know, acknowledging that some only want to know the school curriculum.

12. Another important issue raised was to ask just what is good teaching, and to question whether or not it can be evaluated.

13. In courses in teacher preparation students need to have appropriate "experiences" and university classroom activities that reflect good practice, both pedagogical and mathematical.

14. Assessment practices in teacher preparation should include student portfolios and journals in both mathematics and mathematics education courses. Oral assessment should also be included and other innovative alternatives and practices.

15. The concerns of one group included the need for all countries and participants to make connections between theory and practice, between mathematics in the university and mathematics in schools, between teachers and professors.

16. Attention was drawn to the insufficient content background of teachers; to the level of mathematics anxiety amongst students, especially elementary preservice teachers; the insufficient pedagogical preparation of secondary teachers; the negative role models in many school observations; and the need to make stronger linkages amongst the community of teachers, mathematics educators and mathematics professors.

17. The task of enhancement was seen as a life-long process including adapting to social and technological change as well as the assimilation of research and development in mathematics education by the group that focused on the middle grades.

18. The same perspectives that frame all efforts in education are operative with regard to teacher professional development. These are related to the Pupils, the Teachers, the Subject of study (in this case Mathematics) and Society. Each of these perspectives is associated with a body of accumulated knowledge, experience and theory. This body of knowledge should represent the starting point of work, either to be built upon or consciously modified or rejected. Usually it is ignored and efforts of reform and change repeatedly start "from scratch".

The subgroup identified four general or strategic issues as requiring elaboration:

19. Is professional development equal to training in mathematics together with training in pedagogy? We think there is more, but what exactly is that? Is it mainly attention to the progression in mathematics topics from the lower to the higher from the pupil's perspective?

20. Are there any obvious areas for rapid and marked improvement in mathematics pedagogy? Any quick fixes? We think not, rather there is the need for the careful development of programs over 3 to 5 years to have significant and lasting improvement.

21. How do we measure the effectiveness of teaching approaches and of professional development programs? We tend to dismiss "public currency" measures such as examination results, but the public (or at least the politicians) also dismiss ours (such as pupils' attitudes to the subject and problem solving). We need greater sensitivity to public measures of effectiveness, to differentiate between the bad and good tests and statistics, and to devise well reasoned reforms in this area.

22. How do we devise materials and resources for professional development that are both specific enough to be usable by teachers with benefit, and also promote reflection by teachers on their practice? Resources need to respect the autonomous growth of expertise of teachers within a clear research-based framework in any given field.

23. The common thread of discussions was the need for teachers to be reflective practitioners and for teaching to be a research based

profession. But what should be the subject matter of these reflections? As teachers of teachers we are specifically concerned with:

a). Reflection on the mathematics, and specifically on the progression aspects and misconceptions in each topic. Perhaps most crucial in this area is to distinguish the deeper and bigger ideas from the notation and procedures.

b). Reflection on the learning culture of the mathematics classroom. How to ensure involvement and an active learning environment and interactions. There is the need for evolving a fresh classroom discourse, a set of new professional teaching skills.

c). Reflection on pupils' cognitive development, the changes in the thinking powers (or the mental processing powers) of individual pupils, how to distinguish a pupil's thinking ability from the performance of that pupil on a given task or test? There is a need here for the evolution of a professional discourse amongst teachers on cognitive versus performance issues.

Mathematics Teacher Education and Information Technologies

A range of initiatives making use of the information technologies were reported. They included three main categories of development: interactive CD-ROM, video-conferencing and satellite TV, with the supplementary use of other technologies: video, e-mail, fax etc. The major aim is to use IT as a vehicle or tool for communication in order to change teachers' practice, whether at the pre- or inservice level. The medium only delivers information: further analysis, processing or discussion is required to change teachers' beliefs and practices.

The use of IT to deliver programs at a distance was discussed. Satellite TV and videoconferencing supported by other materials show some potential, but each program creates its own further problems in addressing the dilemmas of providing effective professional development, e.g. provision for interaction, discussion, supervised practice, authentic feedback and so on. Much more developmental work needs to be carried out and documented.

The discussion addressed some of the following:
1. IT should challenge teachers' own views of teaching and present "good" models of teaching. Teachers need to see that there is a problem with their teaching before they can consider changing beliefs and practices

and they need time to develop individual theories of teaching/learning.

2. A range of materials needs to be developed to support individual learning styles.

3. The recording of parallel teaching activities could provide valuable data.

4. Differences between the requirements of preservice and inservice teachers need to be identified and acknowledged (although there are similarities) and the needs of researchers.

5. Provision needs to be made to overcome IT illiteracy among teachers so that IT can be best exploited. Perhaps preservice teachers could be taught how to program software for CD-ROM and related IT as a matter of course.

6. Teachers need support and guidance in using IT to advantage; the metaphor of art critic or guide in an art museum is relevant here.

7. IT must be supplemented with adequate reflective discussion, mentored classroom practice, modelling, coaching etc.

8. Current efforts in using IT may be extended in the near future using the World Wide Web, which places greater demands on quality while creating greater access for teachers. CU-see-me technology is becoming a reality, but raises further issues regarding the quality of interaction and its effectiveness.

9. How IT is used is possibly more important than the fact that IT per se is used. IT promises a lot, but its promises must be qualified.

10. International collaboration using the WWW can assist in exchange of views and information among teacher educators and researchers.

The main purpose of the group was to share knowledge and experience. It was clear that attempts are being made on a number of fronts to use IT in mathematics teacher education at both the preservice and inservice phases. While IT is creating many opportunities for confronting and informing teachers, teacher educators and researchers, it brings with it a number of important dilemmas which must be addressed in order for the art of teaching to be effectively challenged.

Summary: The discussions covered a wide range of issues in mathematics teacher education, some of which were recurring themes in the group presentations on the final working day. These included:
. the low level of mathematics entry requirements for primary teacher education;
. the level of mathematics anxiety amongst teacher education students;
. the importance of teacher (and student) beliefs about and attitudes to mathematics on the teaching and learning of mathematics;
. the identification of good teaching practice and how to evaluate it;
. the problems of negative role models for many school observations;
. the need for teachers to become reflective in their practice and see enhancement as a lifelong process;
. and the growing importance of the role of IT in teacher education.

Marjorie C. Carss
Milan Koman
José Ramón Pascual

EVALUATION OF TEACHING, CENTERS, AND SYSTEMS

EVALUACIÓN DE LA ENSEÑANZA, LOS MEDIOS Y LOS SISTEMAS EDUCATIVOS

Chief Organizer / *Responsable*: David Robitaille (CAN)
Advisory Panel / *Asesores*: Fernando Hernández-Guarch (ESP), Norman L. Webb (USA)
Local Organizer / *Coordinador Local*: Antonio Molano (ESP)

One focus of the Working Group will be on prominent cases of reform activity in mathematics education around the world which emphasize the role of teachers and teacher education in mathematics education, how the role of teachers is changing. A second focus will be on innovative approaches to evaluation including the use of portfolios, perfomance assessment, and others. A panel discussion will be a featur of the first session of the WG, and subsequent sessions will include both paper presentations and group discussions.

THE TEACHING OF MATHEMATICS IN DIFFERENT CULTURES

LA ENSEÑANZA DE LAS MATEMÁTICAS EN LAS DIFERENTES CULTURAS

Chief Organizer / *Responsable:* Jerry P. Becker (USA)
Advisory Panel / *Asesores:* Sunday A. Ajose (USA), Andy Begg(NZL),
T. Fujii (JPN), Martha Villavicencio (PER)
Local Organizer / *Coordinador Local:* Andrés Marcos (ESP)

One hundred thirty-five delegates from 28 countries began their work from the premise that the teaching of mathematics in different countries has commonalities and that there are many aspects to these. Papers that were prepared before the Congress were available from the opening session onwards, along with others that were presented or summarized in the sessions. Other papers were stimulated by the WG and will be added to the proceedings.

In the first plenary session, Professor Terezinha Nunes opened the WG by starting from the idea that mathematics is a cultural practice that is situated in time and space and is defined by the community of mathematicians. According to Nunes, if mathematics is a cultural practice, then to learn mathematics is to become socialized into its particular ways of knowing. Nunes discussed this process of socialization of the mind from a psychological perspective while offering an integrated view of psychological theories and research. The main sections of her presentation were: 1. Is relativism a consequence of a cultural view of mathematical knowledge? 2. The socialization of meanings into mathematical concepts. 3. Mathematical signs as tools for thought. 4. Values associated with the learning of mathematics in and out of school. 5. Implications for mathematics teaching in a multicultural society. The paper set the stage for discussions in subsequent sessions.

Next, Dr. Bill Barton presented a talk in which he mentioned that the aims of mathematics education are inextricably linked with the socio-cultural aims of education. In order to provide a mathematics curriculum that is fair to all students in a multicultural society, it is necessary to unravel these links so that they can be clearly seen, and in this way, minority cultures in the mathematics classroom can be given space and legitimacy. Barton described these links with a model of socio-cultural nets that is used to develop strategies for mathematics course development and delivery in multicultural environments. It was illustrated with the history of Maori mathematics in New Zealand.

In the next two sessions, participants worked in four subgroups, as follows:

Subgroup 1: The Influence of Culture on Teaching and Curriculum -

The five presenters each briefly summarized their papers and discussion then followed. In the discussions, curriculum was included in addition to mathematics, teaching, and culture. Further, the papers and discussions extended the terms sociology, psychology and schemata (webs) from the two initial plenary presentations in the following emergent ways: the possibilities to extend the curriculum by using traditional knowledge that has mathematical components but requires a different approach to curriculum; the prominent differences in teaching styles that exist even between cultures that are similar; the link between all aspects of mathematics and culture and, borrowing from the literature from gender studies, a tentative theoretical framework for the development of culturally inclusive curricula emerged; various problems were shown that can occur with language development; and finally, the language concerns and links between culture and learning styles emerged. The discussion was extended to include the matter of class, especially city/rural and the need to consider the political aspects related to the subgroup's topics.

Overall, the discussions pointed firstly to the need to consider the practical issues that impact on teachers such as overfull curricula and a lack of resources, and secondly, to the rich variation and complexity of the influence of culture even though many similarities exist across disparate cultural groups. [Roslyn M. Frank: "An Essay in European Ethnomathematics and Orality: Celestial Traditions of John Little Bear in Europe and Euskal Herria (The Basque Country)"; Gabriele Kaiser: "Comparative Case-Studies in English and German Mathematics Teaching"; Andy Begg, Salanieta Bakalevu, Roger Edwards, Ana Koloto and Sashi Sharma: "Mathematics and Culture in Oceania"; Franco Favilli and Jama Muse Jama: "Creating a Mathematical Terminology: The Somalia Case"; David Davison: "Issues in the Mathematics Learning of American Indian Students"]

Subgroup 2: Preparing Teachers to Teach to Diversity

The ten presenters each briefly summarized their papers and discussion followed. The papers dealt with the challenge of diversity in one form or another, and all of them directly or indirectly addressed the preparation of teachers for diverse student populations. The main emergent points were as follows:

a) Regarding diversity of cultural expectations, in some cultures a child-centered method of teaching in which the teacher facilitates his/her students' construction of mathematical knowledge is expected. In others, the teacher is expected to be an authority figure, with an answer for every question. Although the latter view may not be considered progressive, it must be respected for instruction to be effective. b) Regarding diversity of students' "webs," it was acknowledged that students bring different "webs" to the classroom. Teaching to diversity means recognition of this fact, taking care not to destroy students' webs while empowering them to modify or extend their webs in ways that will give them greater access to mathematical understanding and competence. c) Regarding the importance of ethnomathematics, the mathematics education of children should begin, when appropriate, with the mathematics of their "cultural practice"; i.e., their ethnomathematics. Two papers actually suggested that ethnomathematics be part of teacher education curricula. Unless this is done, teachers may not see ethnomathematics as "authentic mathematics." The discussions also raised the point that the curricula of teacher education should include courses in minority history, language and culture.

Overall, the papers provided a model for the mathematical enculturation of students along with examples of cultural elements that had mathematical aspects. There was a consensus that for mathematics instruction to be effective, it must be culturally responsive.

[Soo-Hwan <u>Kim</u>: "A Study of the Development of a Teaching/Learning Model for the Mathematical Enculturation of Elementary and Secondary School Students"; Norma <u>Presmeg</u>: "Ethnomathematics and Academic Mathematics: The Didactic Interface";

Ping-Tung <u>Chang</u>: "Mathematics in the 21st Century: A Comparative Study of Teaching Mathematics Between China and the United States of America"; Peggy <u>House</u>: "Preparing Teachers to Recognize Diversity in Students' Mathematical Thinking"; John <u>Suffolk</u>: "Preparing Teachers in Different Countries to Teach a British Inspired Mathematics Curriculum"; Luis <u>Ortiz-Franco</u>: "Integrating

Ethnomathematics in the Teaching of Algebra"; Sunday Ajose: "Culturally Responsive Pedagogy in Mathematics"; Shihu Lu, Mingfu Sun, and Zhongchun Wang: "A Curriculum for Educating Mathematics Teachers for the National Minorities in Northwest China" [Presented by Kenneth Retzer]; Chinglin Hu and Rong Hu: "The Bilingual Teaching Pattern in University Mathematics in the Yi and Han Languages of China"; Geraldo Pompeu: "An In-service Course Based on Ethnomathematics and Modelling as a Methodological Approach to the Teaching of Mathematics"]

Subgroup 3: Cross-cultural Research -

Here it was first recognized that while cross-cultural studies have been done that compare curriculum, teaching methods, or mathematics classroom practices, there still are only a few studies that investigate how students actually learn mathematics under different emphases in classroom teaching. In the first of three presentations, a study of how students incorporate formalized school knowledge and skills into the thinking which they brought into their classroom was reported. Prior to instruction, students' performance on common problems were compared, and during instruction, four students in a U.S. and four in a Japanese classroom were studied using a qualitative research approach. Students' behaviors were synthesized into twelve patterns. There were no great differences in terms of patterns reported. Rather, the differences emerged more in the ways in which students work in their seats: one was the roles of the teacher and peers in the students' process of learning, and the other was the extent to which students were concerned with procedural and representational aspects of the new methods. Students were found to share their strategies that were different from those taught by the teacher.

Another study reported the results of comparative investigations between mathematics classroom practices in the U.S. and Japan. Six lessons in Japan and four in the U.S. were analyzed. The lessons focused on a common mathematical problem. For each lesson, the videotape, transcription and lesson plan were analyzed. The case studies provided evidence of differences between U.S. and Japanese mathematics classroom practices. A discussion emerged regarding a "mathematically convincing" vs. "personally convincing" aspect of the lessons.

It was observed that the Japanese teachers tended to make comments regarding students' work that was based on mathematical sophistication; i.e., which solution is the best mathematically. In contrast, the American teachers regarded each solution as equally important; i.e., they seemed to be accepting of each solution while not evaluating it. An emergent theme was that the Japanese lessons aim at more mathematically sophisticated activity in contrast to the U.S. In the U.S. lessons, most of the time was devoted to group work in problem solving whereas, most of the time in the Japanese lessons was given to comparing and discussing solutions and to summarizing the lessons.

In the third presentation, it was reported that in the U.S. half of fourth-grade students are still in the process of constructing place value concepts, whereas Asian students develop this concept much earlier. Research was conducted in the first grade that incorporated several components from the Japanese curriculum, including a de-emphasis on counting as a strategy, explicit naming of numbers (e.g., "ten-three" for 13), and a subbase of five to make quantities visualizable. There were many significant differences when compared to the control class and to other research. [Keiko Ito-Hino: "Students Constructive Activities During Instruction: Another Look at Classroom Practices in the U.S. and Japan"; Toshiakira Fujii, Yoshinori Shimizu, Koichi Kumagai, and Yoshishige Sugiyama: "A Cross-cultural Study of Classroom Practices Based on a Common Topic"; Joan Cotter: "Constructing a Multidigit Concept in the First Grade Using Explicit Naming and Subbase of Five Without Counting"]

Subgroup 4: Mathematics Learned Outside School-

Three papers were presented and discussed. The main emergent points were as follows: a) In trying to interest children in algebra and in introducing them to algebra, there is a dialectical tension inside mathematics, namely, between formal school mathematics and informal street mathematics. The passage from arithmetic to algebra is a complex process: mapping (1st stage), natural language to formal language (2nd stage), algebraic manipulation (3rd stage), and a proposition of an answer to the problem (4th stage). A didactic sequence was proposed using a two-pan balance scale (that is common in children's lives) to introduce algebra. Based on theoretical considerations and an emphasis on representations, it can be expected that symbolic systems can be conceptual amplifiers--however, they can be misleading and they are not "the real thing." b) When considering models of proportional reasoning among indigenous Maori girls in New Zealand, in the context of cooking, these girls were able to reason and to think mathematically ... and the context is "out of school." By relating the outside school knowledge to the experiences of these girls in school, they can be reasoned about and articulated. In this way, connections and links are more likely to be made, and this may facilitate transfer and generalization across the contexts.c)

Regarding the experience that is concerned with the mathematics that students use outside school and teachers' perspectives of those mathematical activities in students' lives, the discussion revealed that (i) mathematics exists outside of school; (ii) it is useful to introduce or discuss out-of-school mathematics in the classroom to improve a skill(s), and then consciously use it again outside of school; (iii) there is a need to exercise restraint in emphasizing students' reflection on mathematical aspects of their lives, just in case they might stop doing it altogether. [Jorge Tarcísio da Rocha Falcão: "Mathematics Outside School: Interest of Cultural Tools as Metaphors in Algebra Sense-making; Colleen McMurchy-Pilkington: "Turning the Outside into the Inside: Valuing Maori Women's Everyday Mathematical Reasoning"; Joanna Masingila: "What Can We Learn From Students' Out-of-School Mathematics Practice?"]

In the fourth session that was plenary, Professor Richard Pallascio discussed the learning of geometry by Inuit: a problem of mathematics acculturation. Pallascio reported on research that was carried out by Louise Lafortune, Richard Allaire, Pierre Mongeau and himself aimed at developing an understanding of Inuit spatial skills. In the presentation, Pallascio dealt with: 1. The matrix of the development of geometric spatial representation. 2. Types of space. 3.Elements of the theoretical framework. 4. The results and discussion of the research. Subsequently, the researchers carried out a didactical sequence, and in the process, were able to isolate the main characteristics of a contextualized, culturally committed and involved pedagogy that was described.

Though she was not able to come to Seville for the WG, the Organizing Committee was delighted to have a paper (in both Spanish and English) that reported the results of research carried out by Martha Villavicencio that was concerned with mathematical education in Andean bicultural contexts. The conclusion that Villavicencio offered was that the low achievement of boys and girls in Andean bicultural contexts in mathematics was due to (i) a lack of consideration of their cultural sociolinguistic context--it is necessary to carry out qualitative transformations at a technical-pedagogical level, and (ii) the qualitative improvement of mathematical education in contexts of autochthonous sociocultural groups supposes a political decision of the State for the adequate implementation of intercultural programs of good quality. Janet Kaahwa also contributed a paper that was concerned with the need for mathematics educators to explore mathematics in local environments and cultures and to also use it to interest learners in mathematics and to facilitate learning. In her study in Uganda, Kaahwa used cultural objects and explained the mathematics embedded in them both verbally and in diagrams. She concluded that, though ethnomathematics is quite new in Uganda, there is a wealth of mathematics in its culture and environment that can be used to enrich mathematics teaching and learning. D. J. van den Berg also shared a paper in which he indicated that a group-oriented teaching strategy is essential in the South African educational system in order to bring the related skills in line with those required by the modern South African economy. Finally, Tamsin Roberts reported on the development of a mathematics curriculum framework that can be used by individual Aboriginal communities in Australia to develop a curriculum that reflects the needs and aspirations of these communities. [Martha Villavicencio: "Mathematical Education in Andean Bicultural Contexts"; Janet Kaahwa: "Mathematics in Uganda Cultural Objects"; D. J. van den Berg: "A Group-Oriented Approach to the Teaching of Mathematics - An African Perspective"; Tamsin Roberts: "A Mathematics Curriculum Framework for Aboriginal Communities"]

We had only four 1.5-hour sessions in which to deal with many important topics closely linked to teaching mathematics in different cultures. We made very good progress. More time would have made it possible to produce more results from in-depth discussion, and perhaps even make some specific recommendations for further work. However, we had a very high level of attendance, and the plenary papers, short presentations and intensity of discussion led us to conclude that both the format and the WG theme were "on the mark" to achieve our goals: the main papers set the tone, the summaries of papers sparked discussion, and the participants shared and gained insights.

We close by commenting that several people made extraordinary contributions to the success of WG 21: to the Local Organizer, Mr. Andres Marcos Garcia, and to Ms. Estela Villalba Valdayo, a student worker, we express great appreciation for their steady and effective cooperation and support; and to Dr. Luis Ortiz-Franco we express profound appreciation for his translation support in the plenary sessions, as well as in the subgroup discussions--he contributed much to the success of our WG. A proceedings containing the plenary and subgroup papers will be published. Information is available from: Jerry P. Becker, Department of Curriculum and Instruction, Southern Illinois University, Carbondale, Illinois 62901-4610, USA. The e-mail address is JBECKER@SIU.EDU

MATHEMATICS, EDUCATION, SOCIETY AND CULTURE

MATEMÁTICAS, EDUCACIÓN, SOCIEDAD Y CULTURA

Chief Organizer / *Responsable:* Richard Noss (GBR)
Advisory Panel / *Asesores*: Cyril Julie (ZAF), Jean M.Kantor (FRA)
Catherine Vistro-Yu (PHI)
Local Organizer / *Coordinador Local:* José L. Alvarez (ESP)

Presenters at the working group included participants from a wide range of countries including Australia, Brazil, Canada, Colombia, France, Hong Kong, Italy, Malaysia, Morocco, S.Africa, Spain, UK,Ukraine, and USA.

The Group was divided into three panels. In this short report, I merely outine the main themes which were discussed, and provide a one-paragraph summary of the issues. Further details can, of course, be obtained from the authors, and some of the papers presented are available at http://www.ioe.ac.uk/rnoss/WG22.html

PANEL 1: Social and political dimensions

Cyril Julie	Perspectives from S. Africa
Oliverio Herrera	Is a social mathematics possible in pre-school?
Jean-Michel Kantor	Social dimensions of mathematics
Richard Noss	The visibility of mathematics in technological societies
Ubi D'Ambrosio	Socio-political dimensions of mathematics
Sergei Klepko	The flight from mathematics in modern societies

Panel 1 was concerned with macro-level of the relationship between mathematics, mathematics education, and society. The diversity of the presentations is amply reflected in their titles, and illustrate the complexity of the issues concerned. A particularly stimulating discussion concerned the politico-economic role of mathematics, and its place in society including the workplace. Given that so many societies tend to measure their economic success and political influence by the mathematical achievements of their students, it is interesting to ponder how this came to be, how new technologies are influencing the situation (in one direction or another) and how this ties in with the flight from mathematics which is being experienced in much of the developed world.

PANEL 2: Cultures and Criticism

Derek Woodrow	Role of cultural traditions
Habiba Bouazzaoui	Rural communities and mathematics learning
Marta Civil USA	Mathematics and minority students
Gelsa Knijnik	Mathematics Education, power, and the struggle for
land in	Brazil
Frederick Leung	Does culture make any difference to teachers' views of mathematics education?
Kay Owens	Ethnomathematical approaches in Australia

What roles does mathematics play in national cultures? There are two interesting ways ways of looking at the problem, and each was represented in the discussions. The first looks at diversities of culture, and asks whether this culture impinges on the nature of mathematical activity, the attitudes of teachers and curricula in general. The second offers a reverse perspective, and enquires how mathematics — conceived in the broadest sense — acts back either implicitly or explicity on the culture that gives rise to it. Taken together, the twin themes of the panel highlight the dialectical relationship between culture and mathematical activity, in which mathematics shapes and is shaped by the ambient culture.

PANEL 3: Ideology and values

Alan Bishop*	Values education in mathematics classrooms
Lim Chap Sam	Values in mathematics teaching and learning
Malaysian	- a perspective
Peter Gates	Ideology and teacher development
Adalberto Codetta	Research on zero and common sense
Maribel Anacona	Reception of non-euclidean geometries in Colombia
Lionel Slammert	Mathematicians' values
Tony Brown	The role of language

*Unable to present through illness.

In this final session, the relationship between ideologyand mathematics was explored. Emphasis centred on the ways in which mathematics functions as a vehicle for the transmission of social values (alongside its scentific-technological roles), and there were several interesting discussions concerning the ways in which mathematicians and mathematics itself has been (and continues to be) shaped by ideological pressures. As in session 2, the diversity of backgrounds of the participants presented the group with a rich fund of comparative approaches.

COOPERATION AMONG COUNTRIES AND REGIONS IN MATHEMATICS EDUCATION

COOPERACIÓN EN EDUCACIÓN MATEMÁTICA ENTRE PAÍSES Y REGIONES

Chief Organizer / *Responsable:* Bienvenido Nebres (PHI)
Advisory Panel / *Asesores:* Emma García Mora (ESP),
Bernardo Montero (CRI)
Local Organizer / *Coordinadora Local:* Mercedes García (ESP)

John Malone spoke of Australia's key centre for mathematics and school sciences and its work of collaboration among the various regions of Australia and countries on both the Indian and Pacific ocean rims. The centre's purpose is to give access to high-quality graduate programs, to conduct research in mathematics education and its implications for the improvement of teaching and learning and to publish and disseminate results and to promote contact among mathematics teachers nationally and internationally.

Ruth Sweetnam described the International Baccalaureate Curriculum for the final two pre-university years The curriculum is used all over the world. It is examined in English, French and Spanish. This is one example of cooperation among nations using a single curriculum. If WG 23 agrees that a common curriculum is advisable then this is one group that can be of assistance.

Jean-Paul Ginestier agreed to try to form a group of volunteers that would discuss this possibility.

John Egsgard pointed out that a common curriculum among countries, or even in one country, can only be successful if a common examination is taken by students in all the countries concerned.

Wednesday, July 17, 1996

Murad Jurdak spoke of two projects for collaboration among Arab countries. The important conclusions coming from these collaborations were that it is very difficult to impose a standard curriculum and at the same time improve quality. Also one must take into account cultural differences in producing curricula.

Bill Velez described the Southwest Regional Institute in Mathematical Sciences. The attempt of the Institute is to produce a collaboration in research among mathematicians, graduate and undergraduate students and high school mathematics teachers. The task to convince research mathematicians to work with others has been a difficult one.

Aderemi Kuku spoke of the problems of designing a mathematics curriculum for Africa at the tertiary level. The designers must be able to see the whole picture and to know what use will be made of the mathematics. If curriculum design is to be successful there must be more money (for example, through schemes like debt for science), better remuneration for teachers at all levels, and a real attempt to stop the brain drain. Kuku then listed some research projects that are necessary to improve mathematics education globally.

Mark Saul spoke of the collaboration between USA and Russia through the Quantum magazine and translation of mathematics material from Russia. He notes that research mathematicians in Russia work closely with teachers and students at the secondary and elementary level. Groups in the USA are translating Russian Math problems written at an elementary level by research mathematicians.

Kenneth Retzer spoke of a research programme in China looking at the effect of culture among students of mathematics at the elementary and middle school level. They discovered that there is a significant difference between the two cultures (Tibetan and Han) that is not genetic.

He also reported briefly on the work of Prof. Lu Shihu on educating mathematics teachers for the national minorities in northwest China.

Friday, July 19, 1996

Maria Teresa Berhouet from Argentina spoke of cooperation among various regions by means of an olympiad. The olympiad has 400,000 students from ages 12-16 who begin. Six exams take place. In the final exam the 300 best students participate. The organizers have discovered that students near universities have a very great advantage over others. There is hope that the exam will extend to surrounding countries. The result sof the exams are looked at to see what improvement needs to be made in local teaching. Similar difficulties with mathematics in adjoining countries are being worked on together. This cooperation takes place despite the problem of conflict among the countries. Chile and Peru have similar contests.

After the talk, the group began to discuss recommendations:

(1) Establishing Regional Centres for Mathematics Education

The Monash (conference of April 199) recommendations on establishing such centres were endorsed with the following discussions and additions:

(a) Include the role of professional associations

(b) Centres could provide information on different curricula and experiences with curricula for systems looking to a review/ revision of their curricula (what has been tested, what has been found good).

(c) Such centres can also provide support/ assistance for university professors on how to teach.

(2) Establishing databases and an information network on mathematics education on Internet.

(a) The regional centres should develop databases on mathematics education.

(b) These should be made accessible on Internet. (Footnote: There was a poster at the conference on "Internet and Mathematics Education" by Pak-Hong Cheung of the University of Hong Kong. address: phcheung@hku.hk)

(c) This could be a project for ICME 9 and WMY 2000.

(3) Encouraging the role of mathematics departments in developing collaboration among mathematicians, graduate students, undergraduates and high school teachers within and across regions.

ICMI/ IMU should encourage communication across groups as described by Bill Velez. This can be encouraged by policies on grants for projects in teaching and research. Also by university policies supportive of such work as part of a faculty member's work towards promotion and tenure.

Mathematics societies can also encourage such collaboration.

Saturday, July 20, 1996

There was a comment on #1, regional centres, of yesterday saying that emphasis should be on improving teaching rather than writing curricula. (Comment: Curriculum has a wider sense in TIMSS: intended (what ministry of education declares); implemented (what teachers teach); achieved (what students learn)

There is a need to look at what is important in a curriculum for a single or group of cultures before collaboration among cultures takes place. When we look at collaboration, there are three types:

(a) A group of countries with a common culture work on a curriculum.

(b) One country seeks help from another country or culture

(c) A group completely independent of any culture or country such as the International Baccalaureate Association

Groups in (c) should have a more important role, say in ICME 9.

Regional collaboration must precede international collaboration. One area for ICME 9, a WG could work on a model curriculum taking as a reference point the curriculum of the International Baccalaureate Association and/ or other such group such as IEA. This group must discuss the problem that a culture-free curriculum may not be able to be used in various cultures. The results of TIMSS should assist in the work of such a WG.

Popularisation of Mathematics for the WMY 2000.

There were many suggestions in this area; among them were:

(1) Find and examine countries that have successful programmes linking parents and schools.

(2) Find tv programs that do this, showing relevance of math to various areas of life.

(3) Create an interesting spot on www. This will be even more important in year 2000 than in 1996.

(4) Emphasize regional, national and international olympiads.

(5) Get corporations to provide funds for popularisations, eg. puzzle pages in papers.

(6) Example of teacher in Colombia who has prepared a contest for elementary school students using comics as a medium.

Finally, there was a recommendation for two centres for mathematics education in Australasia, one in Japan and another in Australia.

WORKING GROUP 23
ICME 8
PAPERS PRESENTED

Session 1 - July 16, Tuesday

John A. Malone - "Australia's National Key Centre for School Science and Mathematics: Regional Collaboration"
Ruth K. Sweetnam - "A Mathematics Curriculum - Can It Successfully Cross National Boundaries?"
Jean-Paul Ginestier - "Curriculum Across National Boundaries"
John Egsgard - "International Examinations Increasing Cooperation Across Countries"

Session 2 - July 17, Wednesday

Murad Jurdak - "Some Lessons from Two Regional Collaboration Projects in Mathematics Education in the Arab Region"
William Yslas Velez - "Southwest Regional Institute in the Mathematical Sciences (SWRIMS)"
    - "Integration of Research and Education - What does it mean and how can it be accomplished?"
Dr. Kenneth A. Retzer - "China Connections"
Professor Lu Shihu - "A Curriculum for Educating Mathematics Teachers for the National Minorities in Northwest China"
Mark Saul - "Adapting Mathematics Materials from the Soviet Union to Cultural Conditions in the U.S.A."
Aderemi Kuku - "Tertiary Mathematics Education in Africa in Relation to Other Continents"

Session 3 - July 19, Friday

Maria Teresa Berhouet - "Torneos Matematicos de Frontera"
Recommendations from the Forums - ICMI Regional
Conference, Monash University, Melbourne, Australia, April 19-23, 1995

CRITERIA FOR QUALITY AND RELEVANCE IN MATHEMATICS EDUCATION RESEARCH

CRITERIOS DE CALIDAD Y PERTINENCIA EN LA INVESTIGACIÓN EN LA EDUCACIÓN MATEMÁTICA

Chief Organizer / *Responsable:* Kenneth Ruthven (UK)
Advesory Panel / *Asesores*: Robert Davis (USA), Angel Gutierrez (ESP)
Local Organizer / *Coordinador Local*: Salvador Llinares (ESP)

The quality and relevance of research in mathematics education is assessed in different ways for differing purposes. The aim of the working group will be to explore the criteria that are appropriate in assessing research for purposes such as:

- the award of a doctoral degree in mathematics education;
- publication in a refereed journal in mathematics education;
- inclusion in a course aimed at the professional preparation or development of mathematics teachers;
- to inform policy formation in mathematics teaching and the development of professional guidelines;
- to design resources for mathematics teaching, such as textbooks and other classroom materials.

DIDACTICS OF MATHEMATICS AS A SCIENTIFIC DISCIPLINE

LA DIDÁCTICA DE LA MATEMÁTICA COMO DISCIPLINA CIENTÍFICA

Chief Organizer / *Responsable*: Nicolina A. Malara (ITA)
Advisory Panel / *Asesores:* Carmen Azcárate (ESP),Hans-Georg Steiner (DEU), Stephen Lerman (GBR).
Local Organizer / *Coordinadora Local:* María del Carmen Batanero (ESP)

The main aim of the working group was to offer a forum for hightlighting the status of didactics of mathematics as a scientific discipline, focusing on: i) its objects and core; ii) its connections with other fields (anthropology, epistemology, psychology, etc.); iii) its features in the various countries; in order to arrive at delineating a vision of it agreed on internationally.

The group has been organized alternating moments of collective comparison (the opening and closing sessions) and moments of parallel work in groups for remaining of the time, with the aim of maximizing the opportunities for question and discussion. Over 100 Congress attendees partecipated in some portion of the working group and a large part of them (65%) was Spanish native speakers. Because of a strong partecipation of representative from Spanish speaking countries, most presentations and discussions were handled in a bilingual way (English and Spanish) by providing consecutive translation by members of the group. In particular very precious has been the contribution of Carmen Batanero during the common sessions.

THE OPENING SESSION

After a welcome by Nicolina A. Malara, an introduction of her local and international advisors, and the clarification of technical matters, the opening session was focused on the plenary lecture by H. G. Steiner [DEU] Basic Characteristics and Recent Trends in the Development of Didactics of Mathematics as a Scientific Discipline. shortly outlined in the following.

H.G. Steiner started out with some remarks about the names being used for the discipline under consideration. There are basicly two different traditions, the Anglo-American one referring "mathemahics education", and the Continental European one, using, when oommunicating in English, "didactics of mathematics" and otherwise in the various national languages: "didaktik der mathematik", "didattica della matematica", "dydaktyka matematyki", etc. There are problems with the meaning of "didactique des mathématiques" among French researchers a group of whom (Guy Brousseau, Yves Chevallard and others) claim to restrict the term to special phenomena and approaches characterized by key concepts, they have developed, such as "situations didactiques", "contrat didactique", "transposition didactique", "ingénierie didactique". If we indicate this specific meaning by "didactique*", then "didactique* des mathematiques" could be interpreted as a sub domain (actually very important one) of didactics of mathematics and we could declare at an international basis "didactics of mathematics" and "mathematics education" to be synonymous.

H.G. Steiner then shortly described the historical development of didactics of mathematics its beginnings in the 19th century in connexion with the social instituzionalization of schooling and teacher education, the influence of the expansive growth and deep methodological changes in pure and applied mathematics since about 1830, the role of mathematicians and users of mathematics, especially the important contributions by the International Commission on Mathematics Instruction (ICMI) with respect to international exchange of information, coordination of innovative activities, substantial reports and studies, mainly produced in the commission's first working period 1908-1918.

H. G. Steiner stressed that the strongest impulses both with respect to world-wide curriculum changes and related research work in didactics of mathematics came with the New Math Reform, beginning in the late 1950-es and culminating in the 1960-es. Set-theorethical foundations and language, the principles of the axiomatic method, and the central role of the concept of structure together wirh Piaget's genetic epistemology and Bruner's psychology of dicovery learning were the leading orientations. Though in the late 60-es the reform began to be considered as a failure in several of its components and features the innovative impetus had been strong enough to generate a great number of new groups, projects, organizations, institutions, conferences, book series, jounals etc. which contributed to a critical analysis of the past, developed new perspectives and laid the ground for an impressive future growth of research in didactics of mathematics. So in 1968 there were founded among others in France the Instituts pour Recherche sur l'Enseignement des Mathématiques (IREM), which later became the cells for the developement of "didactique des mathématiques", in England The Shell Centre of Mathematics Education at Nottingham, in Germany the Zentrum für Didaktik der Mathematik at Karlsruhe, in Italy the Centro Ricerche Didattiche at Paderno del Grappa and the Nuclei di Ricerca Didattica in various Universities.

H. G. Steiner evidenciated the contribution given to the didactics of mathematics in the sixties by Dienes, Freudenthal and Krigowska and in particular the role of Freudenthal in facing the resistance of mathematicians (worried for the possible involution of mathematics research) with the organization of the first ICME Congress (Lyon 1966) and the foundation of the Educational Studies in Mathematics., and also recalls the foundation of Zentralblatt für Didaktik der Mathematik and in USA the Jurnal for Research in Mathematics Education (1969). Moreover he lists the ICME Congresses underlining their main features: Exter (1972) -centered on the working groups opened to the teachers too-; Karlsruhe (1976) -with the birth of the PME and HME groups (affiliation of ICMI), Berkley (1980) -very ambitious for the large amount of themes in discussion-, Adelaide (1984) -with the birth of the TME group aimed to give theoretical bases to didactics of mathematics-, and the more recent Congresses of Budapest (1988) and Quebec (1992) which consolidated in the present structure.

H. G. Steiner underlined that the strong development of didactics of mathematics as a scientific discipline can be best evidenced from the programs and components of the up-to-now 8 ICMEs. Here H.G. Steiner refferred to ICME 7 held at Quebec, Canada in August 1992 which in many respects is comparable with this present ICME 8. The scientific program with its 23 working and 17 topic groups - each highly differenciated into soubgroups -, with its 4 plenary papers and 45 special lectures on selected themes, its miniconfence on calculators and computers involving 311 congress members for 3 1/2 hours, its special program-components for the 3 ICMI-affi1iated study groups as welll as a presentation and discussion of 3 new ICMI-studies, furthemore the exposition and activation of projects, workshops, special sessions, exhibitions and poster-sessions, and, last but not least, the awarding by Laval University of honorary doctoral degrees to two international leaders in mathematics education, this altogether represent in substance, structure and organization an up to then unreached degree of achievement in giving a lively picture of the high level of progress made internationally in mathematics education as a domain of interconnected research, development and practice. For the first time didactics of mathematics showed itself in great clarity as a scientific discipline which under increasing theoretical orientation and empirical foundation is dynamically growing within an international frame of complex cultural, political and interdisciplinary interrelations. To participate actively - and even only receptively - in this process demands considerable national efforts and support in each single country".

In the discussion many questions were asked in relation to how one can best get acquainted with special research areas and research methodologies. A detailed answer will be given by a list of books in the full proceedings of Working Group 25. H.G. Steiner particularly referred to Bieler et al.1994 [1] .

SUBGROUP 1

Development and status of didactics of mathematics in various cultures.
coordinators: H. G. Steiner [Germany] - J. Sowder [USA]
Contributors: J. Sowder, H. Iwasaki [Japan], J. Novotna [Czech Republic], C. Azcarate [Spain], C. Haucart and M. Schineider [Belgium], E. Gelfman, M. Kholodnaya and R. Cherkassov [Russia], N.A. Malara and M. Menghini [Italy], Gonzales [Venezuela].

The first session was opened by Judith Sowder who spoke about a decade of research in mathematics education in the U.S. She began with the assumption that in terms of paradigms, foci and goals, didactics of mathematics and mathematics education are indistinguishable. She then outlined trends in research interests and in content domains. The influence of the reform movement in U.S mathematics education on teaching, and teacher education, social and cultural change in school mathematics, and assessment and evaluation were next discussed. The changing rule of technology in research and changing research paradigms were also discussed.

Hideki Iwasaki spoke on the theme in a japanese perspective. He noted that mathematics education in Japan is only now beginning to develop a scientific framework and philosophical base. Iwasaki considered some historical events that influenced Japanese thinking, particularly the work at the Lyon ICME in 1969 that facilitated the institutionalization of mathematics education, and the papers by Bigalke and Grisel in 1971 and 1974. The reform movement in mathematics in the

---

[1] R. Bieler, R.W. Scholz, R. Strässer, B. Winkelmann (Eds.): 1994, *Didactics of Mathematics as a Scientific Discipline,* Kluwer Academic Publishers Dordlecht

second decade of the century contributed to an increase in studies of teaching mathematics. After the Second World War the educational system in Japan changed, and research in this field was renewed. It has continued to be influenced by what is happening in Europe and in the United States.

Jarmila Novotna spoke about research in didactics of Mathematics in her country. The report focused on work in the field of arithmetical and algebraic word problems, begun in 1992 in cooperation with researchers in Montreal. The Czech approach to this study area focuses on a students' process of solving problems. The research method is called 'atomic analysis', and uses the students' written solution. The analysis is based on the decomposition of the solution into the smallest units possible -- what is written and what is in the student's mind. A graphical layout of the phenomena discovered was demonstrated, and obstacles and therapies were discussed.

Carmen Azcarate reported on didactics of mathematics in Spain. The domain of "didactics of mathematics" and its departmental organization at the university level was established by the University Reform Law 1983. There are already well-established research groups and postgraduate programs. Spanish researchers are benefiting from the work of researchers in other countries where research groups and programs have a longer history.

In the second session Cristine Hauchart and Maggy Schneider chosed not to separate the question of whether didactics is a scientific discipline from the question of the impact of didactics, and therefore limited to report on a project on teaching mathematical analysis in the last two years secondary school. The guiding principles of this project are to let concepts emerge from mental objects and the exhibit different faults of functions. Several examples were shown the demonstrate these principles. The organizing principle is that there should be no theorizing without necessity and then students should be progressively led to a formalized theory using a sequence of questions going from the familiar to the abstract. The heuristic approach used has been inspired by history in particular ideas of Lakatos.

Raissa Lozinskaia [Russia], representing Emanuila Gelfman et alii, reported on the development of didactics of mathematics in Russia. The presentation included a history of didactics of mathematics in Russia, beginning with the publication of a textbook in 1703; including the all-Russia Congresses of mathematics teachers in 1911 and 1914; the laying out of the scientific foundations of didactics in 1943; the development of a curriculum for mathematics in 1964; and the effects of perestroika beginning in 1985. Russian didactics today is characterized by support of psychological research, in particular by the new discipline called "psychodidactics." Several models, each with its own school of researchers, were described. The Enriching Model," used by the authors of the report, was described in some detail. The model is realized in new textbooks that develops reflection and other metacognitive skills and productive activity through well-chosen tasks. A table comparing traditional didactics with psychodidactics in the context of the enriching model was shown.

Marta Manghini and Nicolina Malara faced the connection between mathematics education and Research in Mathematical Education, exposing a reflection on Italian Studies on the base of the Italian book edited on the occasion of ICME 8[2] , book which involved more then thirtyfour italian researchers. Their analysis focuses on the teaching of mathematics content and was divided into three parts: studies of geometry; studies in the disciplinary areas (arithmetic, algebra, calculus, logic, probability and statistics, and "transversal" kind (e.g., problem solving, mathematics and technology, popularization of mathematics). Of the two concepts of didactics of mathematics as a theoretical and automomous science and didactics of mathematics as an applied science, the second predominates. Nevertheless, the first type also is appearing.

Fredy Gonzalez summarized the state of research in Venezuela. Complex charts were shown of (1) the areas of mathematics education showing their basics in mathematics, and the two branches of mathematics research (teaching and learning) and (2) the complex relationship between the researcher and the teacher. This relationship must be very close with much interaction so that the teacher can understand the teaching of mathematics. To accomplish this, clear links between teaching and research can occur both in teacher preparation at the undergraduate level and at the graduate level.

SUBGROUP 2

Main questions concerning didactics of mathematics as a scientific discipline: objects and core, trends of research. Connections among didactics of mathematics and related fields

coordinators S. Lerman [United Kingdom], Carmen Azcarate [Spain] Contributors: J. Godino and C. Batanero [Spain], S. Lerman [United Kingdom], V. Marafioti [Brasil], J. Gascon [Spain], E. Kopelman [Israel], J. Mousley [Australia], F. Speranza [Italia], J. Ziegenbalg [Germany].

---

[2] Malara, N. A., Menghini, M. and Reggiani, M. (eds.): 1996, *Italian Research in Mathematics Education: 1988-1995*, Litoflash, Roma

In the first session Juan Godino and Carmen Batanero, on the base of the analysis of three investigations, spoke about the dialectic relationships among theory, development and practice in mathematics education. They higthlighted that didactics of mathematics has to be confronted with subtle and complex theoretical problems, whose nature in far away from pratical and technological concerns. Observing and explaing the students difficulties require well designed assessment situations. Overcoming these difficultiese require to organize adequate sentences of teaching situations. All this has to be based on research results, which in its turn, have to be supported in explicite cognitive and epistemological assumptions about mathematics and its learning. But, given that related disciplines do not offer clear and definitive solutions for these foundations, didactics of mathematics needs to integrate different proposals, on even build such teories from its own view and necessities.

Ildar S. Safuanov focused his speech on the similarity between mathematics education and theatrical criticism, as comparing the two parallel four-term schemes: [mathematics education - teaching/learning mathematics - mathematics - nature and objective reality in general]/[Theatrical criticism - theatre - theatrical plays - real life, human relations]. He mantains that mathematics education as well as art studies is a completely applied field, unable to develop independently of practice. The global purpose of such a field might be the creation of certain carefully elaborated system, including in some unity theoretical discoveries and ways of applications, like Stanislavskiy's system in the field of the theatre. In his view, similarity with art criticism still might in some ways enrich and deepen research in mathematics education. For example, affective and emotional aspects of mathematics instruction might be more successfully researched by approaches developed in art studies.

At last Jochen Ziegenbalg spoke on algorithmics and mathematics education. He argued that in mathematical education algorithms play a role on the "object-level", i.e. the level of mathematical content and on the "meta-level" of mathematical methodology. In this latter respect, algorithms (in close connection with the use of computers) are well suited to support:

- experimental mathematics and inductive epistemology
- "operative" methodology (in the sense of Wittmann 1974[3])
- constructive methodology both in the field of problem solving and epistemology (constructive conceptualization)

---

[3] Wittmann, E. Ch.: 1974, *Grundfragen des Mathematikunterrichts,* Braunschweig

- elementarization (in close connection with constructive methodology): the algorithmic method is usually far more elementary than, for instance the method of thinking in terms of "closed solutions";
- cross-connectedness: the algorithmic method is in the center of a vast interconnected web of contents and methodologies; in particular in various fields of art and science transcending the pureley inner-mathematical core.

In the second session Josep Gascón argued that the evolution of didactics of mathematics as a scientific discipline has been produced through successive changes of matters. These changes materialize in successive widenings of the didactical matter which modify the nature of the primary object of the investigation. He delineated a rational reconstruction of the evolution of one of the lines of the development of the didactical matter, without pretending any exhaustivity and objectivity. The methodological principle underlying this reconstruction has its roots in the widening of the didactical matter happened in the Seventies, when the nature of the discipline changed and it was possible for the first time to claim the status of scientific knowledge. In other words he pretended to reconstruct the genesis of the fundamental didactics. In the frame of the fundamental didactics recently was born the anthropological conception of didactics, which permits to integrate a big amount the partial analysis (psychological, sociological, etc.) and to put the teaching-learning processes as aspects of the studyind process. (Chevallard et. al., 1996[4]). Gascón stressed that from this unitary point of view didactics of mathematics can be considered as a science of the study and of the help to study Mathematics.

Evgeny Kopelman suggested that didactics better remain critical, rather than turn pseudoscientific. He reminded the following examples: studies of mathematics learning, which consider it as a purely cognitive phenomenon and thus perceive classroom environment as a psychological laboratory; epistemological research on the ultimate nature of mathematical objects, which leave out historical and cultural content of the latter; development of learning materials, which blindly submits itself to the notions of predefined "goals", "output" and "improvement" of mathematics education.

Judith Mousley was interested in the problem of the understanding of mathematics: she stressed on the "tension" between the realistic con-

---

[4] Chevallard Y, Bosch, M; and Gascón, J.: 1996, *Estudiar Matemática. El eslabon perdido entre enseñanza y aprendisaje,* ed. Horsori, Barcelona

ception (mathematical ideas exist independently from our minds) and the constructivist one (they are products of our mind). These are divergent philosophies which deeply influence our way of thinking: if we wish to be coherent, we must structure the mathematical teaching in a new way. In particular, she analized Plato's writings (realism), and Locke's and Vico's ones, which are clearly constructivist.

Vincente Marafioti Garnica's speaking can be considered as a contribution to the research of the "epistemological status" of didactics of mathematics (which is rooted also in "human sciences"). His analysis was based on the polarity between the "classical"approach to science and the "olistic" one. The former can be dated back to the scientific revolution of the seventeenth century, and is based on a mechanistic conception of the world, and on a reduction of reality to few, simple elements; the latter advocates the necessity of considering reality as an organic whole. Another related contraposition is the one between the quantitative approach to human sciences (e.g. by means of statistic instruments) and the qualitative one. He advocated also the contribution of phenomenologism (Husserl, Heidegger) to the problems of mathematics and mathematics education.

Stephen Lerman's contribution was centered on an analysis of different kinds of epistemologies of mathematics: there are foundational epistemologies, interested in justification of mathematics, and empiricists epistemologies, which are more interested in the context of discovery (this contraposition can be compared with that between absolutist or non absolutist philosophies of mathematics). Our interests can direct us in the choice of an epistemology: in particular, Lerman pointed out the case of epistem logies for and of mathematics education (let's think to the wide range of constructivist philosophies of knowledge), because "epistemologies of mathematics can be seen as resources for mathematics education" (in his contribution he chose an "apparently neutral" approach to the problem of choice).

Francesco Speranza stressed the importance of the clarification of the philosophies which are behind any approach to mathematics and to mathematics education, examining some relevant cases: he classified epistemologies as foundationally, historically or psychologically oriented. In particular, he considered the cases of non -Euclidean geometry and of the concept of space in mathematics, in philosophy and in art as meaningful instances of interaction between philosophy and science. A good choice of a philosophy of mathematics (careful of historical and psychological aspect) can orient also our approach to mathematics education, and can clarify the role of history in it.

THE CLOSING SESSION

The closing session, second and more important moment of collective confrontation, was centered on the round table purposely with the provocative title:"Is didactics of mathematics a Scientific Discipline? Are its connections with related fields (Epistemology, Anthropology, Psichology etc.) incentives or obstacles for its development?". Suggestions from the participants, formulated in advance, brought in some more points to be debate, such as: Is there a need for a comprehensive and concise elaboration of the state of the art in didactics of mathematics in order to facilitate communication and cooperation between researchers and among researchers and teachers? Which is the relation between didactics of mathematics and general didactics and what role should each of them and the relation between the two have in teachers' education and in teachers' practice?

The panelists (S. Lerman [United Kingdom], M. Menghini [Italy] M. Pellerey [Italy], E. Wittmann [Germany], E. Silver [USA] and H. G Steiner [Germany], coordinator) stressed her/his point of view on the themes discussed as reported briefly here below.

Lerman mantained that there is no doubt that didactics of mathematics is a developing academic discipline centrally about the teaching and learning of mathematics (the ICME 8 conference is an indication of that) and he underlined that what we choose to teach, how we choose to examine and judge whether we are improving the teaching and learning of mathematics, etc. are part of the academic activity. As we develop, our discipline takes on more of a life of its own, potentially less and less connected to the teaching of mathematics. He also faced the question in which sense didactics of mathematics can be said a scientific discipline, and mantained that perhaps the critical question, -the criterion of demarcation-, is whether theories in and of didactics of mathematics assume that the teaching and learning of mathematics is governed by laws or principles which can be discovered. He suggested that disciplines which do not make this assumption would not be concerned to call themselves scientific. Thus, in fact, the description 'scientific' is itself a resource (enriching), and a framing (limiting) of the field of study.

M. Menghini reconsidered some points of her presentation in subgroup 2. She claimed that most of the studies in the field of rational geometry are not considered research in didactics of mathematics, while most of the studies on intuitive geometry are considered research and she tried to give some reasons for this. She recalled that rational geometry refers to any aspect of the logical and theoretical organization of the knowledge of geometry: the questions tackled concern problems of theoretical framing for the constitution of a "cultural background" by the teachers, general considerations on the way of setting up the curriculum of Geometry, sometimes in order to face traditional problems of learning. On the other hand the studies concerning intuitive geometry are explicitly focused on geometrical reasoning in the classroom activities, and face more clearly the learning processes. She posed the questions: Is this the difference between what is research and what isn't? Can we say that to face problems of forming a cultural background for teachers, or to make proposals for a piece or for the whole curriculum is useful (good, important, etc.) but is not research; whilst facing problems of teaching-learning processes is always research? (Of course, it may be too easy to say that something is apt to form a cultural background, but isn't the detailed description of a classroom experiment easy too?). There is another difference: researches on learning processes in compulsory school often use tools borrowed from cognitive sciences. Are they therefore research? Her answer is no.

As example she referred to her field of research, i.e. the study of the connections between history of mathematics and teaching (in order to understand cultural or sociological choices, to understand learning difficulties, to analyse epistemological obstacles, etc.). This kind of research is carried on also at secondary school level and is generally not connected to cognitive sciences. But she mantained that it is research and that there is other research with this characteristics, for example the research in advanced mathematical thinking - particularly in algebra. She stressed that this kind of research assigns a clear role to the mathematician (or to the expert of didactics of mathematics). Not because the mathematical level of secondary school is higher, but because one has to analyse the birth and the growth of mathematical ideas.

According to M. Pellerey, didactics of mathematics is a science of practice, the practice of mathematics education. He stressed that the study of a practice can be done in several ways: (a) more theoretical - philosophical, epistemological, and historical; (b) more scientific - psychological, sociological, anthropological, and cultural; or, (c) more tecnnical and practice-oriented. However, the set of questions that characterize such a discipline arizes from the practice. That is to say, the problems faced in the discipline are problems found in the field of practice. Consequently, the plausibility and the validity of the findings and conclusions reached have to be attained - in the same way - in the improvement of practice.

He argued that if we adopt a broad definition of science as a body of knowledge characterized by three main properties (relevance of issues, consistency of arguments and publication of results), didactics of mathematics is certainly a science, but it is a science of practice. The questions posed and the solutions suggested are relevant even if the relevance can be found more at educational and pedagogical level. Didactics of mathematis can develop arguments that are coherent to both the concepts adopted and the argumentation developed, its validity derives from the practice in as much as the conclusions reached can direct and facilitate teaching as well as learning processes. Finally, the questions, the evidence, the arguments and the conclusions must be discussed in a public arena. They can either be supported or falsified, and in the process manifest their plausibility.

Steiner claimed that didactics of mathematics is a scientific discipline which has a variety of domains of reference and actions among which he emphatised three:

- the complex phenomenon mathematics in its historical and actual development and its interrelation with other sciences, areas of practice, technology and culture;
- the coplex structure of teaching and schooling whthin our society, especially the school-subject "mathematics" as a societal and social institution;
- the learner's individual cognitive and social development.

With respect to the first domain he said that one of the fundamental tasks of didactics of mathematics as a scientific discipline is the study of mathematical knowledge in its different forms, representations, metaphors, epistemological structures, foundations, and processes, individual and social constitutions and meanings, in its utilizations, relations to various contexts as well as in its historical changes and the dynamics of its development and growth. This study, which has to be performed in an interdisciplinary way involving logic, psychology, linguistic, epistemology, history, sociology of science and sociology of knowledge, is important for all main areas of didactics of mathematics such as:

- the theory and development of the mathematical curriculum;
- the training of *mathematics teachers;*
- the analysis of *how children learn* and comprehend mathematics.

He considered the need of up-to-date textbooks on didactics of mathematics for students and teachers, as also emerged by the previous discussion, and underlined that there are now at a higher scientific level many attempts at least with respect to subdomains of the discipline, for istance: the series of ICMI-studies, and in particular the recent ICMI Study devoted to delineate mathematics education through its research and results [5] , the monographies related to the work of international study groups such as PME, POME and BACOMET and handbooks such as the one edited by Grouws (1992[6])

In his intervention Silver argued that it was equally important to consider the tension between disciplinary theory and educational practice rather than debating the relative merits of disciplinary dependence and ·disciplinary independence for the field of didactics of mathematics. He pointed out that mathematics education research and scholarship is not unique in experiencing an apparent tension between theory and practice that is related to disciplinary connections. Educational research in general is subject to considerable scrutiny of its potential to produce results that can affect educational improvements. The balancing of disciplinary-oriented and practice-oriented perspectives has been addressed in the context of educational psychology by Fenstermacher and Richardson (1994[7]), who argued that a "dichotomy between allegiance to the discipline and allegiance to the activity of education troubles all foundational studies of education", and they discuss status-related pressures "to be disciplinary" within educational psychology, and ask whether educational psychology will deploy its disciplinary tools and techniques in a morally grounded search for better ways to educate, or whether it will continue to perfect its tools and techniques within its disciplinary boundaries and then sally forth to argue how education should conform to these improved concepts, theories and research findings (p. 53). Silver argued that if the words "didactics of mathematics" or "mathematics education" are substituted for "educational psychology" above, then the issue is likewise posed for our field. Further, he pointed out that a resolution of the theory-practice tension will not be easy to achieve. It is unlikely to be acceptable to choose a focus on one to the exclusion of the other, and so a resolution is likely to come only in striking a balance between the demands of academic theory and educational practice, and he suggested the potential utility of working to create a common discourse among the scholarly research community and the educational practice community. (In this regard, he thinks the Italian research community has much to teach the rest of the world.) The reorientation of our scholarship would involve where research problems are found (i.e.,

[5] Kilpatrick, J. and Sierpinska, A., *What is Research in Mathematics   Education and What are its Results?* ICMI Study, in press

[6] Grouws, D. A.: 1992, *Handbook of Research on Mathematics Teaching and Learning,* Mac Millan, New York

[7] Fenstermaster, G. D. and Richardson, V., 1994, Promoting Confusion in Educational Psychology, *Educational Psychologist,* 29 (1), 49-55

looking at the field of educational practice for significant problems and deriving them solely from theoretical interests) and how they are framed (i.e., casting them in the discourse of educational practice as well as in the discourse of an academic discipline). Such an approach would no doubt constrain the kinds of questions that would be investigated, but it would tie work in the field of didactics of mathematics tightly to the concerns of educational practice without divorcing it entirely from the world of academic scholarship.

Wittmann referred to one of his recent papers where he describes an approach to didactics of mathematics as a "design science"[8] . The main idea of this approach consists in the fact that didactics of mathematics is seen as an interdisciplinary research field amidst a couple of related disciplines. There is a flow of methods and results from these related disciplines to didactics. However, didactics is not an appendix at all to the related disciplines. In order to solve its problems didactics of mathematics must be conceived as a specific field that integrates different aspects into a coherent and comprehensive picture of mathematics learning and teaching and brings them to practical use in a constructive way.

Progress in the very core of didactics is not only due to research into learning, teaching and into various factors of the educational system. It is also due, and in his view even mainly, to the design of innovative learning environments or teaching units. He strongly pleads for addressing the scientific task of didactics not simply as "Research" but as "Design and Research". He underlined that when he argues in favour of design it is not his intention to diminish the importance of other components of mathematics education or of research done without reference to design. It is design in the core of mathematics education and the related areas and a lively interaction between the core and the related areas that represent the full picture of didactics. Of course no mathematics educator can cover the whole field. Everyone has his/her own special field of interest. Nevertheless, he/she should feel responsible for the whole field according to the ecological imperative "Act locally, think globally!" Relating design to research and vice versa increases the relevance of didactics and its relatedness to mathematics and mathematics teaching and helps to link the different components of teacher training to one another.

---

8   Wittmann, E. Ch.: 1995 mathematics as a "Design Science", Educational Studies in Mathematics 29, 355-374

NOTE

Proceedings containing the papers presented to the participants will be published in 1997. Information can be obtained from: Nicolina A. MALARA, Dipartimento di Matematica, Università, via Campi 213/B, 41100 Modena, Italy. Fax (39) 59 370513 , E-mail: MALARA@DIPMAT.UNIMO.IT

This report was prepared by Nicolina A. Malara, Hans Georg Steiner, Judith Sowder and Francesco Speranza.

CONNECTIONS BETWEEN RESEARCH AND PRACTICE IN MATHEMATICS EDUCATION

CONEXIONES ENTRE INVESTIGACIÓN Y PRÁCTICA EN EDUCACIÓN MATEMÁTICA

Chief Organizer / *Responsable:* Beatriz D'Ambrosio (BRA).
Advisory Panel / *Asesora:* Luciana Bazzini (ITA),
Morten Blomhoj (DNK), Sandy Dawson (CAN).
Local Organizer / *Coordinador Local:* Lorenzo Blanco (ESP)

In working group 26 the discussion focused on the connections between research and practice in mathematics education. The speakers (Jaworski, Dawson, Gonzalez, Poli-Mignoni) delivered brief and controversial addresses to the audience inviting the participants to consider issues such as the role of teacher research in bridging the gap between research and practice, the need to support teachers involved in teacher research, the impact of teacher research on theory building, the impact of large scale research on teaching practice, the impact of theory on practice, and mechanisms needed to involve teachers more actively in the dialogue about mathematics education.

Discussions about connecting research and practice often result in the community of academic researchers thinking of ways to "translate" theory and make it more comprehensible to teachers. Fortunately, in this working group the discussion focused on creating mechanisms for accepting teacher-research as a form of scholarship and accepting teacher-research as part of the process of generating the knowledge base about teaching and learning. These two issues were controversial among the working group participants and much time was spent on the debate of these particular issues. The following questions are examples of the issues addressed during the small group discussions: What is the nature of collaborations among teachers and researchers? What is the nature of inquiry projects that teachers pursue? What support mechanisms are needed to support teachers who conduct research in their classrooms and with their students? What are the political implications of teacher-research in countries where there is little freedom of choice for curricular materials? To what degree are teachers' voices considered in large scale studies conducted around the world? How do large scale findings impact practice? How does practice impact the generation and revision of theory? How can teachers' voices become a part of the conversation about mathematics teaching and learning within the community of mathematics education? How can we integrate theory and practice in preservice education? What experiences in preservice education facilitate the development of a future teacher-researcher? Can, and is it necessary that, all teachers become teacher-researchers? While there is no easy answer to any of these questions the discussion and the varying perspectives of the participants provided a rich backdrop for the work of working group 26.

While many themes emerged in the discussions of the participants in WG26, the following themes seem to represent areas of emphasis by the various small break out groups. Each will be briefly summarized here in order to provide the reader with a flavor of the complexity and richness of our interactions during the four day meeting in Seville.

Collaboration:

The collaboration between practitioners and researchers was suggested as a critical component of bridging the gap between research and practice. While the problems of practice are considered of utmost importance to practitioners it is not clear that academic researchers share interest in many of the same questions. Discussions raised many of the barriers to practitioners' involvement in research such as the lack of reward structure for the dissemination of the work of teacher-researchers, the fact that writing and publishing are not part of the expectation of the work of teachers, the fact that teachers' lives are complex and research ends up being an addition to their already extremely busy days, the limited number of appropriate journals and other forums for the dissemination of teacher-research, the lack of a shared language between practitioners and academic researchers, the lack of time for reflection, data collection, and data analysis, and many others. Issues of the power relations implicit in a practitioner/researcher collaboration were also addressed.

Theory and its implications for practice

While it is typical for such a discussion to focus on how to make research accessible to teachers, the direction taken in WG26 focused instead on how to include teachers' voices, their knowledge, and their research activity, in the conversation about mathematics education. One of the main questions addressed and still lingering is how to accept teacher research as a form of scholarship and how to accept teacher research as part of the process of generating the knowledge base about teaching and learning. In order to accept teacher research as scholarship we must look at that body of work as a new genre of research with its own criteria of rigor, unique methodology, form, and style. It also requires a reconsideration of the purposes of research. Teacher researchers do not look to academic research for the accumulated knowledge base about teaching and learning. Instead, academic research serves as a source of intriguing interpretations, conflicting information, multiple conceptual frameworks, confirming or discrepant evidence from other settings, and new questions and problems. As teacher problematize their teaching and seek to understand their classrooms, their students, and their practices they build theoretical frameworks, raise new questions and contribute to the knowledge base on teaching, learning, and research. As a community we face the challenge of including teachers' ways of knowing and understanding in our dialogue about teaching, learning and research.

In this sense another question addressed was how can the research dimension of the life of mathematics teachers be encouraged, supported and nurtured. Without support, encouragement, and nurturing it is unlikely that even a few teachers will value the research component of their work, will take the time to reflect systematically on their practice, or will take the time to share and disseminate their work with colleagues within the mathematics education community. Suggestions for supporting the research of teachers ranged from collaboration with researchers, influence of academic researchers towards convincing society and policy makers of the importance of reflection and time for research as part of the work of teachers, and investigating means of supporting teachers in the pursuit of their professional development.

Finally, it was argued that preservice education must help instill in future teachers the understanding of the role of research as a component of the professional lives of teachers.

Large Scale Studies: Implications for practice

The issues raised in these discussions ranged from the impact of the voices of teachers in large scale studies to the impact of the results of large scale studies on reform and change in education. Discussions centered around how little teachers generally participate in large scale studies, how little impact their voices have and yet, how much impact the results of these studies can have among decision makers and policy makers. There was concern over the extent to which and the forms through which results from these large scale studies have impacted reform and change in the various countries represented in WG26.

In summary, it was clear that the various countries represented in our WG had different experiences with the integration of teachers and the work of teachers into their mathematics education research community. There was considerable variation in forms of collaboration between academic researchers and teachers, in availability of journals accepting the work of teachers for publication, in research conferences involving the presentation of teacher research, and in involving pre-service teachers in research experiences. There were also many different models presented of in-service experiences that engaged practicing teachers in research activity. Finally, there were different approaches to involving teachers and their expertise in curriculum development projects.

Although the many experiences of participants from different countries reveal differences in approaches there were many similarities in the goals and purposes of the activities described. In most cases there was understanding that the knowledge base of teachers is grounded in the articulation of theoretical frameworks, personal histories, and reflection on practice. Teachers' research on teaching and learning provides an insider's perspective on the complexities of the lives of teachers and their students and greatly contributes to the knowledge base of mathematics teaching and learning. It was clear that internationally there is a commitment, although still meager, to include teachers in the community of research in mathematics education, not merely as "collaborators" but as active participants in the process of generating knowledge and understanding about mathematics teaching and learning.

Topic Group 1 / *Grupo Temático 1*

PRIMARY SCHOOL MATHEMATICS

MATEMÁTICAS EN LA ENSEÑANZA PRIMARIA

Chief Organizer / *Responsable:* Régine Douady (FRA)
Local Organizer / *Coordinador Local*: Francisco T.Sánchez-Cobo (ESP)

The first session (divided in 2 parallel sections) was devoted rather to young pupils. The following themes have been discussed :
- first number learning : Bert van Oers from Holland
- the role of problems in the search for meaning of mathematical concepts and strategies of resolution (F.Jaquet from Neuchâtel/Switzerland and L.Grugnietti from Parma/ Italy)
- the notion of unit and the part/whole ratio in measuring magnitudes (work at Universidad del Valle -Cali, Colombie animated by G.Castrillon, cf.also work in Australia described below)
- crucial role of writing in the learning of mathematical reasonning : technical features of mathematics vs narrative features of litterary writing (Colombie).

The second session (2 parallel sections) was concerned with pupils age 9-11 .

One section discussed presentations related to children's understanding of non-integer numbers.

The other was devoted to geometry. Two important topics from mathematical viewpoint, raise difficulties, in the choices of the teacher as well as for conceptualization on the pupil's side:
- the notion of angles : a work of M. Mitchelmore, Sydney, Australia
- geometry in space : geometrical construction of surfaces and solids presented by J.M.Favrat from Montpellier/France.

Let us give a more detailed description of some of the presentations.

First session

Tom Cooper reported a longitudinal study carried out with his colleague Anne Heirdsfield exploring young children's strategies in both algorithmic exercises and word problems. Previous studies have suggested that children use mental procedures in the context of real world problems, and their procedures often do not resemble school-taught algorithms. However, algorithmic presentation of exercises tends to elicit school-taught strategies. The children in this study were interviewed six times across their second and third year of schooling. The children's strategies were identified and compared within each interview and across all interviews. As expected, a greater variety of strategies was used for word problems than for algorithmic exercises. However, these students attempted more word problems than algorithmic exercises, and were more successful on word problems. The one exception to this was three-digit regrouping exercises, which the children attempted more frequently and more successfully in algorithmic form than in word problem form. In general, non-traditional strategies were dominant in the first three interviews, but by the fifth interview, the most popular strategy was a right-to-left calculation as taught in school, especially when problems were presented as algorithmic exercises. The presenter discussed how an understanding of children's spontaneous strategies may be useful in developing more effective mathematics curricula.

Second session

Annette Baturo reported a study carried out by Baturo and Cooper in Australia. The study investigated the knowledge relating to fractions of children about 11 years old in their sixth year of schooling. The focus was on the understanding students had with respect to the part/whole notion of fractions that underlies understanding of decimals, specifically with respect to relations between tenths and hundredths. The study found that students had incomplete, fragmented, or non-existent structural knowledge of tenths and hundredths. Most students relied on syntactic cues to solve problems involving tenths and hundredths. Implications are that instruction should not be limited to prototypes, and that the basic structures of decimals and their genesis in the notion of part/whole relations should be revisited.

Catherine Houdement, from France, reported a complementary teaching study that explored geometric tasks leading to understanding of non-integer numbers. This study was carried out with students 9 to 11 years old in French elementary schools. French students at this level become familiar with non-integer numbers as tools rather than as mathematical objects included in sets of numbers. They are familiar with whole-number operations, and know a little geometry, particularly properties of objects through exploratory activities. Decimal numbers seem to be quite abstract for students, who make many well-documented errors in decimal notation. In this study, fractions were introduced prior to decimals through activities based on the length of line segments and the area of portions of a rectangle.

The first activity had students draw a segment then write instructions to other students to draw a segment the same length. Use of a marked ruler was not permitted; instead, a strip of paper served as the unit of measure. Generally, students had to devise numbers to represent "little bits" of their segment. With the help of the teacher, they folded the unit of measure into halves, fourths, and eighths, and wrote numbers to represent lengths greater than one unit. Their numbers not only represented lengths but also came to represent parts, such as 1/2 being one of two portions of a unit; 1/4 being one of four portions of a unit, and also one of two portions of 1/2.

The second activity used the fact that different shapes can have the same area. Each group of students used whole sheets of paper and smaller pieces of paper to assemble into the same sheet. Each small piece was a fraction 1/n of the whole sheet, but could be of different shapes. The fraction was not given. The students calculated the area of each piece, using the whole sheet as the unit.

In the activity using segments, students came to see 1/n as one of n parts, the partition aspect of fractions. In the area activity, 1/n was seen a quantity which, multiplied n times, gives one, the measurement aspect of fractions. These activities can be followed by others, such as cutting into four pieces a rectangle whose sides are decimal numbers like 1.25 dm. Thus, geometry offers a useful context for making sense of numbers other than integers.

SECONDARY SCHOOL MATHEMATICS.

MATEMÁTICAS EN LA ENSEÑANZA SECUNDARIA

Chief Organizer / *Responsable:* Glenda Lappan (USA)
Local Organizer / *Coordinador Local*: Juan Gallardo (ESP)

This group will focus on research and development issues in the areas of curriculum, instruction, assessment and the alignment of these aspects of secondary mathematics education. The presentations and discussions will focus on work that helps illuminate questions such as the following: What is the interaction between new curricula, new instructional strategies, new assessment strategies and the professional development of teachers? What are the "big" ideas in mathematics at the secondary level and what are compelling contexts that give students access to these ideas? What are the most important research questions that need to be answered to guide change in curriculum teaching, and learning over the next decade? What are the issues of articulation between secondary school and primary school? Between secondary school and o.k. higher education? Between secondary school and the world of work?

UNIVERSITY MATHEMATICS

MATEMÁTICAS EN LA ENSEÑANZA UNIVERSITARIA

Chief Organizer / *Responsable*: Joel Hillel (CAN)
Local Organizer / *Coordinador Local:* José Carmona Alvarez (ESP)

Topic Group 3: 'University Mathematics' included the following themes:

1. Innovative delivery of mathematics, including the use of technology, collaborative learning, and alternative lecture styles.

2. Cognitive research in undergraduate mathematics and its implication for teaching and learning.

3. Curriculum innovations such as the redesigning of traditional courses, the introduction of new courses, and the restructuring of (a substantial part of) the curriculum.

4. A changing role for mathematics department, including means for helping to smoothen the transition from high-school to university, working with under prepared students, and working with prospective mathematics teachers.

The above themes are certainly not independent and most presentations belonged to several themes. Below we give a brief summary of the papers and issues that were discussed in the Topic Group.

Theme 1: Innovative delivery

Presenters described their efforts to change the traditional "chalk and talk" mode of presenting mathematics. I. Cnop (Belgium) reported on small group teaching method in Abstract Algebra where most of the notes containing the theorems and classical examples are produced by the students themselves. He concluded that students show better assimilation and retention of concepts. In a similar manner, J. Frant (Brazil) described an elementary Linear Algebra course in which weekly classes are split between lectures and students' log-book writing related to some theorem or a problem. This format made students' misconceptions more apparent and allowed the instructor to intervene. P. Ferrari (Italy) reported on an Abstract Algebra course for Computer Science students which is much more problem-based than the traditional course and with particular emphasis on different representations of a given concept. As a result of these changes, students' problem-solving ability showed an improvement. R. Burn (UK), exemplified his ideas relating to understanding undergraduate mathematics with special cases, by showing "generic" examples which can serve as entry points into a course in Abstract Algebra.

It was somehow surprising that there was not an emphatic endorsement for the use of computers in any of the presentations of the Topic Group (though computer use was alluded to). But a simple explanation might be that the Working Group on Technology was the preferred venue for discussing technological innovations.

Theme 2: Cognitive reserach

Research related to learning at the undergraduate level was presented by several speakers (We should add that M. Artigue gave one of the invited lectures on research into students' learning of elementary analysis.) G. Ervynck (Belgium) discussed some prevailing concept images of calculus students about meaning and use of the derivative based on a problem concerning the maximum slope of the graph. In the same vein, an analysis of metacognitive behaviour of students solving a problem on the volume of a solid of revolution was made by S. Hegedus (UK), using problem-solving categories elaborated by Schoenfeld.   G. Harel (USA) presented his work on students' cognition schemes related to mathematical proofs. He gave a theoretical perspective based on an epistemological and historical analysis of proof and suggested an instructional approach for helping students refine their own conceptions of justification in mathematics. Harel's work fitted the paradigm for research and development in undergraduate mathematics education, proposed by D. Mathews (US). Mathews described such research as constituting of a theoretical component including an epistemological analysis and a specific learning theory which informs the design of instruction. This is followed by data collection which can trigger a new iteration of the process.

Theme 3: Curricular changes

Changes to the basic calculus and linear algebra courses were reported by B. Pence (USA) and D. Carlson/G. Harel (US). Pence spoke on calculus courses at San Jose State University and the evaluation of students' performance on courses based on learning through exploration and using the Harvard Calculus text, and those of a more traditional calculus courses. Harel summarized recent recommendations about introductory linear algebra. These include increased attention to applicability, the use of computing, and a more "concrete" approach, focusing on n-space and matrices.

P. Kahn (UK) gave a more general survey of recent changes to the honours undergraduate mathematics degree. Based on a questionnaire of 50 departments at the UK and a more detailed analysis of some representative departments, Kahn was able to discern changes which included: reduction of content; introduction of new courses (e.g. Geometry, Problem Solving, Modelling), and changes in perspectives to existing courses (e.g. problem-based lectures, use of computers, project work, linkage to other discipline).

G. Smith (Australia) reported on alternate assessment techniques. Pointing out the lack of consensus among mathematician of what constitutes a "good" answer to a non-traditional question, he described experimentation with several alternative methods, though the issue remains a bit elusive.

Theme 4: Changing clientele and transition courses

The problem of the mathematical preparation of incoming students, their different social-cultural background, age, and expectations is evidently a world-wide phenomenon. The traditional image of a mathematics student as well-prepared, selected, and highly-motivated simply doesn't fit present-day realities. Consequently, mathematics departments find themselves with a new set of challenges.

A way of dealing with insufficient mathematical skills of high-school leavers was discussed by F. Gransard (Belgium) in terms of multimedial computer managed instructional-system which has been in place for 15 years. These bridging courses have been evaluated using pre- and post-testing and have been found to be very effective. Particular concern for students' lack of mathematical discourse skills was brought up by L. Wood (Australia) where a program to develop such skills was instituted. The program borrows from developments in language teaching and attempts to make the language needs of a mathematician more explicit. The same issue of developing appropriate mathematical language was discussed by J. Hillel (Canada). A course of mathematical thinking and proofs, given to all mathematical Majors, emphasizes the different modes of communicating mathematics, where proofs are considered as a particular and privileged mode. K. Austin (UK) also was concerned with developing proof skills of entering students. Rather than have a specific course on proofs, he exemplified an approach which begins at the "shallow end" (e.g.

solving a small finite problem by cases) and then movies to the "deeper end" by giving a situation where testing all possibilities becomes impractical. T. Gardiner (UK) reported that mathematical proofs are missing from pre-university curriculum and that successive reforms didn't seem to increase the population of mathematically-oriented students.

M. Price (UK), reported on a pilot study in which the transition from high school to university of cohort group of 60 students is monitored. The foci of the investigation included individual differences such as educational experiences, attitudes and aspirations; the changing conditions of learning; effective strategies for smoothening the transition.

A more specific clientele of adult learners was considered by M. McGowen (US) who reported on a non-traditional algebra curriculum designed for such students. Centred on the notion of function, the curriculum emphasizes multiple representations and integrates technology and collaborative work. H. Forgasz (Australia) examined the factors influencing mature students' decision to undertake mathematics. Finding that their motivational level was generally high, she argued for offering such students greater opportunity to pursue mathematics.

J. Thomas (Australia) looked at bilingual students in university mathematics, whose first language is not English. She expressed the belief that for such students, their difficulties in mathematics were language-related rather than conceptual.

Summary:

In summary, we could say that the speakers in the Topic Group described various ways in which they, individually, or their departments have tried to undo the shackles of Bourbaki through changes in emphasis, content, course offerings, styles of teaching, and assessment. It was also evident that the problem of under-prepared entering students is quite widespread and that universities are trying to deal with this through various "transition courses". One caveat about generalizing about trends in university mathematics based on the contributions to the Topic Group - most of us who come to ICME are likely not typical members of mathematics departments and it is not always obvious that our concerns are shared by all our colleagues.

I would like to acknowledge the help of I. Cnop, F. Gransard and M. Sward whose notes helped me put this report together.

DISTANCE LEARNING OF MATHEMATICS

MATEMÁTICAS EN LA ENSEÑANZA A DISTANCIA

Chief Organizer / *Responsable:* Haruo Murakami (JPN)
Local Organizer / *Coordinador Local:* José M. Gairín (ESP)

Topic Group 4 on Distance Education met twice under the chairmanship of Professor Haruo Murakami of Konan University, Japan. Introducing the first session, Professor Murakami gave a beautifully succinct description of the situation we find ourselves in.

"Once upon a time a few students would sit at the feet of a wise man, who would impart his wisdom to them in conversation. The teacher and students enjoyed a mutual respect, and knowledge was constructed as a result of their dialogue. Nowadays a university might have classes of 250, or even 500 students, and many of these do not listen to what their teacher is saying. Their minds are elsewhere during lectures, and for them the distance between teacher and student is virtually infinite."

However, over the past two decades the theories and practices associated with distance education have continually changed. At the present moment, with the influence of high technology profoundly affecting both theory and practice, it is difficult to recognise whether it is evolution that has given way to revolution.

Nowadays, no matter what the physical separation between the two parties, if the learner is willing, and can study and communicate electronically -by email, TV, World Wide Web, etc - then the distance between student and teacher is once again effectively zero.

We are living through an information revolution; using modern technology our distance education system will become ever more sophisticated; in fact this is true of education as a whole. The style of education must change in line with these new opportunities, and if these are grasped then the future offers some very exciting prospects."

The first session, and the first part of the second, were devoted to a number of short contributions from participants. The sheer variety of these served to underscore Professor Murakami's remarks.

Kiyoshi Yokochi (Beijin Normal University, China) and Izumi Nishitani (Gunma University, Japan) described the CCV (Computer,Communication and Visual) educational system.. The aim is to develop childrens' creativity and ability in mathematics by using corporate lessons between distant schools. The CCV educational system uses the Internet, multi-media, a TV conferencing system and an 80 inch large projector. Using the system children have lessons which involve talking and looking at other school children through the large screen, all in real time. The project started in October 1995 in collaboration with the Mitsubishi Electric Company. The CCV project team consists of university professors, school teachers and engineers. The CCV project has three steps; the term of each step is 6 months. The first is the preparation of equipment, the content of lessons and testing distance lessons between the elementary school attached to Yamanashi University and the Mitsubishi Land Mark Tower in Yokohama. The second step is to conduct lessons between two distant elementary schools attached to Yamagata University and Yamanashi University (this is currently in progress). Finally the scheme will be extended across national frontiers to have lessons involving schools from two countries.

Judy Ekins (Open University, UK) described the new entry level course which appears to have had an extremely successful start. Noting that the previous OU Mathematics Foundation course was designed for people whose main interest was Mathematics (and who already posessed good algebraic skills), she explained that the content of Mathematics taught in UK schools has changed radically over the last ten years or so. Since the OU is open to all adults, it must become more flexible in its entry assumptions. The new course (MU120 Open Mathematics) aims to offer differententry points to people with different mathematical backgrounds and aspirations. It is a pre-calculus course designed for those who do not have algebraic skills and who lack confidence in Mathematics. It is aimed at those who may not go any further with mathematics as well as those who may wish to do so. The course incorporates the "core skills" of communication and improving thier own learning and performance, in order to provide a more effective preparation for students for distance learning and for using their Mathematics. All mathematical topics are taught in a context from adult life: prices, earnings, maps, music, rainbows, to name but a few. Algebraic and graphical skills are introduced gradually. Much teaching is done via a graphics calculator, which has proved popular with students, half of whom are women. The teaching strategy, assessment and the reactions of students and tutors were briefly described.

David Crowe (Open University, UK) described a six month case study of theuse of electronic conferencing, in conjunction with the algebra pakage Mathcad, to support distance mathematics students. Mathcad enables equations, pictures, graphs and text to be mixed freely on the pages of a document. The resulting file can easily be attached to a message, and the conferencing system FirstClass allows this to be sent either to an individual or to a subgroup. The new OU mathematics foundation course will not have a residential summer school, and a number of students will threfore never meet their tutor or fellow students (either because they are gegraphically remote, or because they suffer from limited mobility). In 1995, twenty four adult students (many of them new to mathematics and to the use of computers) learned to use this technology using distancematerials. They then worked through several chapters of the new OU mathematics foundation course and submitted two assignments electronically.

They were supported throughout (entirely electronically) by a group of tutors. The final phase of the project involved a collaborative modellingexercise in which small groups of students were invited to use the mathematical skills they had learned to produce a simple model of the epidemiology of HIV. In order to do this they accessed data from the World Wide Web and then jointly formulated and improved their mathematical model,using electronic communication to do so. It was pointed out that much of this technology is cheap (a 386 PC + modem is really all that is needed) and so may be of interest to a wider audience in other parts of the world.

Alistair Carr (Monash University, Australia) spoke on supporting learning by distance education. He pointed out that tertiary students of 'service' mathematics by distance education are often working full-time, and come to these subjects with high motivation, wide experience, but limited time. They are adaptable and efficient. While video- and audio-tapes, residential schools, and on-line discussion groups can enhance learning, provision of printed materials is central to effective encouragement of learning. Textbooks can be rich supplements. For a student with limited time, precision and clarity of presentation, illuminating examples, and quick correction of misconceptions, are important. Multimedia software offers several advantages, and a CD-ROM can be 'encyclopaedic'. However, there is a risk of overloading students with bulky and diffuse materials, which by sheer volume or diversity can impede effective learning and development of skills. In institutions which offer subjects simultaneously on-campus and by distance education, the on-campus students reap many benefits from the development of materials for distance education.

Bert Zwaneveld (Open University, the Netherlands) explained the use of Knowledge Graphs in mathematics education. The aim of his research is to develop, test and improve a cognitive tool by which students can be supported in structuring their mathematical knowledge. In mathematics education, in school or in courses to support other disciplines, too little attention is paid to the theory. As a result students do not have optimal advantage, for instance in solving mathematical problems. In a knowledge graph a student can visualize the concepts of some substantial part of a maths course and the relations between these concepts. He has also constructed a model that serves as a prestructured framework. In this model the following aspects are distinguished: a central concept, properties of it, special cases of it, operations on it, and fields of application. He has experimented with small numbers of students who were asked to construct knowledge graphs.

Mark Saul (US) described the work of the Gelfand school. The noted Russian mathematician I.M. Gelfand, while he lived in Moscow, ran a very successful distance learning program for high school students. In its 30 years of existence, it put 70,000 students from the most remote areas of the former Soviet Union in touch with mathematicians and graduate students. The curricular materials Gelfand developed from this school are a valuable contribution to the literature, and a number of well-known mathematicians got their first inspiration from this program. For the past several years, Mark has been working with I.M. Gelfand to adapt his program and materials to American audiences, notably in urban communities. He described the success of the program and the nature of the adaptations which they have had to make for the new audience.

Ted Graham (University of Plymouth, UK) has been working with a colleague in Stockholm to develop and test revision questions for a course in Applied Mathematics. The aim of this work is to provide students with easy access to a bank of problems and solutions that are developed in stages. He feels that the Internet offers a good way to make this material available to students for a number of reasons. In particular that the material can easily be accessed, modified or expanded in the light of student feedback, and that through e-mail links the students can contact their tutors. He has developed a number of questions that are now in use, and an evaluation of the use of the Internet in this way will soon be carried out.

Masahiko Saito (University of the Air, Japan) described the activities of the University of the Air of Japan, which broadcasts about 300 courses by radio and television, including 16 courses in mathematics. About

50,000 people are studying at the University; mathematics courses include the basics such as Calculus, Linear Algebra, Probability Theory, History of Mathematics, and television is particularly useful for topics such as Chaos and Fractals. In calculus, animated graphs on television have facilitated students' understanding of the notion of derivative. One drawback however is that the professor and students do not have face-to-face communication, and this detracts to a certain degree from the efficiency of education.

Hector Medellin (Mexico, currently visiting University of Prague) gave a short address entitled Mathematics into the Internet, Internet into the Mathematics. He pointed out that the availability of new technology must be supplemented by training in its use. There is a future danger of a cultural divide between those who use information technology and those who do not. He urged that as many practising mathematicians as possible freely provide information about themselves and their work for others to peruse.

Ken Clements (The University of Newcastle, Australia) gave a talk entitled "Myths, rhetoric and virtual reality: distance education and the development of links within the international mathematics education community". He proposed that greater cultural awareness and sensitivities are needed if the promises of distance education are to become more than myths and rhetoric. Only when educators learn to appreciate the cultures of others will they value apparently quite different educational practices and theories, and thereby identify what might be appropriate for their ownprograms. In this sense, distance education is the key for opening the door to a new, culturally sensitive, reflective community of international mathematics education scholars and practitioners. However, at present many are merely using distance education and flexible learner modalities to gain a larger share of the international education market. The talk concluded with eight propositions directed at those responsible for developing and implementing mathematics distance education programs.

After each presentation, we had brief but fruitful question, answer and discussion sessions.

One feature of TG4 was that in addition to short presentations, an experiment was made by Professor Murakami and his group. The aim of this experiment was to show how distance education can be enhanced by using computers with mathematical software packages connected to the internet. Immediately prior to the start of ICME, three problems were sent by Internet from Seville to students in several sites around the world. More than 50 answers were received, and in the second session these werediscussed. For brevity we quote here just two of the problems and a few of the many responses to them.

[Problem 2]
(i) You must know that the expression $x^2 + n$ ($n = 1, 2, 3, \ldots$) cannot be factorized into two expressions of the first order unless you use expressions with complex coefficients. Can you prove it?
(ii) What about the story for $x^4 + n$?

Use Mathematica to compute Factor[$x^4 + 1$], Factor[$x^4 + 2$], Factor[$x^4+ 3$] and Factor[$x^4 + 4$]. You will find a surprising result. The expression $x^4 + 4$ can be factorized into two factors with integer coefficients. Is "4" an exceptional number having this property? Or are there many other numbers having this property? Write a suitable command for factorizing the expressions $x^4 + n$ for various n, and find out those n,if there are any, for which the expression can be factorized. (Remember that you are using a computer. Therefore, you can try cases for which n starts from 1 to 3000 or even to 6000 very easily.) If you find values of n, try to represent them in a general form. Furthermore, try to explain why they can be factorized for those specific values of n.

Answer (from a site in Singapore)
n = 4, 64, 324, 1024, 2500, 5184, 9604, 16384, ... or n = 2^2, 8^2, 18^2,32^2, 50^2, 72^2, (Explanation: not given)

(From a site in Japan)
We tried. The answer is
n=4   ($2 - 2x + x^2$)($2 + 2x + x^2$)
n=64   ($8 - 4x + x^2$)($8 + 4x + x^2$)
n=324   ($18 - 6x + x^2$)($18 + 6x + x^2$)
n=1024 ($32 - 8x + x^2$)($32 + 8x + x^2$) n=2500 ($50 - 10x + x^2$)($50 +10x + x^2$) n=5184 ($72 - 12x + x^2$)($72 + 12x + x^2$) ...
therefore we find that n=4 * m^4 (m=integer).

Also, we found that the last digits of the sequence of above numbers n = 4, 64, 324, 1024, 2500, 5184, 9604, 16384, 26244, 40000, ... , for which $x^4 + n$ can be factorized, are 4, 4, 4, 4, 0, 4, 4, 4, 4, 0, 4, 4,4, 4, 0, 4, ...

[Comment: It seems that they found a special case of Euler's theorem for the prime number 5].

[Problem 3]
Factorize the expressions $x^n - 1$ for $n = 1, 2, 3, \ldots$ by using Mathematica, and observe the result.

Let us find any relation between n and factorization of x^n - 1. First, you will find that (x - 1) is a factor of x^n - 1 . Can you explain why? If you observe the result carefully, (x + 1) is also a factor of x^n - 1 if and only if n is an even number. Again, can you explain why?

Try to find other facts which seem to be true for the factorization of x^n- 1. You do not need to prove the facts, but if you could, it would be excellent.

There may be patterns which first seem to be true but actually are false. Again, remember that you are using a computer. It will be easy for you to check your conjectures by testing large values of n (up to, say, n = 500).

Answer (from a site in Australia)
    (i) x^n -1 has the same number of factors as the number of factors of n
    (ii) x^(p-1) + x^(p-2) + x^(p-3) + ... + x^2 + x^1 + x^0 is a factor of (x^n - 1) when p is n's largest prime factor.
    (iii) if n divides m then (x^n - 1)'s factors are a subset of (x^m - 1)'s factors.

(From a site in Singapore)
    (i)   1 is a root for x^n - 1.
    (ii) When n is even, then n = 2m, ((-1)^2)^m = 1, so -1 is a root.
    (iii) conjecture: if n > 2 and n is a prime, then there is no other factor except (x -1).

(From a site in Japan)
    It seems that if n is a prime number, then x^n - 1 = (-1 + x)(1 + x + x^2 + ... + x^(n-1)).

If n is not a prime, and if m is a factor of n, factor of x^n - 1 contains all the factors of x^m - 1. For example, we know that the factors of 12 are 2,3,4 and 6. For n=2, 3, 4 and 6, we have x ^2 - 1 = (-1 + x)(1 + x), x^3 - 1 = (-1 + x)(1 + x + x^2), x^4 - 1 = (-1 + x)(1 + x)(1 + x^2) and x^6 - 1 = (-1 + x)(1 + x)(1 - x + x^2)(1 + x + x^2). And for n=12 we see that x^12- 1 = (-1 + x)(1 + x)(1 + x^2)(1 - x + x^2)(1 + x + x^2)(1 - x^2 + x^4). The last factor is the only new factor appeared for n =12. Also, one feature we found is that the coefficients seemed to be either +1 or -1.

But we later found a striking fact. Namely, for n=105, we have a shocking result. For there are terms whose coefficient is 2 or -2. Same thing happens to n=165. Actually, we have more 2's for n=165. It may have something to do with the fact that 105=3*5*7 and 165=3*5*11, but we do not know what it is. We still do not know if other numbers than 1 or 2 appear for coefficients.

[Comment: More numbers appear as coefficients for larger n.]

The business of TG4 concluded with a lively discussion chaired by Professor Nerida Ellerton, Edith Cowan University, Australia. Four themes were identified for the discussion:

1. A sharing and a celbration of personal experiences in distance teaching of mathematics as described by presenters;
2. The structure of current distance courses in mathematics;
3. The content of these courses;
4. Challenges to the educational and philosophical assumptions which underly the previous three themes.

The question of getting help when 'stuck' on a particular mathematical point was raised, and it was noted that such help must be available quickly if it is to be of use to the student. Another view was that it is more important to teach students a strategy for self-help. Students have different ways and patterns of learning, and a reflective strategy is both useful and important.

The problem of creating networks of learners at a distance was considered, one solution being the bulletin board where problems of any nature may be posted. It was noted that the 'virtual campus' often generates more discussion between students than between student and teacher. Students find it much easier to participate in such a venture if they have met 'face-to-face' beforehand. Though this is certainly desirable, it is probably unattainable when the distances involved are large. Meeting 'electronically' via the World Wide Web was suggested as an alternative way of breaking the ice. The fact that a student has chosen to enroll for a distance course may suggest that such forms of contact may actually be more appropriate.

Use of the various forms of media was mentioned, and it was agreed that text, audio/visual, computers and electronic communications all have their strengths and weaknesses. Work should continue to isolate the advantages and disadvantages of each form.

Some members of the group remarked that lack of access to electronic mail can disadvantage a student, but that this will regrettably remain a possibility for some students for the foreseeable future. This is an important resource issue which must be addressed. Bearing in mind the international nature of future distance education it is also important to take account of the cultural background of the student.

Finally it was noted that use of new technology can obscure important educational issues. There is a danger that concentrating on the media may distract from consideration of course content. Thus using the latest technology one might teach the mathematics of long ago, which would be inappropriate. There was a measure of agreement that all universities will evolve to make some use of distance teaching, and that this process mayhelp to clarify the situation.

EDUCATION FOR MATHEMATICS IN THE WORKPLACE

LA ENSEÑANZA DE LAS MATEMÁTICAS PARA EL TRABAJO

Chief Organizer / *Responsable:* Annie Bessot (FRA)
Local Organizer / *Coordinadora Local:* M. Dolores Eraso (ESP)

The work was organised around the following questions : what is the vocational use of mathematics ? how does mathematical knowledge integrate into vocational situations ? what are the appropriate research methods for the exploration of the vocational use of mathematics ?

Six presentations (10 minutes) per session were grouped by topic so that a 30-minute debate at the end of each session could take place.

The abstracts of these presentations and the main points raised are presented below.

First session

Doing research in the workplace [J.Hogan and W.Morony, Australia]

The Australian Association for Mathematics Teachers is co-ordinating a project to enable us to develop a better understanding of how people use mathematical ideas and techniques for practical purposes.

One part of our project has involved a group of teachers going into a variety of work places around the country and documenting examples of people going about their work.

We set out a methodology that would be useful to others who might want to do some similar research where there were constraints of time and money. We also wanted to develop a methodology which would involve members of mathematics teacher associations around the country.

We described the structure of the research methods and discussed their appropriateness for the exploration of the conventional use of mathematics ; we pointed to the usefulness of the results and looked at the benefits for the teachers who were involved.

Towards a mathematical orientation at work [C.Hoyles, UK]

The mathematisation of intellectual and social life has reached a point where failure to appreciate at least elements of mathematical structures is potentially threatening both for the individual, and for the efficiency of a range of work practices. There is a broadening range of settings, which we will call mathematisable situations where there is 'pay-off' for taking a mathematical perspective, in terms of personal or professional empowerment.

We know that most adults make sense of these situations in ways which differ quite radically from those of the mathematician - such everyday orientations (EOs) tend to be characterised by pragmatic, qualitative descriptions, are geared to solving particular problems, and are framed by the professional practice of the individual. In contrast, a mathematical orientation (MO) tends to search for consistency and generalisation.

In this presentation I described our research which seeks to study EOs in a limited number of scenarios and a small range of practices at work and to construct and analyse appropriate computational activities which will serve simultaneously as a context in which to study individual thinking more closely, and as a means by which individuals might be drawn towards a mathematical approach.

Rôle of mathematical knowledge in vocational training for the building industry [M.Eberhard, France]

In vocational training institutes in France, mathematics teachers wonder about the rôle of mathematical knowledge : where does it fit in at the present time and where could it possibly fit in the future ? When dealing with training for building industry trades that involve skilled workers and foremen, these questions could be formulated in terms of relevance and usefulness : what could be the nature and place of mathematical skills involved on construction sites ? What   relationships exist between mathematical knowledge that is taught and professional aims ?

A study of professional techniques representative of some occupations related to the building trades and linked to a class of tasks which we called "setting-up" was presented. A methodology allowing for making visible mathematical objects present in professional practice was described. It is assumed that this visibility is a requirement for their teachability .

Boundary-Crossing: another look at the possibilities for transfer of learning in mathematics [J.Evans, UK]

Results from a recent study of social science students (generally averse to mathematics) show that these adults do not simply "transfer" their School (or College) Maths learning to solve everyday maths problems in some straightforward way. Rather, they treat the two types of problems as arising in specifically different contexts. Drawing on earlier work (especially Walkerdine, 1988), I outline an alternative position on transfer, using a more promising basis for understanding how people "cross boundaries" between distinct activities - namely, attention to chains of signifiers bearing affective charges. We can be hopeful about the potential for boundary-crossing, if not for learning- transfer as traditionally conceived.

Ethnography and the situatedness of workplace mathematics [R.Zevengergen, Australia]

In this presentation I explored the rationale for using ethnography as a tool to investigate the situatedness of workplace numeracy. A number of investigations of workplace environments provided the basis for this session. The study investigated the numeracy employed by workers across a range of workplace environments. Ethnography provided insights otherwise not accessible through other data collection means. To this end, ethnography provides researchers with valuable insights into workplace numeracies.

Standards for Technical Mathematics [M.Mays and W.Garner, USA]

Students in technical programs should be prepared to function in an ever-changing workplace.Several mathematics organizations in the United States have collaborated on the development of standards for technical mathematics at the introductory post-secondary level. Their conclusions, however, are appropriate for students at the secondary level. While the mathematical preparation of technical students should focus on applications, this preparation should be broad and rigorous enough to provide students with the knowledge and skills necessary for career flexibility.

Discussion

The first discussion concerned the appropriate research methods for the exploration of the vocational use of mathematics. How might we conduct research about mathematics in the work place ? In the presentations many researchers used interviews to obtain data. It seems for some participants that interviews are necessary but not sufficient. Interviews (or other means of data collection) must be located in a theoretical framework for the subsequent interpretation to be useful.

Another point is the need for a great deal of research to build up our knowledge in this area ; for example, we do not know much about transmission of skills, such as the relationship between in-service training and knowledge used at work.

Second session

Mathematics in pre-vocational courses [G.Wake and J.Williams, UK]

The Mechanics in Action Project is developing new courses of mathematics for vocational students in technical subjects such as Engineering, Science, Construction and Manufacturing. The courses are constructed on a new approach to mathematics in which mathematical skills and concepts are organised around clearly useful competencies ("general mathematical competencies") which address a collection of practical problems from the vocational field. Three such units of work have been developed in collaboration with the Nuffield Science in Practice Project and are being trialled by students taking a vocational Science course; we reported on the evaluation of this approach.

An important element in this curriculum design will be the use of practical case studies from students' vocational units of study, and from the relevant world of work which they are preparing for. We have begun to address this through the production of workplace case studies in which we identify the mathematical understanding and skills being used by workers in practice (for example, the work of a sheet-metal worker and a warden of a country reserve).

Searching for Authentic Work-Based Examples [S.L.Forman and L.A. Steen, USA]

What kinds of mathematical tasks truly represent the world of work?

Many so-called "applications" of mathematics are either artificial or academic - useful perhaps for further study, but rarely in the work place. The Mathematical Sciences Education Board (MSEB) at the U.S. National Academy of Sciences is conducting a search for authentic examples of how mathematics is used in the workplace in order to illustrate the kinds of mathematical tasks that students should be able to perform when they leave secondary school. Rationale and selected examples from the MSEB project was presented as stimulus for discussion.

Slow learners, mathematics and professional life [P. van de Zwaart, Netherlands]

The project investigated what mathematical knowledge and skills will be used on the future shopfloor of slow learners in secondary education. This attention for future professional life has implications for textbook development, methodological approaches, teacher training, the official curricula and the examination syllabi. An important part of the development strategy was the design and try-out of teaching materials and materials for internal examinations, based on investigations in the occupational practice and on interviews on the job with professionals. Together with the recently changed curriculum, these experiences were the basis of all other activities of the project.

Teaching mathematics to shop assistant apprentices; choosing appropriate content and didactical situations [C.Hahn, France]

Co-operative education gives the opportunity to link mathematical contents and professional practices. Does it help students to improve their understanding of mathematical concepts ? We studied this question in the case of BEP (a 2-year national curriculum for 16 year olds) for shop assistant apprentices (they spend alternatively one week at school and one week in a jewellery shop).

The first part of this study seeks answers to the following questions : what are the mathematical concepts in use in the shop ? how are they taught at school ? what are the students' skills ? is there a difference between apprentices and non-apprentices ?

In the second part of the study, we try to build didactical situations that will help apprentices to transfer their knowledge. We evaluated the impact of three different situations : word problems in a jewellery shop context, a real situation and a "personalised" situation in which the mathematics course was built on the experience of each apprentice within the framework of a multidisciplinary project.

Mathematical knowledge as vocational qualification [T.Wedege, Denmark] In the Danish Adult Education System it is a general view among educational planners that as a general qualification mathematics is relevant in the context of providing vocational qualifications. Mathematical knowledge does not, however, become a vocational qualification, unless it comprises knowledge, skills and properties that are relevant in relation to technique and work organisation in the working place. In my definition of the concept qualifications I speak of relevant knowledge, skills and properties rather than of necessary knowledge etc. This makes it possible to perceive qualifications from two different points of view: subjective and objective, i.e. from the point of view of individual workers as well as from the point of view of the labour market.

The integration of mathematics into vocational courses -some issues and concerns [J.Gillespie, UK]

I looked at some practical issues concerning the integration of mathematics into vocational courses in the UK. "Application of Number" is a required 'core skill' in all such vocational courses; how can it be embraced by vocational staff and students as a tool to enhance vocational performance rather than just as a cosmetic gloss or be so embedded in the vocational task that the student is unconscious of it ?

Many vocational staff and their students feel threatened by mathematics. Maths learning can be passed over to mathematics specialists, but they can see vocational problems as contexts for demonstrating specific maths techniques. This is often seen as boring and irrelevant by the students. A better approach is to plan students' vocational assignments jointly. I gave examples of this from vocational courses and work in Art and Design and Health and Social Care.

Discussion

Much of the discussion focused on what "authentic" work-based examples actually are. Many participants suggested that authenticity is not possible. Another raised the question as to whether it is sufficient, but claimed it is necessary for practical examples to be given in the classroom if appropriate learning is to take place.

This led into the epistemological problem of differences between: mathematics in vocational knowledge and the mathematics of the mathematician; used knowledge and taught knowledge; learning to use and actually using. What could be the nature and place of the mathematical skills involved in the workplace ?

References

Bessot, A., Eberhard, M. (1995). *Le problème de la pertinence des savoirs mathématiques pour la formation aux métiers du bâtiment,* in G.Arsac et al. (eds) Différents types de savoir et leur articulation, Grenoble: La Pensée Sauvage, 13-32.

Freudenthal, H. (1991) *Revisiting Mathematics Education,* Dordrecht: Kluwer.

Layton D. (1991). *Science education and praxis: the relationship of school science to practical action,* Studies in Science Education, 19, 43-79.

Noss, R., Hoyles C. (1996) *The visibility of meanings : modelling the mathematics of banking,* International Journal of Computers for Mathematical Learning, 1, 3-31.

Nunes, T., Schliemann, A.D., Carraher, D.W. (1993). *Street mathematics and school mathematics,* Cambridge : Cambridge University Press.

Strässer, R.(1996). *Mathematics for work - a didactical perspective,* ICME 8 proceedings.

MATHEMATICS TEACHING FROM A CONSTRUCTIVIST POINT OF VIEW

LA ENSEÑANZA DE LAS MATEMÁTICAS DESDE UN PUNTO DE VISTA CONSTRUCTIVISTA

Chief Organizer / *Responsable*: Ole Bjorkqvist (FIN)
Local Organizer / *Coordinadora Local:* M.V. García-Armendáriz (ESP)

The aim of the group was to give an overview of the state of constructivism in mathematics education as of 1996. Having been a highly valued framework for research in mathematics education for more than a decade, it was expected that constructivism would show signs of maturity or even old age. That would be the case if it were a fad, eventually making way for new popular theories. However, the great interest for this particular Topic Group showed that there are still expectations for constructivism to provide improved understanding of the learning of mathematics and to be a source for new developments in teaching practice.

The 1996 picture of constructivism, regardless if it is emphasized as a philosophy or an epistemology, is one in which social reality is included in a much more explicit way than previously. That is, we may accept that an individual constructs his or her own knowledge; but to have a better theory, we need to include collectivist perspectives of learning and knowledge as well as variables describing social conditions and social change. In 1996, a teacher working within a constructivist framework is much more than a facilitator of learning. Research in the form of classroom studies focuses on interaction and the construction of shared knowledge or meanings. A phrase such as "negotiation of meaning" is used both by interactionists and social constructivists.

In many countries, effectiveness and teacher accountability are stressed as part of a national emphasis on mathematics education. A key question for constructivism is, can it be defended as a framework for better teaching, the way society sees quality in education? In some countries, constructivism has been accepted very well as a philosophy of mathematics education at a national level. The guidelines for the teaching of mathematics include statements that urge you to view students as active learners, etc. However, the practical advice, regarding how to do it, is very scarce. An intentional national curriculum may be very far from an implemented national curriculum. The challenge here is to accomplish large scale change.

The value of constructivism as a theoretical framework for teaching mathematics is connected with its specific ability to provide solutions to didactical problems or clarifications of important issues. Are there situations, e.g., in classrooms, where the unique best description is given by some variant of constructivism? If the answer is negative, "constructivist teaching" might rather be characterized as just a shift in the teacher role in ordinary classrooms. Teacher actions are not deduced from theory, they rather "do not conflict with philosophy".

One of the biggest questions of all is that of assessment. Nothing is thought to influence learning as much as the specific methods of assessment that are used. If one wants constructivist ideas in mathematics education to catch on in society as a whole, one needs to develop methods of assessment that are reasonable to the students, to their parents, to mathematicians – to everyone involved – and that do not compromise with the philosophy of constructivism.

Social constructivism seems to be a theory that resonates well with educators of 1996. This may be so because it appears to sum up a lot of experience and to take into account much more than previous varieties of constructivism. The two sessions of the Topic Group were devoted to presentations in which the influence of social constructivism was very obvious.

The introduction by the chief organizer outlined some of the issues that seemed especially relevant in 1996, including the existence of competing varieties of constructivism and the challenges for constructivism as a framework for teaching mathematics. The main presentations of the first day were then given by Barbara Jaworski, University of Oxford, UK, "Teaching Mathematics as a Social Constructivist" and Carolyn Maher, Rutgers University, New Jersey, USA, "Constructivism and Constructivist Teaching - Can They Co-Exist?".

In her paper, Barbara Jaworski outlined some main competing varieties of constructivism and some alternative theories or frameworks for teaching mathematics. In the actual presentation at the conference, she exemplified the social constructivist perspective in classroom research with her own work on classroom interactions. She described the complexities that are possible to uncover, including the different kinds of tensions involved in teaching mathematics. She also pointed at the implications for teacher education, concentrating on the concept of the practitioner as a researcher.

Carolyn Maher provided a concrete example of "constructivist teaching" in the form a videotape of a group of ten-year old students, focusing on the type of reasoning used by the children to solve a particular problem. The videotape exhibited the way their reasoning was, in different ways, built on the rules used in solving another problem eight months earlier, and it also showed the details of the interaction between the teacher and the students. The study being just a sample of such research, Maher ventured to characterize classrooms that promote "constructivist teaching" by a teacher that (1) provides experiences from which a student can build a powerful repertoire of mental images to draw upon for the construction of representations of mathematical ideas; (2) assesses and estimates the ideas that the student has built by observing their activity (model building) and listening to their explanations; (3) encourages the students to support ideas with justifications and arguments; (4) works to build a classroom culture that encourages the exchange of ideas; (5) pulls out and calls to the attention of students differences and disagreements; (6) facilitates the organization and reorganization of student groups to allow for the timely sharing of information and ideas; (7) encourages student-to-student and student-to-teacher efforts to map representations and develop modes of inquiry that might disclose deeper understanding of discrepancies; (8) provides multiple opportunities for students to talk about and represent ideas; (9) keeps discussion open and revisits ideas over sustained periods of time; (10) seeks opportunities for generalizations and extensions. Finally and most importantly, the "constructivist teacher" treats children and their ideas with dignity and respect.

The first paper of the second day, "An Innovative Approach to the Teaching of Mathematics for Social Science Students" by Paola Valero and Mauricio Castro, Universidad de los Andes, Bogota, Colombia, was presented by the first author. It described the development of a university course in mathematics designed to bridge the gap between mathematics and the social discipline of the student. The course promoted a view of mathematics as a social activity, embedded in the everyday interaction of people with their world and their social environment. Mathematics was constructed as a formalization of this interaction. This general idea conflicted with the student´s initial perception of mathematics as a set of truths, rules and procedures which cannot be questioned or changed. The course also opened the possibility to perform different tasks in which no pre-determined procedure or answer was expected.

In the second presentation, "Exploring the Socio-Constructivist Aspects of Maths Teaching: Using 'Tools' in Creating a Maths Learning Culture", Anna Chronaki, University of Bath, UK, discussed the impact of constructivism in conceptualizing how maths learning takes place. As an example she cited the denunciation of teaching as "transmission of knowledge" and its replacement with teaching as "negotiation of meanings". In the presentation, a teacher's practice was explored in detail paying attention to his actions and intentions during particular classroom episodes. Two issues were discussed, first to what extent the teacher's actions were consistent with his intentions, and secondly the 'fit' of his teaching in a socio-constructivist framework. Data had been collected through ethnographic methods such as observation, videotaping of lessons and extensive interviewing.

The last presentation, "A Study of the Constructive Approach in Mathematical Education", by Tadao Nakahara and Masataka Koyama, Hiroshima University, Japan, was a joint one with the first author providing the fundamental principles of the "Constructive Approach" in mathematical education, the second author presenting a case study of the constructive approach in teaching an introduction to fractions (3rd grade students). The lesson process model of the approach includes the five stages (1) being conscious; (2) being operational; (3) being mediative; (4) being reflective; (5) making agreement. The approach also includes five representational modes for mathematical knowledge. The authors presented their model as a tool for teachers in the construction of mathematics lessons that emphasize the meaning of mathematical knowledge and develop children's autonomy and individuality.

NOTE

The papers presented to the group are available in a volume edited by the chief organizer. For information, contact Ole Bjorkqvist, Faculty of Education, Abo Akademi, PB 311, 65101 Vasa, Finland, e-mail objorkqv@abo.fi

FOSTERING OF MATHEMATICAL CREATIVITY

ESTÍMULO Y DESARROLLO DE LA CREATIVIDAD MATEMÁTICA

Chief Organizer / *Responsable:* Erkki Pehkonen (FIN)
Local Organizer / *Coordinador Local:* Lluis Segarra (ESP)

Summary:

Creativity is a topic which is often neglected within mathematics teaching. Usually teachers think that mathematics need in the first place logic, and that creativity has not much to do with learning mathematics. On the other hand, if we consider a mathematician who developes new results in mathematics, we cannot oversee his/her use of the creative potential. The main method to foster creativity in mathematics seems to problem solving, especially so-called open problem solving, where problem posing plays today an important role.

What is creativity?

Creativity is not a property that is only characteristic artists and scientists, but it is also a part of everyday life. E.g. a do-it-yourself man is realizing creative thinking when he with defective tools is solving many practical problem situations. Therefore, creativity is automaticly part of the "mathematics for all" -program.

Commonly, people think that creativity and mathematics have nothing to do with each other. But the mathematicians disagree strongly. If we observe the performance of mathematicians when they are encountering a new task, we can note that almost all of them are experimenting at first. These first experimentations are random, but they gradually settle in one direction – there is the awakening in the mind of an idea of the possible solution. Based on the experimentations, the mathematicians may set a hypothesis which he tries to prove. So we see that creative performance is an essential part of doing mathematics.

From the very beginning of research on creativity, it has been typical to describe it through such persons' behavior who are generally considered as creative. In the books of creativity, one may read the Heureka experiences of Arkhimedes and Darwin's tedious years of collecting and arranging data before he got the idea of evolution.

In the literature, there are many definitions of creativity, but according to Haylock (1987) there seems to be no commonly agreeable definition. Every scientist has put forward his own version. In the following, we will use the definition of the Finnish neurophysiologist Matti Bergström. He defines creativity "as performance where the individual is producing something new and unpredictable" (Bergström 1984). He introduces the concepts "everyday creativity" and "Sunday creativity": Within the range of the first concept, it belongs the findings of new associations which can be predicted, if we know the elements to be associated. Whereas the real creativity (the latter) demands special circumstances and can neither be achieved through intention nor mechanical methods.

Problem solving as a fostering method

One type of problem solving, the use of so-called open-ended problems has many connections with creativity and its fostering methods. Therefore, it will be considered here briefly. The main idea is, as follows: Pupils are given a situation and a direction to go, with the aid of a (mathematical) problem. The continuation depends on pupils' decisions. Pupils will formulate their own problems within the situation, and try to solve them. And after the solution, they try to generalize their results. Under the concept "open-ended problems", there are several types of problems: investigations, problem posing, real-life situations, projects, problem fields (or problem sequences), problems without question, and problem variations ("what-if"-method).

Of these, for example, problem posing is especially proper to foster creativity. The central idea is here to simulate real situations, since there nobody will formulate the problem for the solver. In reality, he must himself find out and formulate proper problems, and then try to solve them. Problem posing might be difficult for those who have only practiced to solve ready-formulated problems given by others.

The method of using open-ended problems in classroom for promoting mathematical discussion, the so-called "open-approach" method, was developed in Japan in the 1970's (Shimada 1977). About at the same time in England, the use of investigations, a kind of open-ended problems, became popular in mathematics teaching (Wiliam 1994), and the idea was spread more by Cockcroft-report (1982). In the 1980's, the idea to use some form of open-ended problems in classroom spread all over the world, and research on its possibilities is very vivid in many countries.

The idea of using open-ended problems in school mathematics has been written in some countries in the curriculum, in a form or other. For example, in the mathematics curriculum for the comprehensive school in Hamburg (Germany), about one fifth of the teaching time is left content-free, in order to encourage the use of mathematical activities. In California, they are suggesting open-ended problems to be used in assessment beside the ordinary multiple-choice tests. In Australia, some open problems (e.g. investigative projects) are used in the final assessment since the late eighties (Stacey 1995).

A big variety of examples for open-ended problems can be found in the literature. Among others in the ZDM journal, there was a couple of years ago the theme "Using open-ended problems in mathematics" (Pehkonen 1995) which was based on the presentations of the PME discussion group in Japan 1993. Two years later, a booklet about open-ended problems (Pehkonen 1997a) was edited.

Organization of the work in the Topic Group 7

The work in the Topic Group 7 during the ICME-8 conference was realized through short presentations of international specialists and follow-up discussions. Of the two time slots, the first was devoted for more theoretical considerations, whereas the emphazes in the second time slot was in practical school realizations. Our main questions to be discussed were, as follows: What is the meaning of creativity within school mathematics? Which methods could be used to foster mathematical creativity within school situations? What scientific knowledge, i.e. research results, do we have on mathematical creativity?

After my introduction to the theme "The state-of-art in mathematical creativity", the presentation of Prof. Derek Haylock (University of East Anglia, United Kingdom), "Recognising Mathematical Creativity in Schoolchildren" began the program by describing general guidelines for the theory of mathematical creativity. The second main presentation was given by Prof. Edward A. Silver (University of Pittsburgh, USA), "Fostering mathematical creativity through instruction rich in mathematical problem solving and problem posing" which dealt with fostering of problem posing. As the third, Prof. Yoshihiko Hashimoto (University of Yokohama, Japan) described the Japanese problem solving and posing method, the socalled "open-end approach" in his presentation "The methods of fostering creativity through mathematical problem solving".

Prof. Shuk-kwan S. Leung (National Chiayai Teachers' College, Taiwan) "On the Role of Creative Thinking in Problem Posing" began the second time slot by combining creativity and problem posing. The other presentations in this time slot were near school practice: Dr. Hartmut Köhler(Stuttgart, Germany) talked with the theme "Acting Artist-like in the Classroom", Dr. Alice Villar (Montevideo Uruguay) described her mathematics enchantment program "Mathematics for everybody", and Dr. Teh Pick Ching (Darussalem, Brunei) gave a case of fostering creativity in school in "An Experiment to Discover Mathematical Talent in a Primary School in Kampong Air".

Most of the presentations given in the Topic Group 7 are now published in the special theme number of the Journal International Reviews on Mathematical Education (= ZDM), Vol. 3, 1997 edited by myself (Pehkonen 1997b). In this place, I want to express my great gratitude to all presenters of the Topic Group 7 for their cooperation as well as to the audience who was actively discussing.

References

Bergström, M. 1984. *Luovuus ja aivotoiminta. [Creativity and brain function.]* In: Luovuuden ulottuvuudet [Dimensions of creativity] (eds. R. Haavikko & J.-E. Ruth), 159–172. Weilin+Göös: Espoo.

Cockcroft Report 1982. *Mathematics counts*. Report of the Committee of Inquiry into the Teaching of Mathematics in Schools. London: H.M.S.O.

Haylock, D.W. 1987. *A framework for assessing mathematical creativity in schoolchildren*. Educ. Stud. Math. 18 (1), 59–74.

Pehkonen, E. (ed.) 1995. *Using Open-ended Problems in Mathematics Class*. International Reviews on Mathematical Education (= ZDM) 27 (2), 55–72.

Pehkonen, E. 1997a. *Use of open-ended problems in mathematics classroom*. University of Helsinki. Department of Teacher Education. Research Report 176.

Pehkonen, E. (ed.) 1997b. *Fostering of Mathematical Creativity*. International Reviews on Mathematical Education (= ZDM) 29 (3), 63–96.

Shimada, S. (ed.) 1977. *Open-end approach in arithmetic and mathematics – A new proposal toward teaching improvement*. Tokyo: Mizuumishobo. [in Japanise]*

Stacey, K. 1995. *The Challenges of Keeping Open Problem-Solving Open in School Mathematics*. International Reviews on Mathematical Education 27 (2), 62–67.

Wiliam, D. 1994. *Assessing authentic tasks: alternatives to mark-schemes.* Nordic Studies in Mathematics Education 2 (1), 48–68.

* In summer 1997 during the PME conference in Lahti, I heard that the book has been translated into English and published byt the NCTM with the following reference: Becker & Shimada, The Open-Ended Approach, NCTM 1997.

PROOFS AND PROVING: WHY, WHEN AND HOW

DEMOSTRACIONES Y DEMOSTRAR: POR QUÉ, CUÁNDO Y CÓMO

Chief Organizer / *Responsable:* Michael de Villiers (ZAF)
Local Organizer / *Coordinadora Local:* Encarnacion Castro (ESP)

Topic Group 8 was attended by about 150 delegates. Some of the questions addressed during Topic Group 8 were: How are computers and the development of so-called "experimental" mathematics affecting our notions of proof? How can we make proof a meaningful activity for students? What balance should we strike between informal and formal proofs, and how can we assist the transition from the former to the latter? What proof representations do students spontaneously produce themselves? What are students' needs for conviction and explanation? How can we demystify the construction of auxiliary lines in geometry proofs? What contexts can be utilized to present proof as a meaningful activity? Historically, how has the notion of proof and different proof techniques changed and developed over time? Which proofs or logical explanations for results do very young children produce on their own ? What components of proof should be included in the training of mathematics teachers or engineers? Which aspects of proof arise in computer science and mathematical games? Which heuristics are most helpful in assisting students in constructing their own proofs? How should we handle disproof; ie. the generation and use of counter-examples? Which different ways are there of proving the same result and how do they compare?

A list of the papers that were presented are given further on. Gila Hanna (Canada) was also scheduled to give a Plenary talk on "New approaches to Proof and Verification: Implications for Mathematics Education", but unfortunately had to leave Seville early. Dexter Luthuli (South Africa) unfortunately was also unable to attend and would have given a talk on "The use of Auxiliary Lines in the Proof of Euclidean Geometry Riders" in Session 1 of the Concurrent Sessions.

Addresses and telephone numbers of speakers are available from the organizers. A limited publication of the proceedings are being planned which would include most of the papers and all the abstracts. Further details can be obtained from the Chief organizer.

1st Session Friday, July 19, 1996, 12:00 - 13:30. PLENARY.

Chair: Fulvia Furinghetti, Italy Erich Wittmann, Germany: Operative Proofs in Primary Mathematics. (ewittmann@math.uni-dortmund.de). Michael de Villiers, South Africa: The Role and Function of Proof in Dynamic Geometry. (mdevilli@pixie.udw.ac.za).

Nitsa Movshovitz-Hadar, Israel: On striking the Balance between Formal and Informal Proofs. (nitsa@techunix.technion.ac.il).

2nd Session Saturday, July 20, 1996, 12:00 - 13:30. CONCURRENT SESSIONS.

SESSION 1: COMPUTERS & PROOF HEURISTICS
Chair: Ken Retzer, USA Bram van Asch, Netherlands: Does an engineer need proof? (wsinaa@win.tue.nl).
David Ginat, Israel: Design-with-Proof, Loop Invariants, and Mathematical Games. (NTGINAT@WEIZMANN.weizmann.ac.il). Celia Hoyles, UK: Proving and Proof in School Mathematics. (choyles@ioe.ac.uk). Ken Retzer, USA: Proving via Polya. (retzerk@nicanor.acu.edu).

SESSION 2: INFORMAL/FORMAL METHODS OF PROOF
Chair: Erich Wittmann, Germany & Fulvia Furinghetti, Italy Dennis Almeida, U.K.: Proof perceptions and practices of UK mathematics undergraduates. (D.F.Almeida@exeter.ac.uk).
Fulvia Furinghetti & Domingo Paola, Italy: Filling the gap between students' argumentations and mathematical proofs.
(furinghe@dima.unige.it).
John Pegg, Australia: Interpreting students' approaches to geometric proofs: a neo-Piagetian approach. (jpegg@metz.une.edu.au).
Tomas Ortega & M. Ibanes, Spain: Proofs in Mathematics: classification and some examples in Secondary Education (In Spanish). (ortega@cpd.uva.es).
Olga Leon & Dora Calderon, Columbia: Proof in secondary education (In Spanish). (uextern4@colomsat.net.co).

SESSION 3: THE ROLE OF PROOF
Chair: Michael de Villiers, South Africa Evelyn Barbin, France: An epistemological approach to proving: to know why and how we know. (Fax: (33) 1 44 275608).
Paul Goldenberg, USA: Why prove? To understand?.
(PaulG@edc.org).
David Reid, Canada: The Role of Proving: Students and Mathematicians. (dareid@morgan.ucs.mun.ca).
Michael Neubrand, Germany: Proving as part of dealing with theorems. (neubrand@hardy.uni-flensburg.de).
VictorKatz, USA : Proofs by Induction.
(vkatz%UDCVAX.BITNET@VTBIT.CC.VT.EDU).

SESSION 4: LEARNING OF PROOF
Chair: Ana Mesquita, France
Anna Rosa Scarafiotti, Italy: Working out proofs together in the classroom. (DIMAT@polito.it).
Ana Mesquita, France: Deductive reasoning in elementary school geometry: A case study. (Ana.Mesquita@univ-lille1.fr).
Carolyn Maher, USA: Are you convinced? - Proof Making in Young Children. (cmaher@math.rutgers.edu).
Lesley Jones, U.K.: The Process of Learning to Prove.
(aea01lgj@gold.ac.uk).
Yasuhiro Sekiguchi, Japan: What is really special in the Learning of Proof for Students?: An ethnographic analysis.
(ysekigch@ccy.yamaguchi-u.ac.jp).

SESSION 5: TEACHER TRAINING & EDUCATIONAL PRACTICE
Chair: Nitsa Movshovitz-Hadar, Israel Antonio Garnica, Brazil: Fascination for the technical, decline of the critical: a study on rigorous proof and the training of mathematics teachers.
(vgarnica@azul.bauru.unesp.br).
Orit Zaslavsky, Israel: Pitfalls in Generating and Using Counter-Examples in Mathematics. (orit@tx.technion.ac.il).
Guershon Harel, USA: Transformational Reasoning in Proving. (harel@MATH.Purdue.EDU).
Hamutal David, Israel: Making Sense of Reading Proof.
(orgad@techunitechnion.ac.il).
Zsofia Ruttkay, The Netherlands: Proofs and proving in different contexts. (zsofi@cs.vu.nl).

STATISTICS AND PROBABILITY AT THE SECONDARY LEVEL

ESTADÍSTICA Y PROBABILIDAD EN EL NIVEL SECUNDARIO

Chief Organizer / *Responsable:* Brian Phillips (AUS)
Local Organizer / *Coordinador Local:* Eliseo Borrás (ESP)

The aim of this topic group was to highlight issues involved in, and to provide directions for the future of, the teaching of statistics and probability at the secondary level.

The program included an overview of the state of the art of each of these topics, discussions on children's understanding of the basic concepts of probability and statistics, general issues such as the curriculum, assessment, teacher training, the use of technology and how research may affect how these topics are taught in the future.

The format of the sessions allowed participants to focus on either probability, or data analysis. There was a brief forum discussion during the second session.

We list here outlines of the talks with the authors' E-mail to enable contact with the authors for further information. It is intended that the complete texts will be edited and available free by the end of the year from Brian Phillips (to be published by the courtesy of his institution The School of Mathematical Sciences, Swinburne University of Technology, Australia)

Session 1AProbability at Secondary level: Organiser Tibor Nemetz, Hungary <nemetz@math-inst.hu>

1A.1 An overview of the teaching of probability in secondary schools

Tibor summarized responses from several countries to a questionnaire with questions on content- and methodological issues, experiences in classroom practise, inclusion in national school examinations. Manfred Borovcnik (Austria), <manfred.borovcnik@uni-klu.ac.at> discussed and analyzed recent trends both in practise and research.

1A.2 Views on probability as reflected by student-teachers

Yasar Ersoy (Turkey) <yersoy@tutor.fedu.metu.edu.tr> discussed how since the 1960's, when the topic of probability was included in the school mathematics programme, some difficulties arose for teachers. Among others, the introduction of the key probability concept of "independence of events" was of particular concern. A recent survey asked student teachers about their views and experiences from the time they attended secondary school, and how these views were reconsidered when attending a university course. Furthermore, some secondary students were interviewed to get an idea how they identified and interrelated the outcome of independent events and the general beliefs of people. These results were presented and discussed.

1A.3 Statistical Independence - One Concept or Two? John & Kath Truran (Australia) <jtruran@arts.adelaide.edu.au> discussed the ideas of statistical independence which is usually defined as $pr(B|A) = pr(B)$ or $pr(A\&B) = pr(A)pr(B)$. They claimed that this topic is not well understood by students, and often leads to the well-known "Gambler's Fallacy", which denies the obvious fact that a coin has no memory. This paper argued that there are in fact two quite different types of statistical independence. These were defined, and it was shown that such a classification helps to remove some of the common logical and pedagogical difficulties. It then looked at some well-known research results in the light of such a reclassification, and presented other data which suggested that there may be more complex influences on people's predictions than have previously been recognised.

1A.4 A summary of research activities in chance and data by members of the PME 20, Valencia, Spain, July, 1996. Robert Peard (Australia) <r.peard@qut.edu.au> prepared a report on statistical education research from PME. It stated that research in stochastics focused on conception and cognition (including misconceptions), assessment issues and the influence of social and cultural factors. The following lists the reports from PME on statistical education. Jenny Way (Australia) examined strategies that young children use for comparing two types of random generators. Her conclusions generated much discussion about the fundamental nature of chance and whether the recognition of equivalent representations implied intuitive conceptual understanding. C. Batanero (Spain) presented results from a large study of over 300 secondary students' use of heuristics and biases, while Kath Truran (Australia) reported on the use of the same heuristics by younger children. E. Fischbein (Israel) reported that the evolution of probabilistic misconceptions with age is rather divergent. Graham Jones (USA) outlined a large study to determine conceptions of randomness and independence using SOLO taxonomy to analyses responses and make use of the results to inform instruction. John Truran (Australia) presented results about the independence of random generators and misconceptions of young children, including the tendency to assume equal likelihood. Concepts of "independence" and "equal likelihood" appeared in several of the presentations. R. Peard (Australia) claimed that the assumption of equal likelihood when none exists is a type of misconception that is distinct from the others reported in the literature, and is widespread. It was noted in the discussion that in some recent research reports in the field the term "fairness" is used to mean "equally likely", when in fact "mathematical fairness" does not imply this. Furthermore, childrens' informal use of the term usually does not imply equal probability. Most introductory courses in probability start with equally likely situations and it was suggested that further research should be undertaken to examine whether this is an appropriate pedagogy.

In the field of Statistics Education, research focused on the provision of service courses, statistical innumeracy and cultural factors. John Trurin in discussing service courses for economics students spoke of the "social conflict" generated by the modern approach of the "intelligent interpretation of data" in a society that does not encourage critical reasoning. Sue Gorton (Australia) described difficulties in the provision of service courses for nurses and psychologists while Linda Gatusso (Canada) discussed data handling in service courses in which no "mathematics" was required.

A common question in the discussion of such courses was how much mathematics is needed to be able to use statistics. Can one, for example, use a Chi-squared test effectively without any knowledge at all of probability distributions? It was agreed that further research in this area is needed.

Session 1B Data analysis in secondary schools

Organiser Brian Phillips (Australia) <bphillips@swin.edu.au>

1B.1 An international overview of data analysis within the mathematics curriculum

Susan Starkings (UK) <starkisa@vax.sbu.ac.uk> discussed how mathematical education has radically changed, in many countries, over the last decade resulting in the need for mathematically literate students who can function in todays technological society. This has led to many changes in the content of the mathematics curriculum, in particular the statistics content. In the United States the Quantitative Literacy Project placed emphasis on data analysis and this provided the key components of the new mathematics curricula. The National Research Council (1990), suggests, "Most obvious, perhaps is the need to understand data presented in a variety of different forms." The National Curriculum in the United Kingdom also attached a great deal of importance on data analysis, within the mathematics curricula. In developing countries, such as Pakistan, the shift from rote learning of numerical techniques, is currently taking place with data analysis taking a prominent role. The Universities advisors of Pakistan identified the need for the students, within the school system, to be aware of, and become familiar with, the growing developments in data analysis. This paper gave an overview of the implementation of data analysis in various countries; it compared and contrasted data analysis in these countries and elucidated the importance of data analysis within the mathematics curriculum.

1B.2 Curriculum issues in United States Schools

Gail Burrill (USA) <gburrill@macc.wisc.edu> reported how the National Council of Teachers of Mathematics Curriculum and Evaluation Standards reinforced by the Quantitative Literacy Series from the American Statistical Association have had an impact on the curriculum in schools in the Untied States, particularly in the area of data analysis and statistics. Textbooks now include many topics from this area, and teachers are beginning to look for ways to include the concepts in their mathematics programs. Implementation issues, however, are prevalent. Teachers lack the background knowledge to teach the content and often omit it. Many of the texts focus on product answers for example "What is the mean?" and do not build process nor conceptual understanding. Teachers are confronted with many new topics and new ways to teach; they have to make choices in order to "cover" their curriculum. A lack of statistical understanding and erroneous thinking about statistics is evident in many published materials. The National Science foundation has funded a variety of curriculum projects for primary, middle level and secondary students that include data analysis as an appropriate and meaningful part of the curriculum. These projects exemplify in different ways how the tenets of the Standards can be put into practice. Examples selected from several of these projects were used to give some indication about the direction data analysis seems to be taking in the United States and how this is reflected in the schools.

1B.3 Data analysis in secondary education in Hong Kong - curriculum,examination and project

Shir-Ming Shen (Hong Kong) <hrntssm@hkucc.hku.hk> told how during the first five years of the secondary school education in Hong Kong, all students have to learn some descriptive statistics which is taught as part of the compulsory mathematics curriculum. Every year, about 7000 students choose to do more statistics in their sixth and seventh year of study. The syllabus, the way that data analysis is taught and examined, the advantages and disadvantages of the situation were discussed.

1B.4 An Argentinian experience of statistics teaching for masters of high school

Teresita Teran (Argentina) <maverick@rosario.com> discussed how changes are being implemented in Argentina since a 1993 Federal Law defined the Common Basics Contents to be taught throughout the country. These have been organized into 8 blocks, one of which is "statistics and probability notions". In this the aim is for pupils to gather, organise, process and interpret statistical information and understand, estimate and use probability for making the decisions. As the teachers had not studied statistics in their degree, a process of training was organised, through a course that permits them to learn statistics through workshops held throughout the country in the evenings and weekends. These included discussing strategies, formulating conjectures, estimating results, examining alternatives and analyzing the most useful and economic procedures.

1B.5 Emerging Issues for Research on Teaching and Learning Probability & Statistics Mike Shaughnessy (USA) <mike@fpa.lh.pdx.edu> reflected on some of the recent developments in research in the area of stochastics, and raised some issues for future exploration. Past research has concentrated on people's naive beliefs and conceptions of probability and statistics, including both stochastic and deterministic ways of estimating likelihoods or chance outcomes. While there has been some research on the effects of instruction on such beliefs, a good deal more work is needed in this area, especially work on investigating the effect of recent curricular approaches to probability and statistics and middle and secondary levels. An area that is beginning to emerge as quite important is people's understanding of graphs, and the building of a theory of graphicacy. The talk discussed recent work in this area. Directions needed for future research include research on the connections between the teaching and learning of probability and data handling; research on cross cultural differences in probability concepts; and long term classroom studies documenting students' growth in probability and statistics over time.

Session 2. General issues in teaching probability and statistics in Secondary Schools

2.1 Assessing students' interpretations of data: Conceptual and pragmatic issues

Iddo Gal (Israel) <iddo@research.haifa.ac.il> discussed how increased attention has been given in recent years to the development of modern curricula and resources for teaching of statistics in schools. However, little attention has been given to the complex issues involved in assessment of students' emerging knowledge and understanding. This talk examined some conceptual and pragmatic aspects of assessment of students' interpretations of data. The appropriateness of traditional models of assessment (e..g, multiple-choice) in this area was examined, challenges involved in using alternative approaches were discussed, and needs related to future research and to teacher training outlined.

2.2 Teachers of Statistics - Needs and impediments

Anne Hawkins (UK) < ash@maths.nott.ac.uk> claimed that if someone is to teach mathematics, there is a reasonable likelihood that they will have attended courses not only in mathematics itself, but also on how to teach mathematics. In contrast, relatively few teachers of statistics have received adequate training in the statistical equivalents of these areas. For a variety of reasons, some of which were outlined, this state of affairs is persisting. Possible remedies were discussed, and some specific examples of steps that have been taken to improve the situation considered.

2.3 Technology and the teaching of statistics

Kay Lipson (Australia) <kll@stan.xx.swin.oz.au> reviewed the role of technology in statistics education using the following classification (i) technology which enhances the statistical capabilities of the user (ii) technology which aims at developing and furthering the statistical understanding of the user. In this presentation the rationale behind each of the above was elaborated and appropriately illustrated using data obtained from the Internet.

2.4 Forum A forum chaired by Peter Holmes <p.holmes@sheffield.ac.uk>, with panel discussants Rolf Biehler (Germany) <rolf.biehler@hrz.uni-bielefeld.de> and Carmen Batanero (Spain) <batanero@goliat.ugr.es> addressed the question "How statistics and probability can best be incorporated into the overall school program?" In this a number of questions were raised which mainly related to issues of probability and technology.

Carmen posed the questions:

1. Is it possible to understand what is probability using only a frequentist approach?
2. Are the objectives for probability included in new curricula proposals realistic? At what age should an experimental approach be complemented with a mathematical approach?
3. What are the real difficulties for students doing EDA and in understanding the underlying mathematical concepts?
4. Is it possible and reasonable to avoid ideas of chance, probability, and inference when dealing with specific problems?

and Rolf posed the following questions:

1.Do we have a software problem? Lack of adequate programs? For doing statistics? For learning statistics? What are our ideals? (When) do we expect progress?
2. Software use tends to bring in: more different graphs more variables more complex problems & results (How) can we cope with this problem?
3. Which patterns of software use do students develop? How does software use influence their statistical thining? Cultural & gender differences?
4. How can we balance authentic real data analyses and carefully designed learning activities?

A general discussion completed the session.

PROBLEM SOLVING THROUGHOUT THE CURRICULUM

LA RESOLUCIÓN DE PROBLEMAS EN EL CURRICULUM

Chief Organizer / *Responsable:* Kaye Stacey (AUS)
Local Organizer / *Coordinador Local:* José Carrillo (ESP)

Increasingly the success of mathematical education is being judged by the power which it imparts to students to deal with aspects of their lives at work, at home and as informed citizens. This topic group was concerned with theories and practices which give students the power to use mathematical ideas to solve problems arising from within mathematics and from outside mathematics.

In the first session four speakers provoked thinking about how to ensure that mathematics programs give adequate attention to problem solving. In various ways, these speakers each pointed out the need for detailed attention to the four themes which were to be addressed in the second session in separate discussion groups: the challenges to design and administer appropriate assessment of problem solving; the special requirements of problem solving in teacher education; the possibilities of innovative mathematics curricula; and what research has revealed about psychological and social factors relevant to problem solving. The second session was spent in the four discussion groups, which began with short stimulus talks but gave plenty of opportunity for discussion amongst all participants. The proceedings of the topic group were conducted in a mix of Spanish and English with patience and good humour. Before the Congress, many participants had submitted short written contributions which were available for viewing on the world wide web and which served as further input to the four discussion groups.

The first session

María Luz Callejo of Instituto de Estudios Pedagógicos Somosaguas (IEPS), Madrid, Spain, was the first speaker in the first session. Speaking in Spanish with informative English overhead projector slides, she presented a proposal for inservice education which was centred on problem solving and based on recent research on professional development. This proposal has been carried out for eight years at the IEPS, and the effects on the practice of a group of teachers has been studied. Maria Luz presented four principles that guide inservice teacher education activities. She explained how to deal with inservice teacher education in problem solving and reported on experiments carried out in classrooms by groups of teachers undertaking the course.

The second speaker, Hugh Burkhardt of the Universities of Berkeley (USA) and Nottingham (UK) gave a long term overview of the progress that has been made in introducing problems which reflect real applications to mathematics teaching. He examined the type of the tasks that students do as "problem solving" in schools, querying the nature of some tasks which seemed not to demonstrate the power of mathematics. Tasks to encourage problem solving should illustrate how mathematical ideas can be applied to solve problems of interest to students with useful answers that are not known beforehand. Hugh presented examples of problems which illustrated the many different ways in which school problems can relate to the real world, ranging from highly artificial to genuine problems. He also presented some examples of problems which captured a real world spirit but are less pedagogically demanding and can be successfully used by a high proportion of teachers. The ideal of bringing the real world into classrooms is an elusive goal worth striving for. The key ideas of Hugh's talk were delightfully translated by Jose Carrillo.

Koji Yamazaki, a teacher at Setagaya Junior High School associated with Tokyo Gakugei University, Japan, then outlined the principles of "problem situation learning" in the new curriculum in Japan. Illustrating his talk with sample problems and diagrams of teaching processes, he explained the implementation of the open-ended approach and the approach of making up problems. Open-ended problems have multiple correct answers, which the teacher uses to find something new for each pupil. By making up problems (where students work on their own modifications of a basic problem) students can learn to identify what is similar about classes of problems. He showed how Japanese mathematics teachers are attempting to give adequate attention to problem solving by using these two strategies. Koji presented lesson plans of his own and showed how these two strategies enhanced the opportunities that students have to learn to solve problems.

Kaye Stacey (University of Melbourne, Australia) then spoke with two aims - to outline some recent experiences of problem solving in Australia and then to set the scene for the discussion that was to follow on the next day. Kaye presented examples of types of problems now in widespread use in Australia: puzzles unrelated to the usual curriculum to expand students thinking skills; short unusual problems, to be used within the normal curriculum, to get students thinking about mathematics in new ways; extensive investigations where students need to formulate a mathematical model or find relationships in large masses of real data; pure mathematical investigations. Amongst the major successes of teaching problem solving in Australia, Kaye proposed the confidence that many students have developed to attack unfamiliar questions, the intense, creative and co-operative atmosphere that can be found in some classrooms and the way in which students have learned to use technology needed to tackle problems with a lot of data. More students, she proposed, now see mathematics as a purposeful activity which makes sense. Teachers and students alike have a better understanding of the process of mathematical investigation. Students have developed an understanding of the need to consider the reasonableness of results and some have developed an understanding of the criteria for evaluating a mathematical solution. Many students have improved their written communication of mathematics. Some have experienced the joy of posing and solving your own problems.

On the other hand, in some places, time spent on problem solving has been excessive and students and teachers have over-emphasised format and length of written reports instead of coming to grips with the mathematical substance in good problems. Some problems used have been trivial or highly artificial. Some teachers have promoted simple guessing at solutions as a adequate problem solving method and have not demonstrated to students the power of technical skills and clever calculating. In curriculum implementation, there seems to be a trade off between developing adequate technical skill in mathematics or the ability to approach unfamiliar problems. She observed that attempts to teach problem solving had resulted in mixed success and proposed that discussion groups should consider which arrangements maximise benefits and minimise losses.

In setting the scene for the discussion which was to follow in the second session, Kaye posed again the question "How can we ensure that mathematics programs give adequate attention to problem solving?" She drew attention to the four important factors that need to be attended to in order to achieve this aim: curriculum, assessment, a basic understanding of the processes involved and teacher education. Teachers need more advanced skills to teach with a problem solving approach than to teach mechanistically. The session closed with participants deciding which of the four separate discussion groups they would attend on the next day.

The discussions of these are reported below.

Discussion group 1. Assessment of Problem Solving

The discussion on the evaluation of problem solving evolved around three talks. Malcolm Swan (University of Nottingham, UK) discussed the Balanced Assessment Project which produces assessment tasks aligned with objectives, contents, and desired instructional approaches of the curriculum. His remarks centred on balancing the criteria of scaffolding and transparency with the desired goal of students solving unstructured or open problems, illustrating with examples developed by the project. He suggested employing both holistic and point-by-point scoring procedures, emphasising the complementary nature of the information obtained in each case.

Beth Lee (ACT, Australia) spoke about a project that placed problem-solving at the core of mathematical program of a large 11-12 year college and revealed the process and criteria of evaluation that were developed as part of the project. She stressed the development of a portfolio and conferencing and listed evaluation criteria that have been used successfully.

Mary Falk de Losada of the Universidad Antonio Nariño (Colombia) stressed that a concerted effort of the mathematics education community can solve the apparent conflict between constrictions of teacher's time and time required (a priori) to prepare good problems, anticipate routes of solution used by students, as well as that required (a posteriori) to review the actual approaches, processes and arguments employed. Projects similar to the Balanced Assessment Project and well-designed competitions that stress group involvement over time were identified as useful examples. She discussed a competition-based study which suggests that the solidity and creativity of the media used when presenting problems to students will be reflected in the originality and solidity of arguments given by students when solving them. Discussion centred very closely around the presentations with comments, questions and further contributions on the same topics.

Discussion group 2. Teacher Education for Problem Solving

This discussion session, chaired by María Luz Callejo, was conducted principally in Spanish with translation to English. Jose Carrillo (Universidad de Huelva, Spain) presented some of the findings from his recently completed doctoral study in a paper authored jointly with L.C. Contreras and F. Guevara entitled "Un modelo de desarrollo profesional de los profesores de matemáticas". Margaret Taplin (Australia and Hong Kong) gave the second stimulus talk reporting on her investigations of the problem-solving performances of pre-service teachers.

Active participation from the audience, which contained a large number of classroom teachers, ensured that the discussion subjected all ideas proposed to rigorous tests of practicality. Even teachers whose beliefs strongly support problem solving find serious obstacles when they try to put it into practice. It is difficult to manage new aspects of the subject at the same time as new student groupings and to negotiate social norms of the classroom. In some schools, lack of teacher training for mathematical problem solving makes the use of a problem solving based methodology impossible. Teacher education must be conceptualised as a very complex field. The teacher is a complex being and the investigations that researchers carry out can only approach a little towards understanding his or her educational task. A background paper had also been prepared by Neil Pateman and Joseph Zilliox (USA).

Discussion group 3. Innovative Problem Solving Curricula

Ian Isaacs (University of the Northern Territory, Australia) chaired the group looking at changing curriculum. Four papers presented by Giancarlo Navarra (Italy), Katsuhiko Shimizu (Japan), Howard Tanner (Wales) and Lyn English (Australia) served as the basis for discussion of innovations in mathematics curricula specifically related to problem solving. Navarra's paper dealt with his experiences in Italy in a laboratory situation. He taught a class of 11 year old pupils how to improve their linguistic and argumentative competencies by their analysing and discussing word problems which lacked sufficient data. They were also required to construct problems of this type themselves and then have them examined and discussed by the rest of the class under the guidance of the class teacher. Lyn's paper dealt with the teaching of open-ended questions to a group of 10 year old pupils in an Australian school. The teacher initially showed pupils a number of different types of open-ended questions (deductive, combinational and computational) and then they were requested to construct open-ended questions of their own. At the end of the project she found that students preferred deductive type questions, were indifferent to computational type problems and disliked combinational type problems.

Both Howard Tanner (Wales) and Katsuhiko Shimizu (Japan) described large scale projects in their countries. Howard, drawing on a background paper jointly written with Sonia Jones, briefly outlined a project to develop the metacognitive skills of planning, monitoring ongoing evolution of one's progress, and reflection at the end of a problem solving episode. Students in the project classes performed better than the control classes on measures of strategic knowledge and use of metacognitive skills and also continued to do so later. Katsuhiko described a project in which graphics calculators and the Cabri-geometry software package is being used to modify the content of conventional mathematics curriculum by changing closed and directed questions into open-ended, exploratory type investigations. This changed class activities from practice of algorithmic tasks to one of experimental mathematics. Lucia Grungetti and Francois Jaquet had also contributed background paper describing a Mathematics rally in primary school.

The subsequent group discussion focused on the techniques of promoting pupil/student exploration of open-ended questions and the changing of teachers' and students' perceptions of the nature of school mathematics as a necessary social and pedagogical climate to support these innovations in the wider school community.

Discussion group 4. Psychological and Social Aspects of Problem Solving

The discussion group on psychological and social aspects of problem solving was chaired by Kaye Stacey (University of Melbourne, Australia). The session began with two short talks, after which there was general discussion to which all participants contributed. The first presentation was from Zahra Gooya (Iran) who discussed the subtle and varied ways in which cognitive aspects interact with the social aspects of the classroom and of the groups in which students work. She had seen how social factors sometimes inhibited productive problem solving in groups and had developed and investigated strategies for encouraging students to form respectful working relationships with their peers and with the teacher which promoted learning and problem solving. The subsequent discussion showed that her strategies (whole class discussion, journal writing and small group work all carefully implemented) met with widespread approval. There was debate on how to teach children criteria for distinguishing preferred solutions from others. Dianne Siemon (Australia) compared these ideas with findings reported in her background paper, "Social and Cultural Influences on Children's Mathematical Problem Solving".

Nick Scott (Australia) then stimulated a far reaching discussion about results and methodology when he presented a study of different ways in which students made use of numerical examples when they were working on a challenging number theoretic investigation. He found some effective use of examples to test assertions about the underlying structure of the problem. However often, too many examples were generated simply to look for patterns without accompanying analysis of structure. He cited anecdotal evidence suggesting that this approach had been an unintended result of teaching problem solving. This paper raised discussion on methodological issues (e.g. time required to observe problem solving, effect of group structures etc, the degree of difficulty of problems to be used), on the results (e.g. what is "surface-level" and does it relate to a general orientation to learning) and whether such research could be called "psychological". There were three relevant background papers. Philip Clarkson and Lloyd Dawe (Australia) described how a bilingual child rapidly moved between his two languages in various ways during problem solving. E. Gelfman and Z. Matushkina reported on students' development of word problem strategies and Angela Pesci analysed students' argumentation on proportional reasoning problems. Wide ranging discussion followed.

Summary

The vigorous discussion within the groups indicated that the challenge of developing students' problem solving skill is seen as an important issue with much work to be done. In the sessions on problem solving at ICME 5 and 6, most reports had been from the "first wave" of implementation, from countries where problem solving was for the first time becoming a recognised aim of schooling. Many of the 1996 participants were from countries now entering such a first wave phase. Others had seen problem solving become institutionalised in their countries, with good and bad effect and were concerned with the "second wave" issues of realising widespread potential of the innovation. In both cases, participants are faced with the challenge of having problem solving become a significant part of the curriculum and of devising ways for most children to derive substantial benefit from the opportunities that problem solving in the curriculum offers.

THE FUTURE OF CALCULUS

EL FUTURO DEL CALCULO INFINITESIMAL

Chief Organizer / *Responsable:* Ricardo Cantoral (MEX)
Local Organizer / *Coordinador Local* : Jordi Deulofeu (ESP)

The aim of the group is to support the improvement of the teaching Calculus taking into account the differences due cultural context. This group will focus on how the traditional Calculus curriculum is being influenced by phenomenas such as: results of research in mathematics education, new approaches in mathematics and several reform's movement in teaching Calculus. We want to organize the interaction (reflection and discussion), and possibly confrontation, among participants whose views of the discipline are different. We will organize both, short talks on a specific domain of research and a sharing of ideas about the teaching-learning interface of Calculus. Some particular questions will be focused: What are the objectives of a Calculus courses? What are the connections of Calculus courses with courses in Precalculus, Mathematical Analysis, Discrete Mathematics and Differential Equations? Which conceptions of the content of the Calculus and of its teaching are at the base of teaching experiments? How has the new technology affected the teaching Calculus? What does mean "understand" in the Calculus domain?

THE FUTURE OF GEOMETRY

EL FUTURO DE LA GEOMETRÍA

Chief Organizer / *Responsable:* Joe Malkevitc (USA)
Local Organizer / *Coordinador Local:* Francisco Castro (ESP)

The presenters and attendees of Topic Group 12 were asked to react to the following statement: Geometry has grown rapidly beyond its traditional boundary of attempting to give a mathematical description of various aspects of physical space. It now includes such subdisciplines as convexity, graph theory, knots, tilings, and computational geometry, to name but a few. This rapid growth has been accompanied by broadening applicability to robotics, image processing and computer graphics, knotting of DNA, etc. Such dramatic developments create challenges for mathematics educators to integrate these emerging areas with traditional geometry. One important consideration is the use of software systems to help with visualization and geometric explorations.

Six speakers made presentations as follows:

Nuria Gorgorio (Universitat Autonoma de Barcelona)
Keith Jones (University of Southampton)

Title: Elements of the Visualization Process Within a Dynamic Geometry Environment

Istvan Lenart (Hungarian Academy of Sciences)

Title: From Spherical Geometry to Basic Concepts in Algebra

Michael Maryukov (Bryansk State Pedagogical University)

Title: The Role of Computer Technologies in Geometry Research and Their Impact on Geometry Education

Vinicio Villani (University of Pisa)

Title: What is the Usefulness of Teaching Geometry in Upper Grades?

Alexander Soifer (University of Colorado)

Title: Combinatorial Geometry in the Future of Mathematical Education

Joseph Malkevitch (York College of the City University of New York)

Title: Recent Applications of Geometry, K-12

The varied titles of the talks hint at the wide variety of perspectives from which the The Future of Geometry was considered. These perspectives included issues of pedagogy, content (curriculum), and use of technology.

It was apparent that although one can concentrate on a particular issue for a specific discussion, all these facets in approaching geometry must be integrated to provide effective education in geometry at all levels. Put differently, in the final analysis, unless a balanced and well conceived program of geometry is provided, the risk of the trend toward diminished attention to geometry in our schools may continue. This warning made, the following issues emerged within the broad categories of pedagogy, content, and technology.

Pedagogy

It was widely urged that teachers of geometry continue to develop and explore new pedagogical techniques for increasing the understanding of geometry. The need to develop better techniques for understanding three-dimensional phenomena was mentioned. Also, greater attention to developing visualization skills was discussed. Although some saw dangers in the use of computers in complementing traditional approaches to teaching, nearly everyone agreed that new software packages were enhancing our ability to teach geometry in a more varied way. Another aspect of the discussions was the value of choosing stimulating problems in motivating students. To avoid passivity on the part of students, it was urged that students be given challenging work and that experiments with group work be continued.

Content

Although the domain of what is considered geometry has grown dramatically during the 20th century, there was a widespread feeling that traditional topics in geometry still needed to be taught. Not only are traditional Euclidean topics important in everyday life, but also Euclidean geometry has played a special role in intellectual history. However, it also emerged that traditional topics could be employed to discuss newer ideas as well. For example, to study the Voronoi cells of a set of points in the plane (i.e. those points in the plane closer to a given point than any other point) one needs to understand properties of such more traditional geometric objects as circles and perpendicular bisectors. In addition to maintaining the importance of proof in the developing of new content, the importance of discussing modern applications of geometry was raised. The role that geometry is playing in many emerging new technologies (e.g. wireless communication, medical imaging, image processing, robotics, etc.) was mentioned. However, it was widely felt that a balance between traditional and new ideas was required.

Technology

It was widely agreed that new technologies such as graphing calculators, manipulatives, and software offer the geometry teacher a wide variety of ways to augment traditional teaching. In addition to supporting traditional topics, the new technological tools opened up totally new topics and new approaches to traditional topics. For example, in the Cabri or Geometer's Sketchpad environments it becomes possible for students to explore the consequences of sequence of constructions on a geometric figure as the shape of this figure is varied. This enables students to develop problem posing skills (i.e. inventing new geometrical questions), but it was strongly felt that care needed to be taken in showing the role of proof in geometry. It was felt that students should understand the difference between using software to convince one that a certain fact might be true and giving a mathematical proof that it was true.

Some recent works of interest to people in geometry and geometry education are listed below. The book edited by Professor Vinicio Villani is highly recommended for giving a comprehensive treatment of recent and historical developments with regard to the teaching of geometry as well as other developments affecting geometry and the teaching of geometry.

References

Boroczky, K. and G. Fejes Toth (eds.), *Intuitive Geometry,* Elsevier Science Publishing, Amsterdam, 1991.

Malkevitch, J., (ed.), *Geometry's Future, Consortium for Mathematics and Its Applications*, Lexington, 1991.

Mammana, C., (ed.), *Perspectives on the Teaching of Geometry for the 21st Century*, Pre-Proceedings for Catania Conference, Department of Mathematics, U. of Catania, 1995.

Villani, V. (ed.) ICMI Study on Geometry (*Perspective on the Teaching of Geometry for the 21st Century*), Kluwer, (to appear).

ACKNOWLEDGEMENTS

Many thanks go to the speakers, the advisory committee (Maria A. Mariotti (Italy) and Richard Pallascio (Canada)) and the local organizer (Francisco Castro (Spain)) and the many attendees of TG 12 for contributing to and making possible the stimulating discussions about the Future of Geometry.

THE FUTURE OF ALGEBRA AND ARITHMETICS

EL FUTURO DEL ÁLGEBRA Y LA ARITMÉTICA

Chief Organizer / *Responsable*: Joaquín Giménez (ESP)
Local Organizer / *Coordinador Local*: Bernardo Gómez-Alfonso (ESP)

GENERAL APPROACH TO THE SUBJECT

A general approach was given to introduce the existant divorce of arithmetics and algebra in classes and research for mathematics education and presenting a common future of algebra and arithmetics in prior-university studies. Five provocative questions were proposed since the begining: Do we want to keep into the compulsory students' head so big amount of algebra and arithmetics as we have in our curricula? Numbers exist outside school...Does algebra really exist outside school? Does algebra and arithmetic have a separated future for next century schools ? Which kind of new frameworks do we need to have some kind of integration between algebra and arithmetic ?

Two general presentations opened the first session, and three different soubgroups were conducted for presentations and discussions.

Lins and Giménez presentation emphasized that generalisation is not the only need for algebra. Arithmetics needs not to precede algebra and the genral focus should be to produce meaning by several ways. In fact different type of situations give meaning for arithmetics and algebra together: number estimation and big countings; iterative processes; problems "with two conditions"; graph interpretations; code interpretations; explaining the use of technical tools and so on. The war against syntactical difficulties must be converted into a peace with conditions. As it was presented to discuss, new curricular focus for arithmetics and algebra coming together must be guided focussing meaningful approaches by means of interesting activities within and outside schools sense making. In this perspective, there is no previous mathematical object to be exploited, but a situation opened to the students'production. Some examples were presented about the real possibility for children to use early syntactical approach by means of giving sense about what children are doing more than putting the accent on algebraic syntaxis itself.

John Mason [UK] argued that arithmetic was, and still is, the root source for algebra as a tool for expressing generality and controlling the unknown. He started by explaining the tensions between arithmetics and algebra "tensions" as tools, authenticity and motivation, global and local needs. By returning to the historical roots, we can make the best use of whatever technology is available by invoking children's mathematical thinking through being ourselves aware of generality and particularity, of what makes an example exemplary. He proposed in addition that 3000 years of story problems provide a rich cultural resource for provoking students into shifting from arithmetic to algebraic thinking. John Mason added that the future of arithmetic and algebra teaching lies in teacher awareness of the fundamental mathematical thinking process, most particularly, generalisation.

The group was divided to discuss about three topics and goals: (A) Curricular aspects about number sense and algebra problems ; (B) teacher developments and classroom research; (c) epistemological views and other developmental studies .

1. CURRICULAR ASPECTS ABOUT NUMBER SENSE AND ALGEBRA PROBLEMS .

Peter Hilton [USA] contribution emphasized basis for a new pre-college curriculum. The various parts of mathematics must be allowed, indeed encouraged, to interact with each other. One may say that algebra is elementary arithmetic made mathematical, so that universal statements about numbers tend to replace lists of special cases. By using different examples, he concluded that we must teach mathematics so that the students know something really well-what part of mathematics they know really well is unimportant. We must treat our students as intelligent, sensitive human beings and not as embryo computers. Any other form of so called mathematics education is worse than a waste of time.

Mollie McGregor [AUSTRALIA] discussed five aspects of arithmetic knowledge that are essential foundations for learning algebra : ability to focus on the procedure, not only on the answer; understanding how the operations relate to each other; knowing the various interpretations of the equals sign; knowing important properties of numbers; being able to work within the real number system, and not being limited to using small counting numbers.

Group A focused on three main questions : which are the qualities of these journeys running together ? Similar sense and meanings ?

awareness of generality ? new curricular proposals ? emphasizing procedural thinking? common technological use of tools ? And which are the main curricular aspects that could be changed ?

Alex Friedlander's presentation [IL] put the emphasis on experimental situations in which students appear to improve algebraic and arithmetic meanings. After discussion, some points seemed to be clear : Exploring with spreadsheets, was very effective powerful tool for making the transition from arithmetics to algebra ; using investigative activities in order to have the opportunity for giving sense and meaning to superproblems, and consequently acquiring algebraic meaning and number sense.

Professor **Dusan Pagon** [SLO], oferred a different crosscultural perspective about introducing finite structures in the curriculum the last courses before University, using Mapple V. He concluded presenting polynomials as one of the doors for abstract algebra, giving the opportunity for analogies. This presentation shows the continuity of East Countries tradition in Europe on algebraic structures in terms of preparing a curricular basis for technological studies. Even accepting, part of the audience express the difficulties to introduce these experiences in their countries.

2. TEACHER DEVELOPMENT AND CLASSROOM RESEARCH

Group B punt the following questions : which developments and classroom research must be important for the future : common representational problems ? looking for new computational perspectives; no forgetting assessing problems; learning from the past ? Improving living situations since early years ?

James Kaput [USA] pointed out the importance for using different representations, but cybernetic and phisical phenomena must play the central role. His central conclusions were that: (1) the prominence of the manipulable graphical representation as the menas by which phenomena are created and controlled, and (2) that representations are intimately and referentially linked to observable, controllable phenomena. The traditional "big three"- including the algebraic-gain a new life and concreteness that they do not have where they are used simply to represent each other, or are used to represent some situation described via text.

Some specific difficulties about reification -encapsulation processes in the lower grades were focussed by **Dagmar Neuman** [SWE] presentation. After caractherising some proceptual thinking ideas, she pointed out that reification of counting procedures into known facts needs to be seen in an alternative approach. It would be a great advance if researchers interested in problems appearing in the lower grades could form a network. All the isolated pieces of the puzzle, could be put together in such a way that prevent pupils from ending up in a cul-de-sac because they happen to be on the wrong side of a "proceptual divide".

The need for emphasizing assessment was described by **Alan Bell** [UK]. He suggested new assessment perspectives as a view for unifying arithmetics and algebra, and using these ideas as a way for awareness and metacognition . He presented the students constructing tests and mini-debates for reflective thinking approach.

A research presented by **Bill Atweh, Tom J. Cooper and Gillian Boulton Lewis** [AUSTRALIA] shows that regardless of learning algebra tends to act as a stratification agent for the social reproduction of economic differences, necessitating alternative approaches to existing research. Students ressistance to learning algebra could be either to teaching methods or to perceived value of the task, or both. The main conclusion is that the future direction for studying the learning and teaching of algebra based on a collaborative action research beween teachers and university researchers. They need to articulate their intentions and beliefs in order to more fully understand the practice. They argued that therefore, perhaps the disempowerment may be broken.

Montserrat Torra [ES] reflected about teacher training and the use of "stories" as "the three bears" in math lessons for early stages. She argued that the main difficulty lies in the fact that teachers have gone through an academic training which means they are able to identify the factors that influence learning but they can only identify structures in a theoretical manner and do not recognise them in an applied situation. The point is to recognise mathematical structures within real life so that everyday situations can be exploited instead of using.

3. EPISTEMOLOGICAL REFLECTIONS

Five approaches were presented is this group. Luis Radford [CAN] reflected about development of mathematical concepts overcoming reification processes, by using relationhips to sociocultural factors. Through a case study from a history -that of the rise of the algebraic concept of equation- he showed that mathematical reification processes do not happen in abstract spheres reserved for the mind only but are encompassed by sociocultural processes. He argued that the rise of the algebraic concept of an equation was historically related to : (i) the development of writing and (ii) to socially elaborated forms of mathematical explanation.

Alicia Bruno [ES] presented an overview about researches on negative numbers and concluded the need to emphasize the teaching of numbers by means of a unified perspective. The discussion focussed on three aspects: an adequate sequence for extensions (from natural to real numbers), the models and representations used for learning, and problem solving. Future perspectives were also discussed.

A psychological approach of proportional problems was presented by **Alina Galvão Spinillo** [BRA]. In her view different types of knowledge of proportion are used in different tasks : perceptual, covariational and formal, in research studies; but holistic intuitive ideas appear and the accent must be to illustrate how young children   deal with proportion, exploring their initial understanding. She suggested that estimation would play a central role, more exploration is needed by calling children's attention to the relations involved on comparisons... She pointed out that classroom instruction is far from these perspectives, and the emphasis is still on computational skills. Wider mathematical understanding must be introduced.

Liora Linchewski [IL] suggested that there are regularities in the way beginning algebra students interpret the structure of algebraic expressions in a numerical context. The interaction between the structure and the specific number combination seems to explain what Greeno said as random mistakes. Students'difficulty may stem at least in part from the comptetion between the structure and the biasing number combinations.

Len Streefland and Van Ameron [NL] explanations focussed on phenomena of equations in the history of maths. In their proposal, a shift wll be made from the analysis of phenomena from (the history of) mathematics to the intended teaching of equations from the perspective of the didactical phenomenology. This means among others anticipating the teaching of equations in a thought experiment. A system of equations was presented. Many questions were proposed: What is the purpose of such a system of equations? Where does it come from? What phenomena is it supposed to organise ? Which is the meaning of x and y? and so on... Through an example from China, the idea of using linear combinations is used familiarly. The contribution suggested that algebra can be learnt by algebraising, so the future of arithmetic and algebra depends very much on the way in which pupils are confronted with this subjects in school. Although an important aim is the learning of algebra as such, the discourse made clear the importance of the derived aims, namely the involvement of the learners in creating the algebra.

The final discussion in all groups put the emphasis on the need for changing curricular perspectives for compulsory school calling for integrated activities. Everybody accept the need for using computers as an important tool.

NOTE

All the papers of the group are available in a volume: Giménez,Lins and Gómez (eds) Arithmetics and algebra education. The edition can be obtained for US$10 plus postage by Computer Engeniering Dept. at Rovira Virgili University Ctra Salou s/n 43006 Tarragona.Spain , or asking the chief organizer jgr@tinet.fut.es

INFINITE PROCESSES THROUGHOUT THE CURRICULUM

PROCESOS INFINITOS EN EL CURRÍCULUM

Chief Organizer / *Responsable:* Bruno D'Amore (ITA)
Local Organizer / *Coordinadora Local:* M. Carmen Penalva (ESP)

Conclusions

The following seminars were organized as part of the work of T.G. 14. These seminars highlighted various meanings of and various approaches to the didactical use of infinity that are the same across different curricula.

- *"Infinity: A history of conflicts, surprises and doubts. A fertile area for research in Didactics of Mathematics"*, Bruno D'Amore (Italy). [Spanish and English versions of the text of this presentation, including a bibliography of more than 350 titles, were available from the outset.]
- *"Toward infinity step by step: an epistemological approach to the teaching of Analysis"*, Christian Hauchart, Marisa Krysinska, Nicholas Rouche and Maggy Schneider (Belgium).
- *"Infinity: representations, conflicts and analogies"*, Dina Tirosh (Israel).
- *"The importance of recursion"*, Monica Neagoy (USA).
- *"Recent research on the understanding of transfinite numbers"*, M. Carmen Penalva (Spain).
- *"The concept of infinity in teaching and in research"*, Vera W. de Spinadel (Argentina). [This was an introduction to a brief round table discussion that included contributions by Roberto Doberti and Hernan Santiago Nottoli (Argentina).]
- *"Interference between arithmetical infinity and geometrical infinity (at the secondary school level)"*, Ceferino Ruiz (Spain).
- *"The relation between operations and objects in different approaches to infinity in mathematics"*, Raymond Duval (France).

The conclusions of this T.G. can be centred around three distinct points:

1. When the subject under study is infinity, a great variety of contexts and analyses appears, ranging from the student's first conception of infinity to those, most notably relating to the basic ideas of analysis, such as the concept of limit and its applications. This variety is so vast that the question arises: Are there any features of infinity and infinite processes that are common throughout the curriculum? In other words: How can the various approaches to infinity be brought together?

2. In response to such a question we must analyse the mathematical content of every situation, both in school and outside that context, in which infinity makes an appearance, paying attention to the relation that exists between the operations and the (mathematical) objects to which it is applied.

a) The idea of infinity appears when the focus is on the possibility of repeating an operation without being concerned about any drawbacks arising from the properties of the objects involved. For example: (1) adding one (in the context of the natural numbers); (2) dividing a mathematical object (for example, a segment) and then continuing the division, thereby giving rise to a potentially infinite process; or (3) setting up a one-to-one correspondence between infinite collections (for example, between the natural numbers and the integers), thereby bringing infinity itself into consideration.

b) The difficulty of learning about infinity or infinite processes arises when the objects involved seem to call into question the possibility of the operation -- or, rather, its repetition.

Various kinds of difficulties can be considered with regard to the nature of the objects (numbers, measurements, sets, ...) and the operation that is to be performed. Moreover, it has been shown that the epistemological obstacles encountered correspond to different kinds of cognitive obstacles.

We highlight as the main difficulty in learning about infinity the contrast between the nature of the mathematical object and its representation or its written form.

3. As D. Hilbert has already observed, "infinity" is a dynamic idea, not a concept. This is perhaps the reason why infinity stimulates the human mind so much. This aspect should not be forgotten, not only in research, not only when considering infinity as an object, but also when analysing the various levels of the curriculum.

Sometimes "infinity" simply means the possibility of operating (here we have recursion in mind, for example); in other words: sometimes we cannot in fact perform the operation indefinitely, although we are able to control it.

It is important that students be drawn into discussions concerning the finite and the infinite, on the practical aspects of the algorithms, and on the representations of numbers, measurements, sets, etc.

From these points of view we can pose questions on the character -- intuitive or otherwise -- of infinity and on the different kinds of infinity in didactical research.

ART AND MATHEMATICS

ARTE Y MATEMÁTICAS

Chief Organizer / *Responsable:*Dietmar Guderian (DEU)
Local Organizer / *Coordinador Local*: Rafael Pérez-Gómez (ESP)

INTRODUCTION

The idea was to show several roots of the combination between arts and mathematics in different cultures and times during the sessions of the Topic Group. Therefore lecturers from South-America, North-America, Europe, Islamic Africa and Asia were invited. By this it was tried to give a short (standard-) overview on the situation of this subject. An exhibition of art accompanied the work of the Topic Group.

INTRODUCTION TO TG15 AND LECTURE "MATHEMATICS IN CONTEMPORARY ART"

Prof. Dietmar Guderian, Freiburg I. Br., Germany. (guderian@ruf.uni-freiburg.de) In his lecture, Dietmar Guderian first explained how different parts of mathematics are linked to contemporary art, as for instance: numbers (even and uneven numbers, prime numbers,...), series of numbers (arithmetical, geometrical, Fibonacci series,...), combinatorics (permutations, variations, combinations,...), probability (statistics, hazard, chaos, deterministical chaos...), informatics (coding, handling with information, algorithms,...), topology (knots, systems of ways, four-color-problem,...), plane geometry (basic plane forms - square, triangle, circle...), three-dimensional geometry (basic forms - cube, pyramid, sphere,...), mappings (translation, rotation, axial-symmetrical mapping, size changing...). Focussing eespecially on hazard and chaos he explained with the help of artworks of the Polish artist Ryszard Winiarski how such pictures can help to explain what 'deterministical chaos' is. The German artist Rune Mields ignores the existence of chaos at all: a slide of her work "Prime-number Twins" (1986) (the highest in the early eighties known pair of prime numbers twins written by the artist digit by digit) in which she for instance marked the digit '5' in one picture, shows to the uninformed spectator a distribution of this digit beneath all the other nine digits which seems to be given by hazard. And in fact -though a prime number contains only a finite number of digits- it is not possible to prove by any statistical test that the distribution of '5's was not done by hazard.

"DRAWING METHOD OF 'UKIYOE' IN THE EDO PERIOD IN JAPAN AND A COMMENT ON GEOMETRY EDUCATION"

Prof. Kioshi Yokochi. Tokyo, Japan (FAX +81 3 3388 2350)

In his lecture, Kioshi Yokochi gave an overview on the use of perspective as a drawing method during the Edo period after it was brought from China in about 1740. Comparing slides of artworks by Okumura Masanobu (ca. 1740), Maruyamo Ookyo (ca. 1760) with chinese Nengas (pictures for happiness, celebrations, a.o. ca. 1650) it was obvious that Japanese painters were influenced by Chinese pictures at that time. This Chinese painting method was not systematic but informal: For instance, there existed one vanishing point only.

Nearly at the same time (about 1600) systematic perspective was introduced to the Imperial Court through missionaries like Mateo Ricci (1152-1610) or Guiseppe Castiglione (1688-1766). At the same time other Japanese artists like Shiba Kokan (1749-1818) used the systematic method learned from the missionaries and through books imported from Holland. The pictures of these artists often use several vanishing points, and their horizon is often in the middle of the picture. Yokochi exoected mathematics teachers to teach the geometrical drawing method of perspective and oblique projection with historical pictures in their class and was in success with this iniciative.

WESTERN MEDIEVAL ART AND MATHEMATICS

Prof. Doris Schattscheneider, Bethlemem, USA. (schattdo@moravian.edu) "Medieval" means in the lecture of Doris Schattscheneider roughly the time about 500-1500 a.C. She showed that there are many mathematical topics whose study can spring from Western Medieval Art which was influenced by the Christianity (A big lot of these topics were demonstrated by slides): Ruler and Compass geometry (floor plans of castles and cathedrals, constructions f arches, tracery and vaults), basic engineering ideas, symmetry, symbols (manuscript illumination, tapestries, carvings), knots, periodic behaviour (book of hours), perspective (manuscipt illumination, paintings), tesselations (flooring, forniture inlay, halls, courtyards) and even self-similarity.

"RELACIONANDO EL PENSAMIENTO PRECOLOMBINO CON LA ENSEÑANZA DE LA MATEMÁTICA"

Prof. Alicia Villar, Montevideo, Uruguay (FAX + 59 82 60 12 75)In her lecture, she showed some pictures from the Uruguay and modern art of this land. Some slides showed hands curved into the walls of a natural cave by people who lived there in the precolumbian era (possibly used for calculations but more for mythological applications).

"MATEMÁTICA Y ARTE EN LA ARQUITECTURA CONTEMPORANEA"

Prof. Hernán Santiago Nottoli, Buenos Aires, Argentina (FAX +54 1 921 33 85) Prof. Nottoli demonstrated with his impressive collection of slides that, in the architecture of nowadays as well as in former times, elementary three-dimensional forms are used everywhere and especially in worlwide known buidings. In spite of this, he referred as well the pyramid in the court of the Louvre, the 'Grand Arche', a cube in the new quartier "La Défense" in Paris and rectangular constructions in New York. He gave a lot of impulses to the audience to look for applications of three-dimensional forms and their deformations in the neighbourhood of everybody.

EXHIBITION "ARTE Y MATEMÁTICAS"

To complete the work of the Topic Group 15 and in order to have a meeting point connected with mathematics and art during all the congress, the organiser was happy to organise an exhibition on "Mathematics in the Contemporary Art", in the famous Spanish Gallery "Juana de Aizpuru", in Sevilla, which was supported by the financial help of the German "Institut für Auslandsbeziehungen-Bonn". In this gallery, pictures of Rune Mields and Anton Stankowski (especially those, which were explained in the lecture on mathematics in contemporary art) which contained and showed some of the main streams of the connections between mathematics and art were explained to many members of the TG15 as well as to the usual clients of the gallery, by the organiser and a group of assistants during the time of the congress. (The welcome party at the vernissage on top of the gallery in front of the illuminated cathedral was yet visited by about 400 people!).

Beneath the pictures which were (presented by slides there) discussed during the lecture, there were shown some more pictures of Rune Mields dealing with Stone-Age geometry, Evolution, etc, which altogether visualized mathematical ideas in new forms. One of these artwork by Rune Mields showed the sieve of Erathostenes three times: the first in the area between 1 and 12000, the second one in the range of 106 and a third one in the area of 1030. In opposite to the first picture, which visualizes a developed geometrical structure, this structure vanishes nearly in the second picture. In the third one, there rests no structure at all. The prime numbers in this area really seem to be arbitrarely distributed, though the position of each white prime number marked on black ground is exactly and totally determined and calculated. The last of the three pictures shows a distribution of white points which seems to be put there totally by hazard: We have an example of deterministic chaos.

The second artist whose works were shown in this exhibitions was the famous ninety years old German artist Anton Stankowski. It could be seen within some examples, how traditional working constructive-concrete artists (as for instance the Swiss 'Zürcher Konkreten') used elementary mathematical methods (axial-symmetry, rotational symmety, translation...) to let order enter their pieces of art which at the first view seemed to be pieces of art without any order. One of the pictures, for instance, showed "knots of ways": eighteen straight lines, always nine of them connecting one side of the picture to the opposite side, coloured in different colours, these lines seem to search their way, chosen by the artist in a completely subjective manner. But, in fact, all ofnthese lines are strongly connected in one system of orders, building couples of axial-symmetrical lines, parallel couples and so on. All the lines are bound together into a network of elementary geometrical rules. One picture from 1949 (!) showed with the example of the fractals that in the past as well as today it is possible that the artists work parallel to mathematicians and other scientists, or even may be in front of them with their ideas: The picture "Pythagoras" starts with a rectangular triangle with squares erected on the hypotenuse as well on the cathetes. In the next step, the cathetes become hypotenuses of new and smaller rectangular triangles again combined with all the connecting squares. Step by step, the squares become smaller, similar to the development of a fractal. Surely the artist, -not able to paint infinitely small squares- has to stop his work at one final step. With a helpful idea he nevertheless suggests to the spectator that the steps continue infinitely: He lightens the colours of the smaller and smaller getting squares and by this -while they optically nearby vanish- they suggest that the process of constructing smaller squares does never end.

SUMMARY

The work of TG15 as well as the exhibition found the interest as well of comon publications organs (as for instance one of the most important Spanish journals, "El País") as well as of scientific institutions (several universities gave invitations for lectures on this subject in their domains.)

The about 120 members of the topic group were very interested in the subject, got a lot of information from the lecturers and their books, which were also presented.

But nevertheless even now after having discussed this subject during several congresses, it seems to be necessary to give and get more information about these interesting connections between art and mathematics, these two important parts of our culture today.

The idea came up: that during the next ICME9, a working group, instead a topic group, continue this subject, which was begun by other colleagues during ICME7 and was continued by us in Sevilla.

BIBLIOGRAPHY

C.D. Dodwell, *The Pictorial Art of the West, 800-1200.* Yale University Press, 1993

Dietmar Guderian, *Mathematik in der Kunst der letzten dreissig Jahre.* Bannstein-Verlag, 1991. Ebringen (Translated and updated version: Mathematics in the Art of the recent thirty Years), 1996

Paul Lacroix, *The Art in the Middle Ages and the Renaissance.* N.Y. Fredrick Unger, 1964 (original: 1870)

Hernán S. Nottoli, *Notas de Matemática,* FADU -UBA, 1993

Doris Schattschneider, *Visions of Symmetry: Notebooks, Periodic Drawings, and Related Work of M.C. Escher.* W.H. Freeman & Co, 1990

Alicia Villar and A. Bouquet, *Cursos de verano de Geometría*

Kiyoshi Yokochi, *Ukiyoe as seen from Perspective.* Sanseido, 1995

Kiyoshi Yokochi, *Cultural History of Mathematics.* Morikita, Shuppan, 1991.

TEOREMA: ICME 8 FUE UN ÉXITO
Una demostración basada en la semiótica de la imagen

Ismael Roldán Castro
Mª Jesús Serván Thomas

Sea P un conjunto cuyos elementos vienen definidos de la siguiente forma:

$$P = \{ e_m \mid e_m \in \text{ICME 8}\}$$

donde:
e_m = educadores matemáticos
$\in$ = participantes en

Con una probabilidad próxima a la unidad este Teorema no necesitará demostración. Para los elementos de P quizá constituya un perfecto axioma. No obstante, un teorema se vuelve verdadero cuando puede demostrarse que él, o sus consecuencias, concuerdan con los hechos observables.

Nuestra hipótesis parte de un hecho cierto: *ICME 8*, tras de lo cual se afirma una verdad, conclusión o tesis: *que fue un éxito.*

Como en otros teoremas importantes se necesitan algunas demostraciones previas. Y lo que menos podría haberse imaginado Evaristo Galois antes de perecer tan joven y de forma tan lamentable, es que aquel invento suyo denominado *Grupo* pudiese servir 166 años más tarde para una heterodoxa, iconoclasta e inusual demostración. Veamos:

Resulta evidente que el conjunto P es no vacío. Sabemos que Card (P) $\simeq$ 4.000. Además, podemos dotar a P de una operación de composición interna * que vamos a definir:

* = dos o más elementos de P están relacionados por la operación * cuando comparten y comunican la pasión por la innovación y optimización en los procesos de enseñanza y aprendizaje de las matemáticas así como por la prospección e investigación de referentes para el futuro.

Debe resultar evidente que esa operación * es una ley de composición interna, ya que cuando se han relacionado elementos cualesquiera de P las consecuencias afectan (aunque trasciendan) al propio conjunto P[1]. Realmente este es uno de los corolarios del Teorema cuya demostración nos proponemos.

Por otra parte es innegable y debe constituir una de nuestras más preciadas realidades, la asociatividad de los educadores matemáticos sobradamente puesta de manifiesto en ICME 8.

Algunos lectores estarán pensando en la dificultad que pudiera suscitar la búsqueda de un elemento *neutro* único. Y la intuición no les falla. Es necesario encontrar un e_m tal que no modifique aparentemente aquellos elementos que se *relacionen* con él, pero capaz, y esto es lo más difícil, de *neutralizar* los encuentros entre un elemento y su simétrico....

La ausencia de simétrico en el célebre conjunto de los números naturales impidió que aún a pesar de la muy noble ley de composición +, constituyese un Grupo. A los efectos de nuestro Teorema, tuvimos la suerte de encontrar ese elemento único y especial, que por ir más allá de lo natural lo denominamos *sobrenatural* y que tiene nombre propio: *Gonzalo Sánchez Vázquez.* Todo el que se *relacionó* con él siguió siendo él mismo, aunque con una sensibilidad adquirida peculiar que definimos como *humanismo matemático.*

Vistas así las cosas ya no es necesario demostrar que { P, * } es un Grupo Abeliano. La conmutatividad entre los e_m está fuera de toda duda y remitimos a los lectores interesados a cualesquiera imágenes retroactivas de los Happy Hour (ver paso 5º de la demostración).

Como ejercicio dejamos al lector la demostración de P como el *Cuerpo* de educadores matemáticos de ICME 8. Para ello, bastará que definan una segunda ley de composición interna y que comprueben las propiedades correspondientes. Pueden enviar sus soluciones a la SAEM Thales.

---

[1] A modo de ejemplo:Se dieron vínculos emocionales entre azafatos y azafatas durante ICME 8 cuyos potenciales efectos progenitores puede que constituyan una realidad más que trascendente en la actualidad.

«Facing danger»
«Solos ante el peligro»

Although Concha, Lalo, Antonio and José María could predict the magnitude of the event, they would soon discover reality went far beyond their expectations.

Aunque Concha, Lalo, Antonio y José María imaginaban la envergadura del evento, pronto descubrirían una realidad más allá de sus previsiones.

Preternatural element of P, philanthropist, poet and mathematician, major architect of the veracity of the Theorem.

Elemento sobrenatural de P, filántropo, poeta y matemático, principal artífice de la veracidad del Teorema.

Gonzalo Sánchez Vázquez

The necessary external composition relationships between e_m and elements from institutional sets.

Las necesarias relaciones de composición externa entre los e_m y elementos de conjuntos institucionales.

Icme 8 Was A Success
Icme 8 Fue Un Éxito

Proof
Demostración

2nd Step: The Opening
2º Paso: La Inauguración

The setting, the arrival, the beginning
El lugar, la llegada, el comienzo

A geometry-loaded palace welcomes the participants.

Un palacio cargado de geometría recibe a los congresistas.

Top representatives from political and scholarly institutions.

Los máximos representantes de las instituciones políticas y académicas.

Official opening:
a dreamed-of reality.

*La inauguración:
una realidad soñada.*

A few moments
Algunos instantes

Never again would such a dear abscence be more present.

Nunca jamás estaría tan presente una ausencia tan entrañable.

Many-coloured sample of she-elements of P.

Variopinta muestra de elementos femeninos de P.

Unusual advertisement shocked passers-by elements of P.

Inusual valla publicitaria que sorprendería a elementos viandantes de P.

ICME 8 WAS A SUCCESS
ICME 8 FUE UN ÉXITO

Proof
Demostración

3rd Step: The Core
3er Paso: El Núcleo

3.1 Remarkable elements of P
Elementos notables de P

Some remarkable elements of P who contributed to organize the potential texture of Chaos favouring a successful progress.

Algunos elementos notables de P que contribuyeron a ordenar la textura potencial de Caos propiciando un feliz desarrollo.

3.2 Working sessions
Sesiones de trabajo

Finite capacity of session rooms & Infinite attention of participants.
Capacidad finita de las aulas & Interés infinito de los participantes.

When there is no room, it is made up.
Cuando un espacio no existe, se crea.

3.3 Workshops
Los talleres

Elements of P proving the existence of a «homo ludens mathematicae», an essential sub-set in the learning domain.

Elementos de P demostrando la existencia del "homo ludens mathematicae", un subconjunto indispensable en los dominios del aprendizaje.

The workshop on recreational mathematics presented by Juan A. Hans and his students meant a challenge for many a teacher.

El taller de matemática recreativa presentado por Juan A. Hans y sus alumnos supondría un reto para más de un profesor.

3.4 Panels
Los paneles

Mathematics everywhere: geometry in traffic signs (in a more idillic setting than usual)

Matemáticas por doquier: geometría en las señales de tráfico (en un contexto más idílico que el habitual)

A mathematician-to-be considers his mother's explanations.

Un futuro matemático atiende las explicaciones de su madre.

Panels, or the art of compressing so much information within such a limited space.

Los paneles o el arte de comprimir tanta informa-ción en tan limitado espa-cio.

3.5 Exhibitions - Mathematics in art, history and daily life
Las exposiciones - Las matemáticas en el arte, la historia y lo cotidiano

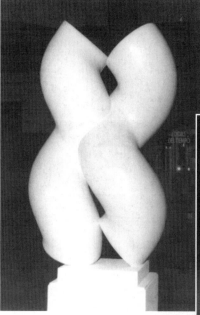

A silhouette by sculptor Javier Carvajal, referring to human shapes or, maybe, also to transversal sines and cosines.

Una silueta del escultor Javier Carvajal que remite a formas humanas o quizá también a senos y cosenos transversales.

Manuel Ibáñez, one life dedicated to time measuring prior to mechanical clocks. A troncoconical clepsydra (1300 b.C.) is shown here.

Manuel Ibáñez o la vida dedicada a la medida del tiempo antes del reloj mecánico. Aquí nos enseña la clepsidra troncocónica (1300 a.C.)

Mathematical archeology: Dauntless members from SEPM «Ventura Reyes Prosper» rescued original instruments for traditional Spanish measures.

Arqueología matemática: Intrépidos miembros de la SEPM "Ventura Reyes Prosper" rescataron piezas originales de medidas tradicionales en España.

Mathematics stamp collecting and photography
Filatelia y fotografía matemáticas

Tiny postal rectangles, conveniently enlarged, full of mathematics history.

Minúsculos rectángulos postales, ampliados a escala conveniente, cargados de historia matemática.

Photography bears witness to the recreation of mathematics in daily life. This lattice-work illustrates ancient aesthetic-geometrical formulae to see and not be seen, or how to masterly solve the inside-outside topological problem.

La fotografía es el fiel testigo de la recreación matemática en la vida cotidiana. Estas celosías ilustran ancestrales fórmulas estético-geométricas para poder mirar sin ser vistos o cómo salvar magistralmente el problema topológico: externo-interno.

Icme 8 Was A Success
Icme 8 Fue Un Éxito

Proof
Demostración

3rd Step: The Core
3er Paso: El Núcleo

3.6 Business
Lo comercial

Together with commercial exhibitions, there also were some non-profit mathematics teachers' societies present. Fractal images set up a highly original visual contrast.

Coexistiendo con las exposiciones comerciales también estuvieron presentes algunas sociedades de profesores de matemáticas sin ánimo lucrativo. Imágenes fractales crearon un contrapunto visual de gran originalidad.

The staff who made the conference newsletter possible: Jesús Casado, Elisabeth Ortega, Auxiliadora Villar, Felipe Villegas, Toñi Sarabia, Juan Rodríguez Cordobés, Marta Sánchez and Ismael Roldán.

El equipo de periodistas que hicieron posible el periódico

del congreso: Jesús Casado, Elisabeth Ortega, Auxiliadora Villar, Felipe Villegas, Toñi Sarabia, Juan Rodríguez Cordobés, Marta Sánchez e Ismael Roldán.

Two readers of the conference newsletter finding out, like the rest of the 3,998 other participants, of the highlights of the day.

Dos lectores del Diario del Congreso informándose, al igual que los aprox. 3.998 restantes, de lo más destacado de la jornada.

Antonio Aranda, another remarkable element of P, responsible for the Scientific Program in the Conference, during an interview done at Canal Sur TV (regional public TV channel).

Antonio Aranda, otro elemento notable de P, responsable del Programa Científico del Congreso, durante una entrevista concedida a Canal Sur TV.

331

Who said mathematicians would not go out, or calmly lie on the grass, or patiently queue for a taste of delicious Spanish cured ham?

¿Quién dijo que los matemáticos no salían nunca a la calle, ni se revolcaban plácidamente en los jardines o formaban pacientes colas para saborear el exquisito jamón ibérico?

The marrow of the Congress
La enjundia del Congreso

The unquestionable secret of a finely tuned orchestra lies in its conductor. A host of 288 "green people" masterly co-ordinated by Juan Núñez Valdés together with Rosana Gallardo and Conchita Paralera.

El secreto indiscutible de una orquesta bien temperada reside en su director. Un colectivo de 288 azafatos magistralmente coordinados por Juan Núñez Valdés acompañado por Rosana Gallardo y Conchita Paralera.

A minute break for some volunteers.

Un instante de respiro para algunos azafatos.

The great Green Orchestra. An unbeatable performance, essential to prove our Theorem.

La gran orquesta de azafatos. Una inmejorable interpretación sin la cual nuestro Teorema no hubiese podido ser demostrado.

Alicia Troncoso, canonical representative of the usual kindness shown by the green people as they started their hard work of the day.

Alicia Troncoso, una representante canónica de la habitual simpatía con la que comenzaban los azafatos la dura jornada de todos los días.

The space of liberty is unpredictable
Los espacios de la libertad son imprevisibles

While Oscar Pacheco is starting one of his demonstrations, others gather strength.

Mientras Oscar Pacheco inicia una de sus demostraciones, otros recuperan energías.

A tribute to geometry: Two women parallel to each other, sip a couple of drinks, also parallel.

Elogio geométrico: Dos mujeres en posición paralela ingieren sendos refrescos también paralelos.

A peculiar power: one man having another as 'exponential' repairs a weather-worn awning.

A wretched reality not to be hidden: sometimes mathematicians make it boring.

Una potencia peculiar: un hombre con otro hombre por exponente reparan un toldo abatido por las turbulencias atmosféricas.

Una triste realidad que tampoco debe ocultarse: a veces los matemáticos, aburren.

ICME 8 WAS A SUCCESS
ICME 8 FUE UN ÉXITO

Proof
Demostración

7th Step: The Unexpected
7º Paso: Lo Insólito

Images to be remembered
Imágenes para el recuerdo

Fermín Novo and Miguel de Guzmán surrounded by granted people. This image shows that solidarity is still possible.

Fermín Novo y Miguel de Guzmán, rodeados de becarios del congreso. Una imagen que demuestra que la solidaridad aún es posible.

La nacionalidad no importa. Las mujeres y las matemáticas conviven con naturalidad superando prejuicios ancestrales.

National origin does not matter. Women and mathematics candidly coexist, thus overcoming ancient prejudice.

Poem: problem solving
Poema: la resolución de problemas

At any moment
At any place
However dressed,
Mathematicians can't help it!
En cualquier momento
Y en cualquier lugar
Con cualquier atuendo,
¡Los matemáticos no lo pueden evitar!

Not by chance, petty fluttering of a myriad of butterflies all too often provoke certain tornadoes, at remote locations...

No por casualidad, los pequeños aleteos de miles de mariposas producen con harta frecuencia y en las más remotas latitudes, ciertos tornados....

The next and impending one will take place at Chiba next millennium.
El más próximo e inminente tendrá lugar en Chiba el milenio que viene.

Que, al fin y al cabo era

Which is, in the end, what we were attempting to prove (QED)

lo que queríamos demostrar(c.q.d.)

No quisiéramos presentar la demostración del Teorema que nos ocupa sin antes hacer una concisa reflexión conjuntista que contribuya a explicar su propia *existencia:*

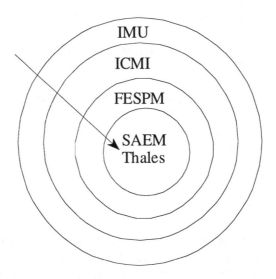

En abril de 1990, el *elemento sobrenatural* de P (Gonzalo Sánchez Váquez), entonces presidente de la FESPM, presentó la candidatura de Sevilla junto a otro emblemático y destacado elemento de gran *peso* específico internacional: el prof. Claudi Alsina. Finalmente, el Comité Ejecutivo del ICMI, en 1991, presidido por el insigne matemático *aúreo:* prof. Miguel de Guzmán, acordó conceder la organización del evento a la FESPM, quien delegaría en la SAEM Thales por último.

Desde entonces hasta hace muy poco, el principal *sufridor* (ahora ya *gozador,* afortunadamente) de las infinitas vicisitudes por las que discurrió nuestro Teorema antes de comprobarse la veracidad del mismo, fue otro elemento fundamental de P, presidente del Comité Ejecutivo y que lo es actualmente de la SAEM Thales: el prof. Antonio Pérez.

Y ya por fin vamos a demostrar el Teorema siguiendo un procedimiento de elevado valor icónico: la imagen fotográfica. Los autores están convencidos de la coherencia en el uso de este recurso para alcanzar el objetivo deseado. Como se estableció al principio, un teorema se vuelve verdadero cuando puede demostrarse que él, o sus consecuencias, concuerdan con los hechos *observables.* El testimonio de esos hechos son las fotografías que hemos seleccionado y que presentamos en modo algorítmico o secuencial como pasos de la demostración:

1er paso: Los preparativos
2º paso: La Inauguración
3er paso: El Núcleo
        3.1 Algunos elementos notables de P
        3.2 Sesiones de trabajo
        3.3 Talleres
        3.4 Paneles (comunicaciones breves)
        3.5 Exposiciones
        3.6 Comerciales
4º paso: Medios de comunicación
5º paso: La distensión
6º paso: Azafatos
7º paso: Lo insólito
8º paso: ICME 9

Ocho capítulos en imágenes. Instantes irrepetibles de una historia colectiva que quedarán perpetuados. Momentos que constituyen tan sólo una muestra discreta del continuum que fue y representa. Una aproximación subjetiva e integradora a un emocionante acontecimiento. En definitiva, una representación gráfica de la función: "felicidad internacional resonante".

HISTORY OF MATHEMATICS AND THE TEACHING OF MATHEMATICS.

HISTORIA Y ENSEÑANZA DE LA MATEMÁTICA.

Chief Organizer / *Responsable* : Louis Charbonneau (CAN)
Local Organizer / *Coordinador Local* : Santiago Fernández (ESP)

The two poles of interest on the subjet of the use of history in mathematics education shall be discussed successively in two sessions. The principal aim is to get some perspective on how history has been applied in the classroom, on the one hand, and in research on mathematics education, on the other hand.

1) The use of history in the classroom : an overview of the different approaches actually experimented, methodological implications of each approach, positive, as well as negative, aspects.

2) The use of history in mathematics education research : fields in which history has been actually used, methodological constraints, evaluation of the effective contribution of history.

MATHEMATICAL MODELLING AND APPLICATIONS

MODELIZACIÓN MATEMÁTICA Y APLICACIONES

Chief Organizer / *Responsable:* Joao Pedro da Ponte (PRT)
Local Organizer / *Coordinador Local:* Carles Lladó (ESP)

The Topic Group 17, Mathematical Modelling and Applications (MMA), met for two one-and-a-half hour slots at ICME 8. In the first day (Friday), there was a plenary session devoted to general themes: the state of the art in MMA concerning curriculum initiatives and research trends and results. In the second day (Saturday), the group met in three separate sessions, arranged by topic and working language, to discuss specific curriculum proposals, teaching experiences, and research reports concerning MMA. Due to late cancellations of contributors and group coordinators, it was necessary to proceed to last minute arrangements in the program and session moderators.

Program description

The first session was held in English and Spanish and moderated by J. P. da Ponte. It had presentations by J. P. da Ponte, H. Pollak, D. Fiorentini and Q. Ye and closed with a period of discussion. In the second session, a first group dealt with secondary school mathematics. This group was held in English and moderated by L. Rogers. It had contributions from H.-W. Henn and H. Doerr. A second group concerned middle and elementary school mathematics. It was also held in English and moderated by G. Pompeu. It had contributions from S. Molyneux and colleagues, J. F. Matos and S. Carreira, and B. Doig, S. Groves and J. Williams. And finally, another group was held in Spanish (also allowing for contributions in Portuguese) and moderated by J. P. Ponte. There were interventions from J. M. Varandas and L. C. Leal, M. C. Domite, and A. Bernardes, M. Saraiva and T. Colaço. All these groups ended with a period of discussion.

In the **Opening remarks: Connecting mathematics with life,** J. P. da Ponte, introduced the theme and program for the topic group. He recalled the main features of the modelling process and indicated that mathematics has an increasing role in society, economy, science, art, and culture and that its relation with every other aspect of the human activity is an essential issue both in learning it and in learning how to use it. The ability to use mathematics in concrete situations and the critical analysis of such use become thus important educational objectives. The author surveyed the contributions to these questions presented to this topic group and sketched possible lines of work for further research and development, stressing the importance of students' assessment and teacher education for MMA.

H. Pollak, in a conference untitled, **Mathematical modelling as part of the school curriculum,** stressed that mathematical modelling can be difficult to teach because the material must be important and correct from the point of view of two different fields: the field of application and mathematics itself. He discussed some of the problems inherent in trying to serve both masters and gave examples of curricula in which modelling is an integral part of the subject matter.

Another presenter, D. Fiorentini, addressed **Brazilian research in modelling.** He discussed the studies produced in Brazil concerning MMA in mathematics teaching. The corpus of data for the analysis were 15 studies carried out until 1994 in master's and doctoral programs. The author indicated that these studies conceive mathematical modelling as a special method of mathematics teaching having as a starting point the study of actual or social problems and tending to a transdisciplinary approach. In his view, they present a relative didactic progress but are, for the most part, intensely prescriptive essays or classroom experiencial reports, lacking a systematic, critical, inquisitorial, and consistent investigative treatment. These studies are more concerned with the uses of mathematical modelling than with the specific aspects of this process. Also, they differ from those made in other countries by their salient anthropological, political, and social-cultural features.

Mathematical contests in modelling and the teaching of mathematical modelling were discussed by Q. Ye. The author described the Mathematical Contest in Modelling (MCM) for college undergraduates, initiated in the United States in 1985 and designed to improve problem-solving and writing skills in a team setting. Each team is presented with two problems and chooses one to work. Once the work begins, the team may not discuss any aspect of the problem with the advisor or anyone else. The competition intends to allow participants to use all information that is currently available. Students may use computers, software packages, libraries, or any other inanimate sources. Problems tend to be open-ended and are unlikely to have a unique solution. Attention must be paid to the clarity, analysis, and design in attempting a solution. Each team should submit a solution paper by the end of three days. Judging takes place three weeks after the contest based on the solution papers. The solutions may be recognized as Successful Participant, Honorable Mention, Meritorious, or Outstanding. There were 320 teams participating in the MCM-95 (teams from 9 countries including 84 teams from China). The China Undergraduate Mathematical Contest in Modelling (CUMCM) started in 1992 and had 1234 teams participating in the 1995 contest. Then the author pointed three common problems in planing to teach a course on MMA: (a) What to teach? how to design the course? what textbooks use? (b) How to teach, especially, how to organize the group study? (c) Who is qualified to teach such a course? He concluded to have greatly benefited from MCM practice and experience, getting a lot good ideas for solving these three problems.

H.-W. Henn addressed **Mathematics at school and in reality.** A new German curriculum, which became effective in the last school year, highlights the importance of application oriented mathematics lessons for all 9 years of the German "Gymnasium" (age 10 to age 19). Extensive tests with computers, especially computer algebra systems, are being evaluated with regard to their ability to improve the modelling activity of students. To fill the curriculum with life in this regard, the students must work with problems which are closer to reality and more open with respect to the possible answer. The central concern must be the process of modelling and not the final result, not only in the classroom and during homework, but also in the central examinations ("mittlere Reife", age 16, and "Abitur", age 19). The author reported some examples of the current efforts.

An integrated approach to mathematical modelling was presented by H. Doerr. She indicated that the typical use of computer modelling in the secondary curriculum involves the manipulation of a previously built model (an expert's model) within some set of parameters. What is less well-understood is the potential effectiveness of engaging students in the actual process of building models using computer-based tools. In a secondary classroom study, she investigated the construction of understanding of the motion of an object down an inclined plane which takes place through the process of model building. The three significant components of the modelling process explored in this study are the action of building representations and relationships from physical phenomena, the use of a simulation environment to explore conjectures, and the iterative process of developing and validating a solution through the use of multi-representational analytic tools. Beginning with a physical setting, students gathered data and conjectured potential relationships between quantities. Through systematic inquiry and the coordination of multiple representations, including those in a simulation environment, the students explored, refined and validated a solution to the posed problem, showing interesting interrelations among these different aspects.

School science: A forum for mathematical modelling was the title of a presentation by S. Molyneux, R. Sutherland, S. Mochon, E. Jinich, and T. Rojano. The authors investigated the mediating role of spreadsheets for expressing and solving MMA problems within physics, chemistry and biology. Using the idea that computer spreadsheets may play a role in students' mathematical practices, they developed and used a series of modelling activities for use in upper school science classrooms. Results of the project show that the spreadsheet offers students a new psychological tool for developing models of scientific situations. Computer feedback provoked students to re-examine their assumptions both about the model and the physical situation being modelled. In this sense, spreadsheet modelling supported students to make links between their informal and formal knowledge. They suggested that spreadsheet models present an intermediate level of abstraction which enables students to move between the formal model and the physical situation. By focusing on a few particular modelling activities, the authors discussed the ways in which students built mathematical models of situations in their science curriculum, how they explored these models and how they constructed meaning from them. The issues raised include: (a) what mathematical modelling means in a school science context; (b) science student perceptions of models and the process of modelling; (c) the development of models for use in the science curriculum; and (d) how student's mathematical practices are influenced by the use of computer spreadsheets.

In another paper, J. F. Matos and S. Carreira addressed **The quest for meaning in students' computer based mathematical modelling activity.** For them, every mathematical model is based on a certain interpretation of reality and this motivates the search and examination of the meanings that support students' modelling activity. In this quest for meaning and its evolution they analyzed one episode extracted from a modelling activity developed by a group of four 10th grade students. To look for meaning in students' modelling activity implies the recognition that students' modelling behavior is fundamentally tied to the setting where the modelling takes place. There are all sorts of mediating elements contributing to the emergence of meaning. The authors identified and discussed some of those elements, namely students' dialogic activity, the role and value of everyday language, its contextualization in the analysis of the situation, as well as the uprising of formal voices, sometimes in a ventriloquism of the voice of reason. They have also looked at the way some of students' models come from their intuitive views of the problem and how they can become rather persistent even in the presence of contradictions. The authors indicate that their results strongly support the conclusion that students' models are mediated by their particular interpretations and dialogic activity, and by their mathematical, technological and symbolical tools.

Mathematization: support or hindrance in young children's science? was addressed by B. Doig, S. Groves, and J. Williams. According to the authors, research indicates that children's spontaneous concepts in mechanics clash with accepted scientific concepts, are remarkable resistant to change, and are already deep-stated by age 10. Their research attempts to identify the features of practical activities which are attended to by the children, investigate the role of mathematical modelling in children's recording and representation of their experiences, and identify opportunities to generalize children's notions and legitimize the formal language of force and motion. They described in detail the mathematization used in one of the activities and discussed the extent to which such modelling appears to support children's development of mechanics concepts, as well as some of the difficulties encountered.

J. M. Varandas and L. C. Leal presented a paper concerning and explora **Investigations tions in the mathematics classroom.** In their view, "knowing" mathematics is "doing" mathematics. This active process is essential if students are to become mathematical problem solvers, learn to communicate and reason mathematically, and value mathematics. Suitable tasks for the classroom are indispensable to attain these goals. The project Mathematics for All aims to create, apply and evaluate investigational and exploratory tasks, addressed to all students and directed related to the Portuguese national curriculum. These tasks intend to promote the development of several abilities and attitudes but they also raise a set of issues related to class management and to the teachers' and pupils' role. The authors considered the potential learning benefits that emerge from these activities, how they help students to broad their perspective, to view mathematics as an integrated whole rather than as an isolated set of topics. The possibility of attaining diverse correct solutions permits that students construct a new understanding of what is mathematics and demands the discussion of ideas and the construction of arguments to support them. They discussed the teacher's role. How must the teacher present these tasks in classroom? At which level must he/she have an active role? How much time will be adequate for the students work? What to do when a group of students is unable to advance? How must the teacher manage the discussion with all the class? The authors also addressed the students' role. What are the reactions of the students to this kind of mathematical experience? Are they feeling that they were making mathematics? Have they learned anything new? Is it worth or it was a waste of time? In what way the real context was decisive to the reactions of the students? These issues were discussed based on an example of a task which draws on a real life context, designed for 14-15 years old students, which has been tried out in the classroom.

M. C. Domite presented a paper on Problematization: **Posing the problem in mathematical modelling** relating the results of a study based in a problematization approach. This is a cognitive movement, not yet clearly delineated, made up of a push and pull between asking and finding of answers to what is hoped will evolve into a mathematical problem. More specifically, this work aims at clarifying the process that occur within pedagogic interaction towards the formulation of the mathematical problem which is discussed/ analyzed/solved through a mathematical modelling process. Indeed, the problematization is one of the very first steps of modelling process. It is important to stress that this process of problematization has a distinct characteristic: is starts in a real situation. By real situation, the author means, "the rest of the world" outside mathematics, i.e., fields of study different from Mathematics, our everyday life and the world around us. Four special strategies have been used to introduce and apply the process of problematization (spontaneous, generative theme, provocative and analogical). Experimental evidence has shown significant effects and positive changes in a 6th grade Mathematics class in which the teacher employed such methods.

A. Bernardes, M. J. Saraiva and T. Colaço addressed **Real situations and applications in the teaching and learning of mathematical concepts.** Working with the new secondary mathematics curricula (during the last two years) led the authors to consider the role of real situations and applications in the teaching and learning of mathematical concepts. In a project work, the population around the school was inquired by the students. This activity led them to learn some statistical concepts. Situations like a launching of a rocket were used to introduce the condition $ax^2 + bx + c > 0$ (a, b, c in R; a $\neq$ 0) and its resolution, using a graphic approach. The authors also used a national newspaper advertisement to introduce, in a case, and to apply, in the other, the arithmetic and geometric sequences. The growing of the world population was a starting point to introduce the derivative concept. The authors worked in group — thinking, discussing and preparing the tasks for the students. Some of the classes were videotaped and then object of reflection. The students were really committed to the proposed tasks and were able to apply and enlarge some mathematical concepts. They constructed mathematical knowledge in a meaningful way.

Topic Group summary

For number of years (that include the period of ICME 6 and ICME 7) the main agenda of those interested in mathematical modelling and applications was establishing the identity and relevance of the field:

• why is MMA important in the teaching and learning of mathematics?
• what are the principal perspectives regarding the teaching of MMA?
• what are the principal obstacles to the implementation of MMA?

Arguments for the teaching and leaning of MMA were put forward (such as the pragmatic, formative, cultural, and psychological) and main orientations for the inclusion of such activities in the curriculum were also identified (e.g., pragmatic, humanistic and integrated). Two main points were stressed as requiring special attention: students' assessment and the preparation of teachers. The computer was seen as potentially important ally in bringing emphasis to MMA, but attention should be paid to several possible dangers. A trend was devised to view this perspective in a broad sense, including many emphasis and varieties. It become increasingly accepted that MMA situations could come in all sorts of formats, scopes, and styles, as part of special course (especially at higher level), integrated into the curriculum, or as a special topic in some points of the curriculum (Blum, 1993).

In this ICME we see much influence of the perspective of mathematical modelling and applications in the work of other topic groups and working groups. Also, some papers related to this topic group were provided as regular lectures reaching therefore wider audiences. It seems that this topic is regarded as important as ever but came to a turning point. From now on the work has to proceed in stronger connection with other topics and issues. There is a need for stronger integration with problems regarding classroom processes, communication, use of technology, teachers' conceptions, etc. However, specific issues regarding MMA are still quite necessary, especially at three levels:

• *philosophical discussions*: epistemology, social, political issues regarding the social and educational role and value of MMA;

• research-based *curriculum development and evaluation;*
• *research* focusing on classroom processes (including strategies to work on MMA, teacher-student interactions, and assessment), students cognitive processes (including metacognition, view and attitudes regarding MMA) and teachers' conceptions, competencies, and professional development.

The work of TG 17 at ICME 8 reflects this transitional situation. Philosophical underpinnings and curriculum perspectives and initiatives continued to receive considerable attention, whereas several papers devoted themselves to research issues related to teachers, students and the teaching and learning of MMA.

ROLES OF CALCULATORS IN THE CLASSROOM

USO DE LAS CALCULADORAS EN CLASE

Chief Organizer / *Responsable*:Pedro Gómez (COL)
Local Organizer / *Coordinador Local*:Juan R. García-Dozaragat(ESP)

The Topic Group 18 'Roles of calculators in the classroom' centered its work on graphing calculators and new hand-held computers and their role in Mathematics Education. Its target population was secondary teachers with little experience with calculators.This group met on two occasions, each of 90 minutes duration. Between 100-150 attended each session.

The purposes of this Topic Group were:

To inform, develop and support reflection and discussion concerning the roles that calculators have played and can play in the teaching and learning of Secondary Mathematics.

To show both why and how teachers would want their students to use hand-held computer technology.

To present the 'state of the art' on calculators and hand-held computers and their role in Mathematics Education.

Each of the two sessions were divided into three activities: two plenary presentations (20 minutes each) in each session; short talks in which specific projects and experiences were presented; the last 20 minutes of each session were used for discussion and questions.

Themes from the plenary conferences

Graphing calculators and mathematics education in developing countries (Pedro Gómez)

By permitting students to experiment with 'new' forms of learning and 'seeing' mathematics, graphing calculators affect the learning process and, as a consequence, can put pressure on teachers and curriculum developers concerning the teaching process. In this way, when adequate conditions are given, this new technology can reinforce the change process that is taking place in the teaching and learning in some areas of mathematics. Nevertheless, in developing countries the necessary conditions to create this dynamic relationship between curriculum and the new technology does not necessarily exist. Therefore the use of calculators present a series of risks and opportunities. The effect that they can have on student behavior and, consequently, on the reflections that teachers make on their own practice, can be used in those countries as a means to initiate and consolidate a process of change through curricular innovation and teacher preparation. Developed countries and the international community can make important contributions in that sense.

Handheld technology & mathematics: Towards the intelligent partnership (Peter Jones)

The pace of technological change is so great that any attempt to focus our attention on a particular technology and its potential impact on the teaching and learning of a particular topic in mathematics is likely to be of transitional value only. Everyday a new and even more sophisticated version of the current technology emerges to take its place. How do we make progress in such a volatile situation? One way is to try and put the problem in a broader perspective by recognizing that we have always used some sort of technology to support mathematical activity in the classroom and to understand what this meant in the past and what are the implications for the future.

Calculators in the classroom: A look to the future (Bert K. Waits, Franklin Demana)

Computer symbolic algebra software on hand-held computers like the Texas Instruments TI-92 will likely become as popular as scientific calculators are today. Many paper and pencil computation methods learned today should become obsolete necessitating many changes in the mathematics curriculum of the future. The mathematics curriculum of the future can focus more on problem solving, applications concepts, and understanding.

Will elementary algebra disappear with the use of new graphing calculators? (José R. Vizmanos)

We begin with an historical look at the development of algebra by Diophantus, Al-Khowarizmi, Lucas Pacioli, Tartaglia, Descartes, etc. Then the relationship is established between the algebraic content and procedures necessary for students in secondary schools, which today can be solved very easily with a graphing calculator. A few examples will be given with the TI-92. Finally, we will insist that even if algebraic procedures will be obsolete in the near future, what will not become obsolete are the algebraic thinking strategies and the reasoning processes that permit us to model as equations situations that are given as verbal descriptions. These not only will not lose their importance with the appearance of graphing calculators; they should, much to the contrary, be the main objective of secondary teaching. Therefore, it appears that a profound revision of the algebra curriculum must be completed in order to adapt it to the future.

Themes from short talks

Short talks dealt with many different issues related to graphic calculators. Some of them were concerned with graphic calculators[1] use in specific areas of mathematics (Berry, Foley, Dick, Resek, Grant, and Lucas). Other short talks dealt with topics related to the mathematics curriculum and its relationship with technology (Scott, Broman, Watanabe, Quesada, Carvalho, and Kissane et al.).

The meetings were coordinated by Pedro Gómez and Bert Waits. Juan Manuel García and Nestor Aguilera helped with the local organization. We want to thank Patrick (Rick) Scott who translated from Spanish two of the papers.

The meeting attracted many people and was quite varied in the issues discussed. The contents of the plenary conferences and the short talks were published in the World Wide Web at the following URL:

http://ued.uniandes.edu.co/roles-calc.html

COMPUTER-BASED INTERACTIVE LEARNING

ENTORNOS INFORMÁTICOS DE APRENDIZAJE INTERACTIVO

Chief Organizer / *Responsable*: Nicolas Balacheff (FRA)
Local Organizer / *Coordinador Local*: Claudio Sánchez (ESP)

In recent years, our computer-based ability to connect and manipulate representations of knowledge in mathematics has become ever more powerful and flexible. The reification of mathematical knowledge in computer-based learning environments, and accompanying enrichment of mathematical experience due to progress in interface design and knowledge representation, widen and deepen access to experiential learning. Some of these environments even involve tools or models that adapt to the learner or guide their learning. Such developments raise questions regarding the use of these tools in the classroom: How can teachers and others assess and make sense of what students learn? How can they manage computer-intensive classroom situations? How is mathematical knowledge transformed when instantiated in such computational environments? How can teachers bridge between low technology and high technology approaches to teaching and learning? Dealing with such questions is essential to the productive use of technology by teachers and designers of instruction.

It was the intention in this Topic Group to examine these questions from the research point of view as well as from practice. Since the design and implementation of computer-based interactive learning environments results from the collaboration of at least two communities, computer scientists and mathematics educators, TG 19 addressed each of them regarding the difficulties and success in the past and the problems to be investigated by research and development in the future.

The Topic Group programme was developped around keynote addresses, short communications, and a panel session, focussing on the state of the art relative to the guiding questions. A special evening session provided the opportunity to demonstrate some of the software underlying the presentation.

An electronic poster session had been organised with the help of the MathForum on a site which is still accessible as of this writing (http://forum.swarthmore.edu/mathed/seville/).

The outcome of the activity of the Topic Group can be summarized along the three following issues: CBILEs and the Construction of Meaning, Designing CBILEs, Effective Use of CBILEs.

CBILEs and the construction of meaning

Because mathematics learning is at the core of our motivation to explore the potential of CBILEs, we addressed first the construction of meaning. Richard Noss explored two theoretical problems, both of which contain important psychological and epistemological kernels. The first problem is that it has long been underscored that mathematical knowledge—like any other—is intimately bound into its setting. The second problem concerns how knowledge is built into mathematical CBILEs—and, critically, how it can be dug out.

Research tells us how particular systems mediate mathematical expression are highly specific. For example, Baruch Schwartz showed, in the case of Algebra, how collaborative construction of meaning could result in the development of the concept of operator (with the OPERA system, which implements a conceptual model), and the concept of algebraic formula (with the spreadsheet-based formal model). Along the same lines, John Olive noted, in the context of the project "Tools for an Interactive Mathematical Activity" (TIMA), that children were able to construct complex operations involving multiplication and division of fractions in TIMA microworlds, but their intuitions differed from the symbolic operations they had learned through their classroom experiences.

This evidence supports the question addressed by Richard Noss: How, exactly, can we systematically specify the relationship between knowledge placed within a system by a designer, and knowledge constructed by a learner as she or he interacts with it?

Designing CBILEs

The collaboration of computer scientists, researchers in mathematics education and teachers is highly needed for the design and the development of CBILEs. Felisa Verdejo, a computer-scientist from Madrid, gave an idea of the richness of the tools offered by AI. But, despite the great efforts to bridge computer-science—especially Artificial Intelligence—and education, the relevance of the tool involved in the development of CBILEs dedicated to mathematics learning is an open question. As Jean-Francois Nicaud emphasized, there is a necessity to build a theoretical framework in order to support the design of CBILEs, starting from elements taken from psychology, didactics, computer science and artificial intelligence.

The main challenge of CBILEs design is to offer students a space in which they can explore freely a virtual world designed to support the construction of some mathematical knowledge. This idea has its early roots in the Logo project and has developed since with a stronger focus on the specific needs of mathematics. A panel on "microworlds and interactive learning" discussed this issue. John Olive discussed the issue with reference to the fractions microworlds TIMA. Nick Jackiw and Jean-Marie Laborde illustrated how geometry may be the domain in which the most impressive progress has been made, with the development of the concept of Dynamic Geometry best examplified by Cabri-géomètre and The Geometer's Sketchpad. The key factor is direct exploration, where the standard paper-pencil environment is replaced with a much more powerfull medium in which geometrical drawings can be seamlessly reshaped via mouse-dragging. This new generation of microworlds offers a novel approach to developing geometric reasoning and analysis skills.

A recent trend of research is to link powerful tools such as theorem provers, to microworlds in order to support students exploration of mathematical properties, testing of conjectures, and searching for counter-examples. Tomas Recio presented the use of the computer algebra software CoCoA to support the exploration of elementary Euclidean geometry theorems, suggesting that this program could be thought as the core of a future intelligent, interactive, learning environment linked to a sketch tool such as Cabri-Géomètre. Philippe Bernat† illustrated this trend in development of CBILEs, which consist of augmenting a microworld with "reasoning tools", with the project CHYPRE which aims to give freedom to explore a problem in any way and to test any plan of problem-solving.

The trend in design is clearly to develop environments specific to mathematics and provide means for students to express their ideas about objects and relations, and possibly their reasoning as well. Some participants expressed their worry that all these developments may be technology pushed, whereas the Panel argued on the contrary that they are user-&-mathematics driven. Mathematics is at the core of modern CBILEs, but the complexity of their contribution to learning is questionable to teachers considering their everyday practice. This issue has also been addressed in a pragmatic way.

The effective use of CBILEs

There are currently no theoretically based tools to address the question of CBILEs use in mathematics classrooms. Action-research is the main answer to current needs, and in some projects it has been systematized so as to provide practical means which can be easily disseminated for pre-service or in-service purposes.

Richard Allen insisted that the principal vehicle through which teachers could reconstruct their pedagogies is the writing and use of teaching scenarios that integrate CBILEs into their teaching These scenarios create inquiry-based, exploratory-oriented teaching situations with a major emphasis on bringing to the forefront mathematical connections. He placed special emphasis on creating laboratory-like teaching environments where both CBILEs and manipulatives are used together to connect and reinforce different ways of teaching old and new curriculum topics.

A similar strategy was presented by Doug McDougall who said that teachers' accounts would be useful to other teachers who may find themselves attempting to integrate computers into their classrooms -- they would be helped to understand the supports that other teachers have needed in similar situations.

Teachers' professional knowledge related to the use of education technologies, and especially CBILEs, was aknowleged by several participants as being a key issue for further research and development, especially in relation to pre-service teacher training.

We are already in the future

The Topic Group exhibited the great progress in the field as well as the rise of complexity, especially in the construction of meaning and teachers' practice. But this is just the indication that we are at the gate of the future. As Jim Kaput, drawing our attention to larger trends, argued in the closing session, we are yet in the early days and have little firm knowledge to guide us, especially since the technology changes the subject matter and all aspects of education so deeply. In this context he also noted the trend of several centuries of needing to teach much more mathematics to many more people, a trend that is accelerating as more mathematics lives in the computational medium, e.g., dynamical systems. He then identified several educational trends: increasing integration of technology in the larger educational enterprise, systematic support for teachers (not only learners), increasing representational pluralism and realism, deeper epistemological penetration by the technology, and integration between levels of technology such as calculators and computers.

Finally, he predicted a continuing transition from Doing (old) Things Better to Doing Better Things. Let us take this last sentence as a challenge for teachers and researchers for the coming decade.

Further readings:

N. Balacheff, J. Kaput (1997) *"Computer-Based Learning Environments in Mathematics",* in : A. Bishop et al. (eds.) International Handbook in Mathematics Education, (pp.469-501), Dordrecht: Kluwer Academic Publisher.

Keitel C., Ruthven K. (eds.) *Learning from computers, mathematics education and technology.* Berlin: Springer Verlag.

Laborde J.-M. (ed.) (1996) *Intelligent Learning Environments, the case of geometry.* Berlin: Springer Verlag.

Noss R., Hoyles C. (1997) *Windows on mathematical meaning. Learning culture and computers.* Dordrecht: Kluwer Academic Publishers.

TECHNOLOGY FOR VISUAL REPRESENTATION

LA TECNOLOGÍA Y LA REPRESENTACIÓN VISUAL

Chief Organizer / *Responsable* : Rosamund Sutherland (UK)
Local Organizer / *Coordinador Local* : Francisco Martín Casadelrrey (ESP)

The advent of fast and sophisticated computer graphics has made dynamic and interactive visual images accessible to mathematics students. This potentially changes the ways students work with mathematics and the mathematics they work with. This topic group will centre around the following themes as they relate to the use of technology for visual representation: the relationship between internal and external visual representations; the role of diagrams (static, dynmic, computerised) in mathematical thinking; using the visual as an analytic tool; cultural differences influencing students' use of visual representations; computational environments which promote the use of the visual.

MATHEMATICS INSTRUCTION BASED ON MANIPULATIVE MATERIALS

ENSEÑANZA DE LAS MATEMÁTICAS BASADA EN MATERIALES MANIPULATIVOS

Chief Organizer / *Responsable*: David Fielker (GBR)
Local Organizer / *Coordinador Local*: Ladislao Navarro (ESP)

The planning of this group was based on two premises:

(i) that spending time hearing about one or two particular materials was counterproductive, and would prevent a discussion about the fundamental issues underlying the use of manipulative materials in the classroom;

(ii) that listening to papers being read was not the best way in which to conduct such a discussion.

Plans were thrown slightly by a last minute discovery that some 150 Congress members had chosen this group! However, we coped with the numbers by making an initial announcement of intent to everyone, and then dividing into smaller discussion groups on the basis of age of students taught, and language of participants - English or Spanish.

Most of the time was spent in discussion, with a brief coming together at the end to encourage feedback to two co-organisers who agreed to publish what was received. This brevity was based on the further premise that active participation in small group discussion was more profitable than listening to summaries of the discussions of others. Indeed, the general organisation of the group as a whole received a round of applause.

Members were given the following paper as a stimulus to discussion.

We shall not be concerned with the merits of any particular materials, but with principles of using materials.

1. It is worth considering what kinds of materials are best to have available, and what the criteria for choice are.

(i) Some materials may help to teach a certain fundamental idea. Is it worth investing in, say, multibase arithmetic blocks, or even just base ten blocks, in order to teach place value?

(ii) Some materials are designed to practise skills, e.g. fraction dominoes, which involve equivalence of fractions; or the "Little Professor", which electronically tested number facts. What do we think about those?

(iii) Some materials are "tools" designed for particular purposes, and are in classrooms anyway: compasses, rulers, protractors. Can these also be used as teaching aids in a more general way?

(iv) The last category could include calculators. How can we make more use of them as teaching aids rather than just as machines which calculate?

(v) Some materials are multipurpose, since even if they were designed originally for particular purposes, they can be used for a variety of different activities at different levels. Does this category include things like Cuisenaire rods, geoboards, Unifix cubes, geostrips?

(vi) Some materials are "everyday", in the sense that they are used outside the classroom, but are readily available. This may include geometrical and measuring instruments, but there are also mirrors, dice, tracing paper, cocktail sticks, rubber bands, sheets of paper, etc.

2. We should also consider what we use materials for.

(i) Some are used, as said above, to practise skills, ...

(ii) ... or to teach particular ideas.

(iii) Some among other things present a structure to be analysed, e.g. logic blocks.

(iv) Some are used as models of a mathematical situation. This includes logic blocks, or Cuisenaire rods, or base ten blocks. Can we model more widely than this? Can we choose our materials to be models?

(v) Some can be used to present problems. This seems a very fruitful idea to discuss. What are the problems? Are they external to the materials, in the sense that the materials are a model? Or can we actually pose problems about the materials themselves?

Although the organisation of the group was welcomed by members, two disadvantages appeared afterwards.

First, as could have been forecast, hardly anything was sent in for publication from the discussion groups! Congress delegates are naturally busy people with many other things to do. On the other hand, perhaps this was further recognition, first that what was important was the discussion at the time, the sharing of ideas and the stimulus of hearing the views of others; and second that such a discussion at one point in time was one of many stages in an ongoing development of anyone's thoughts about the topic. (However, those who did agree to produce something will be contacted.)

Second, as I was filling in as chief organiser as a last minute substitute, I was unaware until much later that a report would be required! This meant that I had not prepared myself by making sure that I knew something of what was going on in the discussion groups. Well, I had intended to do so, and I began with a rapid tour of the rooms in which the groups met. However, one of the discussion groups posed an unexpected problem, which I think has some general relevance to the organisation of ICME.

The group in question consisted largely of local teachers, who had joined the Topic Group expecting to be told what materials to use, and how to use them. My dilemma will be obvious to anyone who has attended previous Congresses. I wondered who was responsible for encouraging such teachers to attend with such expectations, but it seemed essential to do something to fulfill what were obviously desperate needs of thios group, for whom the planned programme seemed totally irrelevant. I attempted therefore to lay on an impromptu in-service course, and in doing so neglected the other discussion groups.

There is occasional talk about encouraging classroom teachers to attend ICME, so that it is not so overpowered by educators in institutions which are concerned with research. I am not suggesting that the purpose of ICME is in-service education of teachers. However, if the Congress is open to classroom practitioners, serious thought needs to be given to provision that is more appropriate for them.

MATHEMATICAL GAMES AND PUZZLES

JUEGOS Y ROMPECABEZAS MATEMÁTICOS

Chief Organizer / *Responsable*: Aviezri Fraenkel (ISR)
Local Organizer / *Coodinador Local*: Manuel García-Denis (ESP)

The Task Group TG22: "Mathematical Games and Puzzles" met twice during ICME-8. Its discussion were very-well attended, and the lectures were translated simultaneously into Spanish. The audience participated actively in the ensuing discussions. The first meeting was chaired by Aviezri Fraenkel, and the second by Thomas Ferguson.

Gillian Hatch reported on a small-scale research which set out to identify the types of advantage which accrue from the use of games in the mathematics classroom.

John Malone reported on the use of games to introduce problems for the benefit of low achieving middle school children (13 year olds), in an effort to motivate them.

Tom Ferguson showed how to use the game of poker to introduce aspects of probability, economics and decision making to undergraduates.

Aviezri Fraenkel illustrated, by examples, the interplay between innovative teaching and mathematical research, where both fruition each other.

David Singmaster reported on the history and development of two interesting diophantine problems.

Challenging chessboard puzzles and problems were presented by Noam Elkies, illustrating several ideas in combinatorics.

Henrik Eriksson presented results on generalizations of the problem of how far a peg can go beyond the straight front of an infinite army of pegs.

Dan Calistrate discussed his results on the partizan game "Domineering" which consists of tiling a board with dominoes, where one player tiles horizontilly, the other vertically.

Kimmo Eriksson showed us how to maneuvre a fodd trolley around tricky corners in the corridors from the Eriksson's family kitchen to their dining room.

The abstracts of the talks follow below.

'A rationale for the use of Games in the Mathematics Classroom'
Gillian Hatch
Didsbury School of Education
Manchester Metropolitan University
UK

This paper describes a piece of small-scale research which set out to identify the types of advantage which accrue from the use of games in the mathematics classroom. This specific issue has not been much studied as a general idea, even though many games to serve particular purposes have been researched. Since it is possible to design a game to use in almost any mathematical topic to attempt to describe their advantages seems to be a relevant task. The game is seen as one of the many strategies available to the teacher of mathematics to teach mathematics amongst which they must choose at any time. The decision to use a game should be influenced by the expected outcomes of the activity. The types of response which can be produced by the use of games are discussed under three headings : learning, ways of working and pupil experience. The games considered are all ones which are designed to teach or practise some aspect of the mathematics curriculum rather than ones played for their value in the development of strategies alone. Groups of children were studied playing games and the outcomes in terms of learning were analysed.

Kimmo Eriksson, KTH, Stockholm: Which is the optimal serving table?

Suppose you're working at a restaurant, with a corridor adjoining the kitchen to the dining room. The corridor has one corner, so it is built up from two straight corridors meeting at some angle. You want to transport food between the kitchen and the dining room on a serving table on wheels. To optimize the amount of food you want to find out the maximum area of a rectangular serving table that can pass by the corner!

At a course in numerical methods at KTH, the students have solved this problem numerically as a small project. During the years, surprising properties were discovered by students, for example that the area of the optimal table is equal for the angles $90º + \alpha$ and $90º - \alpha$. To prove this property was surprisingly hard - until we found the elegant elementary explanation.

I will also discuss the problem of finding the optimal area if the serving table is allowed any shape - and how the problem is related to some simple algebraic geometry.

Joint work with my mother Gerd Eriksson and my father Henrik Eriksson.

Mathematical Models of Poker

Thomas S. Ferguson
Mathematics Department, UCLA

The venerable game of poker is of widespread appeal throughout the world because of its recognition as gambling game in which skill dominates chance. The mathematical theory of poker contains aspects of probability, economics and decision making whose study is valuable for, and accessible to undergraduates. Many mathematical models of poker have been proposed since first introduced in the fundamental book on game theory by von Neumann and Morgenstern. Some of these models are reviewed and several new models are proposed. These new models are designed to illustrate important features of certain games of poker and to shed light on optimal play in practice. Most of the work has been done in collaboration with Christopher P. Ferguson. Some of the models are simple enough to be included in an undergraduate course on game theory.

Lynette McClellan and John A. Malone, Curtin University, Perth, Western
Australia, GAMES IN MATHEMATICS

An innovative activity-oriented approach to problem solving with low achieving middle school children (13 year olds) constitutes the focus of this study. The approach entails introducing problems to students through the medium of games - a strategy which employs manipulative materials to motivate students to participate in the investigation and maintain their interest throughout the problem solving activity.

The approach was developed over a 20 week period in a metropolitan government high school and resulted in the development of a model for enhancing the problem solving ability of these students through games. A sample of 15 students was selected and observed over this period and case studies were conducted on each participant. A variety of games were utilised in the study, but by far the most effective were found to be games that can be created out of the use of pentominoes - specifically, using 5 similar shapes to make as many different design as possible on a square board.

The results of the study indicate that game playing can be effectively employed to introduce and motivate problem solving. Certainly, certain types of games are more appropriate to introduce than others. The model also appeared to enhance students' attitudes towards problem solving and mathematics in general. Teacher response was positive too as they perceived that the use of games in accordance with the thrust of the model not only produced positive results, but also gave legitimacy to the use of games - a consideration which a number of them had hitherto regarded as a"soft" option in promoting students' mathematical understanding and learning.

Dan Calistrate, University of Calgary, Calgary, Alberta

"Domineering" is a two-person game. Left and Right alternately place 2x1 respectively 1x2 (plain) dominoes on an nxm board without overlaping. The first player unable to place a domino loses.

Domineering is the ultimate partizan game; its many features (of being a simple and elegant model for discussing general tactics and strategy concepts as well as an example where the Combinatorial Game Theory applies at full strength) are described here. We give game-values for other types of board shapes and an elementary introduction for actual play on an 8x8 board.

On Pegs and Pebbles by Henrik Eriksson, KTH, Stocholm

Peg solitaire has been analyzed by hundreds of mathematicians from Leibnitz to Conway. If in some row or column two adjacent pegs are next to an empty space, one peg may jump over the other, which is then removed:

This simple rule gives rise to a multitude of difficult problems, among them the following one.

Imagine an infinite army of pegs on one side of a straight line beyond which is an infinite desert. Is it possible to send a peg scout five paces out into the desert? The answer is no, as shown by Conway. If two scouts move four paces out, what is the minimal distance between them? We can now answer these questions not only for a plane board, but for higher-dimensional boards as well, using a joystick, a laser gun and a map of the U.S.A.

In the pebbling game, one starts with a single pebble on the origin and a move consists of replacing any pebble with two pebbles, one above and one to the right of the vanishing pebble: Only one pebble is allowed on each grid point. Chung, Graham, Morrison and Odlyzko proved the surprising fact that the five-point set can never be cleared of pebbles. The full story of such unavoidable sets in the plane and in higher dimension will be told in the lecture.

David Singmaster, Southbank University, London, UK

DIOPHANTINE RECREATIONS

There are several classical Diophantine recreations which have a Diophantine aspect. Usually these lead to equations where only positive (or non-negative) integral solutions are sensible or desired. Another class of problem is determinate, but one asks when integer data produce integer solutions.

After some introduction, I will describe two of the oldest and most interesting examples.

The Hundred Fowls problem originated in China about 475 AD and spread throught the literate world by 900.

The Monkey and the Coconuts problem is an indeterminate form of a determinate problem whose roots go back to the 'aha' problems of the Rhind Papyrus. But the indeterminate form appeared to have arisen independently of the determinate form, in 1907. I have found versions from 850 and have discovered the probable mode of transmission between the 850 and 1907 versions. A few years ago, an alternative formulation of the problem appeared and this leads to four standard versions. Their solutions exhibit some unexpected relationships, one of which I do not understand.

CHESSBOARD MATHEMATICS
Noam D. Elkies, Harvard

The chess board and pieces have given rise to a centuries-old tradition of compelling puzzles and problems, many of which illustrate important ideas in combinatorics and other mathematical disciplines. For instance, chess provides two memorable examples of parity arguments: the 31-domino puzzle and the chessplayer's maxim asserting that ``the Knight cannot lose the move". These also lead naturally to subtler properties and uses of bipartite graphs associated with chessboards, and to questions some of which were settled only within the past few years or remain unanswered. Other chess puzzles and problems illustrate linear recursive sequences, combinatorial game theory a la _Winning Ways_, and issues of computational complexity. We present some of the more striking mathematical chessboard puzzles, starting with classic chestnuts and concluding with a sampling of recent results and open problems.

Aviezri S. Fraenkel, Weizmann Institute of Science, Rehovot, Israel
Mathematical Research Iff Innovative Teaching

We prove that mathematical research leads to innovative teaching, and that innovative teaching leads to nice research results-- by example!

The first example is Chomp, where a simple yet beautiful result of David Gale shows that the first player can win, but nobody seems to know a good strategy for consummating this win.This leads naturally to other poset games where further evidence for impressing young minds with the beauty of mathematics presents itself.

In the opposite direction, we show, by one or two examples (the notion of *strategy* and of *number*), how the quest for simple definitions leads to better and simpler ways of teaching mathematics in general, and mathematical games in particular.

"Paradoxically, we could state that the most valuable part of mathematics consists of the definitions. The learning of mathematics is largely the learning of definitions. Of course, learning the meaning of a definition is a far cry from merely grasping the statement of the definition; the sense of a definition slowly emerges as we master the theory which the definition is intended to bring to life. Such a process of learning may take years, even a lifetime." (G.-C. Rota, Report on the present state of combinatorics, *Discrete Math.* 153 (1996) 289-203.)

FUTURE WAYS OF PUBLISHING IN MATHEMATICS EDUCATION

FORMAS FUTURAS DE PUBLICACIONES EN EDUCACIÓN MATEMÁTICA

Chief Organizer / *Responsable:* Gerhard Koenig (DEU)
Local Organizer / *Coordinador Local*: José Cobos-Bueno (ESP)

We are now at the edge of a major shift in the way that information is disseminated. Books on CD- ROM, programs on diskettes, researchers collaborating over the Internet, and publishing on the World- Wide Web all suggest that the future of publishing in the next century is going to be vastly different from what it was in the past.This was the reason why this topic group was organized in Seville. Under the leadership of G. Koenig, Karlsruhe (Germany) and the local organizer Sixtor Romeo the group discussed the main issues of this topic.

In his introductory presentation, G. Koenig discussed the breakdowns in the traditional system and how to overcome them and presented journals already published electronically as well as available WWW- sites for information in mathematics education.

The shortcomings of the traditional system are the following:

1. There are too many publications and too many journals (keyword: information flood). Most of our journals are written by experts for other experts, but these experts constitute less than 20% of the readership.
2. Authors are increasingly dissatisfied with delays in the publication process. Interested readers are dissatified with the availability of documents on paper.
3. It is an increasingly popular practice among authors to post their manuscripts on publicly-accessible FTP servers at the moment of submission or before.
4. New questions are arising about who will own (or should own) the copyrights when the FTP server will be the author's means of dissemination.
5. Libraries are suffering from reductions of their budgets at a time when subscription prices have been rising faster than inflation and the number of scientific journals has been growin rapidly.

6. Some authors are posting complete collections of their personal works on servers where others can locate them easily simply by knowing the author's name.

The second speaker was the local organizer Sixto Romero Sanchez from the University of Huelva (Spain). His talk in Spanish was "La publicación electrónica como forma de promoción en educación matemática" (The electronic publication as a form of promotion in mathematics education). He discussed the following aspects: * the multimedia interactives and its possibilities * hypertext and hypermedia * the impact of the CD-ROM on teaching and investigation * electronic publications in WWW These are some of the topics that confront in his opinion the mathematician who wants to train his pupils for the integration of a global culture.

Sixto started his talk with the words of Luis Santado in the I CIBEM celebrated in September, 1996: "La misión de los educadores es preparar a las nuevas generaciones para el mundo en que tendrán que vivir. Es decir, impartirles las enseñanzas necesarias para que adquieran las destrezas y habilidades que van a necesitar para desempeñarse con comodidad y eficiencia en el seno de la sociedad con que se van a encontrar al terminar el periodo escolar".

The third speaker addressing general issues in this context was Sigfried Zseby, Berlin,with the talk "How can electronic publishing solve some problems of distribution?"

Some of his points:
1. Archiving: Electronic documents are "living" documents. They can be modified easily, so that several versions of a document can be published.

For archiving purposes it is important to declare a certain version as official. Although archiving of electronic publications is not a trivial task, it should not be more difficult than archiving printed material. 2. Formats: We should not underestimate the problem of mathematical notation. Over thousands of years, mathematicians have developed a sophisticated system of notation. In printed papers we see tables, formulas, diagrams and other graphics. In electronic files we have a variety of formats and it is difficult to decide on certain standards. A first rule could be: Don't use binary format where ASCII is appropriate. 3. Citation: There are certain standards of citation for electronic publications. Two standards are already established:
(1) The MLA (Modern Language Association) Bibliographic Citation Form Guide and (2)The APA (American Psychological Association) Citation

Style. 4. Copyright: Copyright is similar to patent law, at least if you try to understand the legal aspects from a layman's standpoint. There are national, European, US-American (obviously mor than national) and international regulations. Perhaps the most important papers are (1)the US Copyright Act of 1976, as amended (1994) (2) the European Commission's Green Paper on Copyright and Related Rights in the Information Society - COM(95) 382 final. (3)Berne Convention for the protection of literary and artistic works

Siegfried Szeby's talk is available under
http://www.fhw-berlin.de/~zseby/tg23.html

Three other presentation dealt with special problems of the publishing enterprise.

Tsuneharu Okabe from Saitama University Urawa Japan talked about an attempt made at electronic assisted publication of his forthcoming book about geometry. In February 1994, the author published "Illustrated Introduction to Differential and Integral Calculus". Stated in comic strips, this book is designed to let general readers understand the principles underlying differential and integral calculus and their applications to related fields without much pain.

Another book about geometry is now in print. Writing this book involved efforts which no regular writing of academic books would have required. Illustration was left to an illustrator, so the hardest part of the work for the author as a "story teller" was to write the dialogue part of the comic strips. Rewriting was real hard work and there were often cases where he had to rewrite some dialogues after the total illustration was finished. It would have been very convenient if illustration had been fed to the computer via a scanner, the dialogues had been corrected on this basis, and the comic strips had been sent to the publisher as an electronic file. This procedure could be carried out on the internet, which would make proofreading work easier. In fact there are some comic strips (not by mathematics teachers) that use this method, priding theirselves on a beautiful result. Frequently used background scenary and figures are drawn on the CRT screen and saved in the computer. In this respect, mathematics benefits much more from computerization than other fields.

But, to carry this out, a high level scanner and a large memory is needed. The main concern is how to save memory as small as possible.

The method Mr. Okabe adopted is to exchange images with the editor at a low level of density. It takes more time to finish some pieces of original comic strips than the regular one, because each part of the dialogue must be assigned finally to some piece of the original illustration.

The other two special presentations were in Spanish. First, there was the "una empresa docente" research center of the University of los Andes in Bogota, Colombia. The institution has developed a new WWW Mathematics Education site, which is to improve the quality of teaching and learning mathematics by creating a get together place for mathematics teachers and mathematics education researchers, a way of comunication between them and site where users have easy access to research and teaching support information.

The author have gathered different kinds of information about Mathematics Education in one place and made it available to all internet users. The information has been classified in several categories:

* Bibliographical databases
* Information about mathematics education books, journal and magazines
* Projects and research documents
* Articles and papers, original and already published in other media, (authorized)
* Article translations and summaries
* Software
* Future events and fairs
* Information about community: organization, asociations, research cen ters people, etc.
* E-mail lists
* Related places in the web
* News

The URL of this Mathematics Education server is:
http://ued.uniandes.edu.co/

Finally Mari-Claire Ribeiro Pola presented a multimedia project.

The next day there was an vivid discussion on the following topics:

1. How will the web and other electronic forms of communication impact existing mathematics education journals? 2. New electronic journals come into exixtence at a rapid rate. How will these be substained and who will pay for them? 3. How should copyright and issues of intellectual property rights be handled in the electronic environment?

MATHEMATICS COMPETITIONS

COMPETICIONES MATEMÁTICAS

Chief Organizer / *Responsable:* Patricia Fauring (ARG)
Local Organizer / *Coordinador Local*: Pedro J. Martínez (ESP)

Main subjects presented and discussed during the TG 24 sessions:

* The developement of Matematics Competitions follow similar purpouses in different countries.

* Different countries that speak the same language have established new regional competitions, taking advantage of their common language.

* New competitions, for junior students, are arising in different parts of the World. These contests present a new question:
Which kind of problems are adecuated for so young students?

* There were also a very interesting discussion about the use of problems with multiple choice answers in the competitions.

* There is an increasing number of publications (journals) related to Mathematics Competitions. Some of them have a long tradition and others are just starting.

Short presentations were given by:

Alexander Soifer (USA): A problem by Paul Erdos 1932
Kiril Bankov (BGR): Recent trends in Mathematics Competitions for Junior Secondary School in Bulgaria Jordan Tabov & Borislav Lazarov (BGR): Differences between multiple choice questions for competitions and for diagnostics Ljubomir Davidov (BGR): An overview of the Mathematical Competitions for the Secondary School in Bulgaria Anthony Gardiner (GBR) Mark Saul (USA) Veronica Gruenberg(CHL) & Juan Manuel Conde(ESP): La Olimpiada de Mayo, Competencia Juvenil Iberoamericana de Matematica Robert Geretschlager(AUT): 25 Years (and more) of the Austrian Mathematical Olympiad Harold Reiter(USA): Report of the Task Force Ali Rejali(IRN): Statistical Analysis on a GRE-

type Competition Vera Olah(HUN): KOMAL George Berzseny(USA) Maria Gaspar(ESP): Federacion Iberoamericana de Competiciones Matematicas Pedro Martinez(ESP): Olimpiada Matematica THALES de Andalucia

List of papers presented at TG 24:

Kiril Bankov: Recent trends in Mathematics Competitions for Junior Secondary School in Bulgaria Jordan tabov & Borislav Lazarov: Differences betwee multiple choice questions for competitions and for diagnostics Ljubomir Davidov: An overview of the Mathematical Competition for the Secondary School in Bulgaria Veronica Gruenberg: La Olimpiada de Mayo, Competencia Juvenil Iberoamericana de Matematica Robert Geretschlager: 25 Years (and more) of the Austrian Mathematical Olympiad Harold Reiter: Report of the task force Maria Gaspar: Federacion Iberoamericana de Competiciones Matematicas

Patricia Fauring
patri@cbc5.uba.ar

MATHEMATICS CLUBS

CLUBES MATEMÁTICOS

Chief Organizer / *Responsable*: Jenny Henderson (AUS)
Local Organizer / *Coordinador Local:* José Macías Marín (ESP)

What distinguishes a mathematics club from ordinary classroom mathematics? Several conditions usually spring to mind: regular meetings, participants with an interest and ability in mathematics, challenging problem-solving activity, social interaction and fun. The mathematics encountered by students in club activities is generally outside the formal school syllabus, as the intention is to broaden students' skills. Some clubs are associated with competitions, but there are many clubs having no such connection. Seven short talks were given in TG25, revealing quite different approaches from one another and each one filling a particular local need. Further information on any of these talks, which are summarised below, may be obtained by contacting the Chief Organiser of TG25.

Jenny Henderson (Australia) spoke on the Mathematics Enrichment Groups, a network of after-school mathematics clubs for good students aged between 15 and 18. The first group was started in Sydney in 1984 and regularly attracted very large numbers of keen students from all over the city. At present there are 25 such groups in Australia and New Zealand, catering for about 400 students, all of whom are self-selected. The groups have no connection with competitions and exist to promote students' interest and ability in mathematics in a friendly, social setting which can become a regular part of their high school life over several years. Each group has a local organiser (usually a teacher, sometimes a university mathematician) who invites interested students from all nearby schools to meet weekly for 2 hours after school for challenging problem solving activities. There is a deliberate policy of involving students from all types of schools and to make the sessions a social as well as a mathematical event. The groups are linked to one another via the School of Mathematics and Statistics at the University of Sydney, which supplies the problems for the sessions to the local organisers each week by facsimile. Also sent by fax are solutions (for the teachers only, not the students) and a newsletter, which publishes students' solutions to the previous week's problems. Teachers are strongly encouraged not to tell the students too much, on the basis that the struggle to understand a problem and make some progress towards a solution is of more benefit that finding an answer. The faxing of material between university and schools enables quick reporting of solutions and contributes to a sense of belonging to a wider club. Each group contributes $30 per year to the university to cover faxing costs and certificates for the students. The last session of the year in each group is usually a party with maths relays and other games. Local organisers report improvement in problem solving ability in students who attend for a year or more, as well as the development of social skills. Students themselves value being in a situation where they can be open about their interest in mathematics without feeling "different".

In the same country, the establishment of the Academy of Young Mathematicians was motivated by the desire to develop the mathematical talents of gifted high school students in Western Australia. Elena Stoyanova (Australia) reported that the training programs for elite competitions such as the Australian and International Mathematical Olympiads and the Tournament of the Towns cater for only a small fraction of the young people who have the potential to benefit from well-organised enrichment activities. In 1995 a group of mathematicians associated with Edith Cowan University and the University of Western Australia inaugurated a regular program of lectures and workshops for promising high school students, under the name of the Academy of Young Mathematicians. The Academy currently caters for about 50 students in Years 9 to 11, all from Perth, the capital city of W.A. These students are nominated by their schools (from the state and private systems) on the basis of their performance in mathematics. Schools are informed that the goal of the Academy is not to prepare students for competitions nor for the Tertiary Entrance Examinations, but to deepen and enrich their mathematical experience. In 1996 the program consists of 12 sessions held fortnightly in the early evening during school terms, each session lasting for 90 minutes. The material is presented by academics and postgraduate students from local universities and is usually accompanied by small-group work on problem solving. Topics covered include aspects of Geometry, Number Theory, Combinatorics and Polynomials. The cost of the Academy is subsidised by the Department of Mathematics at U.W.A. and the sessions are open to teachers and parents as well as students. There have been some difficulties encountered in the early stages of the Academy. The physical size of the city of Perth means that some students must rely on private rather than public transport to reach U.W.A. Information letters sent to high schools did not always reach the students. Because it is new to the mathematics education scene in W.A., not all high school teachers are familiar with the Academy and its purpose, and so there has not always been encouragement for the students to attend. On the other hand, a few teachers and parents have been enthusiastic enough to bring their students and sit through every session. Future plans of the Academy include the extension of the range of students' ages and levels of work, correspondence work with students in all parts of W.A., the involvement of more high school teachers (contributing to their professional development) and an increase in the number of students participating.

Hungary has more than a century-long tradition of teaching mathematics to talented young students. In her talk, Vera Olah (Hungary) described the formation of the first mathematics club in 1885 in Budapest, called The Round Table of Mathematicians. Members were high school and university teachers who met in a restaurant where they took it in turns to give talks. The Hungarian Mathematical and Physical Society was founded from these meetings in 1891, and 3 years later a high school teacher decided to start a mathematical journal for high school students. This journal, KÖMAL, still exists today and its main goal is the same: to give a wealth of good problems beyond the school syllabus. After the second world war, the mathematical life of the country was organised by Bolyai Mathematical Society, which supported the formation of the first Youth Mathematical Circle by a group of high school students in 1952. Entry was for those students who had demonstrated talent in one of the national competitions. Since 1976 there have been 10-12 such Youth Circles in the country (supported by the Ministry of Education), which provide regular preparation for the International Mathematical Olympiad team. Selection for the Circles is presently based on results in the KÖMAL competitions, in which several thousand students compete each year. Students in each Circle meet for problem-solving sessions 2-4 times a month and all come together in Budapest each month for lectures given by university professors on subjects such as algebraic codes, the geometry of the tetrahedron, axiomatic systems, algebraic numbers and queuing problems.

Tony Gardiner (England) spoke about different types of clubs in the Birmingham area. Events such as mathematics competitions offer valuable occasional enrichment for talented students, especially in the provision of good resource material that can be discussed and thought about in students' own time. In the Birmingham area, there is regular provision of mathematical enrichment at three levels: in schools, at a wider local level and also at regional level. Typical of the school enrichment is a lunchtime maths club, usually run by one or two keen teachers and open to all interested children. For the last 16 years, there have also been local enrichment sessions, commonly held on Saturday mornings. These involve about 50 students aged 12 - 13. They are chosen on the basis of their work in a 6-problem take-home competition, and come each week for about 9 weeks to hear presentations on various topics and to engage in problem solving activities. A feature of this local activity is that because various presenters are involved it is not easy to develop a coherent framework of higher mathematics for the students. The Mathematics Circles were set up in an attempt to develop such a coherent approach, at a regional level. Based on the Eastern European mathematics circles as described by Vera Olah, each one caters for about 20 students aged from 15 to 18. Students are invited on the basis of their results in national competitions (although some are self-selected) and they meet on a monthly basis, for 1.5 - 2 hours, all year. The circles are led by the same teachers each time in order to strengthen and deepen students' understanding, and build on what has gone before. Topics taught include geometry and combinatorics. Since there is no tradition of such enrichment in the U.K., and also since there is (even at this level) quite a range of abilities amongst the students, extra encouragement was needed to keep students coming on a regular basis. It was decided to link the sessions to the Tournament of the Towns, and this provides a focus for the learning and acts as a "cement" to hold the group together.

Quite a different setting for a maths club was presented by Cheryl Maiden (England) in her talk on Maths 100, a program which combines distance learning with group activities, not just for those considered good at maths but also for those considered weak. The Maths 100 philosophy is that children can very often do more than they currently do, and is based on the ideas of Ruddock and Skemp, that children's confidence in their own ability in maths must be increased and that teachers must take note of children's views about their education. Many children, both very good and very weak, need more challenges. The low achievers are given more and more routine practice work and yet also need to do interesting work. The sharpness and shrewdness of students can be harnessed to improve their educational chances. Interviews suggest that under their nonchalance, disaffected students do care about their progress, but lack strategies for effective work. In normal classroom work, teachers leave pupils with summaries only. The pictures and mental maps behind the summaries are not usually remembered. Maths 100 is a program which attempts to remedy this through a combination of individual home-based work and club activities on Saturdays. Modelling workshops are often used and social interaction promoted by setting up groups of 2 students to work together. Concepts are reinforced to build confidence and master classes are conducted to add depth and challenge. These complement and enhance the normal classroom work. There are 3500 students in this program and all are interviewed in advance to ensure that they themselves really want to take part. They have access to a tutor by telephone and are cared for in a wider sense by their own Liaison Officer who phones them regularly. Students' reaction to the attempt to teach them big ideas as well as skills is positive: "It allows me to ask better questions in class."

Carlos D'Andrea (Argentina) reported on two different types of clubs in Argentina. "Euclides" is a student-run club formed in 1992, and based in Buenos Aires. It has about 20 members of ages 15 - 23, all of whom had met in the different stages of various Olympiad programs. One of their present activities is to edit the magazine "Vector", which contains articles about scientific topics. Challenges and games (including computer games) have been specially developed by "Euclides" members for their monthly meetings, which are open to all who are interested. The "Cabri Clubs" are an innovation of the Argentine Olympiad Movement (OMA). They are high school clubs set up to allow students to explore geometry through the computer. There are 15 such clubs in Argentina and 30 in Uruguay, involving about 400 students. The OMA sends questions and challenges to each club, the answers being returned to the OMA for corrections and suggestions. Competitions between clubs are organised to give motivation to their work. The first stage is sent out by mail or fax and about a week is allowed for submission of answers. Clubs which do well in the first stage are invited to complete a 3-hour test, using Cabri in the computer labs. Written proofs as well as a disk containing Cabri constructions must be submitted. The students also give a verbal account of their work. Information about all the activities of the OMA and Cabri Clubs is disseminated through the publication "Lugar Geometrico" which reaches more than 1000 high school students in Argentina, and which is edited by former participants in the OMA.

The last session of TG25 concluded with a short presentation by Esther Ramos (Spain) on behalf of the working group on Mathematical Olympiads "THALES" in Andalucia. They have for 12 years conducted competitions to identify talented pupils for IMO training, with tests given for 13-14 year olds and also for 16 year olds. While these competitions can stimulate interest in mathematics and innovation in mathematics teaching (for example, through the publication of a collection of Olympiad problems) the objectives of the working group have a broader focus. Motivated by Ubiratan D'Ambrosio's notion of education as a process which should convey a sense of dignity to pupils, they aim through their Olympiad work to promote appreciation of mathematics amongst students and to eliminate the unfortunate stereotype that is often associated with students interested in mathematics. Above all, they work towards developing friendship, tolerance and understanding in a non-competitive atmosphere between young people from Andalucia's provinces.

INTERNATIONAL COMPARATIVE INVESTIGATIONS

INVESTIGACIONES INTERNACIONALES COMPARATIVAS

Chief Organizer / *Responsable*: Grabiele Kaiser (DEU)
Local Organizer / *Coordinador Local*: Juan Calderón (ESP)

The sessions of the Topic group provided an overview of the current debate and topical thinking on international comparative investigations in mathematics education. In the first session an overview of previous important studies was given. The second session reflected on the value of these studies from various aspects and perspectives.

Presentation of international comparative studies in mathematics education

The session started with an introduction to the theme given by Gabriele Kaiser (Germany): Firstly the historical development of international comparative investigations was sketched showing the long tradition of comparative education, which goes back to oral reports already by the Greeks and Romans. After a discussion of the various aims of comparative studies, and major problems of comparative studies in general, the remarkable number of international comparative investigations in mathematics education developed in the last thirty years was described, of which a few were presented afterwards in detail. Furthermore the reasons for international comparative studies in mathematics were discussed. One type of reason emphasises the potential of comparative studies concerning the explicit understanding of our implicit theories about how children learn mathematics, which might lead us to question our own traditional teaching practices. Another type of reason aims to identify the relationships between different components of educational systems. The introduction closed with a discussion of difficulties and limitations of such studies like measurement problems, difficulties in defining the curriculum, gender influence and soon.

Afterwards, in concurrent small groups, a few of the most important international comparative studies in mathematics education of the last twenty years were described by contributors who have been involved in those studies.

David Robitaille (Canada) and Al Beaton* (USA) presented the Third International Mathematics and Science Study (TIMSS), the most recent study in a series of educational studies sponsored by IEA (International Association for the Evaluation of Educational Achievement). In 1994-1995, the TIMSS achievement tests were administered to representative samples of more than half a million students in 45 countries. At the same time, context questionnaires were administered to students, teachers, and school principals, eliciting information about their backgrounds, attitudes, and experiences in teaching and learning mathematics and science. TIMSS employed a cross-sectional design, testing students in five grades; population 1 consists of students in the two grades containing the most nine-year-olds; population 2 consists of students in the two grades containing the most 13-year-olds; and population 3 consists of students in the final year of secondary school. Four important questions underlie the study design which was derived from several earlier IEA studies. The first research question explores the ways in which countries vary in the intended learning goals for mathematics and science. The characteristics of the educational systems, schools, and students, and the ways in which these factors influence the development of educational goals are explored. The second question deals with the opportunities provided for students to learn mathematics and science. Variations among nations in instructional practices and the factors influencing these differences are studied within the context of the implemented curriculum. The implemented curricula may be described in terms of concepts, processes, skills, and attitudes, allowing direct comparison between the intended and implemented levels of curriculum. The third question deals with the assessment of the outcomes of learning, that is the mathematics and science concepts, processes, and attitudes that students have actually learned. In this context, the factors linked to students' opportunity to learn are explored, including the learning that was intended and the opportunities that were made available to them. Finally, TIMSS explores the relationship between the intended, implemented, and attained curriculum with respect to the contexts of education, arrangements for teaching and learning, and outcomes of the educational process.

TIMSS builds on several previous IEA studies, including the Second International Mathematics Study (SIMS), which was presented in another concurrent group by Avrum Israel Weinzweig (USA) and Kenneth Travers* (USA). The overall aim of the Second International Mathematics Study (carried out in 1980-82) was to produce an international portrait of mathematics education with a particular focus on the mathematics classroom. SIMS developed a study design to analyse the mathematics

*not present

curriculum at three levels: the intended, the implemented, and the attained level. SIMS considered two age groups, namely students from age 13 to 14 and students in terminal grades of the secondary education. The full design of SIMS was longitudinal in order to measure growth in mathematics achievement. Additionally a detailed questionnaire was developed on teaching methods for selected topics. One of the SIMS findings on the national level is the continued wide discrepancy in the opportunity provided to students to complete secondary education through grade 12 level or equivalent. At the level of the younger population there were many similarities among countries insofar as the content of the mathematics curriculum was concerned, except for geometry. At the level of the older population the differences concerning the mathematics curriculum were remarkable. Students of both populations indicated the belief that mathematics is important, but there were significant differences in their opinions about mathematics.

In another group the Survey of Mathematics and Science Opportunity (SMSO), a developmental project linked to TIMSS, was presented by Curtis McKnight (USA), William Schmidt (USA), Gilbert Valverde* (USA). One of its assigned tasks was to carry out serious, document-based, quantitative curriculum analysis. National or, if necessary, samples of regional and school-type curriculum documents (so-called curriculum guides) and student textbooks were analysed. The following data collection procedures were used: topic-trace mapping documented through expert opinion which topics were covered in which grades and whether they were the focus of special attention; expert questionnaires provided qualitative information in other key contextual issues for mathematics curricula; curriculum guide analysis examined entire curriculum guides but only at the grade levels at which TIMSS would conduct achievement testing; textbook analysis also examined entire textbooks but only at those same selected grade levels; some topics common to most of the TIMSS countries were designated as in-depth topics and analysed in the textbooks at all grade levels. The results of the study show some common patterns among countries, for example concerning the number of topics treated. They show, furthermore, the big variance among the countries in the emphasis of special topics in the textbooks and the curriculum guides or already at the level of the number of the topics covered at particular grades. Globally, the study shows that achievement results must be placed in context and not automatically taken as low yields for educational systems which did not emphasise particular content.

In two more concurrent groups other important studies were presented. Jerry Becker (USA), Toshio Sawada and Yoshinoro Shimizu

(Japan) reported results of the project on U.S.-Japan Cross-national Research on Students' Problem Solving Behaviours. Data were collected at different grade levels in both countries on several non-routine problems. The descriptive nature of the study provided information that helps to document results pertaining to both U.S. and Japanese students on certain kinds of problem solving behaviours, as well as to provide contrasts between U.S. and Japanese students on these behaviours. Further, though various cultural, societal and other factors may play a role in examining the data, results and contrasts between the two countries, there is evidence that what goes on in the classrooms of the two countries is very different with respect to how lessons are crafted, drawing on the thinking of students, teacher-student and student-student interaction, the management of lessons, and the mathematics curriculum itself.

Lianghuo Fan (USA) described a Comparative Study of American and Chinese Textbooks Concerning the Applications of Arithmetic. The study examined the representation of the applications of addition and subtraction in two series of recently published elementary mathematics textbooks, one American and one Chinese, from grade 1 through 6. The results reveal that there are considerable differences and inconsistencies in the patterns of the representations of different types of application problems (limited to addition and subtraction) between the two textbook series, but both paid inadequate attention to applications and did not represent the covered arithmetic operations well.

Discussion of the value and the limitations of international comparative investigations

The second session - organised as panel discussion and chaired by Eduardo Luna (Dominican Republic) - dealt with the question of what can we learn from international comparative investigations. Several experts in the field discussed selected relevant aspects:

Geoffrey Howson (Great Britain) emphasised the value of comparative studies as consensus, but questioned the design of comparative studies, the report of the results and the interpretation of the results, especially by the public and the politicians. Referring to the methods used, he asked for a balance between qualitative and quantitative methods: questionnaires, tests, and national data provide us with 'blurred' objectivity, while expert observation and opinion provide us with 'biased' subjectivity. He claimed that at the level of aims of such studies it is necessary to clarify, whose questions we seek to answer. After listing important variables from the levels context, inputs, and outputs, which have to be considered, some problems of comparative studies were mentioned - such as the question, what do international differences indicate about the success or otherwise of different approaches, or the question what knowledge and which practices are transferable.

Christine Keitel (Germany) discussed the problem of how to consider the aspect classroom reality. She described the TIMSS Videotape Study, in which mathematics lessons in Japan, USA and Germany were videotaped and transcribed. Several questions were posed by her, such as the treatment of the necessarily prejudiced or biased views on such lessons, the possibility of coming closer to reality, the problem of the understanding of culture and so on. She further discussed the underlying fictions of studies, in which opportunities to learn were analysed. Those fictions were among others the assumption of the universal or equal influence of textbooks and curriculum guidelines on classroom practice, the possibility to have constructs like performance expectations and the possibility that comparison means collaboration, not competition, and equity of partners.

The influence of the mathematics curriculum in international comparative investigations was analysed by Jeremy Kilpatrick (USA). He pointed out that international comparative investigations have made increased efforts over the last twenty years to treat the issue of the school mathematics curriculum. He mentioned that some researchers introduced the distinction between intended and implemented curriculum. Others replaced process in the content-by-process matrix (used by earlier investigators to classify performance items) by such dimensions as performance expectation and proficiency level, or added dimensions to capture noncognitive curriculum goals. Kilpatrick emphasised that within each educational system, the mathematics curriculum is an organism that functions at different levels, a factor which has not been considered enough, and he made a plea for a deeper and more serious examination of mathematics curricula in different educational systems, which allows more productive and valid interpretations.

Gilah Leder (Australia) highlighted the intersection between assessment and gender issues, and showed that different strategies to answer a questionnaire are used by females and males. Males seem to be more confident and more prepared to guess an answer than females, even if they are not sure, particularly on difficult questions. This difference is of great importance, because sensible guesses enhance the chances of obtaining a higher score. Males tend to overestimate their performance in contrast to females who often underestimate their performance. Leder closes with open questions on the consequences of these resarch results, such as to stop using multiple choice tests, or train for test-taking, or focus on students' perception to be honest about their performance.

The potential impact of international comparisons on national policy on school mathematics was discussed by Thomas Romberg (USA). He showed that past comparative studies have influenced the policies underlying the current reform movement in school mathematics in the United States. Since some restructuring of school mathematics is going on in most countries, his contention was that information from studies involving comparisons of practices and performances from other countries should be considered for possible changes. However, this will be useful only if the information derived from such studies has clear implications, either for rethinking the goals or modifying the procedures of the nations current system.

Bienvenido Nebres (Philippines) reflected on the role of global cooperation. He proposed considering benchmarking for a national system or for a group of schools, choosing a standard or model which would be used as a measure of a system or group's effort to move towards excellence. International studies and comparative data can give information and precision to the choice of such models, develop realistic measures of efficiency and quality, and learn 'best practices'. Furthermore they can provide assistance for a framework of technology transfer, which may provide a way for more effective international cooperation.

Measurement obstacles to international comparisons, and the need for regional design and analysis of mathematical surveys, were discussed by Richard Wolfe (Canada). His starting point was the public and political attention given to the (average) results in mathematical attainment achieved by each country, which were often treated as 'league tables'. He emphasised that the accuracy of the average achievement was overrated, and that analytic comparisons are valid and useful for subsets of countries where the educational and social conditions are similar. He proposed focusing on smaller regions (economic, geographical, cultural), where conditions are similar and comparisons are interpretable.

The papers presented will be published, together with other contributions on international comparisons, in the following book: Kaiser, G.; Luna, E. & Huntley, I. (Eds.), International Comparisons in Mathematics: The State of the Art. London: Falmer Press, 1998.

ICMI STUDY GROUPS

GRUPOS PERMANENTES DE TRABAJO DEL ICMI

- International Group of the Psychology of Mathematics Education. /
- *Grupo Internacional de Psicologia de la Educación Matemática.*

- International group for the Relations between the History and Pedagogy of Mathematics /
- *Grupo Internacional de Estudio de las relaciones entre la Pedagogia y la Historia de las Matemáticas.*

- International Organization of Women and mathematics Education /
- *Organización Internacional para las Mujeres y la Enseñanza de las Matemáticas*

- Worl Federation of National Mathematics Competitions /
- *Federación Internacional de Competiciones Nacionales de Matemáticas.*

ICMI study

GENDER AND MATHEMATICS EDUCATION

Coordinator:
Gila Hanna
Ontario Institute for Studies in Education of the University of Toronto

The session was devoted to presenting the aims, the scope and the outcome of the seventh ICMI study "Gender and mathematics education." Following an introduction by Gila Hanna and Barbro Grevholm, there were presentations by Liv Berge, Gerd Brandell, Megan Clark, Sharleen Forbes, Kari Hag, Christine Keitel, Gilah Leder, Teresa Smart, and Maria Trigueros.

This ICMI study, as previous ones, had three components:

1. Discussion document

A discussion document setting out the specific agenda of the conference, titled "Gender and Mathematics Education: Key issues and questions," prepared by Gila Hanna and Joyce Nyhof-Young, along with a call for proposals, was published in 1992 in the ICMI bulletin and in a dozen scholarly mathematics education journals and in the newsletters of prominent national and international mathematical education organisations. This was in addition to an initial background document authored by Gila Hanna and Gilah Leder and disseminated to various mathematics education groups during 1990 and 1991, and published in 1991 in both the ICMIö Bulletin and the International Organisation of Women and Mathematics Education (IOWME) newsletter.

2) An international conference

The conference was held in Höör, Sweden, on 7-12 October 1993.

3) Publications

Two books: One presenting the proceedings of the conference

edited by Grevholm, B. and Hanna, G., appeared in 1995 and the other developing further some of the themes discussed at the conference, edited by Hanna, G., appeared in 1996 (see references).

Aims and Structure of the conference

It was generally acknowledged at the conference that the issues of gender and mathematics education are open to multiple interpretations and subject to examination from a number of different perspectives. Indeed, the International Program Committee conceived the conference as a forum in which the participants would not necessarily reach a consensus but would make some progress toward a better understanding of the field and of the often radically disparate existing positions.

The conference held in Höör, Sweden, from October 7 to October 12, 1993, was attended by 80 participants (68 women and 12 men) from some 23 countries. Most of the participants were scholars actively involved in one or more of the following areas of action and investigation: mathematics, mathematics education in general and gender issues in mathematics education in particular, the psychology of gender and learning, feminist issues, educational policy, and the active promotion of women's participation in mathematics.

The scientific program of the conference consisted of plenary sessions, panel discussions, two streams of working groups, and paper presentations, and is summarized below.

Plenary sessions:

Elizabeth Fennema: Scholarship in gender and mathematics education: Past and future

Karin Beyer: A gender perspective on mathematics and physics education: Similarities and differences

Mary Gray: Recruiting and retaining students in mathematics

Panels:

Panel 1: Gender and mathematics education (Gila Hanna, Carl Jacobson, Christine Keitel, Anna Kristjansdottir, Gilah Leder)

Panel 2: Feminist perspectives (Leone Burton, Suzanne Damarin, Ann Koblitz, Beth Ruskai, and summary by Jeremy Kilpatrick)

Panel 3: Role of organisations (Moderator: Christine Keitel; Josette Adda, Gerd Brandell, Kari Hag, Cora Sadosky)

Panel 4: International perspectives (Elfrida Ralha, Hanako Senuma, Teresa Smart, Maria Trigueros)

Panel 5: Research perspectives (Moderator: Maria Trigueros; Karin Beyer, Helga Jungrith, Meredith Kimball, Else-Marie Staberg)

Panel 6: ICMI and equity in mathematics education (Jean-Pierre Kahane, Miguel de Guzman, Jack van Lint)

Working Groups (Streams A and B)

A1:   Students: Personal and psychological factors
This group discussed the ways in which students might be disadvantaged by factors in the learning context, resources, the content of mathematics and its assessment. It also considered the nature of the interactions between gender and other factors such as socio-economic status, ethnicity, and language.

A2:   Mathematics as a discipline
Several aspects of mathematics along with and their possible differential impact on the learning of mathematics by boys and girls were discussed. The group explored the ways in which the image of mathematics becomes important to the learner, and how history, social context and local culture can help present a balanced picture of mathematics.

A3:   Social, economic and technical developments
The following questions were addressed: Could technology provide a way to improve or change mathematics? What are the perceptions of mathematics (of pupils and teachers), and what causes them? Redefining mathematics to relocate its power (hegemony of powerful male mathematicians).

B1:   Assessment and curriculum
The discussions focussed on modes of assessment and their respective potential to be biassed against gender and minorities. The questions addressed included some about new and innovative assessment instruments such as authentic measures and their capacity to better accommodate gender issues.

B2:   Teachers: Personal and psychological factors
The group discussed an image of the teacher as an active investigator, a problem solver in the practice of the ever-changing

classroom situation. After much discussion the group cautioned against the perceived current under estimation of teachers' influence on gender issues in school practice.

B3: Sociological and cultural factors

The group asked the question: How can we change the cultural messages surrounding childhood and elementary mathematics education that seem to leave so many young girls with little confidence in their mathematical abilities? It recommended the adoption of a positive approach that affirms that young girls can so mathematics.

Paper presentations

30 papers were presented (three at a time, in parallel sessions). The presenters discussed research on a number of topics: The role of attitudes, ethnicity and gender differences, applications of selected feminist theories to classroom organisation, policy and equity, gender inclusive teaching, the role of methods of assessment in gender imbalance, and the place of values in teaching and learning. In addition, several presenters reported on the situation in their own country as to the differential participation of girls and boys in mathematics.

Despite the diverse and often conflicting perspectives on gender and mathematics education expressed at the conference, there were a number of important points of similarity. All participants attached a great deal of importance to the continuation of research in gender and mathematics education, and all seemed to agree that both an awareness and an understanding of positions different from their own were an important outcome of this ICMI study.

References:

Hanna, G. (Ed.) (1996) *Towards gender equity in mathematics education: An ICMI study.* Dordrecht: Kluwer Academic Publishers.

Hanna, G., and Grevholm, B. (Eds.) (1995) *Gender and mathematics education: An ICMI study.* Lund: University of Lund.

PERSPECTIVES ON THE TEACHING OF GEOMETRY FOR THE 21ST CENTURY

Vinicio Villani

In recent years Geometry seems to have lost large parts of its former central position in matematics teaching in most countries. However, new trends have begun to counteract this development. First of all, due to an increasing awareness that Geometry plays a key role in matematics and in learning mathematics. Secondly and somewhat paradoxically, because, though Geometry has been eclipsed in the mathematics curriculum, at the same time research in Geometry has blossomed due to new ideas both from inside mathematics and from other disciplines, including computer science.

Starting from this analysis, at the closing session of the 7th International Congress on Mathematical Education in Quebec (1992), on behalf of the ICMI Executive Committee, President Miguel de Guzm\'an proposed the start of a study on the teaching of Geometry.

In response, the Department of Mathematics of the University of Catania offered to host a conference on this subject.

An International Program Committee was appointed, consisting of R\'egine Douady, Vagn Lundsgaard Hansen, Rina Hershkowitz, Joseph Malkevitch, Carmelo Mammana (chair of the local organizing committee), Mogens Niss, Iman Osta, and Vinicio Villani (chair).

A Discussion Document, including a call for papers, was developed and widely circulated during autumn 1994.

The Catania Conference was held from September 27 to October 2, 1995.

Many aspects, significant both for mathematics educators and fo mathematicians were discussed there. E. g.:
What are the main goals of the teaching of Geometry at different school levels
and within different cultural traditions and environments?

What is the impact of new information technologies in Geometry teaching and learning?

What do we know about the processes of learning Geometry?

What should be taught, and why?

How should it be taught?

How should it be assessed?

How should teacher preparation be structured and developed?

Which major trends may be envisaged for the future?

At the end of the Catania Conference, the International Program Committee agreed upon the main gidelines of a volume to be published in the ICMI Study series. The volume will be printed early in 1998.

TABLE OF CONTENTS

Introduction.
1. Geometry: Past and Future.
2. Reasoning in Geometry.
3. Geometry in our World.
4. Computer Technology and the Teaching of Geometry.
5. Geometry in the Classroom.
6. The Evolution of Geometry Education since 1900.
7. Changes and Trends in Geometry Curricula.
8. Assessment in Geometry.
9. Teacher Qualifications and the Education of Teachers.
10. The Way Ahead.
Bibliography

WHAT IS RESEARCH IN MATHEMATICS EDUCATION AND WHAT ARE ITS RESULTS?

A report on the results of this ICMI Study was made by

Jeremy Kilpatrick, Anna Sierpinska, Anna Sfard, Heinz Stenbring, Nicolas Balacheff, Willi Dörfler, Geoffrey Howson./

¿Qué es Investigación en Educación Matemática y cuáles son su resultados?

Jeremy Kilpatrick, Anna Sierpinska, Anna Sfard, Heinz Stenbring, Nicolas Balacheff, Willi Dörfler, Geoffrey Howson.

REGULAR LECTURES

ABRANTES, Paulo (Portugal)
"Project work as a component of the mathematics curriculum"

Current concerns about competencies that school mathematics should develop and belifs about relations between learning and motivation support the idea that project work can play a unique role in the students' mathematical education. Curricular innovations also give contributions to discuss ways to integrate project workin the mathematics curriculum.

ARBOLEDA, Luis Carlos (Colombia)
"The conceptions of Maurice Frechet on mathematics and experience"

We will analyze the philosophical and educational ideas of one of the founders of the theory of abstract spaces, general topology and functional analysis, etc. and we will show relations with certain social epistemology of mathematics and with the social-constructivist approach of mathematics education.

ARTIGUE, Michele (France)
"Teaching and learning processes in elemental analysis"

Didactical research developed around the conceptual field of elementary analysis provides us with efficient means for understanding both students' difficulties and the failure of traditional teaching strategies. In thefirst part of the lecture we present its main results in a synthetic way. Then, we address the fudamental issue of action on educational systems. We show the limits of the epistemological and cognitive approaches mainly used in didactical research in this area, for this purpose and stress the risks of rough transposition of research experimental tools to the educational world.

BALBUENA, Luis (Spain)
"Innovation in Mathematics Education"

We will analyze the existing ideas about the concept of innovation. The classroom is one of the places where any teacher, who wants to do a better qualitative job, may carry out new experimentations. But it seems necessary to clarify many concepts and to give teachers some guides so they know (and become concious) about the criteria of quality concerning their innovative work. Several concrete experiences will be presented.

BARTOLINI-BUSSI, Maria G. (Italy)
"Drawing instruments: historical and didactical issues"

A drawing instrument is a plane articulated system, whose degree of freedom is one (during the motion, the points of the links draws algebraic curves). Drawing instruments have a long history both inside and outside geometry. They constitute a field of experience for geometrical activity in the research project Mathematical Machines for secondary school.

BENDER, Peter (Germany)
"Basic Images and Ways of Understanding of Mathematical Concepts for all Grades"

To primary students, as well as to working mathematicians, mathematical concepts are not mere definitions, but they consist of individual intuitions. These intuitions are formed in processes of imagination andcomprehension, closely depending on each other. The conception of basic images and ways of understanding can help the teacher to create, together with the students, commonly shared kernels of mathematical concepts.

BORWEIN, Jonathan (Canada)
"Virtual Research: The Changing Face of Mathematics"

I aim to illustrate the radical impact that the computer -with the Internet- is having on mathematics and the way mathematicians do mathematics now and in the near future.

BROMAN, Per (Sweden)
"Mathematics Teaching and Learning for the Future"

(Courtesy of CASIO Electronics Co. Ltd.) Society has undergone vast and drastic changes over the last hundred and fifty years, and so have our school system. In the farming society education was considered not only unnecesary, but it was even considered hazardous to society if "common people became half-educated". In the industrial society education became gradually more important, and now you don't have chance to get a job unless you have at least twelve years of education. The society to come will not break this tendency, rather polarise it even more. Since we cannot have children in school for fifty years to make them fit into a new society, we will have to make school more effective. That means, among other things, that we have to take concepts like "knowledge", "learning" and "skills" under reconsideration. In mathematics we have to ask the question "what is true mathematical knowledge, and what is not, even if it looks like it?" To my opinion, the learning process must start with the relevant problems. To my opinion also, too much calculations in algorithms will prevent learning. Calculators should be used from the first day in school to release time for true mathematical learning and to make mathematics a subject for the right half of the brain.

BROUSSEAU, Guy (France)
"The unbalanced conditions of the didactical system"

BRUMBAUGH, Douglas K. (USA)
"Teach Kids for their future, not our past"

I work with teachers about teaching secondary mathematics. If I am going to be telling you how to do it, I need to be out there doing it. I typically have had a class in one of the local schools that is mine for the year. When I discuss teaching mathematics issues with my undergraduate and graduate classes, I can give them examples from a current classroom. Technology is an essential element in my teaching both at the University and in the Secondary School environment. The things I talk with you about work with garden variety students in the 6-12 environment. I have found several features of the Casio CFX 9850G to be particularly helpful:

* Graphing Inequalities.
* Complex Numbers.
* Dynamic Graphing.
* Summation.
* Computational Power.
* Systems of Equations.
* Conics.
* Statistics.
* Calculus

Teach kids for their future, not our past.

CAMPBELL, Patricia F. (USA)
"Transforming mathematics instruction in every elementary classroom: Using research as a basis for effective school practice"

Research on mathematics teaching and learning may support school-based professional development. This session describes how a constructivist perspective was used to improve the quality of mathematics content and pedagogy in every classroom of schools enrolling children of diverse enthnicities and languages. Growth in student achievement and teacher change will be characterized.

COBB, Paul (USA)
"Supporting young children's development of mathematical power"

This presentation focuses on exemplary teacher's proactive role in supporting her six-year-old students' mathematical growth. Particular attention is given to how the teacher communicated to her students what she valued mathematically, and schemes used to symbolize students' explanations and solutions. Excerpts from the classroom will be used as illustrations.

COONEY, Thomas J. (USA)
"Conceptualizing the professional development of teachers"

A rationale and theoretical perspectives for conceptualizing teachers' professional development will be presented. Research from longitudinal studies involving secondary teachers as they progress through their preservice program and into their first year of teaching will be discussed along with specific activities intended to enhance their development.

DALMASSO, Juan Carlos (Argentina)
"Olimpiada Matemática Argentina: past, present and future"

DOUADY, Adrien (France)
"Seeing and reasonning in parameter spaces"

Often a problem boils down to geometry in the space where the solutions are to be found. We will show how this works in the two following problems:

1)Given u, v, w real numbers with u<v, w<v, can one find a monic quartic polynomial f with critical values u, v, w?. Is f unique up to a change of variable x--> x+p?

2)Given an arc of curve A, tangent at both ends to a line L, can one move a straight line D in the plane and bring it back to its position with orientation reversed without having D tangent to A at any time? This problem leads to topology in a Moebius strip. The answer depends on A.

D'AMBROSIO, Ubiratan (Brazil)
"Ethnomathematics: where does it come from and where does it go?"

The history and geography of human behavior allows for us to have a new look into the emergence of mathematical ideas in different cultural environments. With this background, we can develop a conceptual framework for ethnomathematics. Scenarios of the future can lead to considerations about the next steps of the ethnomathematics movement.

DOERFLER, Willibald (Austria)
"Means for Meaning"

Three potential sources from which students could derive meaning and understanding are presented: (i) Mathematical structures viewed as protocols of processes and actions; (ii) Thinking by prototypes for mathematical concepts. (iii) Re-interpreting the mathematical discourse: we speak (and think) as if there were specific objects with the ascribed properties and relations though we only can access so-called representations and verbal descriptions (metaphoric use of the word "object").

ERNEST, Paul (UK)
"Social Constructivism as a Philosophy of Mathematics"

Social constructivism as a philosophy of mathematics is concerned with the genesis and warranting of mathematical knowledge. These processes take place both in the contexts of research mathematics and in the contexts of schooling, where they concern learning and assessment. A theoretical account of these processes situated in human practices will be given, based on the work of Lakatos and Wittgenstein. The resulting theory might be termed a post-modernist philosophy of mathematics, since it dethrones logic as the foundation of mathematical knowledge in favour of decentred human practices and context-bound warranting conversations. Attention will also be devoted to the relations between the philosophy of mathematics and mathematics education. The fact that developments in the philosophy of mathematics and corresponding informal conceptions have important outcomes for mathematics education is widely noted. What is less remarked is that issues of learning and assessment have significant implications, for the discipline of mathematics and for its philosophy, at least from social constructivist and fallibilist perspectives. This will be discussed, together with other relevant issues.

FIRSOV, Victor (Russia)
"Russian standards: concepts and decisions"

FORTUNY, Josep M. (Spain)
"Range of Abilities. Learning and Assessing Geometrical Knowledge in Environmental Context"

We tackle the complex problem of skill's processes in L & A and present a brief historic perspective about research approaches (factorial, conceptual, structural, hierarchical, degrees of acquisition, and cognitive range of abilities). We focus on the design of the learning environment which enhances the development of high order abilities, and on the continuous improvement and adaptation to diversity.

FUJITA, Hiroshi (Japan)
"High lights and shadows of recent Japanese curriculum for secondary schools"

The current Japanese national curricula have been put in force in 1961 for the senior high schools. Its part for SHS mathematics is characterized by double-focused targets (mathematical literacy and mathematical thinking), the Core-Options structure, and introduction of computers. Various difficulties in implementation have come up, while recently we are concerned with "Crisis of mathematics education", of which a main symptom is students' disinclination for mathematics and science.

GALBRAITH, Peter (Australia)
"Issues in Assessment: a never ending story"

This talk does not concern itself with aspects such as instrument design, or with how to make techniques or systems work better. Rather it identifies and elaborates points of debate at technical, practical and political levels that make assessment in mathematics at once an important, a stimulating, and a controversial subject.

GARFUNKEL, Sol (USA)
"Applications reform: a brief history in time.

This presentation will give an historical perspective of the current reform movement in mathematics education from an international perspective. The focus will be on the inclusion of applications of mathematics, the introduction of mathematical modeling, and of contextual approaches to curriculum development at both the secondary and tertiary levels.

GAULIN, Claude (Canada)
"Difficulties and challenges in the implementation of "problem solving" in school mathematics curricula"

Since fifteen years, there has been an increasing international trend to emphasize "problem solving" in school mathematics curricula. What major difficulties have been observed in its implementation? What are the new challenges for research on problem solving? These questions will be discussed in the light of an international survey conducted recently.

GERDES, Paulus (Mozambique)
"Culture and mathematics education in (southern) Africa"

GJONE, Gunnar (Norway)
"A new role for curriculum documents - from inspiration to production plans?"

In many countries new educational thoughts have emerged. Education and research have been increasingly influenced by economic considerations. Education clearly has implications for economic growth, but only in recent years have the models of management i production been adopted for education. We will discuss how curriculum documents reflect this development.

GU, Lingyuan (China)
"An experiment in Qingpu - A report on Math Education Reform of the Contemporary Standard in China"

From the year 1977 to 1992, we developed an experiment on a large scale in education reform in Qingpu county (regarded as an epitome of then China) and made the qualified rate in maths by all county middle school students go up from 16% to 85% and more. The State Education Commission has defined it as the important achievements in basic education reform and decide to spread it out all over the country. The report briefly introduces the unique system of experiment methods suitable for teachers in group and the experiment results of teaching principles and strategy etc. to let all students study efficiently.

HART, Kath (UK)
"What responsability do researchers have to mathematics teachers and children?"

In many countries there is little "Mathematics Education Research". Repeatedly we are told that it has little influence on what happens in the classroom. Perhaps this is because it is insufficiently relevant to the classroom non-generalisable and liable to concerned with theory building.

HOWSON, Geoffrey (UK)
"Mathematics and Commonsense"

What are the relations between mathematics and commonsense? To what extent is it possible to teach mathematics as commonsense and what are the dangers inherent in such an approach?

KEITEL, Christine (Germany)
"Teaching maths anxiety - A circulus of aversion to mathematics with teachers and students"

The way mathematics is taught in study courses for teachers at university level negatively determine perceptions of mathematics and mathematics education and the kind of "transmission" still typical for high school mathematics. Based on research about the social view of mathematics held by teacher students for all school types which were gained by questionnaires at the beginning of university studies, i.e. perceptions mainly determined by school experiences, and later compared with views developed during university at the end of their undergraduate studies, it will be discussed how teachers transform their negative experiences with teaching methods at high school and university explicitly and implicitly into conceptions of aversion or avoidance of mathematics with students which reversely "bequeath" maths anxiety.

KIERAN, Carolyn (Canada)
"The changing face of school algebra"

In the past, school algebra has been viewed chiefly as generalized arithmetic. However, recent attempts to enrich its content by including, for example, problem solving, functional concepts, modeling, and pattern generalization, as well as the use of the computer to encourage algebraic thinking, have all played a role in redefining what we are coming to mean by school algebra.

KIRCHGRABER, Urs (Switzerland)
"On some aspects in the teaching of mathematics at secondary schools in Switzerland"

We briefly describe some specific features of the Swiss secondary school system (upper gymnasium) and we discuss a number of recently developed new tools for teaching under-graduate mathematics.

KRAINER, Konrad (Austria)
"Some considerations on problem and perspectives of mathematics teacher inservice education"

The increasing complexity of discussion in mathematics education changes our view on teacher education and on professional teaching. There are more and more international reports about involving (practicing and prospective) mathematics teachers into research projects and integrating research components into teacher education courses. The self-critical investigation of a teacher into his own teaching will be illustrated.

LEDER, Gilah (Australia)
"Mathematics Education and Gender Issues"

Critical developments in research on mathematics and gender are traced in this session: from early work on recording differences between males and females in performance and participation in mathematics to more recent feminist perspectives which argue that equity for females requires a reevaluation of current social structures, popular values and norms.

MOORE, David S. (USA)
"New Pedagogy and New Content: The Case of Statistics"

Teachers of mathematics at all levels are being urged to adopt a new pedagogy that emphasizes active learning and places more emphasis on group work and communication of results. The call for reform often includes a call to revise our learning objectives to, for example, emphasize flexible problem-solving skills. In statistics, changes in the field itself, driven by technology and professional practice, have moved the content of beginning instruction somewhat away from mathematics toward experience with data. The interaction between these trends has led to rapid change in statistics instruction. This talk will review current trends in statistics teaching and attempt to describe the lessons learned.

NESHER, Pearla (Israel)
"School stereotype word problems and the open nature of applications"

A dilemma is presented to math educators: is problem solving teachable? In most cases, the student learns how to solve problems by working on a variety of examples. Is there a way to teach this proficiency explicitly and in a more articulate way? Findings from cognitive psychology suggest that one should uncover the scheme underlying the problem and that the basic general schemes could be directly taught. Empirical findings will also be presented.

OTEIZA, Fidel (Chile)
"Mathematics in context: an integrated approach for the development of the curriculum"

PAPASTAVRIDIS, Stavros G. and KLAONDATOS, Nick (Greece)
"Assessing the effectiveness of teaching applications of mathematics"

PEREZ FERNANDEZ, Javier (Spain)
"Symbol manipulators in Mathematical Instruction"

Symbol manipulators can and must play an important role in mathematics teaching. With adequate planning they can assist in bettering understanding, studying in depth numerous concepts, be a valuable educational instrument in problem solving and influence curriculum planning in terms of content, selection and order. Their use must be placed within what is known as "experiental mathematics teaching" and must not be hidden in activities aimed at learning as a set of fixed "symbol manipulators" to resolve determined routine exercises. The software in question has been selected on a basis of characteristics accumulated from studies, from students and from other available sources. Alongside an overview of its advantages and inconveniences in relation to its educative tasks, the presentation will incorporate activities directed towards secondary school and university students.

PUIG, Luis (Spain)
"What I have learnt about problem solving from history and research"

There is a wealth of possible worlds of problem solving. Heuristics is the study of one of such worlds. The method of analysis and synthesis, from Pappus through Ibn al-Haytham to Lakatos, has been endowed with the power of leading both the search of solutions and the generation of new problems.

QIU, Zonghu (China)
"Mathematics competitions in China - success and deficiency"

In this talk the activities generated by mathematics competitions in China will be detailed. The influence of mathematics competitions into mathematical education will be examined... and the problems arising when paying too much attention to the mathematics competitions will be discussed.

RICO, Luis (Spain)
"Doctoral and Academic Research programs in Mathematics Education at the Spanish University"

The general content of this lecture will be related to the current development research in Mathematics Education at the Spanish University from 1984 on, with the new universitary estructure derived from the University Reform Law (LRU), the arising of the Knowledge Field of Didactics of Mathematics and the Doctoral Programs in this discipline. In each one of the current programs, a number of Doctoral Thesis have been defended, which state a core of specialized knowledge, academically validated, which conform a well stablished theoretical and practical scientific corpus. In the Spanish Mathematics Educators community, a serious and rigorous scientific field has been settled, with its own entity and inquiry practices. The lecture is aimed to present the backgrounds of the academic research in Didactics of Mathematics, the state of art, with the achievements reached to the present and the major research lines for the next years.

SCHMIDT, Siegbert (Germany)
"Semantic Structures of Word Problems - Mediators Between Mathematical Structures and Cognitive Structures of the Students?"

The existing body of research on semantic structures of word problems concerning addition, subtraction, multiplication, and division on the primary level shall be discussed focussing these problems:
* What epistemological status of such semantic structures does appear to be appropriate?
* What kind of help can such structures provide for the teacher?

SCHUPP, Hans (Germany)
"Regeometrization of school geometry - through computers?"

The decline of geometry at the secondary and its death at the post-secondary level (s. ICME-4) is caused -among others- by the comfortable transition from Euclidean to Cartesian representations and methods. This talk will analyse how the facilities of computer graphics can be used to arouse and to foster genuine geometric intuition and reasoning.

SFARD, Anna (Israel)
"On metaphors and models for conceptual change in mathematics"

Among the many streams that combine into a steadily growing flow of research in mathematics education, one of the most prominent is the study of the development of mathematical concepts. This talk will be devoted to reflections on the past, present, and future of this line of research. More specifically, a critical thought will be given to different metaphors that have been inspiring the study of conceptual change over time. The main focus will be on the ways in which the evolving idea of biological growth have been shaping researchers' approach to the subject since the works of Piaget and Vygotsky.

SKOVSMOSE, Ole (Denmark)
"Critical Mathematics Education - Some Philosophical Remarks"

Mathematics education must serve also as an invitation for participating in democratic life in a highly technological society, in which conditions for democracy may be hampered by exactly the technological development for which mathematics education also serves as a preparation. This challenge signifies the importance of critical mathematics education. However, what then is the nature of critical mathematics education?

STRAESSER, Rudolf (Germany)
"Mathematics for Work - a Didactical Perspective"

The world of work is full of Mathematics. Abstract Mathematics is the most powerful mathematics for work. Computer use implies sophisticated mathematics at work. The average employee / worker must learn (no) mathematics for her / his work. The lecture will comment on these and other slogans on mathematics for / at work.

STREEFLAND, Leen (Netherlands)
"Historical learning for future teaching, or turning a sphere inside out. No kinks"

Stephen Smale made considerable progress in the theory of dynamical systems. His learning process, indeed, is a revealing paradigm. It will be analysed as such. Could its outcomes be exploited for teaching and learning mathematics at different levels, or not? The affirmative answer will be supported by a wealth of examples.

SZENDREI, Julianna (Hungary)
"The role of mother tongue in mathematics learning"

THOMPSON, Alba (USA)
"Conceptual and Calculational Orientations in Teaching Mathematics"

We will contrast two orientations to mathematics teaching, calculational and conceptual, focusing on what instructional patterns characterize the two and the knowledge base that teachers need to draw from in order to teach mathematics conceptually.

TOUBURG, Jens and WAGNER, Soren (Denmark)
"A decade of teaching mathematical modelling"

TRI, Nguyen Dinh (Vietnam)
"Some aspects of the University Mathematics curriculum for engineers"

My talk is based on my experience of mathematics teaching in Hanoi University of Technology for many years. I will address some factors that need to be considered when we design the curriculum of Mathematics for our students of engineering. I would like to insist on this point: one of the main purposes of the undergraduate training for engineers in Mathematics is the encouragement of independence, creativity of students, particularly the abilities in problem posing and problem solving, in modeling and model solving (by mathematics tools). The curriculum of Applied Mathematics for mathematics engineers of our university will be described.

VASCO, Carlos (Colombia)
"A general theory of processes and systems in research in mathematics and in mathematics education"

The task of doing mathematics is viewed as the detection of patterns and regularities in real processes, and the production of systems composed of elements, transformations, relations, in order to explore their behavior. An interpretation of the concepts of structure and dynamics of a mathematical system is proposed, as well as the implications of this general process/systems theory in research in mathematics and in mathematics education.

VERGNAUD, Gérard (France)
"Important cognitive changes in the learning of mathematics. A developmental perspective"

Among all changes that take place in the learning of mathematics, some are most important because they require big qualitative steps from students. The new knoledge may even be counterintuitive. Four examples will be given:

* Addition of numbers when the relatioship rather suggests substraction of one data from the other
* Inversion of quotients of dimensions
* Graphics plotting when the scale chosen does not allow to represent the origin
* Algebraic treatment and interpretation of negative numbers

Teachers should be fully aware of these long lasting difficulties, as there is no hope that students jump over them without repeated and strong examples and explanations.

VICENTE, Jose Luis (Spain)
"Geometry and Simbolic Calculus"

In the last years we have seen a large quantity of research on the applications of simbolic calculus, and its systems, to Geometry. There are several reasons behind this: the growing implementation of the systems of simbolic calculus in research and educational centers and the pure scientific reasons (e.g., invention of new and fast algorithms to do repetitive tasks, computer graphics, data basis...). We will review recent developments in this field, and applications to teaching at various levels. We will dedicate special attention to topics like authomatic proofs in plane geometry, non-euclidean geometries, algebraic curves and surfaces and computer graphics.

VIGGIANI-BICUDO, Maria Aparecida (Brazil)
"Philosophy of Mathematical Education: An Phenomenological Approach."

This lecture will focus the meaning of philosophy of mathematical Education comparing it with that of Philosophy of Education and of Philosophy of Mathematics. Then, it will focus the natural attitude and the phenomological attitude pointing out the ways in which reality and knowledge can be worked out both in the Mathematical Education context.

WANG, Changpei (China)
"Mathematics Education - An Oriental point of view"

The modern reform of Chinese mathematics education has been drived by the two main forces: development of it's own society and the western movement of mathematics education. The report will try to explain how Chinese mathematic education is now moving up to a new paradigm (it is a systematic and profound change towards the 21st century) and how the changing process has to be carefully planed and controled.

CONFERENCIAS ORDINARIAS

ABRANTES, Paolo (Portugal)
"El trabajo de proyecto como un componente del curriculum matemático"

La preocupación actual sobre las competencias que debe desarrollar el curriculum de matemáticas y las opiniones sobre las relaciones entre el aprendizaje y la motivación dan pie a la idea de que el trabajo de proyecto puede jugar un papel importante en la educación matemática del alumnado. Las innovaciones curriculares contribuyen a discutir cómo integrar el trabajo de proyecto en el curriculum matemático.

ARBOLEDA, Luis Carlos (Colombia)
"Las concepciones de Maurice Fréchet sobre matemáticas y experiencia"

Analizaremos las ideas filosóficas y matemáticas de uno de los fundadores de la teoría de espacios abstractos, topología general, análisis funcional, etc. y mostraremos relaciones con cierta epistemología social de las matemáticas y con la aproximación social-constructivista de la educación matemática.

ARTIGUE, Michèle (Francia)
"Procesos de enseñanza-aprendizaje en análisis elemental"

La investigación didáctica desarrollada en el campo conceptual del análisis elemental nos proporciona medios eficientes para entender tanto las dificultades de los alumnos como los fallos en la estrategia tradicional de enseñanza. En la primera parte de la conferencia, presentamos sus principales resultados de forma sintética. Luego, abordamos el aspecto fundamental de la acción en sistemas educativos. Mostramos los límites de los enfoques epistemológicos y cognitivos que se utilizan habitualmente en la investigación en la didáctica de este área y resaltamos los riesgos de una transposición grosera de las herramientas experimentales de investigación al mundo de la educación.

BALBUENA, Luis (España)
"Innovación en Educación Matemática"

Analizaremos las ideas existentes sobre el concepto de innovación. El aula es uno de los sitios donde cualquier profesor que quiera hacer un mejor trabajo puede llevar a cabo nuevos experimentos. Pero parece necesario clarificar muchos conceptos y dar a los profesores algunas guías para que conozcan (y sean conscientes) de los criterios de calidad que conciernen a su trabajo innovador. Se presentarán varias experiencias concretas.

BARTOLINI-BUSSI, María G. (Italia)
"Instrumentos de dibujo: aspectos históricos y didácticos"

Un instrumento de dibujo es un sistema plano articulado cuyo grado de libertad es uno (durante el movimiento, un punto del sistema dibuja curvas algebraicas). Estos instrumentos tienen una larga historia tanto dentro como fuera de la geometría. Constituyen un campo experimental para las actividades geométricas en la investigación del proyecto para secundaria 'Máquinas Matemáticas'

BENDER, Peter (Alemania)
"Imágenes y Formas Básicas de Comprensión de Conceptos Matemáticos en todos los Niveles"

Para los estudiantes de primaria -y para los matemáticos profesionales-, los conceptos matemáticos no son meras definiciones, sino que consisten en intuiciones individuales. Estas intuiciones se forman en procesos de imaginación y comprehensión, que dependen estrechamente entre sí. La concepción de las imágenes y formas básicas de la comprensión puede ayudar al profesor a crear, junto a los estudiantes, núcleos habitualmente compartidos de conceptos matemáticos.

BORWEIN, Jonathan (Canadá)
"Investigación virtual: la cara cambiante de las matemáticas"

La intención es ilustrar el radical impacto que el ordenador -con Internetestá teniendo en las matemáticas y en la forma en que los matemáticos hacen matemáticas, en la actualidad y en un futuro próximo.

BROMAN, Per (Suecia)
'La Enseñanza y el Aprendizaje de las Matemáticas para el Futuro' (Cortesía de CASIO Electronics Co. Ltd)

La sociedad ha experimentado cambios drásticos en los últimos 150 años, y, con ella nuestro sistema educativo. En la sociedad rural la educación era considerada no sólo innecesaria, sino incluso peligrosa para la sociedad si 'la gente corriente se medio-educara'. En la sociedad industrial la educación se hizo cada vez más importante y, de hecho, es casi imposible conseguir un trabajo a menos que se cuente con doce años previos de estudios. En el futuro no se romperá esta tendencia, al contrario, se acentuará. Ya que no podemos mantener a los niños durante 50 años estudiando, tendremos que hacer la escuela más efectiva. Esto significa, entre otras cosas, que tendremos que reconsiderar conceptos como 'conocimientos', 'aprendizaje', 'destrezas', etc. Especialmente en matemáticas tendremos que preguntarnos '(Cuál es el verdadero conocimiento matemático y cuál no lo es aunque lo parezca?.' En mi opinión, el proceso de aprendizaje debe empezar por problemas significativos. Igualmente creo que demasiados cálculos en los algoritmos impedirán dicho aprendizaje. Las calculadoras deberían usarse en el aula desde el primer día para dejar más tiempo disponible para el auténtico aprendizaje matemático y para hacer de las matemáticas un tema a tratar por la parte derecha del cerebro.

BROUSSEAU, Guy (Francia)
"Las Condiciones de Desequilibrio del Sistema Didáctico"

BRUMBAUGH, Douglas K. (EE. UU.)
"Enseñar a los niños para su futuro, no para nuestro pasado"

Trabajo con profesores de matemáticas en secundaria. Si hay que decir cómo hacer algo lo mejor es hacerlo uno mismo; normalmente yo también tengo una clase durante todo el año. Hablaremos del trabajo con alumnos en niveles 6-12. Encuentro las siguientes características de la Casio CFX 9850G especialmente útiles:

* Inecuaciones gráficas.
* Números complejos.
* Gráficos dinámicos.
* Suma de sucesiones.
* Potencia de cálculo.
* Sistemas de ecuaciones.
* Cónicas.
* Estadística.
* Análisis.

Enseñemos a los alumnos pensando en su futuro, no en nuestro pasado.

CAMPBELL, Patricia F. (EE. UU.)
"La transformación de la Educación Matemática en todos los Niveles Educativos: El Uso de la Investigación en la Práctica Escolar Efectiva"

La investigación en la enseñanza matemática puede sostener un desarrollo profesional basado en la escuela. Esa sesión describe cómo una perspectiva constructivista ha sido utilizada para mejorar la calidad del contenido matemático y su pedagogía en todas las aulas de una escuela donde los alumnos presentaban diversas características étnicas e idiomáticas. Se expondrán las mejoras en los resultados de los alumnos y el cambio manifestado en los profesores.

COBB, Paul (EE. UU.)
"Ayuda al desarrollo de la potencia matemática en los niños pequeños"

Esta presentación está enfocada al papel activo que juega una profesora -como ejemplo- en el desarrollo matemático de sus alumnos de 6 años. Se presta particular atención a la manera en que la profesora comunica a sus alumnos lo que ella considera matemáticamente importante y a cómo inicia el desarrollo de esquemas de notación para simbolizar las explicaciones de sus alumnos. Se ilustrará con ejemplos tomados en el aula.

COONEY, Thomas J. (EE. UU.)
"Conceptualización del desarrollo profesional del profesorado"

Se presentan perspectivas racionales y teóricas de la conceptualización del desarrollo profesional del profesorado. Se discutirá la investigación de estudios longitudinales relacionados con profesores de secundaria al progresar en su programa de formación inicial y en su primer año de docencia, con actividades específicas destinadas a mejorar su desarrollo profesional.

DALMASSO, Juan Carlos (Argentina)
"Olimpiada Matemática Argentina: pasado, presente y futuro"

D'AMBROSIO, Ubiratan (Brasil)
"Etnomatemática: ¿de dónde viene y adónde va?"

La geografía y la historia del comportamiento humano nos permite una nueva visión de cómo emergen las ideas matemáticas en diferentes entornos culturales. Con esta base, podemos desarrollar un marco conceptual para la etnomatemática. Futuros escenarios pueden conducir a consideraciones sobre los siguientes pasos del movimiento etnomatemático.

DOERFLER, Willibald (Austria)
"Los medios del significado"

Se presentan tres fuentes que potencialmente pueden proporcionar a los alumnos significado y comprensión:
* i. Estructuras matemáticas vistas como protocolos de procesos y acciones
* ii. Razonamiento por prototipos de conceptos matemáticos
* iii. Reinterpretación del discurso matemático: hablamos (y pensamos) como si hubiera objetos específicos con las propiedades y relaciones descritas, aunque sólo tenemos acceso a las así llamadas representaciones y descripciones verbales (uso metafórico de la palabra 'objeto')

DOUADY, Adrien (Francia)
"Visualización y razonamiento en espacios paramétricos"

A menudo, los problemas se reducen a una forma más sencilla si buscamos las soluciones con la geometría del espacio. Ilustraremos esto con dos ejemplos:

1) Dados tres números reales u, v, w, con u<v y w<v, se puede encontrar un cuatrinomio f, de valores críticos u, v y w?. Es f único respecto a un cambio de variable x --> x+p?

2) Dado un arco de curva A, tangente en ambos extremos a una recta r, (se puede mover otra recta s en el plano hasta devolverla a su posición original, con orientación invertida, sin que sea s, en ningún momento, tangente a A? Este problema conduce a la topología en una cinta de Moebius. La respuesta depende de A.

ERNEST, Paul (GB)
"El constructivismo social como una filosofía de las matemáticas"

Concierne al constructivismo social como una filosofía de las matemáticas la génesis y garantía del conocimiento matemático. Estos procesos tienen lugar tanto en contextos de investigación matemática como en la escuela, donde conciernen al aprendizaje y a la evaluación. Se dará cuenta de forma teórica de estos procesos situados en la práctica humana, basada en los trabajos de Lakatos y Wittgenstein. La teoría resultante podría ser denominada como una filosofía post-modernista de las matemáticas, al destronar a la lógica como fundamento del conocimiento matemático en favor de prácticas humanas descentralizadas y de conversaciones de garantía ligadas al contexto. Se dará también atención a las relaciones entre la filosofía de las matemáticas y la educación matemática. El hecho de que los desarrollos de la filosofía de las matemáticas y su correspondientes concepciones informales tienen importantes aplicaciones en la educación matemática es algo bien sabido. Lo que es menos conocido es que hay aspectos del aprendizaje y la evaluación que tienen implicaciones muy significativas en la propia disciplina matemática y su filosofía, al menos desde perspectivas social- constructivistas y falibilistas. Todo ello será discutido junto a otros relevantes aspectos.

FIRSOV, Victor (Rusia)
"Estándares rusos: conceptos y decisiones"

FORTUNY, Josep Mª (España)
"Rango de capacidades. La enseñanza y evaluación del conocimiento geométrico en un contexto de entorno"

Abordamos el complejo problema de los procesos de destrezas en enseñanza y evaluación y presentamos una breve perspectiva histórica sobre las aproximaciones en investigación de dicho rango (factorial, conceptual, estructural, jerárquica, grados de adquisición y cognitiva). Ponemos el centro de atención en el diseño del aprendizaje en el entorno, que propicia el desarrollo de destrezas de orden superior y en la continua profundización y adaptación a la diversidad.

FUJITA, Hiroshi (Japón)
"Luces y sombras del curriculum japonés en las matemáticas de secundaria"

El curriculum actual japonés fue introducido obligatoriamente en 1961 en las escuelas superiores de secundaria. Se caracteriza por su objetivo final, que es doble (conocimiento matemático y pensamiento matemático), por sus opciones de curriculum central diferenciado y por su introducción a los ordenadores. Han sucedido varias dificultades para su implementación, lo que conocemos recientemente como 'crisis de la educación matemática', de la que es claro síntoma la falta de inclinación hacia las matemáticas y las ciencias por parte de los estudiantes.

GALBRAITH, Peter (Australia)
"Aspectos de la evaluación: la historia interminable"

Esta conferencia no se refiere a aspectos tales como diseño instrumental, ni cómo fabricar técnicas para que el sistema funcione mejor. Más bien identifica y elabora puntos a debatir en niveles prácticos, técnicos y políticos que conviertan de una vez por todas a la evaluación en un objeto importante, controvertido y estimulante.

GARFUNKEL, Sol (EE. UU.)
"Aplicaciones de reformas: una breve historia en el tiempo"

Esta presentación dará una perspectiva del movimiento actual de reforma en educación matemática desde un punto de vista internacional. Se centrará en la inclusión de aplicaciones de las matemáticas, la introducción de modelos matemáticos y los enfoques contextuales para el desarrollo curricular en matemáticas de secundaria y posteriores niveles.

GAULIN, Claude (Canadá)
"Dificultades y retos en la implementación de la "resolución de problemas" en los curricula matemáticos escolares"

Desde hace 15 años, ha habido una tendencia internacional para hacer hincapié en la "resolución de problemas" dentro del curriculum de matemáticas. (Cuáles son las principales dificultades que se han encontrado para su implementación? (Cuáles son los nuevos retos en investigación de este tema?. Se discutirán estas cuestiones a la luz de una encuesta internacional llevada a cabo recientemente.

GERDES, Paulus (Mozambique)
"Cultura y Educación Matemática en Africa del Sur"

GJONE, Gunnar (Noruega)
"Un nuevo papel para los documentos curriculares: ?desde la inspiración hacia los planes de producción?"

Han emergido nuevos pensamientos educacionales en muchos países. La educación y la investigación han sido cada vez más influidos por consideraciones económicas. Claramente, la educación tiene implicaciones en el desarrollo económico, pero sólo durante los últimos años se han adaptado los modelos de producción a la educación. Discutiremos cómo reflejan los documentos curriculares este desarrollo.

GU, Lingyuan (China)
"Un experimento en Qingpu. Un informe de la reforma educativa en matemáticas del estándar contemporáneo en China"

Desde el año 1977 al 1992, hemos desarrollado un experimento a gran escala en la reforma educativa en la región de Qingpu (tomada como epítome de China) y hemos conseguido elevar los resultados positivos de los alumnos desde el 16% al 85% o más. La Comisión Estatal de Educación lo ha definido como un importantísimo logro en la reforma de la educación básica y ha decidido extender la experiencia a todo el país. Este informe introduce brevemente el único sistema de método experimental aconsejable para grupos de profesores y para sus principios docentes, estrategias, etc. que permita a todos los alumnos estudiar con eficiencia.

HART, Kath (GB)
¿Qué responsabilidades tienen los investigadores para con los profesores de matemáticas y los alumnos?.

En muchos países hay poca 'Investigación en Educación Matemática'. Se nos ha dicho con frecuencia que ello tiene poca repercusión en lo que ocurre en el aula. Quizás sea porque es insuficientemente relevante para la clase: no generalizable y responsable de la construcción teórica.

HOWSON, Geoffrey (GB)
"Matemáticas y sentido común"

¿Cuáles son las relaciones entre las matemáticas y el sentido común?. ¿Hasta qué punto es posible enseñar las matemáticas desde este punto y cuáles son los peligros inherentes a este enfoque?

KEITEL, Christine (Alemania)
"Ansiedad al enseñar matemáticas: un círculo de aversión a las matemáticas con alumnos y profesores"

La manera de enseñar las matemáticas en la Universidad a futuros porfesores determina negativamente la percepción de las matemáticas y su enseñanza: la 'transmisión' de conocimientos todavia típica en enseñanza secundaria. Basado en la investigación sobre la visión social de las matemáticas que tienen los futuros profesores de todos los niveles educativos, obtenida con cuestionarios al comienzo de sus estudios universitarios, -esto es, percepciones principalmente determinadas por sus experiencias escolares- y luego comparada con puntos de vista desarrollados durante sus estudios en la Universidad, se discutirá cómo los profesores transforman sus experiencias negativas con los métodos de enseñanza en la escuela y en la propia Universidad explícita e implícitamente en concepciones de aversión o intentos de evitar las matemáticas con los alumnos, lo que a su vez 'lega' la ansiedad en matemáticas.

KIERAN, Carolyn (Canadá)
"La cara cambiante del álgebra escolar"

En el pasado, el álgebra en la escuela era considerada principalmente aritmética generalizada. De todas formas, los recientes intentos de enriquecer su contenido incluyendo, por ejemplo, resolución de problemas, conceptos de funciones, modelos y generalizaciones de patrones, así como el uso de ordenadores para favorecer el razonamiento algebraico han jugado su papel en la redefinición de lo que ha llegado a ser el álgebra en la escuela.

KIRCHGRABER, Urs (Suiza)
"Algunos aspectos de la enseñanza de las matemáticas en secundaria en Suiza"

Describimos brevemente algunos aspectos específicos de la escuela secundaria en Suiza (Gymnasium superior) y discutimos algunas herramientas desarrolladas para la enseñanza de las matemáticas de pregraduado.

KRAINER, Konrad (Alemania)
"Algunas consideraciones sobre los problemas y perspectivas de la formación permanente del profesorado"

La creciente complejidad de la discusión en educación matemática cambia nuestro modo de ver la formación inicial y permanente del profesorado. Hay cada vez más y más informes relacionando profesores de matemáticas (en activo o investigando) en proyectos de investigación e investigaciones integradas en cursos para la formación del profesorado. Se ilustrará un trabajo autocrítico de investigación por parte del profesor.

LEDER, Gilah (Australia)
"La educación matemática y aspectos de género"

Se trazan desarrollos críticos en la investigación sobre 'género y matemáticas': desde los primeros trabajos sobre las diferencias entre chicos y chicas en sus actuaciones y participación en matemáticas hasta las más recientes perspectivas feministas que sotienen que la igualdad entre sexos requiere una reevaluación de las actuales estructuras sociales, valores populares y normas.

MOORE, David S. (EE. UU.)
"Nueva pedagogía y nuevo contenido: el caso de la Estadística"

Los profesores de matemáticas de todos los niveles han de adoptar con urgencia una nueva pedagogía que enfatiza el aprendizaje activo y pone mayor énfasis en el trabajo en grupo y la comunicación de los resultados. Esta llamada a la reforma a menudo incluye una revisión de nuestros objetivos de aprendizaje para, por ejemplo, dar más importancia a destrezas flexibles para la resolución de problemas. En Estadística, los cambios en el propio campo, promovidos por la tecnología y la práctica profesional, han trasladado de alguna manera el contenido inicial matemático a experiencias con datos. La interacción entre ambas tendencias ha producido rápidos cambios en su enseñanza. Esta conferencia revisará tendencias actuales en la enseñanza de la Estadística e intentará describir las lecciones utilizadas.

NESHER, Pearla (Israel)
"Problemas estereotipo de enunciado en la escuela y la naturaleza abierta de las aplicaciones"

Se presenta un dilema a los profesores de matemáticas: ¿se puede enseñar a resolver problemas?. En la mayoría de los casos, los alumnos aprenden a resolver problemas trabajando una cierta variedad de ejemplos. ¿Hay alguna manera de enseñar ésto explícitamente y de forma más articulada?. Los resultados de la psicología cognitiva sugieren que se debería descubrir el esquema subyacente al problema y que los esquemas generales básicos deben ser enseñados directamente. Se presentarán también resultados empíricos.

OTEIZA, Fidel (Chile)
"Matemáticas en contexto: un enfoque integrado para el desarrollo del curriculum"

PAPASTAVRIDIS, Stavros G. , KLAONDATOS Nick (Grecia)
"Evaluación de la efectividad de las aplicaciones didácticas en matemáticas"

PEREZ-FERNANDEZ, Javier (España)
"Los manipuladores simbólicos en la enseñanza de las matemáticas"

Los manipuladores simbólicos pueden y deben desempeñar un papel muy importante en la docencia de las Matemáticas, pueden ayudar (con una adecuada planificación) a una mejor comprensión y profundización de un buen número de conceptos, ser un instrumento valioso en el aprendizaje de la resolución de problemas y deben influir en el diseño de los currícula, en la selección y secuenciación de los contenidos. Su uso debe inscribirse dentro de lo que se conoce como 'enseñanza experimental de las matemáticas' y no debe ser la secuenciación de actividades encaminadas a aprender como un determinado 'manipulador simbólico' resuelve determinados ejercicios rutinarios. El software en cuestión ha de seleccionarse sobre la base de las características de los estudios y de los alumnos, y de los recursos disponibles. Junto a una panorámica sobre sus ventajas e inconvenientes en relación a las tareas educativas, la charla se ilustrará con la presentación de actividades dirigidas a alumnos de secundaria y de universidad.

PUIG, Luis (España)
"Lo que he aprendido sobre resolución de problemas a partir de la historia y la investigación"

Hay toda una riqueza de mundos posibles para la resolución de problemas. La heurística es el estudio de uno de esos mundos. El método de análisis y síntesis, desde Pappus a Lakatos pasando por Ibn al-Haytham ha sido dotado con el poder de dirigir tanto la búsqueda de soluciones como la generación de nuevos problemas.

QIU, Zonghu (China)
"Competiciones Matemáticas en China. Exitos y deficiencias"

Se detallarán las actividades generadas por las competiciones matemáticas en China. Se examinará la influencia de estas competiciones en la educación matemática y se discutirán los problemas que surgen cuando se da demasiada importancia a estas competiciones.

RICO, Luis (España)
"Programas de investigación doctorales y académicos en Educación Matemática en las Universidades españolas"

El contenido general de esta conferencia estará relacionado con los programas de investigación doctorales y académicos en Educación

Matemática en las Universidades españolas desde 1984 en adelante, con la nueva estructura universitaria derivada de la Ley de Reforma Universitaria (LRU), el surgimiento del campo de conocimiento en didáctica de las matemáticas y los programas de doctorado en esta disciplina. En cada uno de los actuales programas, se han defendido varias Tesis Doctorales, lo que asegura un corpus teórico y práctico científico bien establecido. En la comunidad matemática educativa española se ha establecido un campo científico riguroso, con su propia entidad y prácticas de investigación. La conferencia intenta presentar los fundamentos de la investigación académica en Didáctica de las Matemáticas, su estado actual, con los logros alcanzados hasta el presente y las principales líneas de investigación para los próximos seis años.

SCHMIDT, Siegbert (Alemania)
"Estructuras semánticas de los problemas de enunciado. ¿Mediadores entre las estructuras matemáticas y las estructuras cognitivas de los alumnos?"

Se discutirá el corpus existente sobre investigación en estructuras semánticas de problemas de enunciado concernientes a la suma, resta, multiplicación y división en primaria, enfocando estos problemas: -?Qué status epistemológicos de tales estructuras semánticas parecen ser los apropiados? -?Qué tipo de ayuda pueden proporcionar tales estructuras al profesor?

SCHUPP, Hans (Alemania)
"Regeometrización de la geometría en la escuela. ?Con ordenadores?"

El declive de la geometría en secundaria y su muerte en postsecundaria (ICME-4) está causado, entre otros factores, por la confortable transición a la geometría cartesiana desde la euclídea. Esta conferencia analizará cómo las facilidades de los ordenadores gráficos pueden utilizarse para hacer surgir y fomentar razonamientos e intuiciones genuinamente geométricos.

SFARD, Anna (Israel)
"Sobre metáforas y modelos para el cambio conceptual en matemáticas"

Entre las muchas corrientes que forman el flujo creciente y continuo en investigación en didáctica de las matemáticas, una de las más prominentes es el estudio del desarrollo de los conceptos matemáticos. Esta conferencia se dedicará a reflexionar sobre el pasado, presente y futuro de esta línea de investigación. Más específicamente, se dará una visión crítica de las diferentes metáforas que han venido inspirando a lo largo del tiempo el estudio del cambio conceptual. El foco principal estará en las formas en las cuales la idea evolutiva del crecimiento biológico ha venido dando forma a los enfoques de los investigadores de este tema desde los trabajos de Piaget y Vigotsky.

SKOVMOSE, Ole (Dinamarca)
"Educación matemática crítica: algunas anotaciones filosóficas"

La educación matemática debe servir también como invitación a la participación en la vida democrática dentro de una sociedad altamente tecnificada, donde las condiciones democráticas pueden verse impedidas precisamente por el mismo desarrollo tecnológico que la educación matemática facilita. Este reto resalta la importancia de una educación matemática crítica. Sin embargo (cuál es pues la naturaleza de una educación matemática crítica?

STRAESSER, Rudolf (Alemania)
"Las matemáticas en el trabajo. Una perspectiva didáctica"

El mundo del trabajo está lleno de matemáticas. La matemática abstracta es la más potente matemática para el trabajo. El uso de ordenadores conlleva unas sofisticadas matemáticas. El empleado/trabajador medio debe (o no) aprender matemáticas para su trabajo. La conferencia comentará este y otros eslogans en matemáticas para -y en- el trabajo.

STREEFLAND, Leen (Holanda)
"Aprendizaje histórico para futura enseñanza, o volviendo la esfera del revés. Sin arrugas"

Stephen Smale hizo progresos considerables en la teoría de sistemas dinámicos. Su proceso de aprendizaje, desde luego, es un revelador paradigma. Como tal será analizado. ¿Pueden utilizarse sus resultados para enseñar y aprender matemáticas en diferentes niveles, o no?. La respuesta afirmativa será avalada con gran riqueza de ejemplos.

SZENDREI, Julianna (Hungría)
"El papel de la lengua materna en el aprendizaje de las matemáticas"

THOMPSON, Alba (EE.UU.)
"Orientaciones conceptuales y de cálculo en la enseñanza de las matemáticas"

Contrastaremos dos orientaciones en la enseñanza de las matemáticas: la operativa y la conceptual, enfocando en los patrones educativos que caracterizan a ambas y el conocimiento base que el profesor necesita para enseñar matemáticas conceptualmente.

TOUBURG, Jens; WAGNER, Soren (Dinamarca)
"Una década enseñando modelización matemática"

TRI, Nguyen Dinh (Vietnam)
"Algunos aspectos del currículum matemático universitario para ingenieros"

Mi conferencia está basada en mi experiencia como profesor de matemáticas en la Universidad Tecnológica de Hanoi durante muchos años. Expondré algunos factores que han de considerarse a la hora de diseñar un currículo de matemáticas para nuestros estudiantes de ingeniería. Quisiera insistir en este punto: uno de los propósitos principales de la educación pre-graduada de los estudiantes de ingeniería es favorecer la independencia y creatividad del alumno, especialmente las destrezas para proponer y resolver problemas, para proponer y resolver modelos (con herramientas matemáticas). Se describirá nuestro curriculum para las matemáticas de nuestros alumnos de ingeniería.

VASCO, Carlos (Colombia)
"Una teoría general de procesos y sistemas de investigación en matemáticas y en educación matemática"

Se enfoca el hecho de hacer matemáticas como una detección de patrones y regularidades en procesos reales y una producción de sistemas, compuestos por elementos, transformaciones, relaciones, ... para explorar su comportamiento. Se propone una interpretación de los conceptos de la estructura y dinámica de un sistema matemático, así como las implicaciones de esta teoría general de procesos/sistemas en la investigación en matemáticas y en educación matemática.

VERGNAUD, Gérard (Francia)
"Cambios cognitivos importantes en el aprendizaje de las matemáticas. Una perspectiva de desarrollo"

De todos los cambios que están teniendo lugar en el aprendizaje de las matemáticas, algunos son de la mayor importancia ya que requieren grandes pasos cualitativos por parte de los alumnos. Este nuevo conocimiento puede ir incluso en contra de la intuición. Se expondrán cuatro ejemplos:

    * Suma de números donde la relación más bien sugiere una resta de un dato respecto al otro.
    * Inversión de un cociente de dimensiones.
    * Representación de gráficas cuando la escala elegida no permit representar el origen.
    * Tratamiento algebraico e interpretació de números negativos.

Los profesores deben ser muy conscientes de estas duraderas dificultades, pues no hay ninguna esperanza de que los alumnos puedan superarlas sin suficientes ejemplos y aclaraciones.

VICENTE, José Luis (España)
"Geometría y Cálculo Simbólico"

En los últimos años ha habido una gran cantidad de investigación sobre las aplicaciones del Cálculo Simbólico, y sus sistemas, a la Geometría. Las razones son múltiples, yendo desde un crecimiento en la implantación de los Sistemas de Cálculo Simbólico en centros de investigación y educativos hasta otras puramente científicas (por ejemplo, creación de nuevos y rápidos algoritmos para realizar tareas repetitivas, como gráficos por computador y bases estándar). Pasaremos revista a los desarrollos más recientes en este campo, con aplicaciones a la enseñanza en varios niveles. Dedicaremos especial atención a temas como demostración automática de teoremas en geometría plana, geometrías no euclídeas, curvas y superficies algebraicas y gráficos por ordenador.

VIGGIANI-BICUDO, Maria Aparecida (Brasil)
"La Filosofía de la Educación Matemática: un Enfoque Fenomenológico"

Esta conferencia enfocará el significado de la filosofía de la Educación Matemática comparándola con la filosofía de la Educación y con la filosofía de las Matemáticas. Tras ello, enfocaremos la actitud natural y la actitud fenomenólogica apuntando las vías en las que la realidad y el conocimiento pueden trabajarse conjuntamente en el contexto de la Educación Matemática

WANG, Chanpei (China)
"Educación matemática. Un punto de vista oriental"

La moderna reforma de la educación matemática en China ha sido impulsada por dos fuerzas principales: el arrollamiento de su propia sociedad y el movimiento occidental de educación matemática. Este informe intentará explicar cómo se está moviendo la educación matemática en China hacia un nuevo paradigma (es un cambio profundo y sistemático hacia el siglo 21) y cómo los procesos de cambio deben ser cuidadosamente planeados y controlados.

"MATHEMATICS TEACHERS AS DECISION MAKERS: CHANGES AND CHALLENGES".

Report of the ROUND-TABLE at ICME-8

The panel members were:
- Alan J. Bishop (Chair and convenor) is a Professor at the Faculty of Education of Monash University in Melbourne, Australia.
- Gail Burrill, President of the National Council of Teachers of Mathematics in the USA. She is a secondary teacher in Milwaukee, Wisconsin,USA.
- Maria Salett Biembengut teaches at the Universidade Regional de Blumenau in Brazil, and for four years she was the President of the Brazilian Mathematics Education Association.
- Ruhama Even is a senior researcher in the Department of Science Teaching at the Weizmann Institute of Science in Rehovot, Israel.Francisco Hernan is from Spain, and is currently teaching secondary school mathematics at the European School in Brussels, Belgium.
- Tang, Rui Fen from the Department of Mathematics, East China Normal University, in Shanghai, China, was sadly unable to take part and her place was taken by Wang Chiang Pei from the Department of Mathematics, at the Beijing Institute of Education, China.

"Teachers as decision-makers" sounds a very grand idea, and many teachers would not feel that they really are making decisions. But teachers face choices all the time in their professional lives, and they must decide between the choices. The idea of this Round Table discussion was to focus more attention on this idea and to explore the extent to which different countries recognise, take account of, and support the teachers' role in the decision-making which affects the mathematical education of their pupils.

Thus, following an introduction, the Chair posed a series of questions for the panel members which were then discussed by each one in turn:
Qu 1 What do mathematics teachers make decisions about in your country?
And/or What are they allowed to make decisions about?
(1) At the level of the society?
>About the general mathematics curriculum in all the schools?
>Through a mathematics teacher association?
>In a regular consultative process?

(2) Within the school?

    Determining the mathematics timetable/schedule?

    Which pupils/classes they will teach?

    Which textbooks will be used?

    How to assess the pupils?

(3)Within the mathematics classroom?

    Which teaching methods they will use?

    How to deal with pupils learning difficulties?

(Qu 2) How are mathematics teachers trained or educated to make those decisions?

    Within general courses on methodology?

    Within real school experiences?

    Within specific training sessions?

    Within "microteaching" classes or using video material?

(Qu 4) What kinds of changes are now happening in your country which affect the choices which teachers face? Which are the most important changes?

(1) At the level of the society?

    More pupils studying mathematics at university?

    Demographic changes in the population?

    Political changes?

    Economic changes?

    Technological changes?

(2) Within the school?

    Wider range of pupils studying mathematics for longer?

    More subjects competing for time in school?

    More use of computers and calculators?

(3) Within the mathematics classroom?

    Greater range of pupil attitudes?

    Greater range of learning styles?

    More or less emphasis on certain basic skills?

    Variety of pupil access to personal computers and calculators?

(Qu 5) Do you think that teachers in your country will have more responsibility for these kinds of decisions in the future or less?

(1) Do you see greater or less "external" controls in your country:

    - over curriculum?

    - over textbooks and other materials?

    - over assessment?

    - over teaching approaches?

(2) Is there a greater professional responsibility developing among teachers?

> More influential professional teachers associations?
> More teachers creating and writing teaching materials?
> More teacher-directed in-service and professional development?

(3) Is there more individual teacher autonomy and responsibility?

> More professional and academic qualifications sought by teachers?
> Is mathematics teaching still a satisfying profession?
> Is teaching still a vocation?

As may be expected, the questions produced a variety of answers and some consensus. It was clear that the teachers' situations in all the countries represented were becoming more challenging, whether due to the increasing presence of technology, or because of more and more demands being made on the mathematics curriculum, or because of economic or political changes in society. These changes did not seem however to be generally accompanied by any increases in the level of support for in-service education for teachers, nor in the quality or quantity of the teachers pre-service programs.

There was also a recognition among all the panel members that mathematics teachers needed to become, and indeed were becoming, more professionally qualified, more organised and in some way more autonomous. The increased activities of teachers' mathematical associations were welcomed and were needing to be developed further. The support roles of other people in the mathematics education community were also encouraged, and there were calls to reduce the gulf between the teachers and the university members of that community.

PROJECTS SHOWS / EXPOSICION DE PROYECTOS

- A New Elementary School Math Program Using Projets and Calculators
 Patricia Baggett, Andrzej Ehrenfeucht   U.S.A.

- Grupo de Trabalho de Investigacao da Associacao de Profesores de Matemática
 Joa Pedro da Ponte   Portugal

- Centre for Teaching Mathematics
 John S. Berry   United Kingdom

- Matemática y diseño a nivel universitario
 Vera W de Spinadel, Hernan S. Nottoli, Sergio Vainikoff
      Argentina

- Elaboración de materiales instruccionales para Matemáticas I y II
 En la Universidad Nacional (UNA) Abierta de Venezuela
 Mauricio Orellana   Venezuela

- The California Math Show
 Susan Addington, Suzanne Alejandre, Susan Llearn, Yasha Karant   U.S.A.

- Investigación en Educación Matemática y Formación de Profesores
 Isidro Segovia   España

- Projet Display for the Balanced Assessment Projet
 J.E. Ridway   United Kingdom

- Research in the Graduate Program in Mathematics Education
 Marcelo Carvalho   Brasil

- Project Australia!
 Jeff Baxter   Australia

WORKSHOPS / TALLERES

- Using Pop-up Enginnering to teach Mathematics Concepts (TG 21)
  Vivekenand Mohan-Ram (Australia)

- Salón de Juegos Matemáticos
  Juan A. Hans (Spain)

- Papiroflexia y Matemáticas
  Antonio Ledesma (Spain)

- Games in the Mathematics Classroom (TG22)
  Gillian Hatch (U.K.)

- Understanding undergraduate mathematics through special cases (TG 3)
  Robert Burn (U.K.)

- Intuición Espacial
  Floreal Gracia (Spain)

- Matemáticas con Software específico
  Victoriano Ramírez (Spain)

- Mathematics of Chaos
  Daphne Kerslake (U.K.)

- Taller de Calculadoras. CASIO
  CASIO Electronics Co. Ltd.

F.E.S.P.M. EXHIBITS

Taking the opportunity of the icme-8 in Seville, the Spanish Federation of Societies of Teachers of Mathematics made a great effort, both in financing and organization, to offer several exhibitions of materials related to Mathematical Education.

TRADITIONAL MEASURES IN SPAIN (Casino de la Exposición)

Before the general use of the metric system, a great variety of measures were used, often differing from one region to the next one. Many disappeared, but some are still in use. Members of the "Ventura Reyes Prosper" Extremaduran Society of Mathematical Education have compiled and rescued the traditional Spanish measures. All items exhibited are original.

ANTIQUE MATHEMATICS BOOKS (Casino de la Exposición)

Professor Mariano Martínez has made an intensive research along libraries throghout the country to locate books on Mathematics from the earliest days. A wide sample of the material located is exhibited, all original pieces. Books as old as 16 century are included.

It is an exceptional exhibition and very unlikely to be repeated, considering the quality of the material exhibited and the difficulties for their location and transport.

THE MEASURE OF TIME BEFORE MECHANICAL CLOCKS (Casino de la Exposición)

Mr. Manuel Ibáñez has dedicated his life to the restauration and study of timepieces. At his workplace in Galapagar (Madrid), he has produced exact copies of cloks like King Alfonso X's, or an Arabic clock with a complex mechanics and a great beauty of details, presented in this exhibition for the first time.

Items exhibited include a series of posters designed by a team of teachers and students from "Viera y Clavijo" High School (La Laguna, Canary Islands).

PHOTOGRAPHY AND MATHEMATICS (Tobacco Factory)

The project "Photography and Mathematics" has been organized in Andalusia by SAEM THALES and coordinated by Professor Evaristo González for years. A large collection of photographs with a mathematical content, taken by students along special programmed projects. On the other hand, award-winning photographs are exhibited from competitions in different places (Madrid, Canary Islands, etc.), as well as works combining both topics: Photography and Mathematics. A visit to this exhibition will surely prove extremely revealing.

STAMPS AND MATHEMATICS (Tobacco Factory)

Two exhibitions on stamps are presented:
- One prepared by the Emma Castelnuovo" Madrid Society of Teachers of Mathematics, directed by Professor Santiago Gutiérrez; it presents an interesting Spanish / English guide.
- A second one including 150 stamp sheets owned by Professor Edgardo Femández (Bahía Blanca, - Argentina). They are original stamps on different topics related to Mathematics.

DIDACTICAL MATERIALS FOR TEACHERS IN THEIR CLASSROOMS (Biology School Library)

Professor Arturo Mandly presents a series of manipulative materials produced by members of diferent Societies of Teachers of Mathematics in Spain, to be used in the classroom for such aspects as "playful presentation of contents", "towards a more meaningful teaching", "providing the students with research lines" ... A visit to this exhibition will surely provide ideas for the design of, say, Mathematics workshops. Specific materials for the blind are also included.

CALCULATING MACHINES (Casino de la Exposición)

Wide and interesting collection of instruments for analogical and digital calculation. The former are represented by slide rules and calculating cylindres, covering from late 19 c. (Fuller's helix, 1878) to the 70's. Digital instruments include a series of mechanical and electromechanical machines /don't forget there were machines with an electric engine as early as the fist decade of this century). Examples of the three most used systems are included: Odhner's wheel, Leibniz's cylinder and Christel Hamann's intermittent mechanism.

MATHEMATICAL FILMS AND VIDEOS (Engineering School, Lecture Hall)

A big effort was made to compile actual "jewels" in mathematical films. It is worth the while to spend some time watching the material painstakingly collected by Professor José Muñoz.

SCULPTURE AND MATHEMATICS: SHAPE AND NUMBER (Casino de la Exposición)

Works by Javier Carvajal, with a clear mathematical flavour. In collaboration with Fundación Bancaja.

ART AND MATHEMATICS (Juana de Aizpuru Art Gallery, 26 Zaragoza street)

Organized by Professor D. Guderian, sponsored by the Institute für Auslandsbeziehungen (Bonn/Stuttgart).

WORKS ON COPPER

Pieces by French engraver Patrice Jeener will be shown during the Congress at the areas where activities will be held.

EXPOSICIONES DE LA F.E.S.P.M.

Aprovechando la celebración del ICME-8 en Sevilla, la Federación Española de Sociedades de Profesores de Matemáticas hizo un gran esfuerzo, tanto económico como de organización, para ofrecer a los congresistas varias exposiciones de materiales relacionados con la Educación Matemática.

MEDIDAS TRADICIONALES EN ESPAÑA (Casino de la Exposición)

Antes de universalizarse el Sistema Métrico Decimal se utilizaba una gran cantidad de medidas que incluso variaban de unas zonas a otras. Muchas cayeron en desuso pero otras se mantienen aún.
Miembros de la Sociedad Extremeña de la Educación Matemática "Ventura Reyes Prosper" han hecho una recopilación y rescate de medidas tradicionales españolas. Las piezas expuestas son originales.

LIBROS ANTIGUOS DE MATEMÁTICAS (Casino de la Exposición)

El profesor Mariano Martínez ha hecho un barrido exhaustivo por todas las bibliotecas del país para localizar cuantos libros de Matemáticas haya desde los tiempos más remotos. Se ofrece una amplia muestra del material conseguido, todos ellos libros originales. Podrá contemplar libros cuya antigüedad se remonta al siglo XVI.
Se trata de una excepcional exposición que difícilmente podrá volver a repetirse teniendo en cuenta la calidad del material que se expone y las dificultades de localización y transporte.

LA MEDIDA DEL TIEMPO ANTES DEL RELOJ MECÁNICO (Casino de la Exposición)

D. Manuel Ibáñez ha dedicado su vida a la restauración y estudio de relojes. En su taller de Galapagar (Madrid) ha reproducido con total exactitud, relojes como el de Alfonso X el Sabio o un reloj árabe de complicada mecánica y minuciosa belleza que, además, se presenta por primera vez en esta exposición.

Las piezas expuestas se complementan con un conjunto de paneles realizados por un equipo de profesores y alumnos del Instituto de Bachillerato "Viera y Clavijo" de la Laguna - Canarias.

FOTOGRAFIAS Y MATEMÁTICAS (Fábrica de Tabacos)

La Actividad "Fotografia y Matemáticas" la organiza en Andalucía la SAEM THALES y la coordina el prof. Evaristo González desde hace años. Se ha reunido una amplia colección de fotografías de contenido matemático realizadas por alumnos a través de actividades programadas.

Por otra parte, se exponen tambien fotografías que han obtenido premio en concursos celebrados en diversos lugares (Madrid, Canarias, etc.) así como reportajes en los que se combinan los dos temas: Fotografía y Matemáticas. La contemplación de esta exposición puede sugerir muchas ideas.

FILATELIA Y MATEMÁTICAS (Fábrica de Tabacos)

En torno a la Filatelia se presentan dos exposiciones:
- La elaborada por la Sociedad Madrileña "Emma Castelnuovo" de Profesores de Matemáticas bajo la dirección de Santiago Gutiérrez que cuentan, además, con una interesante guía en inglés y español.
- La otra exposición está formada por unas 150 hojas filatélicas propiedad del profesor Edgardo Fernández, de Bahía Blanca - Argentina. Se trata de una amplia colección de sellos originales que abarcan variados temas.

MATERIAL DIDACTICO DEL PROFESORADO EN SUS AULAS (Bibl. Biológicas)

El prof. Arturo Mandly presenta un conjunto de materiales manipulativos que han sido elaborados por miembros de distintas Sociedades de Profesores de Matemáticas de España, útiles para su utilización en el aula aspectos tales como: introducir de forma lúdica determinados contenidos, conseguir una enseñanza más significativa, proporcionar a los estudiantes vías de investigación. Su visita le dará ideas para diseñar, por ejemplo talleres de Matemáticas. Se incluye también material específico para ciegos.

MÁQUINAS DE CALCULAR (Casino de la Exposición)

Amplia e interesante colección de instrumentos del cálculo analógico y digital. los primeros representados por reglas y cilindros de cálculos, abarcando desde finales del siglo pasado (por ejemplo la hélice de Fuller de 1878) hasta los años setenta. los digitales lo forman un conjunto de máquinas mecánicas y electromecánicas (téngase en cuenta que en la primera decena de este siglo ya existían máquinas con motor eléctrico). Podrá contemplar ejemplares de los tres sistemas más utilizados en estos ingenios: la rueda de Odhner, el cilindro de Leibniz y el mecanismo intermitente de Christel Hamann.

FILMS Y VIDEOS MATEMÁTICOS (Sala de Grados de Escuela de Ingenieros)

Se ha hecho un esfuerzo para conseguir una amplia filmoteca matemática. Merece la pena dedicar una parte del tiempo para contemplar el material que ha recopilado con gran tesón el prof. José Muñoz.

ESCULTURA Y MATEMÁTICAS: FORMA Y NÚMERO (Casino de la Exposición)

Esculturas de Javier Carvajal de clara evocación matemática. Colabora la Fundación Bancaja.

ARTE Y MATEMÁTICAS (Galería Juana de Aizpuru, c/. Zaragoza,26)

El Profesor D. Guderian la organiza con el patrocinio de Institute für Auslandsbeziehungen (Bonn/Stuttgart).

TRABAJOS SOBRE COBRE

Serán expuestos por el grabador francés Patrice Jeener durante el congreso en las zonas de desarrollo de las actividades.

MEETINGS / ENCUENTROS

- Founding Meeting of the International Council for Computer Algebra in Mathematics Education (IC-CAME)

- Upliftment initiatives in South Africa: an INSET projet (RUMEP)

- Encuentro conjunto del Comité Interamericano de Educación Matemática y del Comité Iberoamericano de Educación Matemática

- Meeling of World Federation of National Mathematics Education (WFNMC)

- General Assembly of ICMI

- International Baccalaureate: meeting of Mathematics Teachers

- Forum for Officers of National Mathematics Organizations

- Meeting of the International Organization of Women and Mathematics Education (IOWME)

- International Study Group on Ethnomathematics

- Meeting of Journal Editors

- Establishing a European Association of Researchers in Mathematics Education (ERCME)

- Founding Meeting of a European Academy for Teaching Mathematics with Technology

- Booklets presentation of Unione Matematica Italiana and Seminario Nazionale in Ricerca in Didattica della Matematica

- Reunión informativa sobre el desarrollo de la Educación Matemática en el Extremo Sur del Continente Americano:
Las Reuniones de Didáctica de las Matemáticas del Cono Sur.

- Presentation of the Society for the Advancement of Chicanos and Native Americans in Sciense (SACNAS).

- International Mathematics Tournament of Towns

- Encuentro de responsables de Sociedades Iberoamericanas de Educación Matemática.

- Encuentro de la Sociedad Ada Byron

- Sharing Session for Two-Years and Technical Colleges

NON COMMERCIAL EXHIBITIONS
EXPOSICIONES NO COMERCIALES

- Cultural and Historical Perspectives of Mathematics Education in Japan

- Colorado Mathematical Olympiad. Geombinatorics. Books. University of Colorado.

- The Freudenthal Institute of the University of Utrech. (Holland)

- ZDM: Fachinformationszentrum Karlsruhe. (Germany)

- CFEM: Comission Francaise sur l'Enseignement des Mathematiques. (France)

- ATM: Association of Teachers of Mathematics. (UK)

- Teaching in Contest. University of Edinburgh. (UK)

- CIJM: Comité Internacional des Jeux Mathematiques. (France)

- The Mathematics Centre. Chichester Institute of Higher Education. (UK)

- The Mathematical Association. (UK)

- School of Education. University of Nottingham. (UK)

- MOIFEM: Mouvement International pour les Femmes et l'Enseignement Des Mathematics. (France)

- ICTMA8: 8th International Conference on the Teaching of Mathematical Modelling and Applications. (Australia)

- Ada Byron (OECOM): Organización Española para la Coeducación Matemática. (Spain)

- Sociedad Madrileña de Profesores de Matemáticas Enma Castelnuovo. (Spain)

- The Adult Basic Education Resource and Information Service at the National Languages and Literacy Institute of Australia. (Australia)

- Math TALK. (USA)

- EQUALS & Family Math. (USA)

- FESPM: Medidas tradicionales en España. (Spain)

- FESPM: Libros antiguos de matemáticas. (Spain)

- FESPM: Escultura y matemáticas: Forma y Número. (Spain)

- FESPM: La medida del tiempo antes del reloj mecánico. (Spain)

- FESPM: Máquinas de calcular. (Spain)

- FESPM: Fotografía y matemáticas. (Spain)

- FESPM: Filatelia y matemáticas. (Spain)

- FESPM: Material didáctico del profesorado en sus aulas. (Spain)

- FESPM: Films y videos matemáticos. (Spain)

- Rune Mields y Anton Stankowski: Exposición sobre Arte y Matemáticas Art and Mathematics exhibition

- Patrice Jeener: Exposición de grabados sobre cobre / Cooper plates exhibition.

COMMERCIAL EXHIBITION/*EXPOSICION COMERCIAL*

Addlink Software Científico	*España/Spain*
Awr Software	*España/Spain*
Cambridge University Press	*GB/UK*
Casio Inc.	*Multinacional/Multinational*
Comercial Grupo Anaya S.A.	*España/Spain*
Dalin Inc.	*Israel*
DHL	*España/Spain*
Distesa	*España/Spain*
Editorial Síntesis	*España/Spain*
France Edition	*Francia/France*
Fundación O.N.C.E.	*España/Spain*
Grupo Editorial Iberoamérica	*México*
Grupo Hermes	*España/Spain*
Key Curriculum Press	*EE.UU./USA*
Kluwer Academic Publishers	*Holanda/Netherlands*
Librería Díaz de Santos	*España/Spain*
Libros Vicens Vives	*España/Spain*
Marshall Europe	*GB/UK*
Mc Graww-Hill	*España/Spain*
NationalCouncil of Teachers of Mathematics	*EE.UU./USA*
Polydron	*GB/UK*
QED Books	*GB/UK*
Red Olímpica	*Argentina*
Santillana S.A.	*España/Spain*
S.M: Grupo Editorial	*España/Spain*
Soft Warehouse Europe	*Austria*
Springer - Verlag	*Alemania/Germany*
Telefónica de España	*España/Spain*
Texas Instruments	*España/Spain*
Texas Instruments	*Multinacional/Multinational*
Sociedad Andaluza de Educación Matemática Thales	*España/Spain*
Z.D.M.	*Alemania/Germany*

ICME8 NATIONAL PRESENTATION FOR AUSTRALIA

Summary prepared by: Jeff Baxter

Introduction

The purpose of this presentation is to identify research and educational developments in the last four years since ICME7 in Québec. To do this we prepared slides and video presentations which connect with a permanent display, also called Project Australia!, held during the ICME8 congress.

Background

Australia is a country which is home to nearly 20 million people, of whom approximately 75% live in one of seven cities, the state capitals.

Each of Australia's eight States and Territories has an indépendent, democratically elected state legislature which is responsible for the education system in that state. This allows considerable variation within and between states in schooling patterns and styles.

The University and post-high school technical education systems are funded and controlled by the national government.

In each state there is credentialling authority which establishes for every student at the end of year 12, a score which determines University eligibility. Mostly this task is achieved using closed-book, timed examinations, in combination with scores derived from school-based continuing assessment procedures.

Problems Australia must solve

For a country as large and as diverse as Australia, problems arise. They are listed here in no particular order. It is a list not unlike one you might compile for many countries, although differing situations would greatly alter particular aspects. Problems are:

* how to sustain comparability in educational standards and curricula between the different states so that students are not disadvantaged by moving to live in another state

    * how to sustain comparability in educational standards with the rest of the world, particularly of the end-points of schooling so that students can qualify to study wherever they wish in the world

    * the concentration of population in the major cities, and the balance between centralised control of education and diversity of educational experience

    * the isolation of non-city dwellers in smaller towns

    * the more remote learners, often at vast distance even from country centres

    * the education of (often disadvantaged) minorities: gifted learners, our indigenous people (the Australian aborigines), those from other cultures, non-english speakers, educationally disadvantaged, and those disadvantaged by their gender or poverty of circumstance

Steps towards solution

Within the last decade, a much greater awareness, or national view has emerged in education, resulting in national government intervention in the schooling process by the establishment of *National Statements* for curricula in each of the main "discipline" areas of schooling. These do not constitute a National Curriculum, as some other countries have, nor do they have the force of government legislation behind them. Each state and territory has responded in ways that have led to different kinds of progress and growth.

Attempts to interpret what the mathematics framework outlines has led to differing approaches to assessment, of credentialling, of identifying, recording and reporting student progress, of teaching style and of resource development.

One of the educational strengths of Australia is the manner in which we, as a very young country under its current population profile, have drawn upon the older, more traditional, yet often highly innovative Western educational cultures. Australia is developing from these origins, richer for them, but eager for change and growth.

Also, within the past four years, greater recognition and use of ideas and thought streams from our indigenous cultures and those newly represented in the Australian population profile, has started to have influence. This is partly a consequence of the rise of interest since 1984 in ethno-mathematics, which followed the influential plenary address at ICME5, by Ubi D'Ambrosio.

Australians are much more internationally aware than even twenty years ago and now have a mathematics education culture which is a unique blend of many influences: identifying, then remoulding and reshaping ideas from other countries, and incorporating them into the mathematical education of Australians are tricks we have developed skills in, and lately, some expertise in re-presenting to their original owners in ways that are fresh, original and useable.

Fields where this has become an international contribution are alternative assessment practices, professional development resulting from recording and disseminating "best of practice" exemplars, observing and classifying student learning, co-operative and collaborative learning styles, mathematics competitions, activity-based and thematic learning in early years, resource development and dissemination, and incorporating the use of computers and graphics calculators as implicit tools in mathematics learning.

Examples of all this progress were on display at the congress.

Results from a those first steps

Australian practice in classrooms and in research and development centres were presented by video images of interviews with teachers about their practice, of the use of technology in classrooms: databases, email, internet, graphics calculators, software and cdrom exploration and learning.

Images of assessment practices resulting from cooperative and collaborative learning styles, as well as those deriving from traditional teacher-centred instruction were shown. Examples of prodigious talent, of the world-renowned Australian Mathematics Competition, were mixed with images of professional development of teachers: both neophyte and experienced, but each needing to extend their repertoires differently to improve their knowledge bases of both content and style.

Those with specific interests in any of the matters raised were asked to contact the Australian Association of Mathematics Teachers Inc. : fax (+61 8 8362 9288) or the internet: http://www.aamt.edu.au

MATHEMATICS EDUCATION IN HUNGARY

A. AMBRUS, I. LENART, V. OLAH

Hungary is a very small country but rich in mathematicians, in mathematics.

Starting with Farkas and Janos Bolyai (Founder of non-euclidian geometry)there were and there are today also a lot of world famous mathematicians with Hungarian origin. (John Neumann, Paul Erdos,..) Many of Hungarian mathematicians considered as their task to foster the mathematics education in schools. (G. Polya, I. Lakatos, R. Peter,...) Hungary developed its own mathematics education culture, but it was always open to the progressive reform movements of the world. Thank to Tamas Varga the Hungarian mathematics reform movement in the sixties, seventies was not a mechanical copy of New Math, but an original concept, rich in Hungarian traditional characteristics.

The Hungarian school system: Elementary School, Grades 1 - 8 (Age 6 - 14) Secondary School, Grades 9 - 12 (Age 14 - 18). Vocational School, Grade 9 – 11 (Age 14- 17). From 1990 we introduced newly the traditional 8 – years Gymnasium (Secondary Grammar School), Grades 5 - 12 (Age 10 - 18) and the 6 -years Gymnasium, Grades 7 - 12 (Age 13 - 18) . There are about 20 special mathematics classes from Grade 7, with 7 - 9 mathematics lessons in a week.

At the end of the secondary school there is a maturity exam from mathematics in two levels. The higher level is a common maturity and entrance exam to the university. From autumn 1998 we will introduce the new national curriculum. In this curriculum the prescribed compulsory material is only about 50 - 60 %, the other part is free for the teachers.

Some characteristics of Hungarian mathematics education.

The ideas of Tamas Varga influenced the Hungarian mathematics education, first of all in elementary level. These are - Free choice of methods of instruction.

Differentiation, individual treatment. Problemorientedness. Effective use of tools. The role of mother tongue, developing the language of mathematics.

Motivation, the changing role of the teacher. (Teacher as organizer) Formation of personality.

Some additional characteristics of mathematics education in upper secondary level.

Special attention to the talented students. Importance of mathematics as a formal, abstract science. Problemorientedness (many - many problembooks, taskcollections) Neglecting of the real-life problems. Importance of geometry.

Exam orientedness.

COMPETITIONS, PERIODICALS

Hungarian Mathematical and Physical Society was founded in 1891 and 3 years later a high-school teacher Daniel Arany began editing the second mathematical journal for school children on the world. (The first was founded in France 1875)

This journal is named today KOMAL and organizes a competition for secondary schools. For more than a hundred years the periodical is based upon corresponding. Solutions of the best students appear in the journal with their names and photos. Today more than 2000 school children send their solutions from month to month for yearly 200 mathematics and 100 physics problems. There is an English translation of the new problems for more than 30 years in each copy.

After World War II, competitions took up a nation-wide character, accessible for all children. As an outcome there is by now an appropriate form of competition for each child in the age group 9 - 18 years, centrally organized by the Ministry of Education or the Bolyai Society. In addition to these centrally organized occasions a number of local and regional competitions provide further opportunity for the children.

Other famous competition is the KURSCHAK competiton, more than 103 years old, organized annualy. Anybody in the pre-university institution can participate, including holders of a fresh maturity examination certificate.

COMPARATIVE GEOMETRY ON PLANE AND SPHERE, A TEACHING EXPERIMENT.

The idea is to offer a curriculum of geometric activities comparing some basic concepts in plane and spherical geometry, for a fairly wide range of age groups. The activities are carried out by direct manipulation both on plane and sphere. For experiment on the plane, students make use of their regular exercise-book, straightedge, compass, or some kind of computer software, such as Cabri-Geometre or The Geometers Sketchpad. For experiments in spherical geometry, they apply the Lenart Sphere, a manipulative skit that contains a thick, plastic, transparent sphere, about the size of a soccer ball, a supporting torus under the sphere, spherical ruler for drawing and measuring arcs of great circles, spherical compass and center locator for constructing any circles on the sphere, and thin hemispherical plastic transparencies as spherical draft papers, to be fit on the sphere.

Activities in comparative geometry are gathered in Non-Euclidian Adventures on Lenart Sphere, a workbook with blackline masters for the students, and teachers pages with keys and suggestions for the teacher. Student audience are middle- and-high schoolers, with an average level of interest and ability in mathematics. The first results working with this project are encouraging.

References

T. Nemetz: *Mathematics Education in Hungary.* In M.S. Arora (ed.) Moving into twenty-first century. Studies in mathematics education, vol. 8. UNESCO, 1992.

Lenart, Istvan: *Non-Euclidian Adventures on the Lenart Sphere.* Key Curriculum Press, Berkeley, California. 1996

The Lenart Sphere Set. *Construction Materials for Another World of Geometry.* Key Curriculum Press, Berkeley, California. 1996

Centennial issue of the Hungarian Mathematical and Physical Journal for secondary schools. Bolyai Janos Society, Roland Eotvos Physical Society Budapest, 1994

EDUCACIÓN MATEMÁTICA EN ESPAÑA
(Resumen de la Presentación Nacional de España)

Modesto Sierra Vázquez

A la memoria de Gonzalo Sánchez Vázquez

1.- Introducción

España es un país europeo que, según el artículo primero de la Constitución de 1978, se constituye en un Estado social y democrático de Derecho, que propugna como valores superiores de su ordenamiento jurídico la libertad, la justicia, la igualdad y el pluralismo político. La forma política del Estado español es la Monarquía parlamentaria. En virtud de la Constitución, España se organiza en diecisiete Comunidades Autónomas, que gozan de amplia autonomía para su propio gobierno; en particular, en el campo educativo está previsto que el Estado ceda sus competencias a dichas Comunidades en la educación primaria, secundaria y superior, habiéndose completado dichas transferencias en el caso de seis de estas Comunidades.

La población actual de España es de algo más de 39 millones de habitantes de los que casi 9,5 están implicados en el sistema educativo.

En las dos últimas décadas, recuperada la normalidad democrática, España se ha afanado en participar en el concierto de las naciones como lo demuestra nuestra incorporación a la Comunidad Económica Europea, el papel destacado en las relaciones de Europa con los países árabes y los iberoamericanos y la organización de acontecimientos internacionales como la Exposición Universal de Sevilla y los Juegos Olímpicos de Barcelona en 1992.

Esta Presentación Nacional continúa la realizada por el Profesor Claudi Alsina en el ICME de Budapest en 1988 y en ella se pretende exponer los logros de la educación matemática en España en los últimos años.

2.- Sistema educativo español

El actual sistema educativo español se encuentra articulado esencialmente por dos grandes Leyes, la de Reforma Universitaria de 1983 por la que se regula la enseñanza universitaria (L.R.U.) y la de

Ordenación General del Sistema Educativo (L.O.G.S.E.), de 1990, que trata de la educación infantil, primaria, secundaria , profesional y otro tipo de enseñanzas como la enseñanza de idiomas, la artística y la musical, así como de la formación inicial de los profesores de estos niveles. Hasta el curso 2000- 2001 no se implantará en su totalidad la nueva ordenación académica, por lo que actualmente nos encontramos inmersos en un importante cambio del sistema educativo al coexistir estructuras de la nueva ordenación académica con otras residuales del antiguo sistema.

La estructura del nuevo sistema educativo es la siguiente :

a) Educación infantil
Educación no obligatoria entre los 0 y los 6 años dividida en dos ciclos : primer ciclo (0 - 3 años) y segundo ciclo (3 - 6 años)
En el curso 93-94 había 1.077.797 alumnos en este nivel.
Es impartida por profesores (Maestros) especialistas en educación infantil.

b) Educación primaria

Educación gratuita y obligatoria que comprende el periodo 6 - 12 años, con 6 cursos, dividida en tres ciclos: primer ciclo (1º y 2º curso), segundo ciclo (3º y 4º curso), tercer ciclo (5º y 6º curso).

En el curso 93-94, cursaron la educación primaria 4.276.524 , incluyéndose en este número los cursos 7º y 8º de la antigua Educación General Básica.

Es impartida por profesores de primaria (Maestros). La enseñanza de la música, educación física e idiomas extranjeros es impartida por profesores de primaria (Maestros) con la especialización correspondiente.

c) Educación secundaria
Comprende el periodo 12 - 18 años y está dividida en :

c1) .- Educación Secundaria Obligatoria (E.S.O.), para el periodo 12 - 16 años y que como su nombre indica es obligatoria y gratuita para todos los españoles. A su vez está dividida en dos ciclos: primer ciclo (12-14 años) y segundo ciclo (14-16 años). Los alumnos que superen estos dos ciclos obtienen el título de Graduado en Educación Secundaria, necesario para acceder al Bachillerato. Los que no obtienen este título, pueden cursar unas asignaturas en un ciclo llamado Garantía Social para favorecer su incorporación al mundo laboral
En el curso 93-94, había 182.711 alumnos en este nivel.

c2).- Bachillerato, para el periodo 16-18 años. Comprende dos cursos académicos y se estructura en cuatro modalidades con nueve opciones diferentes. Las modalidades son : Artes, Ciencias de la Naturaleza y de la Salud, Humanidades y Ciencias Sociales y Tecnología. Los alumnos que cursen satisfactoriamente estos estudios en cualquiera de sus modalidades obtienen el título de Bachiller, que faculta para acceder a la formación profesional de grado superior y a los estudios universitarios, necesitándose además, en este último caso, la superación de una prueba de acceso.

En el año 93-94, 1.553.616 alumnos cursaron el Bachillerato, incluyéndose en este número los que estaban matriculados en el antiguo Bachillerato Unificado y Polivalente.

Tanto la Educación Secundaria Obligatoria como el Bachillerato son impartidas por Licenciados, Ingenieros o Arquitectos (cuatro o cinco años de estudios universitarios). Además es necesario estar en posesión de un título profesional de especialización didáctica, que se obtiene mediante la realización de un Curso de Cualificación Pedagógica.

d) Formación Profesional

Tiene como finalidad la preparación de los alumnos para la actividad en un campo profesional, proporcionándoles una formación polivalente que les permita adaptarse a las modificaciones laborales que puedan producirse a lo largo de su vida. Recientemente el Ministerio de Educación ha culminado la elaboración de un catálogo de 135 títulos profesionales, repartidos en 22 familias.

Comprende:
d1) Formación profesional específica de grado medio. Se accede al terminar la Educación Secundaria Obligatoria.

d2) Formación profesional específica de grado superior. Se accede como regla general desde el Bachillerato.

Además en la Educación Secundaria y el Bachillerato todos los alumnos reciben una formación básica de carácter profesional.

En el curso 93-94, había 881.174 alumnos en este nivel.
Para impartir la formación profesional específica se exigen los mismos requisitos de titulación que para la educación secundaria.

e) Educación Universitaria

Está regulada en la Ley de Reforma Universitaria de 1983 (L.R.U.) siendo el aspecto mas destacado la autonomía de las Universidades para su organización, administración de recursos, órganos de gobierno, selección de profesorado y elaboración de planes de estudio, entre otras competencias.

Los estudios universitarios se estructuran en tres ciclos. La superación del primero de ellos da derecho a la obtención del título de Diplomado, Ingeniero técnico o Arquitecto técnico; la del segundo ciclo, a la del título de Licenciado, Arquitecto o Ingeniero; la de tercero, a la del título de Doctor.

La duración de los estudios universitarios sigue el sistema de créditos (1 crédito = 10 horas). La obtención del título oficial de Licenciado o Ingeniero exige la superación de un mínimo de 300 créditos . En cuanto al número de años, el primer ciclo tiene una duración de dos a tres años académicos y el segundo ciclo una duración de dos años académicos. Los estudios que conducen a la Licenciatura de ciclo único tienen una duración de cuatro o cinco años. Para cada titulación el Ministerio de Educación establece unas directrices generales mínima y uniformes para todas las Universidades, que en virtud de su autonomía elaboran sus propios planes de estudios

Por lo que se refiere al Doctorado los estudios tienen una duración mínima de dos años durante los cuales el alumno debe cursar 32 créditos. Para obtener el título de Doctor hay que presentar, además, una memoria original de investigación (tesis doctoral)

Actualmente en España hay 44 Universidades públicas y 10 privadas.

En 1976 había 394.094 estudiantes universitarios, en 1985 había 720.419 y en 1995 había 1.444.545 lo que nos da idea del crecimiento espectacular de la población universitaria española.

3.- Formación inicial y permanente del profesorado

Las disposiciones legales señalan distintos niveles para el profesorado: Profesores de Educación Infantil y Primaria (Maestros), Profesores de Enseñanza Secundaria, Profesores Técnicos de Formación Profesional, Profesores de Enseñanzas Artísticas e Idiomas y Profesores de Cuerpos Docentes Universitarios, indicando en cada caso las condiciones de titulación mínima y formación pedagógica requerida para acceder al nivel docente correspondiente.

El profesorado de Educación Infantil y de Educación Primaria requiere el título de Maestro y su formación se realiza en las Escuelas Universitarias de Magisterio o en las Facultades de Educación. El Profesorado Educación Secundaria requiere el título de Licenciado y su formación se realiza en las Facultades o Escuelas Superiores correspondientes. Además, como ya se ha dicho, es necesario estar en posesión del título profesional de especialización didáctica, cuya organización y contenidos se han regulado recientemente. El profesorado de Matemáticas de la Universidad procede en su práctica totalidad de la Licenciatura en Matemáticas completada con el Doctorado.

Hasta el año 1984 la actualización científica y didáctica del profesorado en servicio de educación infantil, primaria, secundaria y formación profesional, se llevaba a cabo principalmente en los Institutos de Ciencias de la Educación(ICEs) dependientes de las Universidades. En ese año el Ministerio de Educación y Ciencia creó los Centros de Profesores como instituciones preferentes para la formación permanente del profesorado, que deben promover el encuentro profesional de los docentes en un marco de participación y colaboración. Recientemente, han pasado a denominarse Centros de Profesores y Recursos (CPRs). Estos Centros cubren todas las áreas del currículo y en particular las Matemáticas.

4.- Matemáticas en la Educación obligatoria

La educación obligatoria comprende el periodo 6-16 años dividido en dos etapas: educación primaria (6-12 años) y educación secundaria obligatoria (12-16 años). En la primaria la dedicación horaria a las Matemáticas es de 4 horas semanales; en la secundaria de 3 horas semanales.

La LOGSE configura un currículo *abierto* con tres niveles de concreción:

Primer nivel: Diseño curricular prescriptivo donde se establecen las enseñanzas mínimas. Segundo nivel: Proyecto curricular de Centro. Tercer nivel : Programación en el aula
Es importante destacar que en los documentos oficiales de nuestro Ministerio de Educación y Ciencia se pone de manifiesto que la formación

matemática en el periodo obligatorio ha sido pensada como un proceso continuo. De este modo, los principios que inspiran el currículo oficial son:

i)Presentar las Matemáticas a los alumnos como un conjunto de conocimientos y procedimientos que han evolucionado en el transcurso del tiempo, y que, con seguridad, seguirán evolucionando en el futuro.

ii) Relacionar los contenidos de aprendizaje de las Matemáticas con la experiencia de los alumnos y presentarlos y enseñarlos en un contexto de resolución de problemas.

iii) Atender equilibradamente los aspectos formativos, instrumental y funcional.

Los contenidos se organizan en conceptos, procedimientos y actitudes y se articulan en torno a los siguientes bloque temáticos:

1.- Números y operaciones. 2.- Medida, estimación y cálculo de magnitudes. 3.- Representación y organización en el espacio. 4.- Interpretación, representación y tratamiento de la información. 5.- Tratamiento del azar (Este bloque está incluido en el anterior en la Educación primaria).

En 4º curso de E.S.O. hay dos opciones que se diferencian fundamentalmente en su enfoque.

Entre los principales problemas de la educación matemática en el nivel obligatorio se pueden destacar los siguientes:

i) Las Matemáticas continúan siendo el punto más débil de los escolares españoles. La evaluación llevada a cabo por el Instituto Nacional de Calidad y Evaluación (INCE) del Ministerio de Educación, en el curso 94-95 sobre una muestra de 10.500 alumnos de sexto curso (11-12 años) dio como resultado que el escolar medio acertó el 50,1 % de las cuestiones planteadas, mientras que en las restantes disciplinas de estudio el porcentaje es mucho mayor. Aunque el déficit en matemáticas no es exclusivo, ciertamente, de los escolares españoles, estos resultados plantean la necesidad de investigaciones que indaguen acerca de las causas de estos resultados y hagan propuestas para mejorar los procesos de enseñanza-aprendizaje de los escolares españoles

ii) En la implantación de la educación obligatoria (6-16 años) los profesores deben darse cuenta que se han producido cambios importantes en lo que se considera conocimiento matemático al destacarse las estrategias para la resolución de problemas y los procedimientos como aspectos con entidad propia ; se ha modificado también el modo de trabajar en el aula y se está revisando a fondo el proceso de evaluación.

iii) La coordinación entre las Matemáticas de la Educación Primaria y las de la Educación Secundaria Obligatoria y entre ésta y el Bachillerato, es un asunto pendiente de resolver.

5.- Matemáticas en el Bachillerato

El Bachillerato regulado en la actual reforma educativa, según se ha señalado, tiene cuatro modalidades: Artes, Ciencias de la Naturaleza y de la Salud, Humanidades y Ciencias Sociales, y Tecnología. Pues bien, en la modalidad de Ciencias de la Naturaleza y de la Salud y en la modalidad de Tecnología aparecen en primer curso, con carácter obligatorio, Matemáticas I y en segundo curso, con carácter optativo, Matemáticas II como materias propias de estas modalidades. En Humanidades y Ciencias Sociales aparecen como materias propias que pueden ser escogidas por los alumnos Matemáticas aplicadas a las Ciencias Sociales I en primer curso y Matemáticas aplicadas a las Ciencias Sociales II en segundo curso.

La dedicación horaria a las diversas asignaturas de Matemáticas es de 4 horas semanales.

Además existe la posibilidad de ofertar asignaturas optativas relacionadas con las Matemáticas.

En cuanto a los contenidos, las Matemáticas I comprenden: Estadística y Probabilidad; Geometría; Funciones; Aritmética y Álgebra y Resolución de problemas. Las Matemáticas II comprenden: Álgebra lineal, Análisis y Geometría.

6.- Matemáticas en la formación profesional

Aunque la nueva formación profesional está en un estado incipiente, podemos asegurar que tanto en la formación profesional de grado medio como en la de grado superior aparecen asignaturas relacionadas con las Matemáticas, dependiendo de la titulación de que se trate. La existencia de 135 titulaciones impide que se pueda llevar a cabo un informe detallado de las mismas.

Hasta aquí se ha presentado, de modo conciso, la situación de la educación matemática en los niveles anteriores a la Universidad. Aceptada la nueva organización del sistema educativo, la reforma correspondiente a Matemáticas ha sido puesta en práctica por el profesorado más activo, generalmente vinculado a movimientos de innovación, mientras que es vista con recelo por alguna parte del profesorado.

7.- La Educación matemática en la Universidad

Al tratar en este informe la educación matemática en la Universidad se van a considerar los siguientes apartados: Departamentos universitarios, Facultades de Matemáticas y Facultades de Educación y Escuelas Universitarias de Magisterio.

a) Departamentos universitarios

La Ley de Reforma Universitaria de 1983 introdujo en el sistema organizativo de la Universidad española dos novedades importantes: la consideración de las áreas de conocimiento y la estructura departamental. Entre las áreas aparece por vez primera la *Didáctica de la Matemática* como uno de los campos de conocimiento básico en torno a los que se va estructurar la Universidad, produciéndose así una total integración de la Educación Matemática en la Universidad española. Por lo que se refiere a los Departamentos universitarios, aunque ya preexistían antes de la LRU es en esta Ley donde se establece decididamente la estructura departamental. De acuerdo con la normativa legal se han constituido Departamentos que incluyen el área de conocimiento Didáctica de la Matemática. Uno de los logros más importantes ha sido la organización y desarrollo de Programas de Doctorado específicos de Didáctica de la Matemática por parte de algunos de los Departamentos constituidos, que ha posibilitado la elaboración y defensa de Tesis Doctorales en Didáctica de la Matemática, produciéndose el reconocimiento institucional de la investigación en nuestra área y de su validez académica.

b) Facultades de Matemáticas

Los estudios superiores universitarios de Matemáticas, que conducen al título de Licenciado, se pueden cursar en veintitrés universidades. Los planes de estudio varían según cada Universidad pero, en general, se puede afirmar que en cuatro o cinco años se obtiene una formación bastante completa en Álgebra, Análisis, Geometría, Topología, Matemática Aplicada, Estadística e Investigación Operativa. Aunque se está introduciendo el lenguaje de los ordenadores, hay poca relación entre Matemáticas e Informática. Los cursos de Física,

Astronomía , etc. casi han desaparecido de los planes de estudio. Por lo que se refiere a la Educación Matemática, varias Universidades ofrecen entre las materias obligatorias y optativas asignaturas relacionas con la Educación Matemática.

c)Facultades de Educación y Escuelas Universitarias de Magisterio
Desde hace ciento cincuenta años existen en España unas instituciones específicas, las Escuelas Normales, para formar Profesores de Educación Primaria (Maestros). Con la Ley General de Educación de 1970 se integraron en la estructura universitaria, situación consolidada actualmente. En 1988 había alrededor de setenta Centros de este tipo entre públicos y privados, siendo los privados un veinte por ciento aproximadamente. En los cinco últimos años algunas de estas Escuelas Universitarias se han integrado en las Facultades de Pedagogía dando lugar a una nueva institución que se denomina Facultad de Educación o Facultad de Ciencias de la Educación según las diversas universidades. En ambos Centros se cursa la titulación de Maestro con tres años de duración. Actualmente hay siete especialidades : Primaria, Infantil, Educación Física, Idioma extranjero, Educación Especial, Educación Musical, Audición y Lenguaje. Pues bien, en las cuatro primeras especialidades *Matemáticas y su Didáctica* es una asignatura fundamental, ofreciéndose también a los estudiantes asignaturas optativas relacionadas con la Educación Matemática.

Además, en otras titulaciones como Pedagogía, Psicopedagogía o Educación Social, aparecen asignaturas optativas elaboradas desde el área de Didáctica de la Matemática.

d) Matemáticas en otros centros.
En casi todos los estudios universitarios, a excepción de lenguas puras, artes y algunos estudios humanísticos, aparecen asignaturas de Matemáticas, fundamentalmente en los dos primeros cursos. El nivel de especialización depende de los estudios. En las carreras técnicas (Ingenierías y Arquitectura) o en las carreras científicas como Químicas y Físicas el nivel es bastante elevado.

8.- Grupos y Sociedades.

Para comprender el desarrollo de la Educación Matemática en España en los últimos veinte años hay que refererirse necesariamente al importante movimiento asociativo que hay en nuestro país y que comenzó a mediados de los setenta con los Grupos de Renovación. Estos grupos actuaron en torno a un proyecto propio, impulsados por alguien con mayor personalidad o carácter, pero con un esquema de trabajo de grupo y con poca o nula ayuda institucional en sus comienzos ; se sostuvieron por la certeza moral de que la tarea emprendida era importante y necesaria .

Por esta misma época hay otros grupos que enfocan las tareas del educador matemático desde una perspectiva más amplia y ven la necesidad de constituir Sociedades de Profesores de Matemáticas con las que abordar un campo de trabajo que se va volviendo cada vez más complejo. Estas Sociedades comprenden la necesidad de aunar sus esfuerzos e inician en 1987 un proceso de federación que culmina en 1989 con la constitución de la Federación Española de Sociedades de Profesores de Matemáticas, integrada por las constituidas en ese momento. Posteriormente se han constituido Sociedades de Profesores en casi todas las Comunidades Autónomas del Estado español que se han integrado en la Federación, a la que pertenecen en este momento 13 Sociedades.

En la perspectiva de sólo siete años desde la constitución de la Federación, se han ido cumpliendo prácticamente todos los objetivos propuestos; se han delimitado grandes áreas de trabajo como docencia, investigación, relaciones de comunicación y difusión y extensión de la cultura matemática. La labor de las Sociedades ha sido muy activa en este periodo promoviendo la mejora de la enseñanza y aprendizaje de las Matemáticas y contribuyendo de modo destacado al perfeccionamiento del profesorado.

La necesidad de articular la investigación en Educación Matemática, ha llevado a la creación, en marzo del presente año, de la Sociedad Española de Investigación en Educación Matemática (SEIEM), uno de cuyos objetivos es mantener un espacio de comunicación, crítica y debate sobre investigación en Educación Matemática, donde plantear cuestiones, transmitir e intercambiar resultados, profundizar en las elaboraciones teóricas , mejorar y validar los diseños metodológicos.

9.- Reuniones, Jornadas y Congresos

Durante los años sesenta y setenta se celebraron en España algunas Reuniones y Congresos sobre Educación Matemática organizados principalmente por la Administración educativa. Durante los años ochenta y noventa se ha producido un cambio, puesto que durante estas dos décadas son las Sociedades de Profesores de Matemáticas y otros colectivos de Profesores los que convocan numerosos Encuentros, Reuniones y Jornadas específicas de Educación Matemática. Por su capacidad convocatoria entre el Profesorado destacamos las Jornadas sobre el Aprendizaje y Enseñanza de las Matemáticas (JAEMs), convocadas por la Federación de Sociedades de Profesores de Matemáticas. Son bianuales y son el foro de encuentro, debate e intercambio de experiencias de los profesores de los distintos niveles del sistema educativo, desde la educación infantil hasta la universidad, habiéndose celebrado hasta ahora siete Jornadas de este tipo.

A destacar el Primer Congreso Iberoamericano de Educación Matemática, celebrado en Sevilla en Septiembre de 1990, organizado por la Sociedad Andaluza de Educación Matemática Thales, en representación de la Federación Española de Sociedades de Profesores de Matemáticas, con la colaboración del Comité Interamericano de Educación Matemática y de la Sociedad Portuguesa de Profesores de Matemáticas.

Además se han celebrado en España numerosos Encuentros, Jornadas y Cursos, siendo imposible hacer un listado de los mismos.

Asimismo hay que destacar la presencia activa de investigadores españoles en Organismos y Encuentros Internacionales, así como los esfuerzos por establecer lazos de cooperación con otros países como lo prueba, por ejemplo, la celebración de Simposios con investigadores de Italia, Portugal y Méjico.

10.-Publicaciones

Las publicaciones sobre Educación Matemática en España han crecido considerablemente en los últimos años

a) Publicaciones periódicas : *Enseñanza de las Ciencias, Epsilon, Números, Suma, Uno*
Además hay otras publicaciones periódicas no específicas de Educación Matemática y que contienen trabajos de nuestro campo , como *Infancia y aprendizaje, Bordón, Perspectiva Escolar, Cuadernos de Pedagogía*

b) Libros
Además de las revistas especializadas se están publicando libros específicos relativos a Educación Matemática. Así, el Ministerio de Educación y Ciencia está editando una serie de documentos dirigidos a los Centros de Profesores sobre el tratamiento metodológico de temas concretos; las Comunidades Autónomas con competencias en materia de

educación están siguiendo una política similar. También el Ministerio de Educación y Ciencia está publicando, en colaboración con editoriales nacionales, traducciones de libros que se han revelado de gran interés para nuestro campo.

Las Sociedades de Profesores editan habitualmente las Actas de los Congresos y Jornadas que celebran. Además, están comenzando a definir su propia política de publicaciones.

Otra iniciativa importante son las colecciones de Educación Matemática de la Editorial Síntesis tituladas *Matemáticas : Cultura y aprendizaje y Educación Matemática en Secundaria,* que constan de sesenta y un títulos y en la que participan alrededor de doscientos autores españoles de todos los niveles educativos.

Las tesis doctorales, tesinas y memorias de tercer ciclo realizadas en Educación Matemática, constituyen una bibliografía específica y valiosa.

Numerosas editoriales publican además libros de texto para los diferentes cursos de los distintos niveles educativos, ofreciéndose en la mayoría de los casos las correspondientes guías didácticas para los profesores. Algunas tienen en su fondo editorial libros de Matemáticas y de Educación Matemática de autores españoles y traducciones de otra lenguas, esencialmente del inglés. Igualmente, existen empresas especializada en la producción y comercialización de materiales didácticos.

Además de las publicaciones periódicas y libros, se están utilizando cada vez los nuevos sistemas informáticos, de modo que ya existen publicaciones, programas de doctorado, etc. que se pueden consultar en Internet.

11.- Extensión de la cultura matemática

Han sido numerosas las actividades que se han llevado a cabo en España en los últimos años, para promover la difusión de las Matemáticas. En primer lugar tengo que citar las *Olimpiadas Matemáticas* para alumnos del último año de la enseñanza básica (13 - 14 años), que comenzaron en Andalucía en el año 1985, y que se han extendido por todo el Estado.

Otro concurso popularizado entre los escolares españoles es el de Fotografía y Matemáticas. Iniciado en Granada en 1988, pronto se extendió al resto de Andalucía con una fase provincial y otra regional. Este concurso ha comenzado a ser organizado por el resto de las Sociedades del Estado.

Las exposiciones constituyen otro de los instrumentos usuales de difusión de la cultura matemática. Durante los últimos años se han realizado numerosas exposiciones.

Además, en los medios de comunicación, prensa, radio y televisión se han realizado actividades de difusión de la cultura matemática.

12.- Consideraciones finales

Al exponer los logros de la comunidad de educadores matemáticos en España se debe mirar hacia el futuro. Algunos de los retos de la Educación Matemática en España son los siguientes :

i) Desarrollo de la nueva organización del sistema educativo emanada de la Ley de Ordenación General del Sistema Educativo: la situación de desconcierto que se está produciendo en algún sector de la sociedad, y en particular en algunos sectores educativos, durante la implantación de esta Ley, necesita clarificarse, planteando el marco más amplio de objetivos que se deben cubrir mediante la adquisición de capacidades matemáticas.

ii) Formación inicial del profesorado de Matemáticas: las nuevas especialidades surgidas con la reforma de planes de estudio de maestros exigen igualmente nuevos planteamiento en la formación matemática de los profesores de primaria haciendo hincapié en la didáctica de nuestra disciplina. En cuanto al profesorado de secundaria, la puesta en marcha del Curso de Cualificación Pedagógica, debe servir para rectificar errores del pasado y para formar en la profesión de profesores de Matemáticas a los alumnos de dicho curso.

iii) Formación permanente del profesorado de Matemáticas: se debe clarificar el papel de los Centros de Profesores y Recursos, así como el de las Universidades a través de sus Departamentos en la formación permanente del Profesorado de Matemáticas.

iv) Investigación en educación matemática: la calidad constrastada de los primeros programas de doctorado debe servir de estímulo a otras Universidades del Estado español para ofertar por su parte nuevos programas. Desde algunas instancias se está reclamando la creación de

Institutos de Investigación en Educación Matemática; pero la investigación no se puede limitar a conocer las circunstancias en las que ocurre la educación matemática sino que tiene que servir para mejorar los procesos de enseñanza- aprendizaje de las Matemáticas en todo los niveles educativos.

v) Consolidación del movimiento asociativo: cada vez debe ser mayor el número de profesores que pertenezcan a las Sociedades de Profesores de Matemáticas. Esto será posible si esas Sociedades saben ofrecer a los Profesores productos que les interesen y les estimulen.

Estos son solamente algunos de los retos que tiene planteada la comunidad de educadores matemáticos en España para los próximos años.

La celebración de este 8º Congreso Internacional de Educación Matemática en Sevilla, muestra la vitalidad de una comunidad, cuyos diferentes estamentos han aunado sus esfuerzos en pro de la mejora de la Educación Matemática en el mundo.

SPECIAL SESSIONS
SESIONES ESPECIALES

- The Cordobese Mean / *La Proporción Cordobesa*
    Rafael de la Hoz

- Asamblea de la S.A.E.M. THALES

- Spanish Mathematicians in the 20th Century /
  Matemáticos Españoles en el Siglo XX
    Alberto Aizpún
        Luis Español, Mariano Hormigón,
        Mariano Martínez, José Luis Vicente

SPECIAL SESSIONS
SESIONES ESPECIALES

SECRETARY'S OBSERVATIONS AND CLOSING REMARKS

Prof. Mogens Niss. ICMI General Secretary

Introduction

Distinguished guests, ladies and gentlemen, dear colleagues and friends,

We all know that we have spent the last week as participants in a most stimulating, intensive, hot, hectic, rewarding, and spectacular event called the 8th International Congress on Mathematical Education, abbreviated ICME-8. We know that we have met some 3500 interesting colleagues from close to a hundred different countries. Some, but certainly not all, of us know that the quadriennial ICMEs –starting with ICME-1 in Lyon (France) in 1969, in retrospect somewhat off the rule which emerged later that the ICMEs are held in leap years– are held on behalf of and under the auspices of ICMI, the International Commission on Mathematical Instruction. It is in my capacity as the Secretary of this Commission that I have the honour of addressing you today.

The Commission was established already in 1908 (but the officers have been changed, even if you might think otherwise listening to me today), with Felix Klein as its first President – but was reconstituted after World War II as a Commission under the International Mathematical Union, IMU. As is the case with IMU, the members of the ICMI are not individual but states, most of which, but not all, are also the members of IMU. Today, 66 countries (excl. Thailand) are members of ICMI. The Commission consists of two bodies: The Executive Committee, p.t. of a total of 10 members, which is appointed by the IMU, and the General Assembly, composed of the National Representatives of the member states, one for each. Both bodies have held meetings during this congress. The current four-year term of the EC will be completed at the end of 1998.

Later in this talk I shall present –briefly, I promise! – the main sorts of activities that ICMI undertakes. Quite a few of them are likely to be of direct interest to the participants in our congress. However, before doing so, I shall, with your permission, take advantage of the privilege it is to address a plenary session of ICME for the last time as the Secretary of ICMI. At the next ICME in 2000, my successor will stand before you on the analogous occasion. What I am going to do next is to put forward and share with you a few observations I have made concerning the development in our field, including certain characteristic features, trends and tendencies which from my observation post have manifested themselves in recent years.

State and trends: Some observations

Mathematics education, or the didactics of mathematics as I prefer to call it, is not a field in which many 'theorems' are proved or indisputable (non-trivial) 'results' are obtained in the classical sense of those terms – although there *are* examples of the latter.

Since the main outcomes of our endeavours cannot easily be stated as theorems or well-defined results established by conclusive evidence, it is not easy to tell 'what is new in the field'. On the other hand, that's what scientific congresses are about, isn't it? Normally, congresses gather to hear about new break-throughs, new specific findings, and to learn what new land has been reclaimed since the last time the participants met. In mathematics education, I submit, we go to congresses for basically the same reason – in addition to the even more important reason: to meet and talk to people. But what kinds of break-throughs, findings, and new reclaimed land are characteristic to our field?

As I see it, the didactics of mathematics is characterised by 'issues of concern', 'areas of interest' and 'fields of attention' in relation to which it doesn't offer many theorems and results but, instead, 'perspectives', 'reflections' and 'insights', all of which are of a somewhat vague and fuzzy nature. If this is true, the new outcomes in our field should be found in the categories just mentioned. So, what are the 'new issues of concern', 'new areas of interest, 'new fields of attention', 'new perspectives', 'new reflections' and 'new insights' in the didactics of mathematics? Attempts to answer this question encounter certain difficulties as well, caused by the vagueness and the fuzziness of the terms. Much of what we have been considering in ICME-8 was considered also in ICME-7, and in ICME-6 too, for that matter. Does this imply that we are simply engaged in disguised repetition of an immense travelling circus concerned with what amounts to be permutations of previous congresses? From my perspective the answer is definitely 'no' even if it is true that in close-up 'yes' might appear to be a tempting conclusion to arrive at. However, to see that the answer is 'no' rather than 'yes' it might be necessary to consider the development not only from one congress to the next, but across a longer span of time, for instance something like two congress terms, i.e. almost a decade. If the observations I am going to present in a minute are valid, we may take this to suggest that development in our field is slow and organic rather than abrupt and mechanical.

I have tried to identify some main lines of development, states and trends by scanning a fair amount of literature from the last decade, roughly, by looking at the programmes of the ICMEs and some other major conferences. My intention is to describe the state of the art, not to make normative claims or appeals. However, what I am offering does not pretend to be the outcome of a scholarly or scientific investigation, but a piece of informal interpretative analysis filtered through the glasses (mental and physical) I happen to wear. In case you will find my considerations and reflections misplaced and ill-justified, you may be pleased to know that they won't take long.

I shall present my observations concerning the evolution in our field by placing a number of key 'areas of interest/attention' in four 'different levels of change in activity and intensity': Areas belonging to the level of *Stagnating or weakening interest/attention*, of *Stable interest/attention*, of *Continued increasing interest/attention*, and of *Interest/attention gaining momentum or emerging*, respectively. Clearly the demarcation lines are not clear-cut, categorical ones; the placing of a certain area on a given level may well be subject of debate. It should be stressed that all items included in the lists below *are* subject to attention in the mathematics education community. The differences lie with their relative weights measured by activity in the area. Put in a simplified, yet illuminating way, it's the derivatives rather than the absolute level of activity which are depicted in the following lists.

Stagnating or weakening interest/attention (initial value: varying; derivative < 0 or ≤ 0)
* curriculum planning and design
* new mathematical topics in the curriculum
* applications and modelling
* links between mathematics and other teaching subjects
* problem solving
* mathematics education and society at large
* testing
* evaluation of systems
* remediation of mathematical anxiety, students' misconceptions and errors
* learning disabilities
* gifted students
constructivist positions in mathematics education

It is worth noticing that the majority of the items in this list occupied key positions in the field of attention of, say, ICMEs 5 & 6 in 1984 and 1988.

Stable interest/attention (initial value: varying; derivative = 0)
* mathematics education in culture (including subcultures)
* cross-cultural studies
* gender issues
* computers and information technology in the teaching of mathematics
* computer-based learning environments
* activity-oriented teaching/learning modes (projects, investigations, explorations)
* the relationship between research and practice in mathematics education

Continued increasing interest/attention (initial value: large; derivative > 0)
* quantitative reasoning and number sense
* images, models, representations of concepts and notions
* ways of thinking, cognitive models, metacognition
* meaning and sense making in mathematics
* understanding mathematics
* (moderately) advanced mathematical concepts and thinking
* communication and discourse in mathematics
* the mathematics classroom
* history of mathematics for mathematics teaching and learning
* pupils'/students' attitudes and beliefs
* teachers' attitudes and beliefs
* mathematics education as a scholarly/scientific discipline

Interest/attention gaining momentum or emerging
* reasoning, proving, proofs
* students' learning strategies
* revitalisation of geometry
* visualisation
* adult education
* design of teaching
* teachers' images of mathematics as a subject
* the professional identity and development of mathematics teachers
* (fairly) advanced mathematical concepts and thinking (emerging)
* university teaching of mathematics (emerging)
* mathematicians and mathematics education (emerging)
* non-constructivist positions in mathematics education (emerging)

The dynamics of these changes is complex and not simple to grasp. Some of the changes are due to novel insights and eye-opening work, others are due to old areas being exhausted, others to search for new virgin land to explore, others –and not the least so– are due to waves of fashion.

In my view, in the mathematics education community time is ripe for paying more systematic attention to the nature, the development and changes, and their underlying dynamics, of our field, not only in the context of ICMEs but at large. Please consider my deliberations as an invitation to continued critical examination of and reflection about mathematics education as a field of research, development and thoughtful practice.

ICMEs

The format of ICME-8 was not basically different from the format of the three previous ICMEs. ICME-5 in Adelaide, ICME-6, and ICME-7 in Québec were all variations of the same template: A fairly substantial component of interactive small group activities in Working Groups and Topic Groups, mixed with lectures, short communications and posters, plus lots of special arrangements. As this format has now been tried out in a number of variations, it might be time to undertake some form of evaluation of the structure –and of course the content– of the ICMEs. On behalf of the ICMI EC I therefore invite you to share your observations, thoughts, concerns and proposal with the organisers of future congresses. Please send your comments and suggestions to me, by letter, fax or e-mail:

Professor Mogens Niss,
Roskilde University,
P.O. Box 260
DK-4000 Roskilde,
DENMARK
Fax: +45 46755065
e-mail: mn@mmf.ruc.dk

Quite a few of you probably already know it, but I am delighted and honoured to officially announce that the EC of ICMI has accepted the invitation of Japan to host ICME-9 in the year 2000. The venue will be Chiba, near Tokyo. We all look forward to yet another magnificent congress, this time organised by our excellent and enthusiastic colleagues in Japan.

When it comes to future ICMEs, beyond ICME-9, no invitations have been received as yet. However, as the task of organising an international congress of the size of an ICMI becomes an increasingly immense, complicated and demanding task, I should like to invite countries which may contemplate to submit a bid to initiate more specific considerations already at this early stage. Even if the decision concerning ICME-10 will be taken by the next EC, 2004 is not as far away in preparation terms as one might tend to think on the verge of leaving ICME-8!

It is true that the ICMEs represent the peak of effort and the most important and spectacular event of the activities held by or on behalf of ICMI. Nevertheless, ICMI's spectrum of activities is broader than the congresses.

ICMI Studies

Since 1986 ICMI has conducted a series of so-called ICMI Studies, devoted to crucial current themes or issues in mathematics education. An ICMI Study is a vector consisting of 5 different components.

(a) A theme/problématique identified by the EC; (b) An International Programme Committee (5-10 members) appointed by the EC to direct the Study; (c) A Discussion Document (10-15 pages) produced by the IPC and distributed worldwide through as many channels as possible. The DD identifies the issues and topics to be dealt with in the study, and invites readers to react in writing to the IPC with reflections, concerns, ideas, proposals, etc. (d) An invited ICMI Study Conference (60-100 participants), summoned by the IPC, to investigate and discuss the theme of the study. Invitations are issued so as to ensure a balance between 'veteran' and 'novice' participants in the area. (e) On the basis of the DD (and the reactions to it) the work done at the Study Conference, papers submitted or commissioned, the final outcome, the ICMI Study volume is produced and published as a separate book in the ICMI Study Series. Typically, the ICMI Study is edited by the Chair, perhaps assisted by one or two members of the IPC.

The state of affairs concerning the ICMI Studies is as follows.
The near past:
Since 1992, the following ICMI Studies have been completed: The ICMI Study on Assessment in Mathematics Education and Its Effects (Study Conference, Calonge, Spain 1991) resulted in two books:

Investigations into Assessment in Mathematics Education (edited by Mogens Niss), Kluwer Academic Publishers, 1993

Cases of Assessment in Mathematics Education (edited by Mogens Niss), Kluwer Academic Publishers, 1993

The ICMI Study on Gender and Mathematics Education (Study Conference, Höör, Sweden, 1993) resulted in:

Towards Gender Equity in Mathematics Education (edited by Gila Hanna), Kluwer Academic Publishers, 1996,

and a separate proceedings volume, outside of the ICMI Study Series proper: Barbro Grevholm & Gila Hanna (eds.): *Gender and Mathematics Education*, Lund University Press, 1995. In a special session in this congress this Study and its outcomes were presented.

The present:
Since 1992 two further Study Conferences have been held and the corresponding Study volumes are under way:

What is Research in Mathematics Education, and What are Its Effects? (edited by Jeremy Kilpatrick and Anna Sierpinska), (Study Conference, College Park, Maryland, USA, 1994). Expected to appear (published by Kluwer Academic Publishers) in 1996

Perspectives on the Teaching of Geometry (editor-in-chief Vinicio Villani), (Study Conference, Catania, Italy, 1995). Expected to appear in 1997. Also these two studies have been presented at this congress.

It should be emphasised that the publications in the ICMI Study Series may be obtained by individuals at a markedly reduced rate if bought through ICMI. If you are interested, simply contact me on the above-mentioned address.

The near future:
The EC has decided to mount the following two studies, with Study Conferences to be held in 1997-98:

The Role of the History of Mathematics in the Teaching and Learning of Mathematics (working title). The Study Conference will most probably be held in France. The IPC is in the process of being appointed.

The Teaching and Learning of Mathematics at University Level (working title). Study Conference venue still to be decided. The IPC is about to be appointed.

The distant future:

The following ideas are being considered by the EC for the next ones on the list of Studies:

The role of proof and proving in mathematics education
Stochastics and probability in mathematics education

Affiliated study groups

Over the years some of the permanent international study groups in mathematics education have been affiliated to ICMI. These are
* HPM, The International Study Groups on the Relations between the History and Pedagogy of Mathematics
* IOWME, The International Organisation of Women and Mathematics Education,
* PME, The International Group for the Psychology of Mathematics Education,
* WFNMC, The World Federation of National Mathematical Competitions, which obtained affiliation during the last congress period (1994).

All four study groups hold separate meetings of their own in addition to staging activities in the ICMEs.

Regional conferences

The 'raisond'être' of ICMI is to be an international organisation. However, we all know that practical, financial, and political constraints, and cultural and linguistic circumstances make internationalism less easily achieved than proclaimed and desired. Therefore, ICMI has always sponsored –morally or financially, the latter, alas!, in symbolic measures only– regional conferences. Since ICME-7, the following regional conferences have been held:

SEACME 6 (South East Asian Conference on Mathematical Education), Surabaya, Indonesia, 1993

ICMI-China Regional Conference on Mathematics Education, Shanghai, China, 1994, on the theme Teacher Preparation in Mathematics

Regional Collaboration in Mathematics Education: An ICMI regional Conference, Melbourne, Australia, 1995

IX IACME, Inter-American Conference on Mathematics Education, Santiago de Chile, Chile, 1995

SEACME 7 (South East Asian Conference on Mathematical Education), Hanoi, Vietnam, 1996

Future meetings

A combined East Asian Regional Conference and a Meeting of East Asian National Representatives to ICMI is under planning. It will be held in Chungbuk, Korea, in 1998.

It is ICMI's hope that within the next few years it will also be possible to hold ICMI Regional Conferences in other parts of the world, such as Africa, the Middle East, Eastern Europe and South Asia. The EC of ICMI would welcome specific proposals and initiatives in this direction.

Solidarity Programme

Those of you who took part in ICME-7 in 1992 may well recall that the President of ICMI, Miguel de Guzmán, announced that ICMI intended to mount a Solidarity Programme and a Solidarity Fund based on contributions from individuals and organisations in mathematics education. The main idea is to support projects which might help the development of mathematics education in a region, country or province, in particular projects which may help the development of a self-sustainable infra-structure (such as preparation of teachers, or researchers in mathematics education; curriculum development; provision of research materials; production of teaching/learning materials; creation of networks; initiation of research activities).

Since 1992, a few small scale projects have been carried out under the auspices of the Solidarity Fund, primarily in Latin America. Although the Fund is still of a fairly modest size, it is growing gradually, and the Steering Committee of the Solidarity Fund would welcome applications concerning projects which conform with the intentions of the Solidarity Programme.

Speaking about solidarity, probably the most spectacular manifestation of international solidarity in mathematics education since 1992 is due to all of you, the delegates of ICME-8. You are probably aware of the fact that the ICME-8 organiser and ICMI agreed to introduce a 10% Solidarity Tax on all registration fees in order to help mathematics educators from less affluent countries to attend ICMI. I am delighted to announce that the Grants Committee was able to support no fewer than 243 delegates from 54 countries. Most of them would not have been able to participate in the congress had it not been for this Solidarity Tax and hence for your help!

Information about ICMI

I hope to have been able to give you a brief, yet comprehensive, survey of the main activities of ICMI, most of which take place in between the ICMEs. Information of ICMI activities and events, and other activities and events in mathematics education, may be found in the ICMI Bulletin which is published by the ICMI Secretariat (i.e. me) twice a year, in June and December. The paper version of the Bulletin is meant to be an internal newsletter for the ICMI family, and thus is neither for subscription nor on sale. Nevertheless, the content is actually available to everybody with access to e-mail or the WWW. You may obtain an electronic version of the Bulletin by contacting me at mn@mmf.ruc.dk or you may find it on the WWW, on the IMU server, by using the URL:

http://elib.zib-berlin.de/imu.icmi.bull[no.].

so far the two most recent issues, no. 39 and 40, have been placed on this server.

Concluding remarks.

Most delightful things come to an end. This is also the case with ICME-8. We have all spent a most intensive and marvellous week. We have taken part in an incredibly rich and complex scientific and social programme. We have enjoyed being together with old and new friends, and we have experienced a Congress being held with as much heat and sun as one would ever want to ask for. Altogether the Congress has been yet another memorable milestone in the history of the mathematics education community.

None of this would have been possible if it weren't for our great Spanish colleagues and friends. Not only have we enjoyed Spanish hospitality in general and Andalucian and Sevillean hospitality in particular. We have also been given a unique opportunity to become acquainted with and to experience crucial aspects of Spanish and Andalusian culture and tradition. For all this we –the Congress participants, the Executive Committee of ICMI, including myself– are grateful beyond the point of verbal expression. Therefore, please bear with me when I am unable to extend our thanks to all who deserve them so much. I have to confine myself to mentioning just a very few token individuals. Please consider them as placeholders for all those known and unknown actors behind the curtains whose tireless efforts were absolutely essential to the success of our Congress. Our most sincere thanks go to

* The Chair of the International Programme Committee, Claudi Alsina, Barcelona, and his colleagues in the IPC.

* The leaders of the Local Organising Committee on behalf of all their colleagues and collaborators in Sociedad Andaluza de Educación Matemática 'Thales', Antonio Pérez, Antonio Aranda, José María Álvarez, Concepción (Concha) García, and all the students in green.

We also wish to extend our sincere thanks to all the sponsors, in particular the Junta de Andalucía (the government of the Province of Andalucía), and the Universidad de Sevilla for their generous support of the Congress.

Finally, but certainly not least, our gratitude and deep sympathy go to the person who strived for years to make it possible for Spain, Andalucía and Sevilla to host this magnificent event:

The President of the Federación Española de Sociedades de Profesores de Matemáticas: Gonzalo Sánchez-Vázquez, on behalf of all his colleagues in the Federación in all of the provinces of Spain. It is terribly sad indeed that a serious illness has prevented Gonzalo Sánchez from attending our –and his– Congress. I want to dedicate my closing statement to Gonzalo.

All those mentioned and their splendid colleagues all deserve our greatest praise. Thank you very much everyone.

At this very end I also want to thank you all, the more than 3000 delegates from about a hundred countries. It has been a great pleasure to be with you in the past week. I look forward to seeing you all again at ICME-9 in Chiba, near Tokyo, Japan in 2000.

In Spanish

Y ahora quiero decir mis palabras de despedida en este Congreso en español.

Hemos disfrutado todos de una intensa y maravillosa semana. Hemos participado en un programa científico increíblemente rico y complejo. Hemos podido gozar de habernos reunido con viejos y nuevos amigos. Y hemos podido también aprender cómo se puede realizar un Congreso, bajo tanto sol y calor como muchos de nosotros pocas veces hemos experimentado.

En conjunto, el Congreso ha sido un hito maravilloso y memorable en la vida de la comunidad de personas que trabajamos en la educación matemática.

Nada de esto hubiera sido posible sin la participación de nuestros magníficos colegas y amigos españoles. No solamente hemos podido gozar de la hospitalidad española en general y de la andaluza y sevillana en particular. También se nos ha proporcionado una oportunidad única de percibir y experimentar aspectos cruciales de la cultura y tradiciones españolas y andaluzas.

Por todo ello nosotros, todos los participantes en el Congreso, el Comité Ejecutivo del ICMI, yo mismo, queremos expresar un agradecimiento que llega más allá que las palabras. Excusadme, por favor, si soy incapaz de transmitir adecuadamente nuestro agradecimiento a todos aquellos que tanto lo merecen. Tengo que reducirme necesariamente a mencionar sólo a unos individuos señalados. Consideradlos, por favor, representantes de todos aquellos actores conocidos y desconocidos, cuyos incansables esfuerzos entre bambalinas han sido absolutamente esenciales para el éxito de nuestro Congreso.

Nuestra gratitud más sincera se dirige

al Presidente del Comité Internacional del Programa Claudi Alsina y a sus colegas en el Comité,

a los directivos del Comité Local de organización junto con todos sus colegas y colaboradores de la Sociedad Andaluza de Educación matemática 'Thales': Antonio Pérez, Antonio Aranda, José María Álvarez, Concepción (Concha) García y a todos los estudiantes de verde.

También queremos hacer extensiva nuestra sincera gratitud a todos los patrocinadores, en particular a la Junta de Andalucía y a la Universidad de Sevilla, por su generoso apoyo a este Congreso.

Y muy especialmente quisiera expresar nuestra gratitud y nuestra más profunda amistad y cariño a la persona que, durante años, se ha esforzado por hacer posible el que este magnífico acontecimiento tuviera lugar en España, en Andalucía, en Sevilla, al Presidente de la Federación Española de Sociedades de profesores de Matemáticas, Gonzalo Sánchez Vázquez, y juntamente con él a todos sus colegas de la Federación en todas las regiones de España. Es ciertamente triste que una seria enfermedad ha impedido a Gonzalo Sánchez Vázquez acompañarnos en este Congreso. Quisiera dedicar muy en particular mis palabras finales a Gonzalo. Él y sus colegas merecen nuestra estima más grande. Gracias a todos y cada uno de vosotros.

Ahora me gustaría pedir a Silvia, la nieta de Gonzalo, que suba a esta tribuna para recibir un pequeño regalo en homenaje a Gonzalo.

Y para acabar quiero también agradeceros a todos vosotros, los más de tres mil participantes de alrededor de cien países. Ha sido un gran placer haber estado con vosotros durante esta semana pasada. Espero con placer veros a todos de nuevo en el ICME-9 en Chiba, junto a Tokyo, Japón, en el año dos mil.

Gracias a todos y un feliz viaje de regreso. Thank you everyone, and have a safe trip back. Goodbye! ¡Hasta la vista! ¡Hasta luego!

HONORARY COMMITTEE / *COMITÉ DE HONOR*

HONORARY PRESIDENCE / *PRESIDENCIA DE HONOR*
S.M. EL REY DON JUAN CARLOS I

Honorary Members / *Miembros Honorarios*
EXCMO. SR. PRESIDENTE DE LA JUNTA DE ANDALUCÍA
D. Manuel Chaves González

EXCMA. SRA. MINISTRA DE EDUCACIÓN Y CIENCIA
Dª. Esperanza Aguirre Gil de Biedma

EXCMO. SR. CONSEJERO DE EDUCACIÓN Y CIENCIA DE
LA JUNTA DE ANDALUCÍA
D. Manuel Pezzi Ceretto

EXCMO. Y MAGFCO. SR.RECTOR DE LA UNIVERSIDAD DE SEVILLA
D. Miguel Florencio Lora

EXCMA. SRA. ALCALDESA DE LA CIUDAD DE SEVILLA
Dª. Soledad Becerril Bustamante

EXCMO. SR. PRESIDENTE DE LA
DIPUTACIÓN PROVINCIAL DE SEVILLA
D. Alfredo Sánchez Monteseirín

EXCMO. SR. DIRECTOR GENERAL DE LA UNESCO
D. Federico Mayor Zaragoza

EXCMO. SR. SECRETARIO GENERAL DE
LA ORGANIZACIÓN DE ESTADOS IBEROAMERICANOS
PARA LA EDUCACIÓN, LA CIENCIA Y LA CULTURA
D. José Torreblanca Prieto

ILMO. SR. PRESIDENTE DE LA COMISIÓN
INTERNACIONAL DE INSTRUCCIÓN MATEMÁTICA (ICMI)
D. Miguel de Guzmán Ozámiz

ILMO. SR. PRESIDENTE DE LA FEDERACIÓN ESPAÑOLA
DE SOCIEDADES DE PROFESORES DE MATEMÁTICAS
D. Gonzalo Sánchez Vázquez

OTHER COMMITTEES / OTROS COMITÉS

ICMI Executive Committee / Comité Ejecutivo del ICMI
Miguel de Guzmán (España), *presidente*
Jeremy Kilpatrick (USA), *vicepresidente*
Anna Sierpinska (Canadá), *vicepresidente*
Mogens Niss (Dinamarca), *secretario*

MEMBERS / *VOCALES*
Colette Laborde (Francia)
Gilah Leder (Australia)
Carlos Vasco (Colombia)
Dianzhou Zang (China)

Ex-officio Members:
David Mumford (USA), Presidente del IMU
Jacob Palis Jr. (Brasil), Secretario del IMU

National Committee / *Comité Nacional*
Executive Committee / *Comité Ejecutivo*
Gonzalo Sánchez Vázquez, Presidente
Concepción García Severón, Secretaria
Luis Balbuena Castellano
Javier Brihuega Nieto
Constantino de la Fuente Martínez
Ricardo Luengo González
Antonio Pérez Jiménez
Luis Puig Espinosa

Members / Vocales
José M. Aroca Hernández
Josechu Arrieta Gallástegui
Francisco Contreras Pérez
José J.Etayo Miqueo
Josep María Fortuny Aymemi
J. Vicente García Sestafe
Nácere Hayek Calil
Rafael Infante Macías
Andrés Marcos García
Antonio Pascual Acosta
José Ramón Pascual Bonís

Antonio Pérez Sanz
Agustín Riscos Fernández
Vicente Riviere Gómez
Juan L. Romero Romero
José A. Rupérez Padrón
Adela Salvador Alcaide
Manuel Torralbo Rodríguez
Florencio Villarroya Bullido

International Program Committee / *Comité Internacional de Programa*

Claudi Alsina (España), *Presidente*
Luis Balbuena (España)
Lida Barrett (USA)
Werner Blum (Alemania)
Zhang Dianzhou (China)
Miguel de Guzmán (España), *Presidente ICMI, ex-officio*
Milan Hejny (Rep.Checa)
Bernard Hodgson (Canadá)
Jeremy Kilpatrick (USA)
Colette Laborde (Francia)
Mogens Niss (Dinamarca), *Secretario ICMI, ex-officio*
Antonio Pérez Jiménez (España)
Luis Rico (España)
Toshio Sawada (Japón)
Anna Sfard (Israel)
Saliou Touré (Costa de Marfil)
Carlos Vasco (Colombia)

Selection Committees (Short Presentations and Projects) / *Comités de Selección (Comunicaciones Breves y Proyectos)*

Ricardo Luengo González
Luis Rico Romero
Luis Manuel Casas García
Aguasantas Guisado Corrales
Faustino Hermoso Ruiz
Mercedes Mendoza García
Manuel Romero Cano-Lares
Cipriano Sánchez Pesquero

LOCAL ORGANIZING COMMITTEE/
COMITÉ LOCAL DE ORGANIZACIÓN

EXECUTIVE / *COMITÉ EJECUTIVO*

Antonio Pérez Jiménez, presidente
José Mª Chacón Iñigo, secretario

SCIENTIFIC PROGRAM AREA
AREA DEL PROGRAMA CIENTIFICO
Antonio Aranda Plata

HUMAN RESOURCES AREA
AREA DE RECURSOS HUMANOS
Juan Nuñez Valdés

GENERAL SERVICES AREA
AREA DE SERVICIOS GENERALES
Concepción García Severón
Fermín Novo Fernández

PROMOTION, DIVULGATION AND TECHNICAL AREA
AREA DE PROMOCION, DIFUSION Y MEDIOS TECNICOS
José Mª Alvarez Falcón
José Gutiérrez
José Muñoz Santonja
Juan Rodríguez Cordobés
Ismael Roldán Castro

ADMINISTRATION AREA
AREA DE ADMINISTRACION
Ladislao Navarro Peinado
Juan A. Suárez Vázquez

P.C.O. SECRETARIAT
SECRETARIA TECNICA
Manuel Luis Salguero Sánchez
Alicia Mateos Morillo
Rocío Yllanes Suárez

MEMBERS/*VOCALES*

Rocío Alonso Gallego
José Mª Ayerbe Toledano
Trinidad Bando Casado
Ricardo Barroso Campos
Bernardo Bueno Beltrán
Martín Cera López
José Carmona Alvarez
Mª Pilar Domínguez Abad
Reyes Domínguez Abascal
Antonio Fernández Aliseda
Jerónimo Ferrer Rodríguez
José Ferrer Rodríguez
Mª Carmen Flores Fernández
Rosa Ana Gallardo Muñoz
Mercedes García Blanco
Mª Angeles Greciano Martín
Manuel Iglesias Cerezal
Adolfo López Gomez
Concepción Paralera Morales
Agueda Porras Ruíz
José A. Prado Tendero
José F. Quesada Moreno
Pilar Rodríguez Peña
Mariano Salmerón Sánchez
Mª Jesús Serván Tomás
José Mª Vicente Carrete
José L. Vicente Córdoba
Jaime Yagüe Castrillo

COLLABORATORS/*COLABORADORES*

Belén Aranda Colubí
Mª José Aranda Colubí
Antonio Durán
Claude Gaulin
Nina H Lauder
Esteban López Martín
Mariano Martínez Pérez
Mogens Niss
Pedro Reyes Columé
Bernd Schedel
Ramón Vellido Arribas
Mariano Ynsa Gómez

OFFICIAL CARRIERS / TRANSPORTISTAS OFICIALES

SPONSORS / *PATROCINADORES*
Institutional Sponsors / *Organismos Oficiales*

AYUNTAMIENTO DE SEVILLA
DIPUTACIÓN DE SEVILLA
CENTRO INFORMÁTICO CIENTÍFICO DE ANDALUCÍA (C.I.C.A.)
DELEGACIÓN PROVINCIAL DE EDUCACIÓN Y CIENCIA DE SEVILLA
INSTITUTO DE CIENCIAS DE LA EDUCACIÓN DE LA
UNIVERSIDAD DE EXTREMADURA
TURISMO DE ANDALUCÍA
ORGANIZACIÓN DE ESTADOS IBEROAMERICANOS
CONSEJO DE EUROPA

Corporate Sponsors / *Empresas Privadas*
CASIO.
(Exclusive calculators sponsor)
(Patrocinador Exclusivo en el ámbito de las calculadoras)
S.M. GRUPO EDITORIAL
FUNDACIÓN EL MONTE
DIARIO DE SEVILLA
TELEFÓNICA DE ESPAÑA, S.A.
CABITEL, S.A.
FUNDACIÓN BANCAJA
COOPERATIVA VINÍCOLA DEL CONDADO S.COOP.AND.
FUNDACIÓN CRUZCAMPO
PEDRO DOMECQ, S.A.
FUNDACIÓN O.N.C.E.

UNIVERSIDAD
de SEVILLA

JUNTA DE ANDALUCIA
Consejería de Educación y Ciencia

Convocan:
FEDERACIÓN ESPAÑOLA DE SOCIEDADES DE
PROFESORES DE MATEMÁTICAS
COMITÉ NACIONAL DE LA I.M.U.

Organiza:
SOCIEDAD ANDALUZA DE EDUCACIÓN MATEMÁTICA THALES

COUNTRIES AND NO. OF PARTICIPANTS

PAÍSES Y NÚMERO DE PARTICIPANTES

ANGOLA	1
ARGENTINA	171
AUSTRALIA	135
AUSTRIA	7
BARBADOS	2
BELGIUM / BELGICA	10
BOLIVIA	8
BRAZIL / BRASIL	190
BRUNEI DARUSSALAM	4
BULGARY / BULGARIA	9
CANADA	56
CAYMAN ISLANDS / ISLAS CAIMAN	1
COLOMBIA	26
COSTA RICA	2
CROACIA	1
CUBA	9
CYPRUS / CHIPRE	2
CZECH REPUBLIC / REPUBLICA CHECA	12
CHILE	28
CHINA	30
DENMARK / DINAMARCA	27
DOMINICAN REPUBLIC / REPUBLICA DOMINICANA	5
EGYPT / EGIPTO	5
EL SALVADOR	4
ESTONIA	3
FINLAND / FINLANDIA	29
FRANCE / FRANCIA	71
GERMANY / ALEMANIA	56
GREECE / GRECIA	16
GUATEMALA	4
GUAYANA	1
HONDURAS	1
HONG KONG	9
HUNGARY / HUNGRIA	13
ICELAND / ISLANDIA	3
INDIA	3

Indonesia	1
Iran	10
Ireland / Irlanda	12
Israel	76
Italy / Italia	51
Ivory Coast / Costa De Marfil	2
Jamaica	1
Japan / Japon	169
Kenya / Kenia	1
Korea / Corea	13
Kuwait	5
Lebanon / Libano	1
Lituania	3
Luxenbourg / Luxemburgo	2
Macau	1
Malawi	2
Malaysia / Malasia	7
Mauritania	1
Mexico	38
Moldavia	1
Morocco / Marruecos	2
Mozambique	3
Netherlands / Holanda	49
New Zealand / Nueva Zelanda	17
Norway / Noruega	29
Pakistan	4
Palestinian Authority / Autoridad Palestina	1
Panama	2
Papua New Guinea / Papua Nueva Guinea	3
Paraguay	30
Peru	14
Phillipines / Filipinas	4
Poland / Polonia	11
Portugal	110
Puerto Rico	4
Qatar	1
Romania / Rumania	3
Russia / Rusia	25
Saudi Arabia / Arabia Saudi	1
Singapore / Singapur	6
Slovakia / Eslovaquia	1
Slovenia / Eslovenia	4
South Africa / Sudafrica	52

SPAIN / ESPAÑA	1008
SWAZILAND / SUAZILANDIA	1
SWEDEN / SUECIA	61
SWITZERLAND / SUIZA	15
TAIPEI - CHINA	7
THAILAND / TAILANDIA	33
TRINIDAD & TOBAGO	1
TUNISIA / TUNEZ	1
TURKEY / TURQUIA	6
U.S.A. / ESTADOS UNIDOS	328
UGANDA	2
UKRAINIA / UCRANIA	7
UNITED ARABIAN EMIRATES / EMIRATOS ARABES UNIDOS	1
UNITED KINGDOM / REINO UNIDO	222
URUGUAY	19
VENEZUELA	24
VIETNAM	1
YEMEN	1
ZIMBABWE	1

Totals / Totales:

98 countries / *países*   **3467** participants / *participantes*

LIST OF PARTICIPANTS / *LISTA DE PARTICIPANTES*

AARNES, RANDI; [NOR]

ABADIA AZNAREZ, Mª JOSEFA; [ESP]

ABALLE VILLERO, MIGUEL ANGEL; [ESP]

ABDELNUR, VICTORIA; [ARG]

ABDOUNUR, OSCAR JOAO; [BRA]

ABDUL HAMID, HAZIMAH; [MYS]

ABDULCARIMO, ISMAEL; [MOZ]

ABDUL-JALBAR BETANCOR, BEATRIZ; [ESP]

ABEL, MICHAEL; [USA]

ABELE, ALBRECHT; [DEU]

ABELS, MIEKE; [NLD]

ABOUTALEBI, MOHAMMAD; [IRN]

ABRAHAM, MIRTA CELIA; [ARG]

ABRAHAMS, LANCE ROWEN; [ZAF]

ABRAIRA FERNANDEZ, CONCEPCION; [ESP]

ABRAMOVICH, SERGEI; [USA]

ABRAMSKY, JACK; [GBR]

ABRANTES, PAULO; [PRT]

ABREU MENDES, [IRN]; [BRA]

ABREU SILVA DE SOUSA TUDELLA, ANA C.; [PRT]

ABRIERO VILLACIORIA, CARMEN; [ESP]

ABSHIRE, GEORGE; [USA]

ACCASCINA, GIUSEPPE; [ITA]

ACCOLA, EMANUELE; [ITA]

ACEITUNO SERRANO, DOLORES; [ESP]

ACOSTA FERNANDEZ, MIGUEL A.; [ESP]

ACUÑA RODRIGUEZ, CARMEN GADOR; [ESP]

ACZEL, JAMES; [GBR]

ADAMS, PAUL; [ZAF]

ADDINGTON, SUSAN; [USA]

ADHAMI, MUNDHER NUMAN; [GBR]

ADROVER LLINARES, MATILDE; [ESP]

AFANASJEV, JURI; [EST]

AFFLACK, RUTH; [USA]

AFONSO MARTIN, Mª CANDELARIA; [ESP]

AFONSO MARTINEZ, BEATRIZ; [ESP]

AG ALMOULOUD, SADDO; [BRA]

AGRASAR, MONICA; [ARG]

AGUADO DUQUE, ROSALIA; [ESP]

AGUEL DI MERLO, ROSSANA LOURDES; [URY]

AGUILAR CALDERON, Mª TERESA; [ESP]

AGUILAR HUERGO, MARIA ASUNCION; [ESP]

AGUILAR ROMANOS, ANA MARIA; [ESP]

AGUILERA, NESTOR; [ARG]

AGUILO GOST, FRANCISCO; [ESP]

AHARONI, DAN; [ISR]

AHLM, LILIAN; [SWE]

AHMED, AFZAL; [GBR]

AHRENS, RICHARD; [GBR]

AHRENS, SUSAN; [GBR]

AHUJA, MANGHO; [USA]

AIZPUN LOPEZ, ALBERTO; [ESP]

AJOSE, SUNDAY; [USA]

AL - HUSSEINAN, KHALED; [KWT]

AL - SARRAF, ALI; [KWT]

ALANIS, JUAN ANTONIO; [MEX]

ALARCON RUIZ, PETRA; [ESP]

ALBARRACIN GONZALEZ, ARMANDO; [COL]

ALBERT, LILLIE; [USA]

ALBERT, JEANNE; [ISR]

ALCALA DEL OLMO PEREZ, ANGEL M.; [ESP]

ALCALA HERNANDEZ, MANUEL; [ESP]

ALCALDE ESTEBAN, MANUEL; [ESP]

ALCANTARA GARCIA, INMACULADA; [ESP]

ALCARAZ, CRESCENCIO; [PAR]

ALCAZAR LEDESMA, FCO JAVIER; [ESP]

ALDERFER, EVAN; [USA]

ALEJANDRE CHAVERO, MANUEL JOSE; [ESP]

ALENCAR MORENO, MARIA; [BRA]

ALEXANDER, JOHN; [USA]

ALEXANDROY, SMARO; [GRC]

ALFARO CARPANETTI, RUTH; [CHL]

ALGABA EXPOSITO, PILAR; [ESP]

ALGABA EXPOSITO, ESPERANZA; [ESP]

ALIENDRO, ESTELA SONIA; [ARG]

ALM, LENA; [SWE]

ALMATO BARBANY, ADOLFO; [ESP]

ALMEIDA, MARIA; [PRT]

ALMEIDA, ERONALDO; [BRA]

ALMEIDA, DENNIS; [GBR]

ALMEIDA RODRIGUEZ, ANGEL; [ESP]

ALMIRALL DE POCHAT, MARTA ANA; [ARG]

ALONSO, LUIZ ANTONIO; [BRA]

ALONSO CANOVAS, DIEGO; [ESP]

ALONSO ESPEJO, ISABEL; [ESP]

ALONSO LOPEZ, Mª OLGA; [ESP]

ALONSO MOLINA, FERNANDO; [ESP]

ALONSO RUIZ, FCO.JAVIER; [ESP]

ALPERS, KARSTEN; [DEU]

ALSINA CATALA, CLAUDI; [ESP]

ALSINA KIRCHNER, JORGE; [ESP]

ALSON HARAN, PEDRO; [VEN]

ALVARADO MARTINEZ, ARMANDO; [VEN]

ALVARENGA BARBOSA, KARLY; [BRA]

ALVAREZ, MARIO LUIS; [ARG]

ALVAREZ ALCAIDE, SERGIO; [ESP]

ALVAREZ CARRASCOSA, MARIA ISABEL; [ESP]

ALVAREZ ESCUDERO, FCO. JAVIER; [ESP]

ALVAREZ FALCON, JOSE Mª; [ESP]

ALVAREZ FONTENLA-GAYOSO, FCO J.; [ESP]

ALVAREZ GARCIA, JOSE LUIS; [ESP]

ALVAREZ GAVIRIA, JAIRO; [COL]

ALVAREZ LEIVA, JUAN ANTONIO; [ESP]

ALVAREZ LOPEZ, ALBERTO; [ESP]

ALVAREZ SOLANO, VICTOR; [ESP]

ALVES, OTAVIANO; [BRA]

ALVES DE SOUSA AMARAL, ELZA M.; [PRT]

ALVES DUTRA, ERCI; [BRA]

ALVES PEREIRA, NUBIA; [BRA]

ALVES RIBEIRO, MARIA LENIR; [BRA]

ALLAN, FATHI; [PAL]

ALLARD, JOANE; [CAN]

ALLEN, RICHARD; [USA]

AMADOR BRUNHEIRA, LINA MARIA; [PRT]

AMBRUS, ANDRAS; [HUN]

AMIT, MIRIAM; [ISR]

AMORIM, ISABEL; [PRT]

AMORNWONG, CHALIDA; [THA]

ANACONA, MARIBEL P.; [COL]

ANAZAWA, YOKO; [JAP]

ANCIERBERG, BENGT; [SWE]

ANDERBERG, BENGT; [SWE]

ANDERSEN, STIG; [DNK]

ANDREINI, CHARLOTTE; [USA]

ANDZANS, AGNIS; [CYP]

ANEGON MARTIN, FRANCISCO JOSE; [ESP]

ANGHILERI, JULIA; [GBR]

ANGULO DIAZ, CLARA; [ESP]

ANIDO DE LOPEZ, MERCEDES ALICIA; [ARG]

ANILLO RAMOS, FCO JOSE; [ESP]

ANSAROV, ROBERT; [USA]

ANTHONY, GLENDA; [NZL]

ANTIBI, ANDRE; [FRA]

ANTONIOU, ANDREAS; [CYP]

ANTUNES, ANTONIO; [PRT]

ANTUNES M. A. ROCHA, Mª ISABEL; [PRT]

ANTUNEZ ALPERIZ, MARIA ISABEL; [ESP]

APARECIDO DE OLIVEIRA, MAURICIO; [BRA]

APIOLA, HEIKKI; [FIN]

ARAGON, ANA TADEA; [ARG]

ARAGONES GUILLEN, JESUS; [ESP]

ARAI, HIDEO; [JAP]

ARAM, SALEH AWADH; [YEM]

ARANDA BALLESTEROS, F. DAMIAN; [ESP]

ARANDA COLUBI, BELEN; [ESP]

ARANDA DE ROVIRA, CLYDE LILIAN; [ARG]

ARANDA PLATA, ANTONIO; [ESP]

ARANHA, ALVARO; [BRA]

ARANTES SAD, LIGIA; [BRA]

ARAUJO SOUSA FERNANDEZ DUARTE, Mª I.; [PRT]

ARAVENA DIAZ, MARIA; [CHL]

ARBELAREZ ROJAS, GABRIELA; [COL]

ARBOLEDA APARICIO, LUIS CARLOS; [COL]

ARCAVI, ABRAHAM; [ISR]

ARDILA ACUÑA, ANALIDA ISABEL; [PAN]

ARENAS OROPESA, ANTONIO; [ESP]

ARESE OLIVA, Mª CARMEN; [ESP]

ARGÜELLO PASTOR, ANA Mª PILAR; [ESP]

ARIAS CABEZAS, JOSE MARIA; [ESP]

ARITA, YASUHO; [JAP]

ARMAS GUTIERREZ, JULIA; [PER]
ARMSTRONG, PETER; [GBR]
ARQUEROS GOMEZ, JOSEFA; [ESP]
ARRANZ SAN JOSE, JOSE MANUEL; [ESP]
ARRIAGA CARPIO, JESUS; [ESP]
ARRIERO VILLACORTA, CARMEN; [ESP]
ARRIETA GALLASTEGUI, JOSE JOAQUIN; [ESP]
ARRIOLA PANGUA, IÑAKI; [ESP]
ARROYO MOLAS, CARMEN DELIA; [PAR]
ARTAVIA CAMPOS, EDWIN; [CRI]
ARTIGUE, MICHELE; [FRA]
ASADA, TERUKO; [JAP]
ASCURRA, LORENZA E.; [PAR]
ASENSIO CAZORLA, JULIAN JOSE; [ESP]
ASHE, SEAN; [IRL]
ASHOUR, ATTIA A.; [EGY]
ASKEW, MICHAEL; [GBR]
ASTURIAS, HAROLD; [USA]
ATKINS, WARREN; [AUS]
ATWEH, BILL; [AUS]
AUB, MARTIN; [JAM]
AUDEOUD, ANNE; [CHE]
AUGUST-ROTHMAN, PHYLLIS; [ISR]
AUSAVATERAKUL, MONGKON; [THA]
AUSTIN, WILLIAM; [USA]
AUSTIN, A. KEITH; [GBR]
AVEDISSIAN, ZAROUHI; [ARG]
AVERBUCH, HAIM; [ISR]
AVERNA, CARLOS ALBERTO; [ARG]
AVITAL, SHMUEL; [ISR]
AVIVA, YONATAN; [ISR]
AXELSSON, CARINA; [SWE]
AYALA ZELADA, Mª ANGELICA; [PAR]
AYOUB, AYOUB B.; [USA]
AYUSO GARCIA, GEMA; [ESP]
AZCARATE GIMENEZ, CARMEN; [ESP]
AZCARATE GODED, PILAR; [ESP]
AZEVEDO VASCONCELOS E SOUSA, Mª F.; [PRT]
AZNAR SANCHEZ, ENCARNA; [ESP]
BABOLIAN, ESMAIL; [IRN]
BACELLA DE AGUILERA, SUSANA B.; [ARG]
BACELLA DE HUGONETT, RAQUEL E.; [ARG]
BAENA RUIZ, JULIAN; [ESP]

BAEZ ROJO, ASCENSION; [ESP]
BAEZA SALAS, ANTONIO; [ESP]
BAGGETT, PATRICIA; [USA]
BAGNALL, SUSAN; [AUS]
BAHALUL, HANNAH; [ISR]
BAILLE, PHILIPPE; [CAN]
BALACHEFF, NICOLAS; [FRA]
BALBUENA ARTILES, OFELIA; [ESP]
BALBUENA CASTELLANO, LUIS; [ESP]
BALDERAS CAÑAS, PATRICIA ESPERA; [MEX]
BALDINO, ROBERTO; [BRA]
BALDRICH ALVAREZ, JORDI; [ESP]
BALENZATEGUI HERNANDEZ, I.; [ESP]
BALESTRINI DE AGRIELLO, MARTA I.; [ARG]
BALTANAS ILLANES, JOSE PABLO; [ESP]
BALLANTYNE, MARK; [FRA]
BALLERINI, SARA; [ITA]
BANDO CASADO, TRINIDAD; [ESP]
BANERJEE, BHARATI; [IND]
BANKOV, KIRIL; [BGR]
BARAHONA DROGUETT, MANUEL; [CHL]
BARBA SANCHEZ, JUANA; [ESP]
BARBERA GREGORI, ELENA; [ESP]
BARBERA SENDRA, ABELARD; [ESP]
BARBIN, EVELYNE; [FRA]
BARBOUR, ROBERT; [GBR]
BARCO BERNAL, PEDRO; [ESP]
BARDADYM, VICTOR; [UKR]
BARDOULAT, JEAN-PAUL; [FRA]
BARGUEÑO SANCHO, JESUS JAVIER; [ESP]
BARNARD, TONY; [GBR]
BARNETT, JANET; [USA]
BARON GORRETO, MIGUEL ANGEL; [ESP]
BARRA, MARIO; [ITA]
BARRAGUES FUENTES, JOSE IGNACIO; [ESP]
BARRALLO CALONGE, JAVIER; [ESP]
BARRANTES LOPEZ, MANUEL; [ESP]
BARREIRO CLARO, OLGA MARIA; [BRA]
BARRERA PULIDO, ALVARO; [ESP]
BARRERO RIPOLL, MANUEL; [ESP]
BARRETO PEREZ, JOSE; [ESP]
BARRETT, LIDA; [USA]
BARRON DUQUE, IGNACIO; [ESP]

Barroso, Leonidas; [BRA]
Barroso Campos, Ricardo; [ESP]
Bartlett, Dawn; [AUS]
Bartolini, MªGiuseppina; [ITA]
Barton, Shelley; [CHE]
Barton, Bill; [NZL]
Basadien, Soraya; [ZAF]
Basarte Anguiano, Pilar; [ESP]
Bashmakov, Mark; [RUS]
Basso, Milena; [ITA]
Bastan, Marta Haydee; [ARG]
Bastid, Vincent; [FRA]
Bastos, Rita; [PRT]
Batanero Bernabeu, Carmen; [ESP]
Baturo, Annette; [AUS]
Bauer, Carole; [USA]
Baxter, Jeff; [AUS]
Bayer, Nina; [USA]
Baza, Eugenia; [ESP]
Bazik, Edna; [USA]
Bazzini, Luciana; [ITA]
Beal, Susan; [USA]
Beaulieu, Sylvie; [CAN]
Beck, Pamela; [USA]
Becker, Joanne; [USA]
Becker, Jerry; [USA]
Bechara Sanchez, Lucilia; [BRA]
Beeney, Gill; [GBR]
Begg, Andy; [NZL]
Bejar Narvaez, Mª Jose; [ESP]
Bekenkamp, Arthur; [CHE]
Belal, Ibrahim; [SAU]
Belsom, Christopher; [GBR]
Beltra Salas, J Carlos; [ESP]
Beltran Aguilera, Manuel Jesus; [ESP]
Bell, Pamela; [NZL]
Bell, Alan; [GBR]
Bellido Huertas, Mª Jesus; [ESP]
Bello Landeira, Francisco; [ESP]
Bello Rodriguez, Luis; [ESP]
Bellot Rosado, Francisco; [ESP]
Bell-Lloch Bell-Lloch, Aurora; [ESP]
Benarroch, Martin; [ARG]

Bender, Peter; [DEU]
Benedicto Juste, Mª Dolores; [ESP]
Benedicto Juste, Carmen; [ESP]
Benedicto Martin, Cesar; [ESP]
Benetti, Eva Beatriz; [ARG]
Benevicius Auliso, Adriana; [URY]
Bengtsson, Gunilla; [SWE]
Benito Gomez, Manuel; [ESP]
Benjumea Gonzalez, Carlos David; [ESP]
Benjumea Moreno, Carmen; [ESP]
Benn, Roseanne; [GBR]
Bentele, Brigitte; [USA]
Ben-Chaim, David; [ISR]
Ben-Zvi, Dani; [ISR]
Berdonces Escobar, Maravillas; [ESP]
Berenguer Cruz, Luis; [ESP]
Berenguer Maldonado, Maria I.; [ESP]
Berenguer Maldonado, Javier; [ESP]
Berezin, Boris; [RUS]
Berg, Gene; [USA]
Berge, Liv; [NOR]
Berger, Margot; [ZAF]
Bergillos Aguilar, Javier; [ESP]
Berhouet, Maria Teresa; [ARG]
Berinde, Vasile; [ROM]
Berio, Adriana Beatriz; [ARG]
Berlin, Donna; [USA]
Bermejo Gonzalez, Macarena; [ESP]
Bermejo Mora, Ivana; [ESP]
Bernat, Philippe; [FRA]
Berova, Maria; [SVK]
Berral Yeron, Joaquina; [ESP]
Berry, John; [GBR]
Bertoldi, Cleyton Cesar; [BRA]
Berzsenyi, George; [USA]
Bessot, Annie; [FRA]
Beukes, Cecil; [ZAF]
Bezerra, Jose; [BRA]
Bibby, Neil Leonard; [GBR]
Bibby, Tamara; [GBR]
Bibby, John; [GBR]
Bickmore-Brand, Jennie; [AUS]
Bicudo, Maria Aparecida; [BRA]

Biehler, Rolf; [DEU]
Bilbao Buñuel, Rosalia; [ESP]
Biltchev, Svetoslav; [BGR]
Birdsall, Maryann; [USA]
Bisbal De Labato, Mª Cristina; [ARG]
Bishop, Alan; [AUS]
Bitter, Gary; [USA]
Bjerneby Hall, Maria; [SWE]
Bjork, Lars-Eric; [SWE]
Bjorkqvist, Ole; [FIN]
Bjorkqvist, Eivor; [FIN]
Blair, Richelle; [USA]
Blair, Monika; [GBR]
Blancas Alvarez, Mª Elena; [ESP]
Blanco Del Can, Mª Concepcion; [ESP]
Blanco Nieto, Lorenzo J.; [ESP]
Blanton, Maria; [USA]
Blazey, Graham; [AUS]
Blazquez Martin, Sonsoles; [ESP]
Blithe, Thora; [NZL]
BlomhOj, Morten; [DNK]
Bloomfield, Alan Paul; [GBR]
Blum, Werner; [DEU]
Blumenkranz, Rahel; [ISR]
Blumenthal, Gladis; [BRA]
Boaler, Jo; [GBR]
Boavida, Ana Mª; [PRT]
Bodin, Antoine; [FRA]
Boettger Giardinetto, Jose R.; [BRA]
Boieri, Paolo; [ITA]
Bolea Olivan, Jose Angel; [ESP]
Bolite Frant, Janete; [BRA]
Bolt, Brian; [GBR]
Bolletta, Raimond; [ITA]
Bonacina, Marta Susana; [ARG]
Bonenberger, Niva Helena; [BRA]
Bonilla Estevez, Martha Alba; [COL]
Bonotto, Cinzia; [ITA]
Boondao, Sakorn; [THA]
Boonraksa, Somchai; [THA]
Booth, Drora; [AUS]
Borba, Marcelo; [BRA]
Borgersen, Hans Erik; [NOR]

Borges, Jeronimo Aug.; [BRA]
Borges, Alvaro; [BRA]
Borges Nascentes Coelho, H.; [BRA]
Borja Sanz, Nicolas; [ESP]
Borovcnik, Manfred; [AUT]
Borralho, Antonio; [PRT]
Bortolato, Gustavo Dante; [ARG]
Bosch, Erik A.C.; [NLD]
Bosque Mates, Carmen Mª; [ESP]
Boswinkel, Nina; [NLD]
Botana Ferreiro, Francisco; [ESP]
Botelho, Jurema Lindote; [BRA]
Botero De Meza, Maria M.; [COL]
Boudine, Jean Pierre; [FRA]
Boufi, Ada; [GRC]
Boulton-Lewis, Gillian; [AUS]
Bowers, Janet; [USA]
Bowie, Lynn; [ZAF]
Boye, Anne; [FRA]
Braathe, Hans Jorgen; [NOR]
Bradley, Jennifer; [AUS]
Bradshaw, John; [GBR]
Brady, Alan; [AUS]
Bragg, Sadie; [USA]
Branco Pinheiro, Luis Jose; [PRT]
Brandell, Gerd; [SWE]
Bravo Aguilar, Luis; [BOL]
Bravo De Mansilla Jimenez, A.; [ESP]
Brekke, Gard; [NOR]
Brenci Ascoli-Bartoli, Maria T.; [ITA]
Brew, Christine; [AUS]
Bridger, Mark; [USA]
Bridger, Maxine; [USA]
Bridy, Anna; [USA]
Briggs, Mary; [GBR]
Brihuega Nieto, Javier; [ESP]
Brin, Philippe; [FRA]
Brinkworth, Peter; [AUS]
Brito, Marcia Regina; [BRA]
Brito Oliveira, Mª Alice; [PRT]
Brito Sabedra, Mariela Angela; [URY]
Britto Gonçalves, Lucinei A.; [BRA]
Broman, Per; [SWE]

BROOMES, DESMOND; [BAR]

BROUGHTON, MICHAEL; [GBR]

BROUSSEAU, GUY PIERRE; [FRA]

BROWN, SUZANNE; [USA]

BROWN, DAVID LAUGHLIN; [CHE]

BROWN, ROBERT BRUCE; [USA]

BROWN, ROGER; [AUS]

BROWN, DAWN; [USA]

BROWN, MARGARET; [GBR]

BROWN, LAURINDA; [GBR]

BROWNE, RICHARD; [GBR]

BROWNING, CHRISTINE; [USA]

BRUMBAUEH, DOUGLAS; [USA]

BRUNO CASTAÑEDA, CARLOS; [ESP]

BRUNO CASTAÑEDA, ALICIA; [ESP]

BUCKLAND, GARETH H; [GBR]

BUDIENE, VIRJINIJA; [LIT]

BUENDIA CASTIÑEIRA, Mª GUADALUPE; [ESP]

BUENO BELTRAN, BERNARDO; [ESP]

BUENO FERNANDEZ, JOSE ANTONIO; [ESP]

BUENO GUISADO, ANTONIO F.; [ESP]

BUNYAPARATAYUT, SIWAPORN; [THA]

BURGOS MALUENDA, CLEMENTINA; [ESP]

BURGUES FLAMARICH, CARMEN; [ESP]

BURKHARDT, HUGH; [GBR]

BURN, ROBERT; [GBR]

BURNS, SUE; [GBR]

BURREL CELAYA, FLORENCIO; [ESP]

BURRIL, JOHN; [USA]

BURRIL, GAIL; [USA]

BURSCHEID, HANS J.; [DEU]

BUSSER, ELISABETH; [FRA]

BUSTOS DE RIZO, NORA BEATRIZ; [ARG]

BUYS, KEES; [NLD]

BYRON, MARIA; [TRI]

CAAMAÑO ESPINOZA, CARLOS LEON; [CHL]

CABALLERO RUBIO, SALVADOR; [ESP]

CABAÑAS NAVARRO, GUILLERMO; [ESP]

CABELLO CABELLO, CARLOS; [ESP]

CABELLO PEREZ, MARIA TERESA; [ESP]

CABRAL, TANIA CRISTINA; [BRA]

CABRAL DE VELAZQUEZ, MARIA; [PAR]

CABRERA PADILLA, LUZ LUCIA; [ESP]

CABRERA SUAREZ, FRANCISCO; [ESP]

CABRERIZO ROMERO, MIGUEL ANGEL; [ESP]

CACHAFEIRO CHAMOSA, LUIS CARLOS; [ESP]

CAETANO DA FONSECA, HELENA I.; [PRT]

CAGIGAS RODRIGUEZ, J. ANTONIO; [ESP]

CAI, DA-YONG; [CHN]

CAIANELLO, EVA; [ITA]

CALABUIG SERRA, TERESA; [ESP]

CALDEIRA, ADEMIR; [BRA]

CALDERON, DORA INES; [COL]

CALDERON BLAZQUEZ, JUAN AGUSTIN; [ESP]

CALVO ALDEA, CARMEN; [ESP]

CALVO MARTIN, MERI EMILIA; [ESP]

CALVO PENADES, CONSUELO; [ESP]

CALLEJO DE LA VEGA, Mª LUZ; [ESP]

CALLEJON GALLEGO, Mª DEL PILAR; [ESP]

CALLIS FRANCO, JOSEP; [ESP]

CAMACHO MACHIN, MATIAS; [ESP]

CAMBRONERO SANCHEZ, JOSEFINA; [ESP]

CAMPBELL, PATRICIA F.; [USA]

CAMPI ABERGO, MARIA RAQUEL; [URY]

CAMPISTROUS PEREZ, LUIS AUGUSTO; [CUB]

CAMPO ANDION, MODESTA; [ESP]

CAMPON RODILLO, PETRA; [ESP]

CAMPOS, TANIA M.M.; [BRA]

CAMPOS HERRERA, ANDRES; [ESP]

CANALS TOLOSA, Mª ANTONIA; [ESP]

CANAVARRO, ANA PAULA; [PRT]

CANJURA LINARES, CARLOS; [SAL]

CANNELL, DIANE; [GBR]

CANNIZZARO, LUCILLA; [ITA]

CANO CAZORLA, MIGUEL ANGEL; [ESP]

CANO DE HARO, FRANCISCO JOSE; [ESP]

CANO IVORRA, MARIA; [ESP]

CANTERO JIMENEZ, Mª TERESA; [ESP]

CANTERO TOMAS, ANGEL; [ESP]

CANTORAL, RICARDO; [MEX]

CAÑIGUERAL BLANCO, MANUEL; [ESP]

CAÑIZARES, MARIA JESUS; [ESP]

CAPDEVILA, MIRIAM; [ARG]

CAPPO, MARGE; [USA]

CARABUS DE MARTINEZ, OLGA N.; [ARG]

CARAZO DIAZ, BORJA; [ESP]

CARDEÑOSO DOMINGO, JOSE MARIA; [ESP]
CARDONA PERIS, SALVADOR; [ESP]
CARLAVILLA FERNANDEZ, JOSE LUIS; [ESP]
CARLON MONROY, ASELA; [MEX]
CARMONA, ABEL; [ARG]
CARMONA ALVAREZ, JOSE; [ESP]
CARMONA ARIZA, ENRIQUETA; [ARG]
CARNALL, JEAN; [GBR]
CARO CHAPARRO, ANDRES; [ESP]
CARO DORANTES, MILAGROSA; [ESP]
CARPENTER, THOMAS; [USA]
CARR, ALISTAIR; [AUS]
CARRANZA DE FORESI, GRACIELA I.; [ARG]
CARRANZA GONZALEZ, CARMEN O.; [ESP]
CARREIRA, SUSANA; [PRT]
CARRERA DE ORELLANA, INES; [VEN]
CARRETERO CASTAÑO, JOSE EUGENIO; [ESP]
CARRETO RODRIGUEZ, VICTOR; [ESP]
CARRILLO GALLEGO, DOLORES; [ESP]
CARRILLO YAÑEZ, JOSE; [ESP]
CARRINGTON, ANNE; [AUS]
CARRION PEREZ, JOSE CARLOS; [ESP]
CARROLL, WILLIAM; [USA]
CARSS, MARJORIE; [AUS]
CARTER, MICHAEL; [NZL]
CARUBA, GIOVANNELLA; [ITA]
CARVALHO, CAROLINA; [PRT]
CARVALHO E SILVA, JAIME; [PRT]
CASADO BARRIO, Mª JESUS; [ESP]
CASALS COLLDECARRERA, MERCEDES; [ESP]
CASAS GARCIA, LUIS MANUEL; [ESP]
CASAS SILES, Mª DEL MAR; [ESP]
CASERTA DE AGUIAR, JORGETE; [BRA]
CASQUETE MEDINA, JOSE LUIS; [ESP]
CASTEJON SOLANAS, Mª ANGELES; [ESP]
CASTELNUOVO, EMMA; [ITA]
CASTELO BRANCO, FERNANDA MARIA; [PRT]
CASTELLANO QUIROGA, Mª ANGELICA; [ARG]
CASTELLANO QUIROGA, MªANGELICA; [ARG]
CASTELLO ESNAL, Mª JOSE; [ESP]
CASTELLS CABALLOS, CARLOS JAVIER; [ESP]
CASTIGLIONE DE RENOLFI, DELIA I.; [ARG]
CASTILLA MARTINEZ, YOLANDA; [ESP]

CASTILLEJO CARRASCO, EVA; [ESP]
CASTILLO CASTRILLO, MAXIMILIANO; [ARG]
CASTILLO COLOMA, PEDRO EDUARDO; [PER]
CASTILLO VIZCAINO, CATALINA; [ESP]
CASTIÑEIRA PALOU, ROSER; [ESP]
CASTRILLO GUERRA, LEONOR BEATRIZ; [VEN]
CASTRILLON CASTRO, GLORIA; [COL]
CASTRO, VERA LUCIA; [BRA]
CASTRO CASTRO, SANTIAGO; [MEX]
CASTRO CASTRO, FERNANDO; [MEX]
CASTRO GUTIERREZ, FERNANDO; [VEN]
CASTRO JIMENEZ, FRANCISCO; [ESP]
CASTRO MARTINEZ, ENCARNACION; [ESP]
CASTRO MARTINEZ, ENRIQUE; [ESP]
CASTRO OCHOA, NATALIA; [ESP]
CATALAN, MARTA CECILIA; [ARG]
CAVALLARO, MARIA INES; [ARG]
CAZENAVE BERNAL, Mª LUISA; [ESP]
CAZENAVE BERNAL, Mª PILAR; [ESP]
CEFET - BA, ; [BRA]
CEMELI DURAN, IGNACIO; [ESP]
CENART, ISTVAN; [HUN]
CEPEDA ABECIA, ANGELES; [ESP]
CERDA BONOMO, FRANCISCO; [CHL]
CERDA FRANCES, ANGEL BLAS; [ESP]
CEREZO RAMIREZ, ANTONIO; [ESP]
CERRADA MIGUELA, ROSA MARIA; [ESP]
CERVANTES, RITA; [ARG]
CESAR, MARGARIDA; [PRT]
CESTARI, MARIA LUIZA; [NOR]
CIANCONE, TOM; [CAN]
CIBEIRA BELTRAN, LAURA; [ESP]
CIGNONI, EDNEIA POLI; [BRA]
CILLERO JIMENEZ, BELEN; [ESP]
CIMADEVILLA LOPEZ, ADELINA; [ESP]
CIVIL, MARTA; [USA]
CIVIT CONDE, JORGE; [ESP]
CLACKWORTHY, MICHAEL; [ZAF]
CLARK, MEGAN; [NZL]
CLARKE, DAVID; [AUS]
CLARKE, DAVID; [GBR]
CLARKSON, PHILIP; [AUS]
CLEAVES, CHERYL; [USA]

CLEMENTS, KEN; [AUS]
CLOSE, JOHN; [IRL]
CLOSE, GILL; [GBR]
CNOP, IVAN; [BEL]
COADY, CARMEL; [AUS]
COATES GOTHBERG, GRACE; [USA]
COBACHO DE ALBA, MILAGROSA; [ESP]
COBB, PAUL; [USA]
COBO MERINO, BELEN; [ESP]
COBO MUSATADI, MARIA LUISA; [ESP]
CODETTA RAITERI, ADALBERTO; [ITA]
CODINA PASCUAL, ROSER; [ESP]
COHEN, DIANA; [GBR]
COHEN, GILLES; [FRA]
COHEN GOTTLIEB, FRANCA; [BRA]
COLAÇO, Mª TERESA; [PRT]
COLAGRECO, GRACIELA MARINA; [ARG]
COLATAREI, OLGA CRISTINA; [ARG]
COLOMA SUERO, GUACOLDA; [CHL]
COLOMA SUERO, G. NINOSKA; [CHL]
COLOMBAT, HUBERT; [DEU]
COLWELL, DHAMMA SUSAN; [GBR]
COMITI, CLAUDE; [FRA]
CONCEIÇAO E ALMEIDA, EMA; [PRT]
CONDE CALERO, JUAN MANUEL; [ESP]
CONDE CASAS, AURELIO; [ESP]
CONROY, JOHN; [AUS]
CONSTANTINESCU, GABRIELA; [ESP]
CONSTANTINESCU, ELIODOR; [ESP]
CONTRERAS DE LA FUENTE, ANGEL; [ESP]
CONTRERAS GONZALEZ, LUIS CARLOS; [ESP]
CONTRERAS PASCUZZO, EDUARDO A.; [VEN]
COOK, FRANCIS; [NZL]
COOKE, TRACEY; [GBR]
COONEY, THOMAS; [USA]
COOPER, WILLIAM; [USA]
COOPER, TOM; [AUS]
CORBALAN YUSTE, FERNANDO; [ESP]
CORBERAN SALVADOR, ROSA MARIA; [ESP]
CORDANO RIPAMONTE, ROSANNA; [PER]
CORDEIRO, MARIA JOSE; [PRT]
CORDOVA, JOAN KAREN; [USA]
CORNELISSEN, MERCIA AMELIA; [ZAF]

CORONADO BALLESTEROS, TEODORO; [ESP]
CORONADO SANTANA, FRANCISCO; [ESP]
CORONILLA MUÑOZ, SILVIA; [ESP]
CORRALES, JULIA EDITH; [ARG]
CORREA, JANE; [BRA]
CORREA DUTRA, FABIO; [BRA]
CORREA LEITE, LIDUINA; [BRA]
CORSO, AMALIA MONICA; [ARG]
CORTEGOSO IGLESIAS, MANUEL; [ESP]
COS REIS MARTINS, JOSE AFONSO; [PRT]
COSTA, SUELI; [BRA]
COSTA VARGENS, EUGENIO MUNIZ; [BRA]
COSTELLO, JOHN; [GBR]
COSTOYA RAMOS, Mª CRISTINA; [ESP]
COTTER, JOAN; [USA]
COTTON, ANTHONY; [GBR]
COUPLAND, MARY; [AUS]
COURELA, SUZETE AFONSO; [PRT]
COUSINS, LIZ; [AUS]
COWEN, CAROL; [ZAF]
COX, SHERRY; [USA]
CREUS MOREIRA DOS SANTOS, E.; [PRT]
CRIADO SIERRA, FRANCISCO; [ESP]
CRISOSTOMO DOS SANTOS, JESIEL; [BRA]
CRITON, MICHEL; [FRA]
CRONJE, LEFINA S.; [ZAF]
CROSS, KATHLEEN; [GBR]
CROWE, DAVID; [GBR]
CROWE, ANGELA; [NLD]
CROWLEY, LILLIE; [USA]
CRUZ, CIPRIANO; [VEN]
CRUZ, GLORIA; [ARG]
CUDMORE, DONALD; [GBR]
CUDUGNELLO ARAGUNDE, INES G.; [ARG]
CUNHA, CLEUZA MARTINS; [BRA]
CUNHA LEAL, LEONOR; [PRT]
CUNILLERA SALA, DOLORES; [ESP]
CURCIO, FRANCES R.; [USA]
ÇAGLAR, MEHMET; [TUR]
ÇOBAN, OYA ARZU; [TUR]
CHACKO, INDIRA; [PNG]
CHACON FERNANDEZ, Mª CASIMIRA; [ESP]
CHACON IÑIGO, JOSE MARIA; [ESP]

Chamoso Sanchez, Jose Mª; [ESP]
Champion, Alverna; [USA]
Chang, Ping Tung; [USA]
Chang, Ching-Kuch; Changhua - [CHN]
Chankong, Totsaporn; [THA]
Chankong, Prateep; [THA]
Chanpariyavateewong, Nongnuch; [THA]
Chapman, Olive; [CAN]
Charbonneau, Louis; [CAN]
Charles-Christie, Desiree; [CAY]
Chaseling, Janet; [AUS]
Chasiotis, Christos; [GRC]
Chatsuksiridat, Somsak; [THA]
Chavez De Diego, Mª Jose; [ESP]
Cheeseman, Jill; [AUS]
Chen, Shi You; [CHN]
Chena De Epelbaum, Leonor; [ARG]
Cherinda, Marcos; [MOZ]
Cherkas, Barry; [USA]
Cherry, Paul; [GBR]
Cheung, Pak; [HKG]
Chillemi De Mingues, Ana Maria; [ARG]
Chinn, Phyllis; [USA]
Chi-Benedetti, Monica; [USA]
Choe, Young Han; [KOR]
Chow, Wai Man Raymond; [HKG]
Christiansen, Iben; [DNK]
Christoffersen, Torben; [DNK]
Chronaki, Anna; [GBR]
Da Conceiçao Ventura Viana, M.; [BRA]
Da Costa Xavier, Renilda; [BRA]
Da Cruz, S. Secatto; [BRA]
Da Rocha-Falçao, Jorge; [BRA]
Da Silva Rabello, Ricardo; [BRA]
Da Silva Reis, Frederico; [BRA]
Da Veiga Fernandez, Carmen; [ESP]
Daconto, Edvige; [ITA]
Dalmasi Muñiz, Lidia; [DOM]
Dalmasso, Juan Carlos; [ARG]
Daniel, Coralie; [NZL]
Danjo, Koichi; [DEU]
Daroca Eguizabal, Graciela; [ARG]
Das Neves E Sousa C. St Aubyn, M.; [PRT]

Daviaud, Daniel; [FRA]
David, Hamutal; [ISR]
Davidov, Ljubomir; [BGR]
Davis, Robert; [USA]
Davis, Gary; [GBR]
Davis, Lorraine; [AUS]
Davison, David; [USA]
Dawe, Lloyd; [AUS]
Dawson, A.J.Sandy; [CAN]
De Bock, Dirk; [BEL]
De Carrera, Elena; [ARG]
De Freitas Ferreira, Edilma; [BRA]
De La Calzada Galvez, Ramon; [ESP]
De La Cruz, Yolanda; [USA]
De La Fuente Martinez, C.; [ESP]
De La Fuente Martos, Miguel; [ESP]
De La Plaza, Eva Maria; [ESP]
De La Rocque Palis, Gilda; [BRA]
De La Rosa Onuchic, Lourdes; [BRA]
De La Rosa Sanchez, Maria; [ESP]
De La Torre Fernandez, Enrique; [ESP]
De La Villa, Agustin; [ESP]
De Lange, Jan; [NLD]
De Liefde, Peter; [NLD]
De Los Santos Gonzalez, Felix; [ESP]
De Los Santos Rojas, Hugo; [BRA]
De Miguel Perez, Miguel Angel; [ESP]
De Monicault, Gonzague; [FRA]
De Neverlee, Leila; [FRA]
De Oliveira Junior, Ailton Paulo; [BRA]
De Oliveira Pontes, Gilvanise; [BRA]
De Oliveira Pontes, Mª Gilvanise; [BRA]
De Simon Caballero, Mª Luisa; [ESP]
De Sousa E Silva, Mary; [BRA]
De Villiers, Michael David; [ZAF]
Dechardilok, Dechar; [THA]
Defence, Astrid; [CAN]
Deitcher, Rachel; [ISR]
Dejgaard, JOrgen; [DNK]
Del Aguila Del Aguila, Yolanda; [ESP]
Del Grande, John; [CAN]
Del Olmo Escalante, Mª Dolores; [ESP]
Del Olmo Romero, MªAngeles; [ESP]

Del Pozo Medel, Juan Carlos; [ESP]
Del Rey, Patricia; [USA]
Del Rio Mendez, Pilar; [ESP]
Del Rio Mendez, Victoria; [ESP]
Del Valle Leo, Maria; [CHL]
Delaney, Kev; [GBR]
Delgado De Ortiz, Mirta Lilian; [ARG]
Delgado Gomez, Amelia Damasia; [PAR]
Delgado Recio, MaJosefa; [ESP]
Dell Ducas, Ivonete Luzia; [BRA]
Della Morte, Claudia; [ARG]
Demana, Franklin; [USA]
Dengra Barroso, Jose Luis; [ESP]
Denton, Brian; [GBR]
Denux, Christian; [FRA]
Denys, Bernadette; [FRA]
Desquith, Etienne; [CIV]
Dettori, Giuliana; [ITA]
Deulofeu Piquet, Jordi; [ESP]
Devesa Fernandez, Laura; [ESP]
Devoto De Cortes, Maria G.; [ARG]
Dexeus Millo, Josefina; [ESP]
Dias Coutinho, Marcos Juliano; [BRA]
Dias De Castro, Ilka; [BRA]
Dias Ferreira, Catarina; [PRT]
Diaz, Nestor Alberto; [ARG]
Diaz, Jose Eliseo; [ARG]
Diaz Boils, Pau; [ESP]
Diaz Canto, Elisa; [ESP]
Diaz Fernandez, Irene; [ESP]
Diaz Flores, Miguel Antonio; [CHL]
Diaz Gil, Jose Miguel; [ESP]
Diaz Godino, Juan; [ESP]
Diaz Mariscal, Ma Rosario; [ESP]
Diaz Martinez, Maria R.; [ESP]
Diaz Molina, Ma Angeles; [ESP]
Diaz Morales, MaConcepcion; [ESP]
Diaz Moreno, Leonora; [CHL]
Diaz Quezada, Maria Veronica; [CHL]
Diaz Romero, Maria Del Rocio; [ESP]
Diaz Tegerina, Ma Luisa; [ESP]
Dibut Toledo, Lazaro Salomon; [CUB]
Dick, Thomas; [USA]

Diego, Fridrik; [ISL]
Diegues Jasso, Ma Del Carmen; [MEX]
Dieschbourg, Robert; [LUX]
Diez, Elsa Beatriz; [ARG]
Diez Barrabes, Ma Mercedes; [ESP]
Diez Fernandez, Alice; [ESP]
Diez Fernandez, Adela; [ESP]
Diez Rubio, Fernando; [ESP]
Dimitrova, Radost; [BGR]
Dixon, Colin; [GBR]
Do Conto Lopes, Ilda Ma; [PRT]
Do Couto Lopes, Ilda Maria; [PRT]
Doberti, Roberto Eduardo; [ARG]
Doerr, Helen; [USA]
Dogan, Necla; [TUR]
Doig, Brian; [AUS]
Dolores Flores, Crisologo; [MEX]
Domenech I Cabre, Josep; [ESP]
Domenico, Ettiene Guerios; [BRA]
Domingo, Irene M.; [BRN]
Dominguez Abad, Ma Pilar; [ESP]
Dominguez Abascal, Ma Reyes; [ESP]
Dominguez Alarcon, Juan Jose; [ESP]
Dominguez Marin, Patricia; [ESP]
Dominguez Marmol, Aurea Maria; [ESP]
Dominguez Muro, Mariano Julio; [ESP]
Dominguez Rodriguez, Ana Ma; [ESP]
Dominguez Rubio, Ma Isabel; [ESP]
Dominguez Viñas, Josefa; [ESP]
Donlan, Margaret; [USA]
Donoghue, Eileen; [USA]
Doorman, Michael; [NLD]
Dorfler, Willibald; [AUT]
Dorier, Jean-Luc; [FRA]
Doritchenko, Serghei; [RUS]
Dorta Jimenez, Candelaria; [ESP]
Dos Santos Campanha, Eneida; [PRT]
Dossey, John; [USA]
Douady, Adrien; [FRA]
Douady, Regina; [FRA]
Douari, Rached; [TUN]
Dreyfus, Tommy; [ISR]
Drijvers, Paul; [NLD]

DROUHARD, JEAN PHILIPPE; [FRA]
DU PLOOY, LEONARD LIONEL; [ZAF]
DU TOIT, DAWID JOHANNES; [ZAF]
DUARTE, TANIA; [BRA]
DUARTE, MARTA RAFAELA; [ARG]
DUARTE CANO, PASCUALA RAMONA; [PAR]
DUBOURG, XAVIER; [FRA]
DUFFIN, JANET; [GBR]
DUGDALE, SHARON; [USA]
DUMONT, SILVIA A.; [ARG]
DUNKLEY, RONALD; [CAN]
DUPUIS, FRANCIS; [FRA]
DURAN, PHILIPPE; [DEU]
DURAN TORRES, SOFIA Mª; [ESP]
DURE ROLON, AMANDA MARLENE; [PAR]
DUVAL, RAYMOND; [FRA]
DWEK, ALBERT; [ISR]
DEGRAW, MISHAA; [USA]
D'AMBROSIO, UBIRATAN; [BRA]
D'AMBROSIO, BEATRIZ; [USA]
D'AMORE, BRUNO; [ITA]
D'ANDREA, CARLOS; [ARG]
D'ANGELI, LILIANA ROSA; [ARG]
D'HALLUIN, CHANTAL; [FRA]
EAMORAPHAN, SUCHAVADEE; [THA]
EBBUTT, SHEILA; [GBR]
EBEID, WILLIAM; [KWT]
EBERHARD, MADELEINE; [FRA]
EDVINSSON, BENGT; [SWE]
EDWARDS, JULIE-ANN; [GBR]
EDWARDS, LAURIE; [USA]
EEROLA, RIITTA LIISA; [FIN]
EGELAND, HELGE; [NOR]
EGSGARD, JOHN; [CAN]
EGSGARD, LYN; [CAN]
EHRLICH, AMOS; [ISR]
EISENBERG, TED; [ISR]
EKINS, JUDITH; [GBR]
EKSTIG, KERSTIN; [SWE]
EL BOUAZZAOUI, HABIBA; [MAR]
EL TOM, MOHAMED ELAMIN; [QAT]
ELFVING, JAN; [SWE]
ELKIES, NOAM; [USA]

ELLERTON, NERIDA; [AUS]
ELLIS, JILL; [NZL]
EMORI, HIDEYO; [JAP]
ENFEDAQUE ECHEVARRIA, JESUS; [ESP]
ENGLISH, LYN; [AUS]
ENGLUND, TOR; [SWE]
ENGSTROM, LIL; [SWE]
ENGSTRÖM, ARNE; [SWE]
ENGUIX GONZALEZ, ALICIA; [ESP]
ENRIQUEZ DE SALAMANCA GARCIA, J. M.; [ESP]
ENTRENA AGUILERA, MARIA; [ESP]
ERASO ERRO, MªDOLORES; [ESP]
ERIKSSON, HENRIK; [SWE]
ERIKSSON, KIMMO; [SWE]
ERNEST, PAUL; [GBR]
ERSOY, YASAR; [TUR]
ERVYNCK, GONTRAN; [BEL]
ESCALONA FUENMAYOR, MARIA J.; [VEN]
ESCALONA SERRANO, EVA; [CUB]
ESCOFIER, JEAN-PIERRE; [FRA]
ESCRIBANO RODENAS, Mª CARMEN; [ESP]
ESCUDERO PEREZ, ISABEL; [ESP]
ESCUTIA BASART, PILAR; [ESP]
ESPAÑOL GONZALEZ, LUIS; [ESP]
ESPINEL FEBLES, Mª CANDELARIA; [ESP]
ESPINOZA SALFATE, LORENA; [ESP]
ESPLUGAS GRAU, MERCE; [ESP]
ESPONA, PATRICIA EUGEN.; [ARG]
ESPONA DONES, JORDI; [ESP]
ESTEBAN ARIAS, FRANCISCO; [ESP]
ESTELA BALLESTER, Mª VICTORIA; [ESP]
ESTEPA CASTRO, ANTONIO; [ESP]
ESTEVE PUNTI, JORDI; [ESP]
ESTEVES, FATIMA; [PRT]
ESTRADA ROCA, Mª ASUNCION; [ESP]
ETCHEGOYEN DE OLIVERAS, SUSANA N.; [ARG]
ETTER, DAVID; [GBR]
ETTINGER, PIERRE; [FRA]
ETXEBARRIA ARRAETA, JON; [ESP]
EVANS, JEFF; [GBR]
EVANS, WARWICK; [GBR]
EVEN, RUHAMA; [ISR]
FABRA LASALVIA, MARGARIDA; [ESP]

FACAL ABELEDO, XOSE Mª; [ESP]
FADAEE, MOHAMMAD REZA; [IRN]
FAKIR MOHAMMAD, RAZIA; [PAK]
FAMILIAR RAMOS, PRIMITIVO; [ESP]
FAN, LIMING; [CHN]
FAN, LIANGHUO; [USA]
FARFAN, ENRIQUE; [ESP]
FARIA NETTO, CARLOS H.; [BRA]
FARIÑA DE MACHUCA, BASILIA; [PAR]
FASANELLI, FLORENCE; [USA]
FAURING, PATRICIA; [ARG]
FAUVEL, JOHN; [GBR]
FAVA, NORBERTO ANGEL; [ARG]
FAVILLI, FRANCO; [ITA]
FAVRAT, JEAN-FRANÇOIS; [FRA]
FAVRE, PIERRE; [CHE]
FEDER, TREVOR; [AUS]
FEDERICO, CARLOS VICENTE; [ARG]
FEDORENCO, IGOR; [RUS]
FEDRIANI MARTEL, EUGENIO MANUEL; [ESP]
FEDRIANI MARTIN, EUGENIO; [ESP]
FELIZ MARRERO, GENOVA; [DOM]
FENG, XIAN; [CHN]
FERGUSON, THOMAS; [USA]
FERGUSSON, ANDREW; [AUS]
FERNANDES, ELSA; [PRT]
FERNANDES, MARIA HELENA; [PRT]
FERNANDES NUNES MATIAS, TERESA E.; [PRT]
FERNANDEZ ALONSO, MARIA JOSE; [ESP]
FERNANDEZ BARBERIS, GABRIELA M.; [ESP]
FERNANDEZ BENITO, INMACULADA; [ESP]
FERNANDEZ BRAVO, JOSE ANTONIO; [ESP]
FERNANDEZ CHACON, ANTONIO JESUS; [ESP]
FERNANDEZ DEL CAMPO SANCHEZ, JOSE E.; [ESP]
FERNANDEZ DOMINGUEZ, JESUS; [ESP]
FERNANDEZ FERNANDEZ, SANTIAGO; [ESP]
FERNANDEZ FERNANDEZ, L. MANUEL; [ESP]
FERNANDEZ GAGO, JOAQUIN; [ESP]
FERNANDEZ GARCIA, GABRIEL; [ESP]
FERNANDEZ GARCIA, FRANCISCO; [ESP]
FERNANDEZ GUERRERO, M MERCEDES; [ESP]
FERNANDEZ GUTIERREZ, MANUEL J.; [ESP]
FERNANDEZ MARTINEZ, JOSE Mª; [ESP]

FERNANDEZ MENA, Mª LUZ; [ESP]
FERNANDEZ MONTERO, ROSA Mª; [ESP]
FERNANDEZ MUÑOZ, COLUMBA; [ESP]
FERNANDEZ NODARSE, FRANCISCO; [CUB]
FERNANDEZ ORTEGA, MIGUEL; [ESP]
FERNANDEZ PEREZ, ANA MARIA; [ESP]
FERNANDEZ PORTERO, ANTONIO; [ESP]
FERNANDEZ PRADA, JUAN ANTONIO; [ESP]
FERNANDEZ SANCHEZ, LUIS FCO.; [ESP]
FERNANDEZ STACCO, EDGARDO LUIS; [ARG]
FERNANDEZ TERNERO, DESAMPARADOS; [ESP]
FERNANDEZ VILLANUEVA, MARISA; [ESP]
FERNANDEZ-ALISEDA REDONDO, A.; [ESP]
FERNANDEZ-BLANCO, INMACULADA; [ESP]
FERRARI, PIER LUIGI; [ITA]
FERRARI, SUSANA ALICIA; [ARG]
FERREIRA, ANETE MARTINS; [PRT]
FERREIRA, MARTA DE ASSIS; [BRA]
FERREIRA DA SILVA, ISABEL A; [PRT]
FERREIRA DE SOUSA, AURELIO; [PRT]
FERREIRA DOS SANTOS, ELIETE; [BRA]
FERREIRA MARTINS SALVADOR, M.; [BRA]
FERREIRA NEVES, Mª AUGUSTA; [PRT]
FERREYRA, RAFAEL; [ARG]
FEY, JAMES; [USA]
FIDALGO BENAYAS, CONCHA; [ESP]
FIDALGO RODRIGUEZ, MANUEL; [ESP]
FIELDS, EWAUGH; [USA]
FIELKER, DAVID; [GBR]
FIGUEIRA, ELISA MARIA; [PRT]
FIGUEIRAL SILVA, Mª LURDES; [PRT]
FIGUEIRAS OCAÑA, LOURDES; [ESP]
FIGUEIREDO, VERA LUCIA; [BRA]
FIGUEIREDO GONZALEZ, MARIA LUIZA; [BRA]
FIGUEREDO DE FRUTOS, MARTA C.; [PAR]
FILIPASIC, SUZANA; [CRO]
FILIPE, LEONOR; [PRT]
FILIPE MATIAS, BERNARDO; [ANG]
FIOL MORA, Mª LUISA; [ESP]
FIORENTINI, DARIO; [BRA]
FIORITI, GEMA INES; [ARG]
FIRSOV, VICTOR; [RUS]
FITZHARRIS, ANDREW; [GBR]

FITZSIMONS, GAIL; [AUS]
FLEMING, RICHARD; [GBR]
FLEMMING, DIVA MARILIA; [BRA]
FLORENCIO LORA, MIGUEL; [ESP]
FLORES, Mª ALBERTINA; [PRT]
FLORES, GRISELDA ESTELA; [ARG]
FLORES CASTRO, LETICIA; [MEX]
FLORES FERNANDEZ, Mª CARMEN; [ESP]
FLORES MARQUEZ, PEDRO JESUS; [ESP]
FLORES MARTINEZ, PABLO; [ESP]
FLORESCU, MARCEL; [ROM]
FLOWER, JEAN; [GBR]
FOLEY, GREGORY; [USA]
FOLOMEYEVA, ELENA; [RUS]
FONG, HO-KHEONG; [SGP]
FONSECA BON, CECILIO; [ESP]
FONSECA SOARES, ROOSEWELT; [BRA]
FONT MOLL, VICENÇ; [ESP]
FORBES, SHARLEEN; [NZL]
FORGASZ, HELEN; [AUS]
FORMAN, SUSAN; [USA]
FORTUNY AYMENI, JOSEP M; [ESP]
FRADE BELLO, ROGELIO; [ESP]
FRAENKEL, SHAULA; [ISR]
FRANCIS, NASIF; [ISR]
FRANCISSEN, DORIEN; [NLD]
FRANCO LEIS, DANIEL; [ESP]
FRANK, ROSLYN; [USA]
FRANKE, MARIANNE; [DEU]
FRANKS, DOUGLAS; [CAN]
FRAU GARCIA, MARIA DOLORES; [ESP]
FREDERICK, BETZ; [USA]
FREDERICK, HAROLD; [USA]
FREEMAN, CINDY; [USA]
FRENNESSON, SVEN-AKE; [SWE]
FRIEDLANDER, ALEX; [ISR]
FRIEDLI, BEATRIZ MICAELA; [ARG]
FRIEDLI, BEATRIZ; [ARG]
FROIDCOEUR, MAURICE-DENIS; [CHE]
FUENTEALBA ACUÑA, CLAUDIO; [CHL]
FUENTES FUENTES, RAUL ARNALDO; [CHL]
FUENTES GIL, INMACULADA; [ESP]
FUENTES GONZALEZ, WILDA; [CHL]

FUENTES VERDERA, MARIA JESUS; [ESP]
FUEYO TIRADO, FERNANDO; [ESP]
FUGLESTAD, ANNE BERIT; [GBR]
FUJII, SHIRO; [JAP]
FUJII, TOSHIAKIRA; [JAP]
FUJITA, YOSHIKO; [JAP]
FUKAYA, HIDESHI; [JAP]
FUKUOKA, YAEKO; [JAP]
FUNG, CHUN-IP; [HKG]
FURINGHETTI, FULVIA; [ITA]
GABRIELSSON, GERT; [SWE]
GADEMAN, JOHAN; [NLD]
GAGO DE OLIVEIRA BRITO, Mª C.; [PRT]
GAIRIN GALLAN, JOSE Mª; [ESP]
GAITAS FILLO, JOSE; [BRA]
GAL, IDDO; [ISR]
GALAN OLLOQUI, JOSEFINA; [ESP]
GALBRAITH, PETER; [AUS]
GALDO, CONSTANZA; [ARG]
GALDOS IRAZABAL, CLARA; [ESP]
GALINDO NAVARRO, RUTH; [CHL]
GALITO BERENGUER, Mª TERESA; [ESP]
GALLARDO CALDERON, JUAN; [ESP]
GALLARDO GUTIERREZ, EVA; [ESP]
GALLARDO GUTIERREZ, AGUSTIN; [ESP]
GALLARDO MUÑOZ, ROSA ANA; [ESP]
GALLEGO GARCIA, JOSE LUIS; [ESP]
GALLEGO SAAVEDRA, SANTIAGO; [ESP]
GALLON CARDONA, LUIS HUMBERTO; [COL]
GALLOU-DUMIEL, ELISABETH; [FRA]
GAMBOA BRENES, MARIA; [ESP]
GAMEZ MELLADO, FRANCISCO PEDRO; [ESP]
GANDIT, MICHELE; [FRA]
GANDOLFO FERREIRA, ELIZABETH; [URY]
GARCIA ALVAREZ, BEGOÑA; [ESP]
GARCIA AMADEO, GRACIELA; [ARG]
GARCIA ARMENDARIZ, Mª VICTORIA; [ESP]
GARCIA BARBANCHO, MANUELA; [ESP]
GARCIA BAREA, JOSE; [ESP]
GARCIA BLANCO, MERCEDES; [ESP]
GARCIA CARRION, Mª ENCARNACION; [ESP]
GARCIA CAZORLA, ANGELES; [ESP]
GARCIA CORDOBA, ANA MARIA; [ESP]

GARCIA CRUZ, JUAN ANTONIO; [ESP]
GARCIA CUESTA, SERAPIO; [ESP]
GARCIA DE COCIÑA, ANDREA; [ARG]
GARCIA DE FRUTOS, INMACULADA; [ESP]
GARCIA DENIZ, MANUEL; [ESP]
GARCIA DOZAGARAT, JUAN MANUEL; [ESP]
GARCIA FERNANDEZ, Mª TERESA; [ESP]
GARCIA GARCIA, FRANCISCO JESUS; [ESP]
GARCIA GARCIA, FCO. JAVIER; [ESP]
GARCIA GARCIA, Mª ELENA; [MEX]
GARCIA GARCIA, Mª LUISA; [ESP]
GARCIA GARCIA, Mª ISABEL; [ESP]
GARCIA GARCIA DE ANDOIN, LUISA; [ESP]
GARCIA GONZALEZ, Mª CARMEN; [ESP]
GARCIA GONZALEZ, ISABEL; [ESP]
GARCIA HERNANDEZ, ANGEL IVAN; [MEX]
GARCIA HITA, JOSE FRANCISCO; [ESP]
GARCIA JIMENEZ, JUAN EMILIO; [ESP]
GARCIA LOPEZ, ANA; [ESP]
GARCIA LOPEZ, ALFONSA; [ESP]
GARCIA LORITE, MIGUEL JOSE; [ESP]
GARCIA LLAMAS, MªCARMEN; [ESP]
GARCIA MANCILLA, SYLVIA; [MEX]
GARCIA MARTINEZ, FERNANDA; [ESP]
GARCIA MAZARIO, FRANCISCO; [ESP]
GARCIA MIGUEL, MERCEDES; [ESP]
GARCIA MIRANDA, Mª DE LA VILLA; [ESP]
GARCIA MONDARAY, DIEGO A.; [ESP]
GARCIA MOYA, Mª BELEN; [ESP]
GARCIA MURILLO, RICARDO; [ESP]
GARCIA NETO, OSMAR; [BRA]
GARCIA PEDRO, JOSEFA; [ESP]
GARCIA PERALTA, ENCARNI; [ESP]
GARCIA PEREZ, JESUS ROBERTO; [MEX]
GARCIA POLANCO, PILAR EUGENIA; [ESP]
GARCIA PORTA, JOSE ANTONIO; [ESP]
GARCIA PORTABALES, Mª DOLORES; [ESP]
GARCIA PRIETO, ESTHER; [ESP]
GARCIA RIBEIRO, Mª ELISA; [ESP]
GARCIA RODENAS, RICARDO; [ESP]
GARCIA RUBIO, MARIA JOSE; [ESP]
GARCIA RUIZ, MARGARITA; [ESP]
GARCIA SEVERON, CONCEPCION; [ESP]

GARCIA - HERREROS AGORRETA, F.; [ESP]
GARCIADIEGO DANTAN, ALEJANDRO; [MEX]
GARDINER, ANTHONY; [GBR]
GARFUNKEL, SOLOMON; [USA]
GARNER, WANDA; [USA]
GARRIDO RODRIGUEZ, MªDEL MAR; [ESP]
GARRISON, LIONEL; [USA]
GARRISON, SUSAN K.; [USA]
GARRONE PIOVANOTTI, EDISON W.; [URY]
GARTON, ISABEL M.; [PRT]
GASCON BLANCO, EVA MARIA; [ESP]
GASCON PEREZ, JOSEP; [ESP]
GASSER, EDDA; [CHE]
GATES, PETER; [GBR]
GATTUSO, LINDA; [CAN]
GAUDREAULT, LS-PHILIPPE; [CAN]
GAULIN, CLAUDE; [CAN]
GAVILAN IZQUIERDO, JOSE MARIA; [ESP]
GAVILAN RECHE, ELISA; [ESP]
GELFMAN, EMANUILA; [RUS]
GELLERT, UWE; [DEU]
GENAO CHAVES, ROSARIO; [ESP]
GEORGE, ACCAMMA; [USA]
GEORGE GONZALEZ, JOSE KELME; [COL]
GERDES, PAULUS; [MOZ]
GERETSCHLAGER, ROBERT; [AUT]
GERLING, MAX; [USA]
GHAZALI, MUNIRAH; [MYS]
GHOLAM, GHADA; [EGY]
GHORAISHI, SEYED SAEED; [IRN]
GIANSANTI, SILVIA PALMIRA; [ARG]
GIL, BEATRIZ SUSANA; [ARG]
GIL, FABIAN; [ARG]
GIL CUADRA, FRANCISCO; [ESP]
GILEAD, SHOSHANA; [ISR]
GILI RIPOLL, MARIONA; [ESP]
GILIS, DANIEL; [FRA]
GILLESPIE, JOHN A; [GBR]
GILLOT LABBE, ANTONIO ERNESTO; [GTM]
GIMENEZ, CLAUDIA ANDREA; [ARG]
GIMENEZ MARTINEZ, INMACULADA; [ESP]
GIMENEZ RODRIGUEZ, JOAQUIN; [ESP]
GIMENEZ ZARACHO, MIRYAN NANCY; [PAR]

GINAT, DAVID; [ISR]
GINBAYASHI, KO; [JAP]
GINESTIER, JEAN-PAUL; [NOR]
GINSBURG, LYNDA; [USA]
GINSHIMA, FUMI; [JAP]
GIORDANO, LILIANA; [ARG]
GIOVANNONI, LAURA; [ITA]
GIRETT DE SERVIN, ZUNILDA; [PAR]
GIRONDO PEREZ, Mª LUISA; [ESP]
GJONE, GUNNAR; [NOR]
GLAZER, EVAN; [USA]
GLEIZER, GRIGORI; [RUS]
GLOVER, OWEN HUGH; [ZAF]
GOBEA LLAMAS, FRANCISCO JAV.; [ESP]
GODDEN, GAIL; [AUS]
GODDIJN, AAD; [NLD]
GODOY DELGADO, DOLORES; [ESP]
GOETZ, ALBERT; [USA]
GOFFREE, FRED; [NLD]
GOIFFON, REGIS; [FRA]
GOIKOETXEA MAIZTEGUI, Mª JOSE; [ESP]
GOLAN, ANA Mª; [USA]
GOLDBERG, DOROTHY; [USA]
GOLDEN, THOMAS; [USA]
GOLDENBERG, E.PAUL; [USA]
GOLDSCHWARTZ, MAXIMILIANO; [ARG]
GOMES, MARCIA REGINA; [BRA]
GOMES, MARILDA TRECENT; [BRA]
GOMES, MARILDA TRECENT; [BRA]
GOMES, MIGUEL; [PRT]
GOMES BRANCO, ISABEL Mª; [PRT]
GOMES DA SILVA, MARIA REGINA; [DEU]
GOMEZ, PEDRO; [COL]
GOMEZ ALCARAZ, GUILLERMO; [MEX]
GOMEZ ALFONSO, BERNARDO; [ESP]
GOMEZ BERNAL, LOURDES; [ESP]
GOMEZ BERROCAL, FRANCISCO JOSE; [ESP]
GOMEZ CASADO, PILAR; [ESP]
GOMEZ CHACON, INES Mª; [ESP]
GOMEZ I URGELLES, JOAN; [ESP]
GOMEZ JURADO, INMACULADA; [ESP]
GOMEZ LORA, MARIA; [ESP]
GOMEZ MARTINEZ, MARIA; [USA]

GOMEZ MONGE, Mª DOLORES; [ESP]
GOMEZ MORILLA, MIGUEL ANGEL; [ESP]
GOMEZ MURIANA, BASILIO; [ESP]
GOMEZ VAZQUEZ, Mª ISABEL; [ESP]
GOMIS MIQUEL, MISERICORDIA; [ESP]
GONZALEZ, FREDY ENRIQUE; [VEN]
GONZALEZ ABRIL, LUIS; [ESP]
GONZALEZ ARAVENA, JORGE; [CHL]
GONZALEZ ASTUDILLO, MªTERESA; [ESP]
GONZALEZ BENEYTO, Mª JESUS; [ESP]
GONZALEZ CARMONA, ANA ROSA; [MEX]
GONZALEZ DAZA, NADIA; [VEN]
GONZALEZ DE LORA, SARAH; [DOM]
GONZALEZ DIAZ, ROCIO; [ESP]
GONZALEZ DIAZ, MªEDUVIGES; [ARG]
GONZALEZ DOMINGUEZ ADAME, LUZ; [ESP]
GONZALEZ FERNANDEZ, LUCIANO; [ESP]
GONZALEZ GARCIA, ANTONIO E.; [ESP]
GONZALEZ GONZALEZ, EVARISTO; [ESP]
GONZALEZ HENRIQUEZ, JUAN JOSE; [ESP]
GONZALEZ IGLESIAS, ANA ROSA; [ESP]
GONZALEZ LOPEZ, Mª JOSE; [ESP]
GONZALEZ MAGALLANES, MARTA; [ESP]
GONZALEZ MARTINEZ, ALEJANDRO; [ESP]
GONZALEZ RAMIREZ, JORGE ANTONIO; [ESP]
GONZALEZ SANCHEZ, MARIA DEL MAR; [ESP]
GONZALEZ VARELA, Mª CARMEN; [ESP]
GONZALEZ-MENESES LOPEZ, JUAN; [ESP]
GOÑI, NELVA EDITH; [ARG]
GOÑI ZABALA, JESUS MARIA; [ESP]
GOODALL, JONATHAN EDWARD; [ZAF]
GOODWIN, JEFFREY; [GBR]
GOOS, MERRILYN; [AUS]
GOOYA, ZAHRA; [IRN]
GORDILLO LOBATO, JUAN; [ESP]
GORDON, SUE; [AUS]
GORGORIO, NURIA; [ESP]
GORMAZ GORMAZ, Mª NIEVES; [ESP]
GOULDING, MARIA; [GBR]
GOURDEAU, FREDERIC; [CAN]
GOVEA FONTANILLA, AMPARO; [ESP]
GRACIA ALCAINE, FLOREAL; [ESP]
GRAÇA FERREIRA, ELVIRA; [PRT]

Graeber, Anna; [USA]
Graf, Andrea; [DEU]
Graham, Edward; [GBR]
Grandes Arnaiz, Mª Begoña; [ESP]
Grando, Regina Celia; [BRA]
Grandsard, Francine; [BEL]
Grant, Fiona; [GBR]
Gras, Regis; [FRA]
Graumann, Gunter; [DEU]
Gravemeijer, Koeno; [NLD]
Gravina, Maria Alice; [BRA]
Gray, Edward; [GBR]
Gray, Mary; [USA]
Gray, Michael; [AUS]
Greciano Martin, Angeles; [ESP]
Green, David Robert; [GBR]
Green, Kevin Norman; [AUS]
Green, Sylvia; [GBR]
Green, John; [AUS]
Greer, Brian; [IRL]
Gremillion, Danny; [USA]
Grevholm, Barbro; [SWE]
Grigoriu Rocha, Juana Maria; [BOL]
Groninger, Don S.; [USA]
Gros Ezquerra, Mª Jose; [ESP]
Gross, James; [USA]
Grosso De Sala, Carmen Haydee; [ARG]
Grou, Maria Alice; [BRA]
Grouws, Douglas; [USA]
Groves, Susie; [AUS]
Gruenberg, Veronica; [CHL]
Grugnetti, Lucia; [ITA]
Guala, Graciela; [ARG]
Guanuco, Maria Del Valle; [ARG]
Guderian, Dietmar; [DEU]
Gudovich, Irina; [RUS]
Guedes, Eliana Maria; [BRA]
Güemes Alzaga, Mª Belen; [ESP]
Guerra Mota, Ana Clotilde; [PRT]
Guerra Quintana, Nicanor; [ESP]
Guerrero Garcia, Pablo; [ESP]
Guerrero Hidalgo, Salvador; [ESP]
Guerrero Ojeda, Jesus; [ESP]

Guichard, Jacqueline; [FRA]
Guichard, Jean-Paul; [FRA]
Guidili, Barbara; [USA]
Guil Soto, Rafael; [ESP]
Guillen Soler, Gregoria; [ESP]
Guimaraes, Henrique; [PRT]
Guo, Chorng-Jee; [TPI]
Gura, Ein-Ya; [ISR]
Gusev, Valery; [RUS]
Gustafsson, Lars; [SWE]
Gutierrez, Jose; [ESP]
Gutierrez Alvarez, Horacio; [ESP]
Gutierrez Carballude, Mª Isolina; [ESP]
Gutierrez Carrizo, Fernando; [ESP]
Gutierrez Castillo, Mª Teresa; [ESP]
Gutierrez Lopez, Consuelo; [ESP]
Gutierrez Naranjo, Miguel A; [ESP]
Gutierrez Pereda, Guadalupe; [ESP]
Gutierrez Perez, Jose; [ESP]
Gutierrez Rodriguez, Mª Elena; [ESP]
Gutierrez Rodriguez, Angel; [ESP]
Gutierrez Rubio, David; [ESP]
Gutierrez Vazquez, Santiago; [ESP]
Guttman, Karin; [SWE]
Guzman, Raymond; [USA]
Guzman, Marta Elena; [ARG]
Guzman Ozamiz, Miguel De; [ESP]
Guz', Nikolai; [UKR]
Gvozdeva, Elena; [RUS]
Gysin, Liliana Mabel; [ARG]
Haack, Joel; [USA]
Haanos, Marianne; [NOR]
Haase, Christian; [ESP]
Habibullah, Saleha; [PAK]
Hachiya, Kiyotaka; [GBR]
Hadas, Nurit; [ISR]
Hadnagy, Eva; [HUN]
Hag, Per; [NOR]
Hag, Kari; [NOR]
Haga, Monica; [NOR]
Hahn, Corine; [FRA]
Haines, Christopher; [GBR]
Hairault, Jean-Pierre; [FRA]

Hakansson, Susie; [USA]
Hakim, Victor; [CHE]
Hakonsson, Erik; [DNK]
Halai, Anjum; [PAK]
Hale Tamayo, Rosa; [MEX]
Halevi, Tirza; [ISR]
Hall, Neil; [AUS]
Halliday, James; [BAR]
Hamid, Chaachova; [FRA]
Hamm, Susan; [CAN]
Hammond, Brenda; [USA]
Hammond, Pamela Marion; [AUS]
Hammontree, Jane; [USA]
Handa, Toru; [JAP]
Hang, Kim Hoo; [SGP]
Hanna, Gila; [CAN]
Hanrahan, James P.; [CAN]
Hans Martin, Juan A.; [ESP]
Hansen, Hans Christian; [DNK]
Harboe, Baard; [NOR]
Harding Rojas, Ines; [FRA]
Hardy, Tansy; [GBR]
Harel, Guershon; [USA]
Harpaz-Robin, Yael; [ISR]
Hart, Kathleen; [GBR]
Hartmann, Jens; [DEU]
Hartz, Viggo; [DNK]
Hashimoto, Yoshihiko; [JAP]
Haskins, James; [USA]
Hastad, Matts; [SWE]
Hastings, Anne; [AUS]
Hatch, Gillian; [GBR]
Hatfield, Larry; [USA]
Hatfield, Mary; [USA]
Hatori, Asako; [JAP]
Hatton, Joyce; [GBR]
Hauchart, Christiane; [BEL]
Haugland, Lena Sjursen; [NOR]
Hawkins, Anne; [GBR]
Haworth, Anne; [GBR]
Hayashi, Susumu; [JAP]
Hayashi, Juichi; [JAP]
Hayes, Robert; [AUS]

Haylock, Derek; [GBR]
Hayter, John; [GBR]
Hedren, Rolf; [SWE]
Heerebout, Berry; [NLD]
Hegedus, Stephen John; [GBR]
Heid, M. Kathleen; [USA]
Heide, Torkil; [DNK]
Heidema, Clare; [USA]
Heikkurinen, Tuulikki; [FIN]
Hein, Nelson; [BRA]
Hejny, Milan; [CZR]
Henderson, Jenny; [AUS]
Henn, Hans Wolfgang; [DEU]
Henning, Herbert; [DEU]
Henriquez, Luis; [DOM]
Henriquez Rodriguez, Lucia Esther; [ESP]
Henry, Michel; [FRA]
Heraud, Bernard; [CAN]
Herbst, Patricio; [USA]
Hermans, Victor; [NLD]
Hernaez Medina, Juana Simona; [PAR]
Hernandez Aguirre, Leopoldo; [MEX]
Hernandez Amador, Agustina; [ESP]
Hernandez De Fontes, Heloisa; [BRA]
Hernandez De Ortega, Maria V.; [VEN]
Hernandez Dominguez, Josefa; [ESP]
Hernandez Fernandez, Herminia T.; [CUB]
Hernandez Garcia, Amparo; [ESP]
Hernandez Guadarrama, Rafael; [MEX]
Hernandez Guarch, Fernando; [ESP]
Hernandez Lopez-Carpeño, Rosa M.; [ESP]
Hernandez Real, Maria De Jesus; [MEX]
Hernandez Ruano, Mª Victoria; [ESP]
Herrera, Terese; [USA]
Herrera Carrera, Consuelo; [MEX]
Herrera Ejarque, Jose Antonio; [ESP]
Herrera Ejarque, Pilar; [ESP]
Herrera Govantes, Javier; [ESP]
Herschel, Deborah; [USA]
Hershkowitz, Rina; [ISR]
Hess Andersson, Anna; [SWE]
Hevia De Fernandez, Alicia Susana; [ARG]
Hewitt, Dave; [GBR]

HIBBARD, THOMAS; [ARG]
HIDALGO CARRANZA, Mª JOSE; [ESP]
HIDDLESTON, PATRICIA; [MWI]
HIGUCHI, TEIICHI; [JAP]
HIGUERA MAYORAL, CECILIA; [MEX]
HINDS, KIRSTEEN; [GBR]
HIRAHATA, CHIEKO; [JAP]
HIRANO, YUICHI; [JAP]
HIRAYAMA, YASUO; [JAP]
HIRST, ANN; [GBR]
HIRST, KEITH EDWIN; [GBR]
HITCHCOCK, GAVIN; [ZWE]
HITOTSUMATSU, SHIN; [JAP]
HOBBS, MARGIE; [USA]
HOCKMAN, MEIRA; [ZAF]
HODGSON, BERNARD; [CAN]
HODGSON, BRIAN; [AUS]
HODNIK, TATJANA; [GBR]
HOGAN, JOHN; [AUS]
HOLDEN, NORMAN L.; [CHE]
HOLMES, PETER; [GBR]
HOLMQUIST, MIKAEL; [SWE]
HOLTON, DEREK; [NZL]
HOLLAR, JEANNIE; [USA]
HOOGLAND, KEES; [NLD]
HORMIGON BLANQUEZ, MARIANO; [ESP]
HORNE, MARJ; [AUS]
HORTOBAGYI, ISTVAN; [HUN]
HOSPESOVA, ALENA; [CZR]
HOSPITAL VALERO, FRANCISCO; [ESP]
HOUDEBIME, JEAN; [FRA]
HOUDEMENT, CATHERINE; [FRA]
HOUSE, PEGGY; [USA]
HOVDEN, EIVIND; [NOR]
HOWSON, GEOFFREY; [GBR]
HOYLES, CELIA; [GBR]
HOYOS GOMEZ, ALBERTO; [ESP]
HUANG, MEN-TON; [TPI]
HUANG, WEI; [CHN]
HUANG, XIANG; [CHN]
HUANG, KEMING; [CHN]
HUBER, ARLA; [USA]
HUDSON, BRIAN; [GBR]

HUERTA PALAU, M. PEDRO; [ESP]
HUERTOS RODRIGUEZ, MANUEL; [ESP]
HUESO PAGOAGA, JOSE LUIS; [ESP]
HUETINCK, LINDA; [USA]
HUGHES, MARTIN; [GBR]
HUMBERT DE MIRANDE, ROSA MARIA; [ARG]
HUMPHREY, GEORGE; [IRL]
HUNTER, MARK DALGLIESH; [GBR]
HUNTING, ROBERT; [AUS]
HUSSEIN, MANSOUR; [KWT]
HYDE, ROSALYN; [GBR]
HYUN, JONG-IK; [KOR]
IBAÑES JALON, MARCELINO; [ESP]
IBAÑEZ LOZANO, JOSE ANTONIO; [ESP]
IBAÑEZ ORTS, VICENTE; [ESP]
IBAÑEZ VARELA, RAUL; [ESP]
IBRAHIM, EDUARD MIKHAIL; [EGY]
ICHINOSE, KOGI; [JAP]
IGARASHI, KAN; [JAP]
IGLESIAS BRAVO, MARIA ELENA; [ESP]
IGLESIAS BRAVO, EVA Mª; [ESP]
IGLESIAS CEREZAL, MANUEL; [ESP]
IGLESIAS DE ALBANEZ, HAYDEE; [SAL]
IGLESIAS GARCIA, JOSE LUIS; [ESP]
IIDA, TATSUHIKO; [JAP]
IIDA, SHINJI; [JAP]
IITAKA, SHIGERU; [JAP]
IKEDA, FUMIO; [JAP]
IKEDA, TOSHIKAZU; [JAP]
IKONEN, LEENA; [FIN]
ILANY, BAT-SHEVA; [ISR]
ILICASU, GONCA; [TUR]
IMAI, TOSHIHIRO; [JAP]
IMPERIANO DA SILVA, ROOSEVELT; [BRA]
INABA, MISTUKO; [JAP]
INACIO PIRES PEREIRA, HENRIQUE; [PRT]
INAFUKU, ANDRE MINORU; [BRA]
INFANTE MACIAS, RAFAEL; [ESP]
INGOLFSDOTTIR, ASDIS; [ISL]
INKPEN, SARAH; [CAN]
INPRASITHA, MAITREE; [JAP]
IOANNOU, DIMITRIOS; [GRC]
IPPOLITO, DANIELA; [GBR]

ISAACS, IAN; [AUS]
ISHIDA, JUNICHI; [JAP]
ISHIDA, TADAYUKI; [JAP]
ISMAIL, ZALEHA; [MYS]
ISODA, MASAMI; [JAP]
ITO, YOSHIHIKO; [JAP]
ITOH, SETSURO; [JAP]
ITO-HINO, KEIKO; [JAP]
IVANOV, OLEG A.; [RUS]
IWASAKI, HIDEKI; [JAP]
IWASAKI, HIROSHI; [JAP]
IZARD, JOHN; [AUS]
IZCUE ANCIN, MARAVILLAS ANA; [ESP]
IZQUIERDO BERNAL, ESPERANZA MAC.; [ESP]
IZUMORI, HITOSHI; [JAP]
JORGENSEN, ANNA; [DNK]
JABLONKA, EVA; [DEU]
JACKIW, NICHOLAS; [USA]
JACKSON, NAN; [USA]
JACOBS, MARILYN SYBIL; [ZAF]
JACOBSEN, EDWARD; [USA]
JADUR, CAMILO ALBERTO; [ARG]
JAFFER, SHAHEEDA; [ZAF]
JAHN, ANA PAULA; [FRA]
JAIME PASTOR, ADELA; [ESP]
JAKOBSSON, DAN; [SWE]
JAMES, MARGARET; [GBR]
JANSSENS, DIRK; [BEL]
JAPON VAZQUEZ, Mª CARMEN; [ESP]
JAQUET, FRANCOIS; [CHE]
JARA DE CABALLERO, MIRIAM; [PAR]
JAREONSILAVAT, PUNYAWEE; [THA]
JAWORSKI, JOHN; [GBR]
JAWORSKI, BARBARA; [GBR]
JEENER, PATRICE; [FRA]
JENSEN, CLAUS; [DNK]
JENSEN, BOB; [USA]
JEWSEN, BIRGIT HOLMER; [DNK]
JEZIK, IVAN; [AUT]
JI, DA WEI; [CHN]
JIMENEZ ALARCON, AURELIO DAMIAN; [ESP]
JIMENEZ ALEIXANDRE, Mª EUGENIA; [ESP]
JIMENEZ CRUZADO, JESUS MANUEL; [ESP]

JIMENEZ JIMENEZ, Mª ESPERANZA; [ESP]
JIMENEZ RODRIGUEZ, Mª JOSE; [ESP]
JIN, CHAIHUA; [CHN]
JIRMAN, PHILIP; [GBR]
JIROTKOVA, DARINA; [CZR]
JOEL, HILLEL; [CAN]
JOHANSSON, ANN-MARGRET; [ESP]
JOHANSSON, BENGT; [SWE]
JOHN, ALAN; [GBR]
JOHNSEN, VESLEMOY; [NOR]
JOHNSEN-HOINES, MARIT; [NOR]
JOHNSON, PHILLIP; [USA]
JOHNSON, DAVID C; [GBR]
JOHNSON, HOWARD; [USA]
JOHNSTON, BETTY; [AUS]
JOHNSTON, JAYNE ELIZABETH; [AUS]
JOJOT DE DEMESTRI, AVELINA C.; [PAR]
JONES, GRAHAM A.; [USA]
JONES, LESLY; [GBR]
JONES, KEITH; [GBR]
JONES, MARGARET; [GBR]
JONES, ANTHONY; [AUS]
JONES, SONIA; [GBR]
JONES, THERESE; [USA]
JONES, PETER; [AUS]
JONG SOO, BAE; [KOR]
JONSDOTTIR, KRISTIN; [ISL]
JOVER MONTIANO, ANTONIO; [ESP]
JUAN GARCIA, JOSE FERNANDO; [ESP]
JUAN RIVAYA, FRANCISCO; [ESP]
JUAREZ RODRIGUEZ, ELEAZAR; [MEX]
JULIA, MARTHA; [ARG]
JULIE, CYRIL; [ZAF]
JUNCAL SAEZ, IRMA; [ESP]
JUNDA, ZHANG; [CHN]
JUNQUEIRA, MARGARIDA; [PRT]
JURADO ANTUNEZ, PURIFICACION; [ESP]
JURADO RODRIGUEZ, JOSE FRANCISCO; [ESP]
JURDAK, MURAD; [LBN]
JUSTEL, MARIANA; [ARG]
KAAHWA, JANET; [UGA]
KAGESTEN, OWE; [SWE]
KAHN, PETER; [GBR]

KAISER, GABRIELE; [DEU]
KAJIKAWA, YUJI; [JAP]
KAKIAGE, ATSUSHI; [JAP]
KAKIHANA, KYOKO; [JAP]
KALDRIMIDOU, MARIA; [GRC]
KALIN, ROBERT; [USA]
KALLGARDEN, EVA-STINA; [SWE]
KAMIN, HEDVA; [ISR]
KANETA, TAKASHI; [JAP]
KANG, WAN; [KOR]
KANG, OK-KI; [KOR]
KANO, HIROKO; [JAP]
KANTOR, JEAN-MICHEL; [FRA]
KAPUT, JAMES; [USA]
KAREEMEE, SOMNUEK; [THA]
KARLSSON, SOREN; [SWE]
KARLSSON, BARBRO; [SWE]
KASLOVA, MICHAELA; [CZR]
KATSURA, TAKEO; [JAP]
KATZ, VICTOR; [USA]
KAUFMAN FAINGUELERNT, ESTELA; [BRA]
KAUR, BERINDERJEET; [SGP]
KAWAMURA, JUN-ICHIRO; [JAP]
KAZAMA, KIMIE; [JAP]
KAZIM, MAASSOUMA; [EGY]
KAZIMA, MERCY; [MWI]
KEIJZER, RONALD; [NLD]
KEITEL-KREIDT, CHRISTINE; [DEU]
KELLY, SUSAN; [GBR]
KEMP, MARIAN; [AUS]
KENNEWELL, STEPHEN; [GBR]
KENT, PHILLIP; [GBR]
KERANTO, TAPIO; [FIN]
KERSLAKE, DAPHNE; [GBR]
KETTLER, MARILYN; [USA]
KHOLODNAYA, MARINA; [RUS]
KIERAN, CAROLYN; [CAN]
KIERNAN, JAMES F.; [USA]
KILIAN, HANS; [DEU]
KILPATRICK, JEREMY; [USA]
KIM, SOO HWAN; [KOR]
KIM, BYUNG MOO; [KOR]
KIM, YOUNG KUK; [KOR]

KIMURA, YOSHIO; [JAP]
KINDT, MARTIN; [NLD]
KING, LONNIE; [ZAF]
KINNUNEN, LIISA; [FIN]
KIRCHGRAVER, URS; [CHE]
KIRKBY, DAVID RICHARD; [GBR]
KIRO, SARA; [ISR]
KISHIMOTO, TADAYUKI; [JAP]
KISSANE, BARRY; [AUS]
KITAHARA, TOMIKO; [JAP]
KIVINUKK, ANDI; [EST]
KJELLSTROM, KATARINA; [SWE]
KLAKLA, MACIEJ; [POL]
KLAOUDATOS, NICOS; [GRC]
KLASA, JACQUELINE; [CAN]
KLEIN, MARJUNIA EDITA; [BRA]
KLEINER, [ISR]; [CAN]
KLEIVE, PER-EVEN; [NOR]
KLEPKO, SERHIY; [UKR]
KLING, LILI ANN; [SWE]
KLOPP, RENE; [LUX]
KLÜSENER, RENITA; [BRA]
KMETIC, SILVA; [SLN]
KNIGHT, GORDON; [NZL]
KNIJNIK, GELSA; [BRA]
KNOCHE, NORBERT; [DEU]
KNUDTZON, SIGNE; [NOR]
KOBAYASHI, ICHIRO; [JAP]
KODERA, TAKAYUKI; [JAP]
KOEBISU, TETSURO; [GBR]
KOEHLER, HARTMUT; [DEU]
KOIRALA, HARI; [USA]
KOLBE, LISA; [USA]
KOMAN, MILAN; [CZR]
KONGCHAREON, FUANGSAK; [THA]
KONIG, GERHARD; [DEU]
KONSTATINOV, NIKOLAI; [RUS]
KOO, KWANG JO; [KOR]
KOPELMAN, EVGENY; [ISR]
KOSEKI, KEIKO; [JAP]
KOSOUM, MONTIRA; [THA]
KOSS, ROBERTA K.; [USA]
KOSTYRKO, JACEK; [USA]

KOTA, OSAMU; [JAP]
KOTAGIRI, TADATO; [JAP]
KOUTLIS, MANOLIS; [GRC]
KOVACS, ZOLTAN; [HUN]
KOYAMA, MASATAKA; [JAP]
KOZAR, EVELYN; [USA]
KRAINER, KONRAD; [AUT]
KRAUTHAUSEN, GUNTER; [DEU]
KREVISKY, STEPHEN; [USA]
KRONFELLNER, MANFRED; [AUT]
KRUPANANDAN, DANIEL; [ZAF]
KRUSE, FABIO; [BRA]
KRUSIQUE, JOSE LUIZ; [BRA]
KRYSINSKA, MARIZA; [BEL]
KUBINOVA, MARIE; [CZR]
KUCZMA, MARCIN EMIL; [POL]
KUENDIGER, ERIKA; [CAN]
KUIJK, LUC; [NLD]
KUKU, ADEREMI; [ITA]
KULESHOVA, LINA; [RUS]
KUMTIENTONG, RATREE; [THA]
KUNAKOVSKAYA, OLGA; [RUS]
KUNIMOTO, KEIYU; [JAP]
KUNIMUNE, SUSUMU; [JAP]
KUPARI, PEKKA; [FIN]
KURAMITSU, HIROFUMI; [JAP]
KURINA, FRANTISEK; [CZR]
KUROSAKI, TAMAMI; [JAP]
KURTH, INA; [DEU]
KUSUMOTO, ZENNOSUKE; [JAP]
KUTSCHER, BILHA; [ISR]
KUWATA, HARUMI; [JAP]
KWAN, TJIOE; [USA]
KYNIGOS, POLYCHRONIS; [GRC]
LABORDE, COLETTE; [FRA]
LABORDE, JEAN MARIE; [FRA]
LABRAÑA BARRERO, ANTON; [ESP]
LABRIE, JEAN-MARIE; [CAN]
LABROUSSE, CAROLE; [FRA]
LACAMPAGNE, CAROLE; [USA]
LACASTA ZABALZA, EDUARDO; [ESP]
LADOUCEUR, ANDRE; [CAN]
LAGARES BARREIRO, PAULA; [ESP]

LAGRANGE, JEAN-BAPTISTE; [FRA]
LAHTI, UNO; [SWE]
LAIRD, STUART; [NZL]
LAKOMA, EWA; [POL]
LAMAR, LIDER-MANUEL; [USA]
LAMON, SUSAN J; [USA]
LANGBORT, CAROL; [USA]
LANGDON, NIGEL; [GBR]
LANKIEWICZ, BOGUSLAWA; [POL]
LANZ, EURICO; [BRA]
LANZ, IARA HELENA; [BRA]
LAPPAN, GLENDA; [USA]
LARIDON, PAUL; [ZAF]
LARSSON, MONICA; [SWE]
LARSSON, INGER; [SWE]
LARSSON, STIG; [SWE]
LASELVA, RITA DE CASSIA; [BRA]
LATORRE, ADRIANA; [ARG]
LAURINOLLI, TEUVO; [FIN]
LAVADO GOMEZ, IRENE; [ESP]
LAVARING, BRYANT; [AUS]
LAVEAULT, SERGE; [CAN]
LAW, CHIU - KEUNG; [TPI]
LAWRIE, CHRISTINE; [AUS]
LAZARNICK, SYLVIA; [USA]
LAZAROV, BORISLAV; [BGR]
LE CADRE, JEAN-YVES; [FRA]
LE ROUX, PATRICIA; [ZAF]
LEAL MARTIN, JOSE LUIS; [ESP]
LEBRE, ANA MARIA; [PRT]
LEBRON GALLARDO, TERESA; [ESP]
LEDER, GILAH; [AUS]
LEDESMA LOPEZ, ANTONIO; [ESP]
LEDESMA MUÑOZ-REDONDO, JOSE; [ESP]
LEE, BETH; [AUS]
LEE, YOUNG-SUK; [JAP]
LEE, PENG YEE; [SGP]
LEFEVRE MAIDEN, CHERYL; [GBR]
LEIKIN, ROZA; [ISR]
LEITAO ALEGRE, PAULA DE FATIMA; [PRT]
LEITE, OLIMPIO; [BRA]
LEITE VISSOTO, OLIMPIO RUDININ; [BRA]
LEIVA, MIRIAM; [USA]

LEIVA ENRIQUE, EVA ANGELICA; [PAR]
LEON CORREDOR, OLGA LUCIA; [COL]
LEON GOMEZ, NELLY; [VEN]
LEON MELENDEZ, RAFAEL; [ESP]
LEON VELASCO, Mª INMACULADA; [ESP]
LEONOVA, GALINA; [UKR]
LERMAN, STEPHEN; [GBR]
LESH, RICHARD; [USA]
LEU, YUH - CHYN; [TPI]
LEUNG, SHUK-KWAN; CHIAYI - [CHN]
LEUNG, FREDERICK K.S.; [HKG]
LEVENBERG, ILANA; [ISR]
LEVIN, ZIVA; [ISR]
LEVY, AZRIEL; [ISR]
LI, YUWEN; [CHN]
LI XUN, LI XUN; [CHN]
LIDEN, FOLKE; [SWE]
LIDEN, KERSTIN; [SWE]
LIM, PENG SEAH; [MYS]
LIM, CHAP SAM; [MYS]
LIMA MONTENEGRA, SYLVIA; [CUB]
LIMPRASIRT, URAIPRON; [THA]
LIN, FOU - LAI; [TPI]
LINARES ARANDA, MANUELA; [ESP]
LINCHEVSKI, LIORA; [ISR]
LINDBERG, LISBETH; [SWE]
LINDEN, NORA; [NOR]
LINDENSKOV, LENA; [DNK]
LINDGREN, M.I. SINIKKA; [FIN]
LINDQUIST, MARY; [USA]
LINDSAY, VICTORIA; [USA]
LINDSTROM, JAN-OLOF; [SWE]
LING, SIU - HING; [HKG]
LING, JOSEPH; [CAN]
LINGEFJARD, THOMAS; [SWE]
LINS CONCEIÇAO, SHIRLEI; [BRA]
LINUWIH, SUSANTI; [INS]
LIPSON, KAY; [AUS]
LIRA DE CARLOROSI, GRACIELA; [ARG]
LIRES RODRIGUEZ, Mª LUISA; [ESP]
LISSONI, ANGELO; [ITA]
LITHNER, JOHAN; [SWE]
LIU, YIZHU; [CHN]

LIU, ANDY; [CAN]
LIZARAZO, CARLOS WILSON; [COL]
LO CICERO, ANA M.; [USA]
LOBO GARCIA, BELEN; [ESP]
LOFSTRAND, BENGT; [SWE]
LOIACONO, STELLA MARY; [ARG]
LONG, MADELEINE; [USA]
LOPES, ANTONIO JOSE; [BRA]
LOPES DE OLIVEIRA, ROSALBA; [BRA]
LOPEZ, BLANCA SILVIA; [ARG]
LOPEZ, PAULINE G; [USA]
LOPEZ BRITO, Mª BELEN; [ESP]
LOPEZ DE LOBATTI, IVETTE CELIA; [PAR]
LOPEZ ESTEBAN, Mª DEL CARMEN; [ESP]
LOPEZ FERNANDEZ, JORGE M; [PRI]
LOPEZ GARCIA, Mª LUZ; [ESP]
LOPEZ GOMEZ, ADOLFO; [ESP]
LOPEZ GUERRERO, MIGUEL ANGEL; [ESP]
LOPEZ HERNANDEZ, ANGELES; [ESP]
LOPEZ LOPEZ, JOSE; [ESP]
LOPEZ MARTIN, ESTEBAN; [ESP]
LOPEZ MOJARRO, MIGUEL; [ESP]
LOPEZ MONZON, MARIA; [ESP]
LOPEZ PEREZ, MARCELA; [ESP]
LOPEZ RODRIGUEZ, ALBERTO; [ESP]
LOPEZ SOLIGO, NATIVIDAD; [ESP]
LOPEZ SUTIL, Mª CARMEN; [ESP]
LOPEZ VIZCAINO, Mª ESTHER; [ESP]
LOPIZ CANTO, PEDRO; [ESP]
LÖRCHER, GUSTAV ADOLF; [DEU]
LORELEY PION, LAURA; [URY]
LORENZ, DAN; [ISR]
LORENZ, JENS HOLGER; [DEU]
LORENZO, MARCELO DANIEL; [ARG]
LORY COSTA, Mª JOSEFA; [PRT]
LOSADA RODRIGUEZ, MARGARITA; [ESP]
LOTTERING, MARJORIE; [ZAF]
LOUREIRO, Mª CRISTINA; [PRT]
LOURO ALMEIDA PIRES, FERNADO A.; [PRT]
LOVE, ERIC; [GBR]
LÖWING, MADELEINE; [SWE]
LOZANO FERNANDEZ, LUIS M.; [ESP]
LOZANO LOZANO, MATILDE Mª; [ESP]

LOZANO MORENO, CHARO; [ESP]
LUCAS, JOHN; [USA]
LUCERO FIGUEROA, MAGDALENA; [SAL]
LUCIA T. A. DE AZEVEDO, REGINA; [BRA]
LUE, YUANG - TSWONG; [TPI]
LUEDEMAN, JOHN; [USA]
LUELMO VERDU, Mª JESUS; [ESP]
LUENGO GONZALEZ, RICARDO; [ESP]
LUKACS, JUDIT; [HUN]
LUNA, EDUARDO; [USA]
LUNA, CHARITA; [PHI]
LUNA OCHOA, SELENE GUADALUP; [MEX]
LUNA ROMERO, MARISA; [ESP]
LUTKUS, ALEX; [BRA]
LUZ, NATIVIDADE; [PRT]
LYNESS, PAUL; [USA]
LYNGYUAN, GU; [CHN]
LYONS, JERRY; [USA]
LLINARES CISCAR, SALVADOR; [ESP]
LLORENS FUSTER, JOSE LUIS; [ESP]
LLORO LONGAS, Mª JESUS; [ESP]
LLOVET VERDUGO, JUAN; [ESP]
LLUELMA LAYNEZ, ANTONIO; [ESP]
MACGREGOR, MOLLIE; [AUS]
MACIAS GIL, CRISTOBAL; [ESP]
MACIAS GONZALEZ, TOMAS; [ESP]
MACIAS RIVERO, JUAN PABLO; [ESP]
MACINTYRE, THOMAS; [GBR]
MACINTYRE, CAROLE; [GBR]
MACKIE, DIANA; [GBR]
MACNAMARA, ANN; [GBR]
MACHADO RIBEIRO, Mª DO ROSARIO; [PRT]
MACHIDA, SHOICHIRO; [JAP]
MADAN, V.D.; [IND]
MADDALOSSO, MIRELLA; [ITA]
MADROÑERO DE LA CAL, ADELA; [ESP]
MADRUGA, Mª DO ROSARIO; [PRT]
MAGDALENA LOPEZ, PILAR; [ESP]
MAGINA, SANDRA MARIA; [BRA]
MAGNUSSON JUNIOR, MARIO; [BRA]
MAHER, CAROLYN; [USA]
MAKINEN, JUKKA; [FIN]
MALARA, NICOLINA; [ITA]

MALATTO TORRES, MªANGELICA; [CHL]
MALKEVITCH, JOSEPH; [USA]
MALONE, JOHN; [AUS]
MALVEIRA ALVES, LINALDO; [BRA]
MALVITANO, NELIDA B.; [ARG]
MAMMANA, CARMELO; [ITA]
MANCERA MARTINEZ, EDUARDO; [MEX]
MANDLY MANSO, ARTURO; [ESP]
MANEEROD, RUTSAMEE; [THA]
MANGUBAT, THELMA M.; [BRN]
MANN, GIORA; [ISR]
MANSFIELD, HELEN; [USA]
MANSILLA, CARLOS ALBERTO; [ARG]
MANTIS, ADRIANA AZUCENA; [ARG]
MANZANO RODRIGUEZ, ANTONIO; [ESP]
MARAFIOTI GARNICA, ANTONIO; [BRA]
MARCANO COELLO, GISELA; [VEN]
MARCOS GARCIA, ANDRES; [ESP]
MARCHETTI, STELLA MARIS; [ARG]
MARIJUAN REBOLLO, Mª ANGELES; [ESP]
MARIM, VLADEMIR; [BRA]
MARIN DEL MORAL, ANTONIO; [ESP]
MARIN RODRIGUEZ, MARGARITA; [ESP]
MARQUEZ GARCIA, Mª CARMEN; [ESP]
MARR, BETH; [AUS]
MARRERO DEL TORO, DANIEL; [ESP]
MARROQUIN, JOSE FRANCISCO; [SAL]
MARSHALL, DAVID; [USA]
MARTIN, PETER; [AUS]
MARTIN, DAVID; [AUS]
MARTIN ADRIAN, ANTONIO RAMON; [ESP]
MARTIN CASALDERREY, FRANCISCO; [ITA]
MARTIN DIANA, ALEJANDRO; [ESP]
MARTIN FERNANDEZ, MANUEL; [ESP]
MARTIN MARTIN, ALICIA; [ESP]
MARTIN OLALLA, GONZALO; [ESP]
MARTIN OLALLA, EMILIO; [ESP]
MARTIN SANCHEZ, MARIA ESTHER; [ARG]
MARTIN STICKLE, MIGUEL; [ESP]
MARTIN STICKLE, ANTONIO; [ESP]
MARTIN YAGÜEZ, Mª DEL CARMEN; [ESP]
MARTINEZ, HUGO; [ESP]
MARTINEZ, ELISEO; [CHL]

MARTINEZ, MARIANO; [ESP]
MARTINEZ CASADO, RAFAEL; [ESP]
MARTINEZ DEL VALLE, FATIMA; [ESP]
MARTINEZ DIAZ, MANUEL; [ESP]
MARTINEZ FERNANDEZ, PEDRO JOSE; [ESP]
MARTINEZ GONZALEZ, ROCIO; [ESP]
MARTINEZ LUACES, VICTOR; [URY]
MARTINEZ MENENDEZ, AGUSTIN; [ESP]
MARTINEZ MORENO, JOSEFINA; [ESP]
MARTINEZ NAVAS, PILAR; [ESP]
MARTINEZ PEDREÑO, AGUSTIN; [ESP]
MARTINEZ PEÑA, PILAR; [ESP]
MARTINEZ PUNZANO, GREGORIO; [ESP]
MARTINEZ RECIO, ANGEL; [ESP]
MARTINEZ RESINO, Mª ROSA; [ESP]
MARTINEZ SANCHEZ, Mª ANGELES; [ESP]
MARTINEZ SARRASAGUE, MARIA I.; [ARG]
MARTINEZ TAVORA, MACARENA; [ESP]
MARTINEZ TELLEZ, MARIA; [MEX]
MARTINEZ TORRES, FCO. JAVIER; [ESP]
MARTINI, BERTA; [ITA]
MARTINON CEJAS, ANTONIO; [ESP]
MARTINS, MARIA PAZ; [PRT]
MARTINS PAIVA, SUZANA; [BRA]
MARTIN-CHARLEBOIS, HELENE; [CAN]
MARYUKOV, MICHAEL; [RUS]
MASCARELLO, MARIA; [ITA]
MASINGILA, JOANNA; [USA]
MASON, JOHN; [GBR]
MASSOT, CHRISTIAN; [FRA]
MASTUCCI, SILVANA NOEMI; [ARG]
MASUDA, MIKIO; [JAP]
MATESANZ FRANCH, PURIFICACION; [ESP]
MATHEWS, DAVID; [USA]
MATHISON, GRANT; [GBR]
MATO GALBARRO, JOSE JAVIER; [ESP]
MATOS, JOAO FILIPE; [PRT]
MATOS, JOSE MANUEL; [PRT]
MATOS G.S. DELFIM, Mª LUISA; [PRT]
MATSUMOTO, SEIICHI; [JAP]
MATSUMOTO, SHIGEKI; [JAP]
MATSUMURA, TORU; [JAP]
MATSUO, NANAE; [JAP]

MATSUZAWA, MASAO; [JAP]
MATTHEWS, LYNNELL; [USA]
MATTO MUZANTE, MAURO ENRIQUE; [PER]
MATUTE AZPILLAGA, Mª MAGDALENA; [ESP]
MAULE FERNANDES, SILVIA ELIZABET; [BRA]
MAURICIO CAZORLA, IRENE; [BRA]
MAYES, ROBERT; [USA]
MAYOBRE ANTON, JOSE LUIS; [ESP]
MAYS, MARILYN; [USA]
MAZA GOMEZ, CARLOS; [ESP]
MBOKAZI, ZAKHELE; [ZAF]
MBOYIYA, THANDI; [ZAF]
MCARTHUR, A. GREIG; [AUS]
MCBRIDE, MAGGIE; [USA]
MCCLELLAN, LYNETTE; [USA]
MCGRATTAN, PETER; [IRL]
MCINTOSH, ALISTAIR; [AUS]
MCLAREN, DAVID; [GBR]
MCLOUGHLIN, ANN ISABEL; [GBR]
MEAVILLA SEGUI, VICENTE; [ESP]
MEDELLIN HERNANDEZ, HECTOR; [MEX]
MEDGHALCHI, ALIREZA; [IRN]
MEDINA RODRIGUEZ, CECILIA; [ESP]
MEEDER, MARJA; [NLD]
MEFFERT, C.WILFRIED.M.; [NLD]
MEIRA, LUCIANO; [BRA]
MEISSNER, HARTWIG; [DEU]
MEKHMANDAROV, IBBY; [ISR]
MELCER, ELSA; [ARG]
MELENDRERAS PELAEZ, MARCELINO; [ESP]
MELGAR PINTO, LUIS ALBERTO; [PER]
MELROSE, JEAN; [GBR]
MEL'NYK, TARAS; [UKR]
MELLEMA, WILBUR; [USA]
MELLO, REGINA SONIA; [BRA]
MENCHIK, NOAMI; [ISR]
MENDES MOREIRA GOULART, JUSSARA; [BRA]
MENDEZ GUTIERREZ, Mª JESUS; [ESP]
MENDEZ HERRERA, Mª DEL MAR; [ESP]
MENDOÇA DOMITE, MARIA DO CARMO; [BRA]
MENDORI, TOSHIHIKO; [JAP]
MENDOZA DIANEZ, MARAVILLA; [ESP]
MENESES RAMOS, ROLANDO; [MEX]

MENGHINI, MARTA; [ITA]
MENIZ SANCHEZ, ISABEL; [ESP]
MENNE, JULIE; [NLD]
MENON, RAMAKRISHNAN; [SGP]
MERCIER, ARMEL; [CAN]
MERMELSTEIN, EGON; [USA]
MESA NARVAEZ, VILMA MARIA; [USA]
MESQUITA, ANA; [FRA]
MEVARECH, ZEMIRA; [ISR]
MEWBORN, DENISE; [USA]
MEYER, MEHL; [ZAF]
MEYER, JOERG; [DEU]
MEYLER, MARGARET; [AUS]
MICHEL-PAJUS, ANNIE; [FRA]
MIGUEL, ANTONIO; [BRA]
MIKOLAJCZYK, MALGORZATA; [POL]
MILTON, KEN; [AUS]
MILLAR, MICHAEL; [USA]
MILLER, JOE; [GBR]
MILLER, DAVID; [GBR]
MILLER-REILLY, BARBARA; [NZL]
MILLETT, ALISON; [GBR]
MINATO, SABURO; [JAP]
MING, HE; [CHN]
MIÑANO RUBIO, RAFAEL; [ESP]
MIQUEL BERTRAN, ESTER; [ESP]
MIRALLES VALLBONA, ANNA; [ESP]
MIRANDA DIAZ, ISABEL; [ESP]
MIRELES, MIRIAM; [VEN]
MIRO IBARS, EMMA; [PAR]
MISO SANCHEZ, BEATRIZ; [ESP]
MISROLE, GLORIA; [ZAF]
MITCHEL, PETER; [GBR]
MITCHELMORE, MICHAEL; [AUS]
MITSUMA, YOSHIE; [JAP]
MITTELBERG, DAVID; [ISR]
MIYAKAWA, ATSUKO; [JAP]
MIZOGUCHI, TATSUYA; [JAP]
MIZZAU DE GARCIA, ELIZABETH; [ARG]
MKHONTA, SIBUSISO SAMUEL; [SWZ]
MOELLER, REGINA; [DEU]
MOFFAT, JENNIFER; [GBR]
MOGENSEN, ARNE; [DNK]

MOGI, ISAMU; [JAP]
MOHAN-RAM, VIVEKANAND; [AUS]
MOK, AH-CHEE IDA; [GBR]
MOLANO ROMERO, ANTONIO; [ESP]
MOLERO LUQUE, ALICIA; [ESP]
MOLINA CARRION, ENRIQUE; [ESP]
MOLINA PEREZ, ROQUE; [ESP]
MOLINA SANCHEZ, ISABEL MARIA; [ESP]
MOLNA'R, JOSEF; [CZR]
MOLYNEUX, SUSAN; [GBR]
MOLLA PINO, ALFREDO; [ESP]
MOLLEDA SANCHEZ, LAURA; [ESP]
MOLLEHED, EBBE; [SWE]
MOLLER, HERBERT; [DEU]
MOMPO I SIRVENT, ARIEL; [ESP]
MONAGHAN, JOHN; [GBR]
MONCADA ANDINO, CLARA REGINA; [HON]
MONCECCHI, GIANFRANCO; [ITA]
MONCHO PELLICER, ALFRED; [ESP]
MONSERRAT BORDES, MONICA; [ESP]
MONTANO MIDENCE, ROBERTO; [GTM]
MONTANUY FILLAT, MANUEL; [ESP]
MONTERO, PATRICIO; [CHL]
MONTERO CAMPUZANO, RAFAEL; [ESP]
MONTERRUBIO PEREZ, CONSUELO; [ESP]
MONTESINOS SIRERA, JOSE LUIS; [ESP]
MONTILLA DIAZ, JOSE ENRIQUE; [ESP]
MONZO DEL OLMO, ONOFRE; [ESP]
MOORE, DAVID S.; [USA]
MORA ESPEJO, Mª LUISA; [ESP]
MORA MUÑOZ, LUISA; [ESP]
MORA SANCHEZ, JOSE ANTONIO; [ESP]
MORAIS, TULA MARIA; [BRA]
MORALES FIGUEROA, BERNARDO; [GTM]
MORALES GONZALEZ, AGUSTIN; [ESP]
MORALES HARO, FRANCISCO; [ESP]
MORALES RODRIGUEZ, Mª SOLEDAD; [ESP]
MORANGE, GEORGES; [FRA]
MORANTE CALDERON, JORGE EDUARDO; [PER]
MORAR, NIRUPA; [ZAF]
MORATALLA ESTEVE, FRANCISCO; [ESP]
MORBELLO, GIANPIERO; [ITA]
MORCILLO DELGADO, NICOLAS; [ESP]

MOREIRA, LEONOR; [PRT]
MOREIRA TRINDADE, DENISE; [BRA]
MORENO CARRETERO, MªFRANCISCA; [ESP]
MORENO FERNANDEZ, MARIA DEL MAR; [ESP]
MORENO GOMEZ, PILAR; [ESP]
MORENO GONZALEZ, Mª AUXILIADORA; [ESP]
MORENO INFANTE, IGNACIO; [ESP]
MORENO LOPEZ, DOLORES; [ESP]
MORENO LORENTE, MARIA JOSE; [ESP]
MORENO MARQUEZ, MATILDE; [ESP]
MORENO MARTEL, CARMEN OLGA; [ESP]
MORENO MARTEL, Mª DOLORES; [ESP]
MORENO MORENO, MARIA DEL MAR; [ESP]
MORENO PEREZ, ROBLEDO; [ESP]
MORENO SANCHEZ, BERNARDA; [ESP]
MORENO TERNERO, JUAN DE DIOS; [ESP]
MORENO VERDEJO, ANTONIO; [ESP]
MORETTO, VASCO PEDRO; [BRA]
MORIENA DE MANNARINO, SUSANA; [ARG]
MORIKAWA, IKUTARO; [JAP]
MORILLA SOUSA, DIEGO; [ESP]
MORILLO GORDILLO, Mª CARMEN; [ESP]
MORIMOTO, AKIRA; [JAP]
MORIN, HELENA; [PRT]
MORLAND-KALININA, TATJANA; [NLD]
MORLEY, STEPHEN; [GBR]
MORO GONZALEZ, OLGA; [ESP]
MORONY, WILL; [AUS]
MORROW, LORNA; [CAN]
MOSCOSO FRANCO, ANA MARIA; [ESP]
MOSCHKOVICH, JUDIT; [USA]
MOSIMEGE, MOGEGE DAVID; [ZAF]
MOSQUERA, JULIO; [VEN]
MOTOYA, YOSHIKO; [JAP]
MOUNTWITTEN, MALCA; [ISR]
MOURA ESTEVES, ANABELA; [PRT]
MOUSLEY, JUDITH ANNE; [AUS]
MOVSHOVITZ-HADAR, NITSA; [ISR]
MOYA, Mª MERCEDES; [ARG]
MOYA MOLINA, GABRIEL; [ESP]
MUKHERJEE, ARUDHATI; [IND]
MUKHOPADHYAY, SWAPNA; [USA]
MULGREW, MADELEINE; [USA]

MULLER, ERIC; [CAN]
MULLIGAN, JOANNE; [AUS]
MUNN, PENELOPE; [GBR]
MUNRO, JOHN E.M.; [AUS]
MUNSHIN, SARA; [USA]
MUNTER, JACOB; [NOR]
MUNTHER, ROLAND; [SWE]
MUÑIZ MENDIONDO, JOSE LUIS; [URY]
MUÑOZ ALMARAZ, FCO.JAVIER; [ESP]
MUÑOZ CANO, FRANCISCO JESUS; [ESP]
MUÑOZ DELGADO, FCO JAVIER; [ESP]
MUÑOZ FONSECA, JULIO FERNANDO; [ESP]
MUÑOZ SANTONJA, JOSE; [ESP]
MUÑOZ VELASCO, EMILIO JOSE; [ESP]
MUÑOZ VELASCO, EMILIO J.; [ESP]
MURAKAMI, HARUO; [JAP]
MURILLO GALAN, ANA MARIA; [ESP]
MURPHY, CATHERINE; [USA]
MUSIKARAK, PANNEE; [THA]
MUYOR PIÑERO, Mª DOLORES; [ESP]
MCCABE, JOHN; [GBR]
MCCLAIN, KAY; [USA]
MCCLEW, EDWARD; [USA]
MCCLURE, JAN; [AUS]
MCDOUGALL, DOUGLAS; [CAN]
MCGOWEN, MERCEDES; [USA]
MCLEOD, DOUGLAS; [USA]
MCMURCHY - PILKINGTON, COLLEEN; [NZL]
NAATANEN, MARJATTA; [FIN]
NABORS, WANDA; [USA]
NAGAI, TSUNEO; [UAE]
NAGANO, AZUMA; [JAP]
NAGATA, CHIGUSA; [JAP]
NAGY, MARGARETHA; [HUN]
NAIDOO, KERSERI; [ZAF]
NAKAHARA, TADAO; [JAP]
NAKAMURA, MICHIMASA; [JAP]
NAKAMURA, YOSHIO; [JAP]
NAMIKAWA, YUKIHIKO; [JAP]
NASSER, LILIAN; [BRA]
NATSOULAS, ANTHULA; [USA]
NAVA MONTES, FREDEFINDA; [VEN]
NAVARRA, GIANCARLO; [ITA]

NAVARRETE CUADRA, CRISTOBAL; [ESP]
NAVARRO DE MENDICUTI, TERESA; [MEX]
NAVARRO OLMO, ROSA MARIA; [ESP]
NAVARRO PEINADO, LADISLAO; [ESP]
NAVARRO RAMIREZ, ISABEL; [ESP]
NAVAS ALABARCE, FCO. JOSE; [ESP]
NAVOZ RUBIO, MARIA ROSARIO; [ESP]
NAWROCKI, JAN; [POL]
NDABA, LESLIE; [GBR]
NEAGOY, MONICA M.; [USA]
NEBREDA, V.FEDERICO; [ARG]
NEBRES, BIENVENIDO; [PHI]
NEGHISHI, HIDE; [JAP]
NEMETZ, TIBOR; [HUN]
NESHER, PEARLA; [ISR]
NET, GABRIELA P.; [ARG]
NEUBRAND, MICHEAL; [DEU]
NEUBRAND, JOHANNA; [DEU]
NEUMAN, DAGMAR; [SWE]
NEVES, PAULO; [BRA]
NGUYEN, DINH TRI; [VNM]
NIANGO, NIANGO DONATIEN; [CIV]
NICAUD, JEAN-FRANCOIS; [FRA]
NICKSON, MARILYN; [GBR]
NICHOLS, ROSALIE; [USA]
NICHOLSON, JAMES; [IRL]
NIEHAUS, JANSIE; [ZAF]
NIELSEN, LENE; [DNK]
NIETO BACO, SUSANA; [ESP]
NIETO HIDALGO, ESPERANZA MAC.; [ESP]
NIETO NIETO, PEDRO; [ESP]
NIEWALD, JOHN; [GBR]
NINA DE FARIA MARTINS, Mª CARLOTA; [PRT]
NING, TZYH-CHIANG; MINGSHONG - [CHN]
NIQUINI, HELTON; [BRA]
NISBET, STEVENS; [AUS]
NISHIMOTO, TOSHIHIKO; [JAP]
NISHIMOTO, KOOE; [JAP]
NISHIMOTO, YUKIE; [JAP]
NISHINE, TAKANORI; [JAP]
NISHITANI, IZUMI; [JAP]
NISHIUCHI, HISANORI; [JAP]
NISS, MOGENS; [DNK]

NOBUHIKO, NOHDA; [JAP]
NOMACHI, TADASHI; [JAP]
NOMDEDEU MORENO, ROSARIO; [ESP]
NOMEN XATRUCH, MISERICORDIA; [ESP]
NORWOOD, KAREN; [USA]
NOSS, RICHARD; [GBR]
NOTESTINE, RONALD; [JAP]
NOTTOLI, HERNAN SANTIAGO; [ARG]
NOVOTNA, JARMILA; [CZR]
NOWAKOWSKA, AGNIESZKA; [POL]
NTULI, MIKE; [ZAF]
NULTY, BRUCE; [AUS]
NUNES, TEREZINHA; [GBR]
NUÑEZ, ADOLFO; [USA]
NUÑEZ, MIRIAM DANIELA; [ARG]
NUÑEZ CASTAIN, ANGELA; [ESP]
NUÑEZ PAÑOS, CARMEN; [ESP]
NUÑEZ VALDES, JUAN; [ESP]
NYGAARD, JETTE OVESEN; [DNK]
NYSTROM, PETER; [SWE]
OBANDO ZAPATA, GILBERTO JESUS; [COL]
OBERMAN, JOHN; [ISR]
OCAÑA ESCOLAR, LUIS; [ESP]
OCEJO VALENCIA, TULIO; [PER]
OGAYAR MORAL, CIPRIANO; [ESP]
OHSAWA, HIRONORI; [JAP]
OHTAKE, NOBORU; [JAP]
OHTANI, MINORU; [JAP]
OJEDA GARCIA, JUAN; [ESP]
OJEDA MARTINEZ DE CASTILLA, IGNACIO; [ESP]
OJEDA VIZCAINO, MANUEL; [ESP]
OKABE, TSUNEHARU; [JAP]
OKUNO, HIROSHI; [JAP]
OLAH, VERA; [HUN]
OLAYA BENITES, MARIA ELENA; [IRL]
OLDHAM, ELISABETH; [IRL]
OLIVE, JOHN; [USA]
OLIVEIRA, HELIA MARGARIDA; [PRT]
OLIVEIRA, FATIMA REGINA; [BRA]
OLIVEIRA, SILVIA DE LIMA; [BRA]
OLIVEIRA BRITO B. MARTINS, ANA C.; [PRT]
OLIVEIRA CUNHA, Mª HELENA; [PRT]
OLIVEIRA DA SILVA, MARILENE; [BRA]

Oliveira e Cunha, Maria Helena; [PRT]
Oliveira Pereira, Candida Mª; [PRT]
Oliveras Contreras, Mª Luisa; [ESP]
Olivetto, Beatriz Susana; [ARG]
Olivier, Yves; [FRA]
Olivier, Alwin; [ZAF]
Olmo Jimenez, Mª Jose; [ESP]
Olmo Olmo, Manuel; [ESP]
Olmos Sabater, Amparo; [ESP]
Olofsson, Bo; [SWE]
Olofsson, Gunilla; [SWE]
Olofsson, Hans; [GBR]
Olssen, Kevin; [AUS]
Olssen, Helen; [AUS]
Oltra Ortuño, Dolores; [ESP]
Ong, Lay Gek; [SGP]
Onyango-Otieno, Vitalis P.; [KEN]
Ordoñez Cañada, Lourdes; [ESP]
Ordoñez Vargas, Jose D; [ESP]
Orellana, Ines; [VEN]
Orellana Chacin, Mauricio; [VEN]
Oria De Chouhy Aguirre, Mª M.; [ARG]
Oropesa, Leticia; [USA]
Orsega, Emilio F.; [ITA]
Ortega Del Rincon, Tomas; [ESP]
Ortega Gutierrez, Manuel; [ESP]
Ortega Lopez, Rodrigo; [ESP]
Ortega Millan, Concepcion; [ESP]
Ortega Moya, Juan; [ESP]
Ortega Sanchez, Belen; [ESP]
Ortego Rojo, Mª Del Mar; [ESP]
Ortiz Capilla, Mª Angeles; [ESP]
Ortiz De Haro, Juan Jesus; [ESP]
Ortiz De Trangoni, Ana Maria; [ARG]
Ortiz Montoya, Antonia Maria; [ESP]
Ortiz Rios, Monica; [ESP]
Ortiz Vallejo, Maria; [ESP]
Ortiz-Franco, Luis; [USA]
Osburg, Thomas; [DEU]
Oshrat, Dafna; [ISR]
Osimo, Guido; [ITA]
Otarola Valdivieso, Victoria Y.; [PER]
Otarola Valdivieso, Flor; [PER]

Oteiza Morra, Fidel; [CHL]
Otero Baamonde, Anton; [ESP]
Otero Mazoy, Carmen; [ESP]
Otsuka, Kenichi; [JAP]
Otsuka, Kayo; [JAP]
Ould Jidomou, Ahmedou; [MAU]
Outhred, Lynne; [AUS]
Outon Ruiz, Jose Manuel; [ESP]
Ovelar De Smith, Maria Stela; [PAR]
Owa, Sumio; [JAP]
Owens, Kay; [SWE]
Oyaneder Soto, Ana Mª; [CHL]
Oyon Aguado, Nieves; [ESP]
Ozejo Valencia, Tulio Antonio; [PER]
O'Brien, Thomas; [USA]
O'Donoghue, John; [IRL]
O'Neal, Judy; [USA]
O'Reilly, Declan; [GBR]
Paasonen, Johannes; [FIN]
Pacios, Amabile; [BRA]
Pacheco Rios, Oscar; [BOL]
Padron Chao, Ricardo; [ESP]
Paes, Francisca Mª; [BRA]
Paez Jimenez, Raul; [ESP]
Pagon, Dusan; [SLN]
Painchaud, Caroline; [CAN]
Paiva, MªAuxiliadora V; [BRA]
Palacian Gil, Emilio; [ESP]
Palacios De Burgos, Mª Jesus; [ESP]
Palarea Medina, Mª Mercedes; [ESP]
Palm, Torulf; [SWE]
Palomares Alvariño, Luis; [PER]
Pallascio, Richard; [CAN]
Panchishchina, Valentina; [RUS]
Pantozzi, Ralph; [USA]
Paola, Domingo; [ITA]
Papastavridis, Stavros; [GRC]
Papay De Alonso, Stella Maris; [ARG]
Paralera Morales, Concepcion; [ESP]
Pareja, Silvia; [ARG]
Park, Kyungmee; [KOR]
Park, Han-Shick; [KOR]
Parker, Bill; [USA]

Parnizari Espasandin, Rosina; [URY]
Parra Sandoval, Hugo Enrique; [VEN]
Parsons, Anthony; [GBR]
Parsons, Victor; [GBR]
Parzysz, Bernard; [FRA]
Pasadas Rodriguez, Mª Encarnacion; [ESP]
Pascual, Pedro Luis; [ARG]
Pascual Acosta, Antonio; [ESP]
Pascual Bonis, Jose Ramon; [ESP]
Pastor Grueso, Mª Mercedes; [ESP]
Pateman, Neil; [USA]
Patkin, Dorit; [ISR]
Paul Escolano, Pedro Jose; [ESP]
Paz Samudio, Alfonso; [COL]
Pazo Muñoz, Eugenia; [ESP]
Pazos Crespo, Manuel Ricardo; [ESP]
Pead, Daniel; [GBR]
Peard, Robert; [AUS]
Pearn, Catherine; [AUS]
Peatfield, John David; [GBR]
Pecal, Michele; [FRA]
Pedregal Mateos, Mª Angeles; [ESP]
Pedreira Mengotti, Alicia; [ESP]
Peerboom, Eugenie; [AUS]
Pegg, John; [AUS]
Pehkonen, Erkki; [FIN]
Pekelharing, Mark; [GBR]
Pelaez Garcia, Rosa Mª; [ESP]
Peled, Irit; [ISR]
Pellerey, Michele; [ITA]
Penalva Martinez, Mª Carmen; [ESP]
Pence, Barbara; [USA]
Pengelly, Helen; [AUS]
Penn, Doreen Margaret; [GBR]
Penteado Silva, Miriam; [BRA]
Peñalver Lopez, Monica; [ESP]
Perales Rodriguez, Manuel; [ESP]
Pereira, Maria Da Graça; [BRA]
Pereira Figueroa, Jose; [ESP]
Pereira Figueroa, Dolores; [ESP]
Pereira Lopes, Valdemar; [BRA]
Perelberg, Liberman; [BRA]
Perelli, Mariapia; [ITA]

Perero, Mariano; [USA]
Perez Bernal, Luis; [ESP]
Perez Coronel, Tomas; [ESP]
Perez Cuenca, Pascual; [ESP]
Perez Fernandez, Fco Javier; [ESP]
Perez Jimenez, Antonio; [ESP]
Perez Lopez, Mª Trinidad; [ESP]
Perez Lorenzo, Ana; [ESP]
Perez Marquez, Agustin; [ESP]
Perez Martinez, Mª Felisa; [ESP]
Perez Morilla, Carmen; [ESP]
Perez Olivan, Mª Jesus; [ESP]
Perez Ortoneda, Melchor; [ESP]
Perez Peña, Alejandro; [ESP]
Perez Perez, Jose Antonio; [ESP]
Perez Perez, Melquiades; [ESP]
Perez Vazquez, MªDictinia; [ESP]
Perry, Mike; [USA]
Perry Carrasco, Patricia Ines; [COL]
Persson, Sven-Olov; [ESP]
Persson, Ingvar O.; [SWE]
Perz, Gottfried; [AUT]
Pesci, Angela; [ITA]
Pesonen, Martti E.; [FIN]
Pesonen, Silja; [FIN]
Peter, Andrea; [DEU]
Petit Vila, Maria; [ESP]
Petocz, Dubravka; [AUS]
Petocz, Peter; [AUS]
Phensuwaphap, Nuansee; [THA]
Phillips, Richard; [GBR]
Phillips, Eileen; [CAN]
Phillips, Brian; [AUS]
Phythian, Ted; [PNG]
Picard, Luc; [CAN]
Piceno Rivera, Juan Carlos; [MEX]
Picker, Susan; [USA]
Piedra Garcia, Mª Angeles; [ESP]
Piedras Martos, Mª Angustias; [ESP]
Pietrocola, Norma Cristina; [ARG]
Piloto, Olga Graciela; [ARG]
Pillay, Subasani; [ZAF]
Pimenta, Adelino Candido; [BRA]

PIMM, DAVID; [GBR]
PIND, PERNILLE; [DNK]
PINEDA NARVAEZ, DOLORES; [ESP]
PINEL, ADRIAN; [GBR]
PINILLA FERNANDEZ-CASTAÑON, Mª C.; [ESP]
PINTO DOS SANTOS, MADALENA; [PRT]
PINTO GONZALEZ, ALEJANDRO; [ESP]
PINTOR BERMUDEZ, MACARENA; [ESP]
PINTOS, ZULLY HAYDEE; [ARG]
PIRES, MANUELA; [PRT]
PIRIE, SUSAN; [CAN]
PIROLA, NELSON ANTONIO; [BRA]
PITTA, DEMETRA; [GBR]
PLASENCIA CRUZ, INES; [ESP]
PLATA CASAIS, AURORA; [ESP]
PLAZA MENENDEZ, PEDRO; [ESP]
POBLETE LETELIER, ALVARO; [CHL]
POLETTINI, ALTAIR F.F.; [BRA]
POLO GARCIA, BEATRIZ; [ESP]
POLLAK, HENRY O.; [USA]
POLLARD, GRAHAM; [AUS]
POMPEU JR., GERALDO; [BRA]
PONCE DE LEON, ADRIANA ROSA; [ARG]
PONCE DE LEON, JULIO ALEJANDRO; [ARG]
PONTE, JOAO PEDRO; [PRT]
PONZA, Mª VICTORIA; [ARG]
PORFIRIO, JOANA; [PRT]
PORRAS BOCANEGRA, FERMIN; [ESP]
PORRAS RUIZ, AGUEDA; [ESP]
PORTA DE BRESSAN, ANA MARIA; [ARG]
PORTEOUS, JOYCE; [GBR]
POSSAMAI RIBEIRO, ELIZETE MARIA; [BRA]
POTARI, DESPINA; [GRC]
POTIVICHAYANONT, KANJANA; [THA]
POULOS, ANDREAS; [GRC]
POURKAZEMI, MOHAMMAD HOSSEN; [IRN]
POVOA RAFAEL, Mª AMELIA; [PRT]
POWELL, BETH; [AUS]
POZO DURAN, FERNANDO JESUS; [ESP]
PRADO RIBEIRO, JOAQUIM F.; [BRA]
PRATT, DAVE; [GBR]
PREFUMO DE ACOSTA, NELLY; [ARG]
PRESMEG, NORMA; [USA]

PREZENS, MARJORIE; [ZAF]
PRICE, MIKE; [GBR]
PRICE, JACK; [USA]
PRICE, NIGEL; [GBR]
PRIETO ANDRES, ANGEL; [BRA]
PRIETO GONZALEZ, LEONISA; [ESP]
PRIETO GUTIERREZ, IGNACIO J.; [ESP]
PRIETO RODRIGUEZ, ALICIA; [ESP]
PRISTA, MARILIA; [PRT]
PROENZA GARRIDO, YOLANDA; [CUB]
PRUSAK, NAOMI; [ISR]
PUENTE CRESPO, MANUEL; [ESP]
PUERTA GARCIA, FRANCISCO; [ESP]
PUIG ALSINA, XAVIER; [ESP]
PUIG ESPINOSA, LUIS; [ESP]
PUIG GARCIA, JAUME; [ESP]
PUIG MOSQUERA, LUIS; [ESP]
PUIG PORTAL, JACINTO ELOY; [CUB]
PULIDO, RICARDO; [MEX]
PULIDO DEL RIO, JUAN ANTONIO; [ESP]
PUTKONEN, HELLEVI; [FIN]
QIU, ZONGHU; [CHN]
QUADROS DA SILVA, EDUARDO; [BRA]
QUEIROZ E SILVA COUTINHO, CILEDA; [BRA]
QUERALT LLOPIS, TOMAS; [ESP]
QUESADA, ANTONIO R.; [USA]
QUESADA MORENO, JOSE FRANCISCO; [ESP]
QUILEZ ROYO, EMILIO; [ESP]
QUINLAN, ELIZABETH; [CAN]
QUINN, MADGE; [UGA]
QUINTANA, JULIO; [PRI]
QUINTANA ALBALAT, JORDI; [ESP]
QUINTANA MONTESDEOCA, Mª DEL PINO; [ESP]
QUINTANILLA GONZALEZ, JULIETA; [BOL]
QUINTERO RIVERA, ANA HELVIA; [PRI]
QUIROS MARIN, ALBERTO; [ESP]
QUTUB, CAROL HOTELLING; [USA]
RABASCO RODRIGUEZ, MARGARITA; [ESP]
RADFORD, LUIS; [CAN]
RADNAI SZENDREI, JULIANNA; [HUN]
RAINHO, AVELINA; [PRT]
RAITZ, CESAR; [BRA]
RAKOV, SERGEY; [UKR]

Ralston, Anthony; [GBR]
Ramil Alvarez, Jose; [RUS]
Ramires Sapata, Elisabete; [BRA]
Ramirez, Betty; [PRI]
Ramirez Campos, Rosa Ana; [ESP]
Ramirez Fajardo, Maria; [ESP]
Ramirez Gonzalez, Victoriano; [ESP]
Ramirez Lopez, Francisco; [ESP]
Ramirez Maldonado, Cynthia A.; [PAR]
Ramirez Martin, Manuel Luis; [ESP]
Ramirez Olmedo, Elvira; [ESP]
Ramirez Pastor, Alicia; [ESP]
Ramos Gonzalez, R.Esther; [ESP]
Rampazo, Renata; [BRA]
Ramsden, Jenny; [GBR]
Ramsden, Philip; [GBR]
Randhawa, Bikkar; [CAN]
Randolph, Tamela; [USA]
Ransom, Peter; [GBR]
Rasmussen, Steve; [USA]
Raya Hidalgo, Lourdes; [ESP]
Rayo Leon, Herminio; [ESP]
Rebolo Varela, Ana Mª; [ESP]
Recalde, Luis Cornelio; [COL]
Recalde Caicedo, Luis Cornelio; [COL]
Recio Muñiz, Tomas; [ESP]
Rechimont De Gonzalez, Estela E.; [ARG]
Redondo Cruz, Araceli; [ESP]
Reguera Doblado, Maria Dolores; [ESP]
Reid, David; [CAN]
Reid, Gay; [AUS]
Reillo Palacios, Jose Manuel; [ESP]
Reilly, Ivan; [NZL]
Reina De Aguilar, Silvia Susana; [ARG]
Reinoso Valdivia, Raquel; [ESP]
Reis, Marcia Rita; [BRA]
Reis Mendonça, Adelaide; [BRA]
Reiter, Ashley; [USA]
Reiter, Harold; [USA]
Rejali, Ali; [IRN]
Remillieux, Marie-Claire; [FRA]
Rene De Cotret, Sophie; [CAN]
Repo, Sisko; [FIN]

Resek, Diane; [USA]
Resende Oliveira, MªFernanda; [PRT]
Retzer, Kenneth; [USA]
Revilla Martinez, Domingo; [ESP]
Reyes Colume, Pedro; [ESP]
Reyes Iglesias, Mª Encarnacion; [ESP]
Reynolds, Anne; [USA]
Ribeiro Da Fonseca, Ubaldo Luiz; [BRA]
Ribeiro Pola, Marie-Claire; [CAN]
Ribeiro Terra, Edmir; [BRA]
Rickey, Fred; [USA]
Rico Rodriguez, Carmen; [ESP]
Rico Romero, Luis; [ESP]
Richards, Ann; [AUS]
Richardson, Bill; [GBR]
Ridgway, Jim; [GBR]
Riehs, Robert; [USA]
Riemersma, Martinus; [NLD]
Riggio, Miguel Angel; [BOL]
Riley, Sheryl; [USA]
Rincon De Rojas, Felix; [ESP]
Rios Collantes De Teran, Ricardo; [ESP]
Rios Valledepaz, Javier; [VEN]
Rios Villar, Mª Celia; [ESP]
Riquelme Fernandez, Blanca; [PAR]
Risacher, Billie; [USA]
Riscos Fernandez, Agustin; [ESP]
Risnes, Martin; [NOR]
Risuenho, Valeria; [BRA]
Ritson, Rene; [IRL]
Rivera Reyes, Mario; [ESP]
Rivero Rodriguez, Alejandra; [ESP]
Rivero Toledo, Roberto Ramon; [ARG]
Roberts, Tamsin; [AUS]
Roberts, Gareth; [GBR]
Robertson, Isobel; [GBR]
Robinson, Derek; [GBR]
Robitaille, David; [CAN]
Rodas Garcete, Ramona F.; [PAR]
Roddier, Jean-Alain; [FRA]
Rodrigues, Ana Maria; [PRT]
Rodrigues, Margarida; [PRT]
Rodrigues, Luciana; [BRA]

Rodrigues Neto, Francisco Per.; [BRA]
Rodrigues Pereira, Ismael; [BRA]
Rodriguez, Luz Marina; [VEN]
Rodriguez, Norma Leonor; [ARG]
Rodriguez, Michel; [FRA]
Rodriguez Arevalo, Mercedes; [ESP]
Rodriguez Bellido, Maria Angeles; [ESP]
Rodriguez Benito, Eva; [ESP]
Rodriguez Biehn, Guillermo; [ESP]
Rodriguez Carreira, Maria-Luz; [ESP]
Rodriguez Cesar, Cristobal; [ESP]
Rodriguez Chamizo, Ana; [ESP]
Rodriguez Escobar, Manuel; [ESP]
Rodriguez Fernandez, Jose Luis; [ESP]
Rodriguez Gomez, David; [ESP]
Rodriguez Gonzalez, Miguel A.; [MEX]
Rodriguez Mato, Mª Dolores; [ESP]
Rodriguez Minarsky, Etda Luisa; [URY]
Rodriguez Nogueiras, Maria; [ESP]
Rodriguez Nuñez, Mª Carmen; [ESP]
Rodriguez Peña, Pilar; [ESP]
Rodriguez Perez, Jose Antonio; [ESP]
Rodriguez Rava, Beatriz; [URY]
Rodriguez Rita, Francisco A.; [ESP]
Rodriguez Rodriguez, Mª Carmen; [ESP]
Rodriguez Rodriguez, Jose; [ESP]
Rodriguez Rufo, Pedro Antonio; [ESP]
Rodriguez Soalleiro, MªDolores; [ESP]
Rodriguez Suarez, MºDel Pilar; [ESP]
Rodriguez Teijeiro, Mª Carmen; [ESP]
Rodriguez Vitoria, Ana Maria; [URY]
Rodriguez-Moldes Rey, Covadonga; [ESP]
Rogers, Leo; [GBR]
Rojas, Silvia Aurora; [ARG]
Rojas Dominguez, Marta Beatriz; [PAR]
Rojas Garzon, Pedro Javier; [COL]
Rojas Pardillos, Pilar; [ESP]
Roj-Lindberg, Ann-Sofi; [FIN]
Roldan Castro, Ismael; [ESP]
Rolph, Cheryl; [USA]
Roman Campos, Javier; [ESP]
Romberg, Thomas; [USA]
Romero Bogado, Ignacia; [PAR]

Romero Infante, Jose Manuel; [ESP]
Romero Jimenez, Alvaro; [ESP]
Romero Lopez, Olalla; [ESP]
Romero Martin, Juana; [ESP]
Romero Palacios, Eulalia; [ESP]
Romero Rico, Montserrat; [ESP]
Romero Romero, Olivia De Jesus; [MEX]
Romero Rubio, Eduardo; [ESP]
Ron, Gila; [ISR]
Rondero Guerrero, Carlos; [MEX]
Rosado Rivas, Silvia; [ESP]
Rosanova, Svetlana A.; [RUS]
Rosas P.P. Da Costa, Maria Cecilia; [PRT]
Roscoe, Jorge Edgardo; [ARG]
Rosen, Linda P.; [USA]
Rosich Sala, Nuria; [ESP]
Rosier, Ronald; [USA]
Rosolen, Rosana; [BRA]
Rososhek, Semen; [RUS]
Rosov, Nicolas; [RUS]
Rossouw, Lynn; [ZAF]
Rouan, Omar; [MAR]
Rowlands, Stuart; [GBR]
Rubio Avello, Trinidad; [ESP]
Rubio Prieto, Alejandro; [ESP]
Ruddock, Graham; [GBR]
Rueda Perez, Sonia; [ESP]
Rui Fen, Tang; [CHN]
Ruibal Isla, Cristina; [ESP]
Ruiz, Mari-Jo P.; [PHI]
Ruiz Cervera, Antonio Manuel; [ESP]
Ruiz Garrido, Ceferino; [ESP]
Ruiz Higueras, Mª Luisa; [ESP]
Ruiz Lopez, Mª Pilar; [ESP]
Ruiz Ruiz, Mª Eugenia; [ESP]
Ruperez Padron, Jose Antonio; [ESP]
Ruthven, Kenneth; [GBR]
Ruttkay, Zsofia; [NLD]
Ruwisch, Silke; [DEU]
Ryder, Jane; [USA]
Saa Perez, Evaristo; [ESP]
Sacramento, Mercia Helena; [BRA]
Sachdev, Sohindar; [USA]

SADOLIN, VIGGO; [DNK]
SAEKI, AKIHIKO; [JAP]
SAEZ MARTINEZ, ALEJANDRO; [ESP]
SAFAK, NILGUN; [AUS]
SAFFORD, KATHERINE; [USA]
SAFUANOV, ILDAR; [RUS]
SAIF, KHAYRIA; [KWT]
SAIFULLAH, KHALID; [PAK]
SAINZ, MARIA INES; [ARG]
SAITO, MASAHIKO; [JAP]
SAKONIDIS, HARALAMBOS; [GRC]
SALAS ACOSTA, MARIA DOLORES; [ESP]
SALAS ALVAREZ, CARMELO; [ESP]
SALAS MARTINEZ, HUMBERTO; [MEX]
SALAZAR GALLARDO, FRANCISCO; [ESP]
SALCEDO MORALES, ALBERTO; [ESP]
SALERNO, ELISA; [ARG]
SALETT BIEMBENGUT, MARIA; [BRA]
SALINAS [PRT], Mª JESUS; [ESP]
SALINAS SERRANO, SILVIA Mª; [ESP]
SALMERON SANCHEZ, MARIANO; [ESP]
SALORT SERRA, LAURA; [ESP]
SALVADOR ALCAIDE, ADELA; [ESP]
SALVADOR DAROS, FRANCESC; [ESP]
SALVADOR MARIN, EVA MARIA; [ESP]
SAMPSON, CECIL; [ZAF]
SANCHEZ ALBALA, JULIAN; [ESP]
SANCHEZ ALEGRE, Mª LUZ; [ESP]
SANCHEZ BALLESTEROS, Mª DOLORES; [ESP]
SANCHEZ BALLESTEROS, ISABEL; [ESP]
SANCHEZ BORREGO, ISMAEL; [ESP]
SANCHEZ CATALAN, ANGEL; [ESP]
SANCHEZ CERRATO, LUIS; [ESP]
SANCHEZ COBO, FCO. TOMAS; [ESP]
SANCHEZ CHAPARRO, PILAR; [ESP]
SANCHEZ FERNANDEZ, JOSE; [ESP]
SANCHEZ FIGUEROA, DOMINGO; [ESP]
SANCHEZ GARCIA, VICTORIA; [ESP]
SANCHEZ GOMEZ, MERCEDES; [ESP]
SANCHEZ GOMEZ, CARMEN; [ESP]
SANCHEZ GRANDE, JOSE M.; [ESP]
SANCHEZ HEREDIA, NEILA; [COL]
SANCHEZ MARQUEZ, ANDRES; [ESP]

SANCHEZ MARTINEZ, Mª CARMEN; [ESP]
SANCHEZ MOLINA, JOSE MARIA; [ESP]
SANCHEZ NAVAS, RAMON; [ESP]
SANCHEZ NUÑEZ, MARIA HELVECIA; [URY]
SANCHEZ PALOMO, SONIA; [ESP]
SANCHEZ PESQUERO, CIPRIANO; [ESP]
SANCHEZ SEGOVIA, ANGELES; [ESP]
SANCHEZ VALADES, RAQUEL; [ESP]
SANCHEZ VAZQUEZ, GONZALO; [ESP]
SANCHEZ VAZQUEZ, MANUEL; [ESP]
SANCHEZ-LIROLA ORTEGA, FRANCISCO; [ESP]
SANCHEZ-LIROLA ORTEGA, MARIA GRACIA; [ESP]
SANCHO ROCHER, JULIO; [ESP]
SANDER, HANS-JOACHIM; [DEU]
SANDERS, MALCOLM; [GBR]
SANDERS, SUSAN ELISABETH; [GBR]
SANDIN, PETER; [SWE]
SANDOVAL SIERRA, PILAR; [ESP]
SANGIORGI, MARIA CHIARA; [ITA]
SANGUINETI, MARGARITA; [ARG]
SANGUINETI DE SAGGESSE, NORMA; [ARG]
SANTA MARIA, GRACIELA; [ARG]
SANTA OLALLA TOVAR, JOSE MARIA; [ESP]
SANTAGUEDA RUIZ, LIDIA; [ESP]
SANTAMARIA BRITO, FELIX JOSE; [ESP]
SANTANA, TANIA JUSSARA; [BRA]
SANTANA DE AZANZA, GLORIA MARIA; [ARG]
SANTIAGO DO AMARAL CARVALHO, REGINA C.; [BRA]
SANTOFIMIA NAVARRO, Mª ELENA; [ESP]
SANTONJA GOMEZ, FRANCISCO JOSE; [ESP]
SANTOS, VANIA MARIA; [BRA]
SANTOS, VINICIO DE M.; [BRA]
SANTOS CRESPO, IGNACIO; [ESP]
SANTOS DE SOUZA, HAMILTON R.; [BRA]
SANTOS HERNANDEZ, ARNULFO; [ESP]
SANTOS MARQUEZ, Mª DEL ROCIO; [ESP]
SANTOS NEJM, ESTELA D'ALVA; [BRA]
SANTUCCI, DAVID; [USA]
SANT'ANNA F.PARRACHO, NEIDE; [BRA]
SANZ DOMINGUEZ, Mª ISABEL; [ESP]
SANZ GILSANZ, Mª TERESA; [ESP]
SANZ PEREZ, JAVIER; [ESP]
SAÑAS RODELLAS, JOAN; [ESP]

Saraiva, Manuel Joaquim; [PRT]
Sargenti, Ada; [ITA]
Sarmiento, Olga Ines; [ARG]
Sartori Remedi, Mª Del Carmen; [URY]
Sasaki, Tetsurou; [JAP]
Sasuwan, Kasama; [THA]
Sato, Yoshitaka; [JAP]
Sato, Kazutaka; [JAP]
Sato, Katsuhiko; [JAP]
Sato, Tsutomu; [JAP]
Sattathumgul, Yongyuth; [THA]
Saul, Mark; [USA]
Savora, Simona; [SLN]
Sawada, Toshio; [JAP]
Sawiran, Moho Sahar; [MYS]
Sbaragli, Silvia; [ITA]
Scarafiotti, Annarosa; [ITA]
Scimemi, Benedetto; [ITA]
Scomparim De Lima, Valeria; [BRA]
Scott, Margaret; [USA]
Scott, Patrick; [USA]
Scott, Joy; [AUS]
Scott, Deb; [AUS]
Scott, Nicholas; [AUS]
Scruton, Paul; [GBR]
Schaar, Richard; [USA]
Schattschneider, Doris; [USA]
Schedel, Bernd; [ESP]
Scheffer, Nilce Fatima; [BRA]
Scheibler, Andre; [CHE]
Scherer, Petra; [DEU]
Schmidt, Siegbert; [DEU]
Schmitt, Lynn; [USA]
Schneider, Maggy; [BEL]
Schneider, Joel; [USA]
Schomacker, Gert; [DNK]
Schramm, Ruben; [ISR]
Schulz, Wolfgang; [DEU]
Schumann, Heinz; [DEU]
Schupp, Hans; [DEU]
Schuring, Henk; [NLD]
Schurle, Arlo; [USA]
Schuster, Eva; [DEU]

Schwartz, Judah L.; [USA]
Schwarzkopf, Patricia; [USA]
Schwarzkopf, Elisabeth; [ARG]
Schwenk, Elizabeth; [USA]
Searl, John; [GBR]
Sebastiani Ferreira, Eduardo; [BRA]
Sebela, Mokgoko Petrus; [ZAF]
Seeberg, Tom Cato; [NOR]
Segawa, Hisahito; [JAP]
Segovia Alex, Isidoro; [ESP]
Segovia Isasi, Juana Julia; [PAR]
Segovia Ordoñez, Carmen; [ESP]
Segurado, Mª Irene; [PRT]
Seino, Sadanobu; [JAP]
Seitz, Richard; [USA]
Sekiguchi, Yasuhiro; [JAP]
Selden, John; [USA]
Selden, Annie; [USA]
Seliktar, Miriam; [USA]
Selinger, Michelle; [GBR]
Selma I Juan, Fatima; [ESP]
Selter, Christoph; [DEU]
Selvik, Bjorj Kristin; [NOR]
Semadeni, Zbigniew; [POL]
Semenov, Andrei; [RUS]
Semenov, Alexei L.; [RUS]
Sendova, Eugenia; [BGR]
Senk, Sharon; [USA]
Senuma, Hanako; [JAP]
Seo, Hye Sook; [JAP]
Seppala, Reino; [FIN]
Seppala, Mika; [FIN]
Sequeira, Clara Felicidad; [ARG]
Sereno, Fernando; [PRT]
Serra Santasusana, Teresa; [ESP]
Serrano Czaia, Isabel; [ESP]
Serrano Garcia, Antonio; [ESP]
Serrano Gil, Vicenta; [ESP]
Serrano Gomez, Inmaculada; [ESP]
Serrano Romero, Luis; [ESP]
Serrazina, Mª De Lurdes; [PRT]
Servan Thomas, Mª Jesus; [ESP]
Servat Susagne, Jordi; [ESP]

SEVERINO, LILIANA; [ARG]
SFARD, ANNA; [ISR]
SHAFROTH, CHANTAL; [USA]
SHAHAM, ZIVA; [ISR]
SHAHVARANI - SEMNANI, AHMAD; [IRN]
SHAKESPEAR DE SCHMITT, MONICA B.; [ARG]
SHANE, RUTH; [ISR]
SHANNON, ANN; [USA]
SHARP, JENNY; [GBR]
SHAUGHNESSY, MICHAEL; [USA]
SHAW, PAMELA; [AUS]
SHAYER, MICHAEL; [GBR]
SHEALY, BARRY; [USA]
SHEATH, GEOFF; [GBR]
SHECHTER, BAT-SHEVA; [ISR]
SHEFFIELD, LINDA; [USA]
SHEFI, YAEL; [ISR]
SHELLY, BARBARA; [USA]
SHEN, SHIR-MING; [CHN]
SHEN, MING ZHE; [CHN]
SHIBANO, HIROKI; [JAP]
SHIBATA, MASANORI; [JAP]
SHIBATA, SHIGERU; [JAP]
SHIDA, MASAO; [JAP]
SHIGEMATSU, KEIICHI; [JAP]
SHIHU, LU; [CHN]
SHIM, JAE - UNG; [KOR]
SHIMIZU, TOMOKO; [JAP]
SHIMIZU, SHIZUMI; [JAP]
SHIMIZU, YOSHINORI; [JAP]
SHIMIZU, TOSHIAKI; [JAP]
SHIMIZU, NORIHIRO; [JAP]
SHIMIZU, KATSUHIKO; [JAP]
SHIN, HYUN-SUNG; [KOR]
SHIU, CHRISTINE; [GBR]
SHMUKLER, ALLA; [ISR]
SHOAF-GRUBBS, MARY MARGARET; [USA]
SHOWALTER, CAROLYN; [USA]
SHULTE, ALBERT; [USA]
SHULTZ, HARRIS; [USA]
SHULTZ, JANICE; [USA]
SIEMON, DIANNE; [AUS]
SIERPINSKA, ANNA; [CAN]

SIERRA VAZQUEZ, MODESTO; [ESP]
SILFVERBERG, HARRY; [FIN]
SILVA, MELQUISEDEC FCO; [BRA]
SILVA DE GIUDICI, ROSA; [VEN]
SILVA FERNANDES, JOSE ANTONIO; [PRT]
SILVA FERREIRA, SIVANILDES; [BRA]
SILVA GRAÇA, Mª MARGARIDA; [PRT]
SILVA LABARCA, LILA; [CHL]
SILVA PRECATADO, Mª ADELINA; [PRT]
SILVA ROSENDO, ANA ISABEL; [PRT]
SILVEIRA, BRANCA MARIA; [PRT]
SILVER, EDWARD; [USA]
SILLERO ARROYO, ALFONSA; [ESP]
SIMONS, FRED; [NLD]
SIMONSEN, JORGEN - TOFT; [DNK]
SIMPSON, DONNA; [USA]
SINGER, MIHAELA; [ROM]
SINGMASTER, DAVID; [GBR]
SINKINSON, ANNE; [GBR]
SINNEMAKI, JUSSI; [FIN]
SINTES MARCO, BARTOLOME; [ESP]
SIU, MAN-KEUNG; [HKG]
SIVAKUL, ANUSORN; [THA]
SIVERTSEN, PER; [NOR]
SIWEK, HELENA; [POL]
SKEATH, ANN; [USA]
SKILLMAN, REBECCA; [GBR]
SKOVSMOSE, OLE; [DNK]
SLAMMERT, LIONEL; [ZAF]
SMART, TERESA; [GBR]
SMIT, CORNELIS P.; [NLD]
SMITH, PAULINE; [GBR]
SMITH, GEOFF; [AUS]
SMITH, DRONALD; [AUS]
SMITH, JOHN BARRY; [CHE]
SNIDER, JAMES; [USA]
SNYDERS, MARITZ; [ZAF]
SOARES, VALDETE CARLOS; [BRA]
SOBRADO CROS, MONICA MARIA; [ESP]
SOBRINO REYES, MANUEL; [ESP]
SOCAS ROBAYNA, MARTIN MANUEL; [ESP]
SÖDERHOLM, EVA; [SWE]
SODERSTROM, JAN-GUSTAV; [ESP]

Soifer, Alexander; [USA]

Sol Puig, Manuel; [ESP]

Sola Bohigas, Josep; [ESP]

Solar, Claudie; [CAN]

Solbakken, Harald; [NOR]

Solbes, Dolores Regina; [ARG]

Soledade, Jose Ruy Freire; [BRA]

Sologuren, Santiago; [BOL]

Soria, Laura Cristina; [ARG]

Soria Gamez, Pedro; [ESP]

Soriano Molinero, Marisa; [ESP]

Sorvali, Tuomas; [FIN]

Sosenke, Fanny; [USA]

Soto Luque, Manuel; [ESP]

Sottomayor, Miguel; [ESP]

Sousa P.S. Passos Marques, Mª. Helena;[PRT]

Sousa Varela E Silva, Albano Antonio; [PRT]

Southwell, Beth; [AUS]

Southwood, Sue; [ZAF]

Southwood, Susan; [ZAF]

Souza, Jose Messias; [BRA]

Souza Alves, Angela Christin; [BRA]

Souza Gastaldi Sardinha, Luciana; [BRA]

Sowder, Judith; [USA]

Spanneberg, Rose; [ZAF]

Sparron, Len; [AUS]

Speier, Peter; [USA]

Spence, Mary; [GBR]

Speranza, Francesco; [ITA]

Spinillo, Alina Galvao; [BRA]

Spiro, Lea; [ISR]

Spresser, Diane; [USA]

Spyker, Geert; [AUS]

Sritongsook, Nuansawat; [THA]

Staal, Henk; [NLD]

Stacey, Kaye; [AUS]

Stange, Plinio; [BRA]

Starkings, Susan; [GBR]

Stastna, Viena; [CAN]

Steen, Lynn; [USA]

Stehlikova, Nada; [CZR]

Steinbring, Heinz; [DEU]

Steiner, Hans-Georg; [DEU]

Steinweg, Anna Susanne; [DEU]

Stepan, Lumidla; [MOL]

Stephens, Max; [AUS]

Stevens, Pierre; [CAN]

Stevenson, Richard David; [PRT]

Stivale, Diana Elisa; [ARG]

Stortz, C.B.; [USA]

Stoyanova, Elena; [AUS]

Straesser, Rudolf; [DEU]

Streefland, Leen; [NLD]

Strnad, Milena; [SLN]

Stupp, Jonathan; [ISR]

Suarez Barrio, Mª Araceli; [ESP]

Suarez Bracho, Estrella J.; [VEN]

Suarez Rodriguez, Alejandro; [ESP]

Suarez Vazquez, Juan Antonio; [ESP]

Suchich, Laima; [LIT]

Suda, Hiroshi; [JAP]

Suffolk, John; [BRN]

Suger Cofiño, Jose Eduardo; [GTM]

Sugiyama, Yoshishige; [JAP]

Suhit, Gloria; [ARG]

Sukthankar, Neela; [PNG]

Sullivan, Kelly Marie; [EGY]

Sullivan, Robert P.; [AUS]

Sullivan, Peter; [AUS]

Sun, Wen-Hsien; [TPI]

Sundberg, Ritva; [SWE]

Sunkel, Veronica; [ARG]

Sunzunegui De Iglecia, Elena; [ARG]

Sutabutr, Charuni; [THA]

Sutherland, Rosamund; [GBR]

Swafford, Jane; [USA]

Swan, Malcolm; [GBR]

Swanepoel, Jon; [ZAF]

Sward, Marcia; [USA]

Sweetnam, Ruth; [GBR]

Sykora, Vaclav; [CZR]

Szendrei, Janos; [HUN]

Sznajder, Maria; [POL]

Szöllösyne-Somfai, Zsuzsa; [HUN]

Tabata, Sigqibo; [ZAF]

Tabesh, Yahya; [IRN]

Tabov, Jordan; [BGR]
Taflin, Eva; [SWE]
Taiana Marques, Aida Lucrecia; [ARG]
Takahashi, Tadashi; [JAP]
Takahashi, Akihko; [JAP]
Takao, Horoshi; [JAP]
Takasaka, Jun; [JAP]
Takeda, Tetsuji; [JAP]
Takenouchi, Osamu; [JAP]
Takeya, Makoto; [JAP]
Tall, David Orme; [GBR]
Tan, Leonida; [USA]
Tan, Peter; [GYN]
Tanaka, Hiroshi; [JAP]
Taneki, Tateo; [JAP]
Tanner, Howard; [GBR]
Tantivit, Boonua; [THA]
Tapia, Leandra; [DOM]
Taplin, Margaret; [HKG]
Tararykova, Tamara; [GBR]
Tarp, Allan; [DNK]
Tarvin, James; [USA]
Tarzia, Domingo Alberto; [ARG]
Tavares Da Costa, Paulo Sergio; [BRA]
Taylor, Kelvin; [USA]
Taylor, Peter; [AUS]
Taylor, Teresa; [GBR]
Teague, Daniel J.; [USA]
Tease, John; [GBR]
Techapiwat, Patra; [THA]
Teeguarden, Janet; [USA]
Teh, Pick Ching; [BRN]
Teijeiro Couce, Berta; [ESP]
Teixeira, Mª Paula; [PRT]
Tejada De Castillo, Mª Guadalupe; [PAN]
Tejedor Hernandez, Alicia; [ESP]
Tennison, Rosemary; [GBR]
Teppo, Anne; [USA]
Ter Heege, Hans; [NLD]
Terada, Fumiyuki; [JAP]
Teran, Teresita; [ARG]
Teran, Tesesita A.; [ARG]
Tertuliano, Waldivina; [BRA]

Teruel Marti, Vicent; [ESP]
Thomaidis, Yannis; [GRC]
Thomas, Noel; [AUS]
Thomas, Claire; [USA]
Thomas, Jan; [AUS]
Thomas, Lindsay; [AUS]
Thompson, Denisse R.; [USA]
Thompson, Patrick; [USA]
Thompson, Alba; [USA]
Thornton, Carol A.; [USA]
Ticha, Marie; [CZR]
Tinoco, Lucia; [BRA]
Tinto, Patricia; [USA]
Tirosh, Dina; [ISR]
Tirosh, Chaim; [ISR]
Tokmakidis, Anastassios; [GRC]
Toledo Montiel, Jose Fernando; [CHL]
Toledo Ortiz, Enrique; [ESP]
Tolmie, Julie; [AUS]
Tomazos, Dianne; [AUS]
Tominaga, Yasuo; [JAP]
Tomita, Koichi; [JAP]
Tompa, Klara; [HUN]
Toni, Paolo; [ITA]
Tormenta Bastos Calvario, Maria Lidia; [MAC]
Tornero Checa, Antonio; [ESP]
Torra Bitlloch, Montserrat; [ESP]
Torralbo Rodriguez, Manuel; [ESP]
Torregrosa Girones, German; [ESP]
Torregrosa Ortiz, Antonia; [ARG]
Torres, Mª Julia; [PRT]
Torres, Roberto W.; [ARG]
Torres Alonso, Mª Del Carmen; [ESP]
Torres Marin, Mª Magdalena; [ESP]
Torroja Bendito, Jesus; [ESP]
Torruella, Mirta Teresa; [ARG]
Tortora, Roberto; [ITA]
Tortosa Lopez, Antonio; [ESP]
Toschi Bambicini, Elisabeth; [BRA]
Totten, Jim; [CAN]
Toubassi, Elias; [USA]
Touborg, Jens Peter; [DNK]
Tout, Dave; [AUS]

Tovar, Ensony Jose; [VEN]
Traça Duarte M.V. Gomes, Mª Jose; [PRT]
Trafton, Paul; [USA]
Trankjaer, Ib; [DNK]
Traverso Garcia, Fco. Javier; [ESP]
Travis, Betty; [USA]
Tregub, Nina; [UKR]
Trejo, Mª Luisa; [ARG]
Trigueros Gaisman, Maria; [MEX]
Troncoso Lora, Alicia; [ESP]
Truedson, Conrad; [GBR]
Trujillo Pascual-Vaca, Jesus; [ESP]
Trujillo Vega, Juan Vicente; [ESP]
Truran, Kath; [AUS]
Truran, John; [AUS]
Tsamir, Pessia; [ISR]
Tshongwe, Themba; [ZAF]
Tsuji, Hiroko; [JAP]
Tsukahara, Kumiko; [JAP]
Tsuyuki, Shigeru; [JAP]
Tucker, Diane; [ZAF]
Turbiani, Edson; [BRA]
Turegano Moratalla, Santiago; [ESP]
Turegano Moratalla, Pilar; [ESP]
Turnbull, Susan; [AUS]
Tzekaki, Marianna; [GRC]
Tzoulakis, Stavros; [GRC]
Tzur, Ron; [USA]
Ubuz, Behiye; [TUR]
Uchida, Kiyoshi; [JAP]
Uchiyama, Mamoru; [JAP]
Udomphoch, Boonsri; [THA]
Uegaki, Wataru; [JAP]
Ueikul, Pornpod; [THA]
Ueno, Miho; [JAP]
Uetake, Tsuneo; [JAP]
Urrutia, Fernando; [ESP]
Urrutia Salgado, Inmaculada; [ESP]
Urschel De Prieto, Liliana E.; [ARG]
Usiskin, Karen; [USA]
Usiskin, Zalman; [USA]
Usnick, Virginia; [USA]
Usui, Masataka; [JAP]

Utairat, Suwattana; [THA]
Uudelepp, Helgi; [EST]
Uus-Leponiemi, Markku; [FIN]
Uus-Leponiemi, Tuula; [FIN]
Uy, Frederick; [USA]
Vaaje, Audhild; [NOR]
Vadas, Robert; [AUS]
Vadell, Dalila; [ARG]
Vaello I Sebastia, Anna M.; [ESP]
Vagner, Soren; [DNK]
Vale, Isabel; [PRT]
Valella, Julio; [USA]
Valencia Carrascal, Gabriel Ferney; [COL]
Valente Nogueira, Joao Manuel; [PRT]
Valente Pires, Isabel; [PRT]
Valenzuela Paz Soldan, MªAntonieta; [BOL]
Valenzuela Quijada, Jaime Belisario; [CHL]
Valenzuela Quinta, Juan Manuel; [ESP]
Valenzuela Salazar, Jaime Antonio; [CHL]
Valero Correa, Alejandro; [ESP]
Valero Dueñas, Paola Ximena; [COL]
Valero Tejedor, Isabel; [ESP]
Valiente Guerrero, Alicia; [ESP]
Valverde Fernandez, Carmen; [ESP]
Valverde Ramirez, Lourdes; [CUB]
Valldeperes Y Coma, Carmen; [ESP]
Vallecillos Jimenez, Angustias; [ESP]
Van Asch, Bram; [NLD]
Van Den Brink, Jan; [NLD]
Van Den Heuvel-Panhuizen, Marja; [NLD]
Van Der Kooij, Henk; [NLD]
Van Der Westhuizen, Gert; [ZAF]
Van Der Zwaart, Pieter; [NLD]
Van Dormolen, Joop; [ISR]
Van Etten, Bertus; [NLD]
Van Galen, Frans; [NLD]
Van Groenestijn, Mieke; [NLD]
Van Heeswijck, Lutgarde; [BEL]
Van Leeuwen, Ingeborg; [ESP]
Van Lent, Gerben; [NLD]
Van Oers, Bert; [NLD]
Van Schalkwijk, Louis; [NLD]
Van Wijk, Peter; [NLD]

VAN ZOEST, LAURA; [USA]
VANDENBERG, DANIEL; [ZAF]
VANDERLEI SILVA, FELIX; [BRA]
VANHILLE, BRUNO; [FRA]
VARA PIRES, MANUEL C.; [PRT]
VARANDAS DE CARVALHO DA SILVA, JOSE M.; [PRT]
VARGAS LOAYZA, FRANZ JACINTO; [BOL]
VARO GOMEZ DE LA TORRE, ANTONIO J.; [ESP]
VASCO URIBE, CARLOS EDUARDO; [COL]
VASINO DE BORGHIANI, SUSANA MARIA; [ARG]
VASSILEV, PETER; [BGR]
VAZQUEZ DE LA TORRE PRIETO, JOSE M.; [ESP]
VAZQUEZ DE TAPIA, NELLY ESTHER; [ARG]
VAZQUEZ MARTINEZ, TERESA; [ESP]
VEGA RESTREPO, MYRIAM; [COL]
VEGUIN CASAS, Mª VICTORIA; [ESP]
VELAZQUEZ MANUEL, FIDELA; [ESP]
VELEZ, WILLIAM; [USA]
VELIKOVA, EMILIA; [BGR]
VELOSO MENDARO, GUADALUPE; [ESP]
VENHEIM, ROLF; [NOR]
VENTURA HERNANDEZ, DAVID; [ESP]
VENTURA MARTIN, MANUEL; [ESP]
VERA DE ALCARAZ, AURORA; [PAR]
VERA YEGROS, OSCAR; [PAR]
VERASTEGUI RAYO, DOROTEO; [ESP]
VERDUGO DIAZ, JULIETA; [MEX]
VERDUN, ARMANDO; [ARG]
VERGARA MANZANO, GUADALUPE; [ESP]
VERGNAUD, GERARD; [FRA]
VERHAGE, HELEEN; [NLD]
VERMANDEL, ALFRED; [BEL]
VERMEULEN, NELIS; [ZAF]
VERON, Mª ANGELES; [ARG]
VIANA, JOSE PAULO; [PRT]
VICENTE, LINA MARIA; [PRT]
VICENTE ALONSO, EVA; [ESP]
VICENTE CARRETO, JOSE MARIA; [ESP]
VICENTE CORDOBA, JOSE LUIS; [ESP]
VICENTE FERNANDEZ, Mª ESTRELLA; [ESP]
VICENTE SUAREZ, JORGE; [ESP]
VICENZO, BONGIOVANNI; [BRA]
VIDAKOVIC, DRAGA; [USA]

VIDAL, MARTA CECILIA; [ARG]
VIDAL ARIAS, ANTONIO; [ESP]
VIEIRA, ELAINE; [BRA]
VIEIRA DA SILVA, MAGDA; [BRA]
VIEIRA LOPES, ANA; [PRT]
VIEIRA TEIXEIRA, MARCOS; [BRA]
VIGIER, NOELE; [FRA]
VIGIL FERNANDEZ, JUAN CARLOS; [ESP]
VILA CORTS, ANTONI; [ESP]
VILAPRINYO PAYCHERE, FRANÇOIS; [ESP]
VILCHES ALARCON, JOSE ANTONIO; [ESP]
VILCHEZ LOPEZ, SILVERIO; [ESP]
VILE, ADAM; [GBR]
VILHENA DE MORAES, INES; [BRA]
VILLA DE BENITEZ, ANA MARIA; [PAR]
VILLAFRANCA YESTE, INMACULADA; [ESP]
VILLAGRA DE ALEGRE, MARGARITA D.; [PAR]
VILLALBA VALDAYO, Mª ESTELA; [ESP]
VILLALBA VILLALBA, Mª JOSE; [ESP]
VILLALOBOS SANCHO, LESLIE; [CRI]
VILLAMAYOR RAYNAL, NANCY ELIZABETH; [PAR]
VILLANI, VINICIO; [ITA]
VILLANUEVA CUEVA, Mª CARMEN; [ESP]
VILLANUEVA FERNANDEZ, FCO. MANUEL; [ESP]
VILLAR, ALICIA SARA; [ARG]
VILLAR ICASURIAGA, MARIA ALICIA; [URY]
VILLARREAL, MONICA ESTER;
VILLARROYA BULLIDO, FLORENCIO; [ESP]
VILLAVICENCIO, MARTHA ROSA; [PER]
VILLAVICENCIO HIGUERA, VERONICA; [MEX]
VILLELLA, JOSE AGUSTIN; [ARG]
VINK, ANDERS; [NLD]
VISTRO-YU, CATHERINE; [PHI]
VITHAL, RENUKA; [ZAF]
VIVONO, NORMA ALICIA; [ARG]
VIZMANOS BUELTA, JOSE RAMON; [ESP]
VOIT, KATHRYN; [USA]
VOLQUIND, LEA; [BRA]
VOLLMER, NATALIE; [DEU]
VON STERNBERG, HAYDEE; [USA]
VONGNITIPHAT, MONTIRA; [THA]
VORONEL, YAEL; [ISR]
WADA, FUMIOKI; [JAP]

Waddingham, Jo; [GBR]
Wagner Fort, Javier; [URY]
Wagner Fort, Javier Gustavo; [URY]
Waits, Bert; [USA]
Wake, Geoff; [GBR]
Walser, Hans; [CHE]
Walsh, Angela; [GBR]
Wang, Chang Pei; [CHN]
Wang, Liguan; [CHN]
Wang, Kun Xin; [CHN]
Ward, Patricia; [IRL]
Watanabe, Shin; [JAP]
Watanabe, Tad; [USA]
Watkins, Anthony; [GBR]
Watson, Anne; [GBR]
Watson, Richard; [IRL]
Watson, Jane; [AUS]
Way, Jenni; [AUS]
Webb, Norman; [USA]
Wedege, Tine; [DNK]
Weidig, Ingo; [DEU]
Weigand, Hans-Georg; [DEU]
Weinzweig, Aurum [ISR]; [USA]
Weissman, Shulamit; [ISR]
Welna, Boguslawa; [AUS]
Wenger, Ronald; [USA]
Wennerholm, Barbro; [SWE]
Wheeler, Robert; [USA]
White, Alvin; [USA]
White, Arthur; [USA]
Whitenack, Joy; [USA]
Wick, Cathy; [USA]
Widmer, Connie; [USA]
Wieland, Gregor; [CHE]
Wiernik, Aviva-Rosa; [ISR]
Wilder, Peter; [GBR]
Wiliam, Dylan; [GBR]
Wilkinson, Patricia; [USA]
Wilson, Patricia; [USA]
Wilson, Dave; [GBR]
Wilson, David; [GBR]
Wilson De Jesus, Juana; [USA]
Williams, Honor; [GBR]

Williams, Julian; [GBR]
Willis, Vivienne; [GBR]
Willis, Sue; [AUS]
Wimbish, Glenn; [USA]
Winbourne, Peter Charles; [GBR]
Winicki Landman, Greisy; [ISR]
Winitzky De Spinadel, Vera Martha; [ARG]
Winston, Bente; [USA]
Winter, Jan; [GBR]
Winteridge, David; [GBR]
Wisbrun, Hans; [NLD]
Wit De, Paul; [NLD]
Wittmann, Erich Ch.; [DEU]
Woloszyn, Mabel Graciela; [ARG]
Wong, Ngai Ying; [HKG]
Wong, Ka Ming Patrick; [HKG]
Wood, Terry; [USA]
Wood, Leigh; [AUS]
Woodrow, Derek; [GBR]
Xavier, Marcelo Fco.; [BRA]
Xifre Arroyo, Angel; [ESP]
Yaakub, Baidurian; [MYS]
Yabar Madinavieitia, Jose Manuel; [ESP]
Yackel, Erna; [USA]
Yagüez Castrillo, Jaime; [ESP]
Yamada, Atsushi; [JAP]
Yamagishi, Kazunori; [GBR]
Yamaguchi, Takeshi; [JAP]
Yamanaka, Kazuhito; [JAP]
Yamashita, Hajime; [JAP]
Yamashita, Kazuyuki; [GBR]
Yamazaki, Koji; [JAP]
Yañez Canal, Gabriel; [COL]
Yao, Jing; [CHN]
Yasugi, Mariko; [JAP]
Yates, Elizabeth; [USA]
Yazlle, Jorge Fernando; [ARG]
Ye, Qi-Xiao; [CHN]
Yerushalmy, Michal; [ISR]
Ynsa Gomez, Mariano; [ESP]
Yokochi, Kiyoshi; [JAP]
Yokoyama, Hiroyuki; [JAP]
Yoshida, Minoru; [JAP]

YOSHIDA, HAJIME; [JAP]
YOSHIKAWA, YUKIO; [JAP]
YOSHIKAWA, SHIGEO; [JAP]
YOSHIMURA, SATORU; [JAP]
YOSHINO, HIROYUKI; [JAP]
YOUN GKHONG, DANAI; [THA]
YOUNG, JAMES; [GBR]
YOUNG, KIANG - CHUEN; [USA]
YRJONSUURI, KAIJA; [FIN]
YRJONSUURI, YRJO; [FIN]
YU, WEI; [CHN]
YUPANQUI YUPANQUI, CESAR DIEGO; [PER]
YUSTY LOPEZ DE MENESES, MARIA; [ESP]
ZABULIONIS, ALGIRDAS; [LIT]
ZACK, VICKI; [CAN]
ZAERA CAPSIR, IMMACULADA; [ESP]
ZAFRA GARCIA, Mª ESTHER; [ESP]
ZALAZAR, LAURA CRISTINA; [ARG]
ZAMORA DOMINGUEZ, SONIA CARMEN; [CHL]
ZAMORA LORENTE, MERCEDES; [ESP]
ZANIRATTO, ARIOVALDO A.; [BRA]
ZARAGOZA FREIRE, Mª ASUNCION; [ESP]
ZARAGOZA SANTOS, JOSE DAMIAN; [ESP]
ZARZYCKI, PIOTR; [POL]
ZASLAVSKY, ORIT; [ISR]
ZAWOJEWSKI, JUDITH; [USA]
ZAYA GRILO, ALICIA; [ESP]
ZEHAVI, NURIT; [ISR]
ZEVENBERGEN, ROBYN; [AUS]
ZHANG, DIANZHOU; [CHN]
ZIEGENBALD, JOCHENS; [DEU]
ZILLIOX, JOSEPH; [USA]
ZISKIN, CLARA; [ISR]
ZOFIO PEREZ, MARIA LUISA; [ESP]
ZORN, PAUL; [USA]
ZSEBY, SIEGFRIED; [DEU]
ZUNINO DE TORO, MELISSA; [URY]
ZWANEVELD, GIJSBERTUS; [NLD]